W9-CGV-506

# Trade Theory, Analytical Models and Development

# Trade Theory, Analytical Models and Development

Essays in Honour of Peter Lloyd, Volume I

*Edited by*

Sisira Jayasuriya

*Director, Asian Economics Centre, Department of Economics, University of Melbourne, Australia*

**Edward Elgar**
Cheltenham, UK • Northampton, MA, USA

Published by
Edward Elgar Publishing Limited
Glensanda House
Montpellier Parade
Cheltenham
Glos GL50 1UA
UK

Edward Elgar Publishing, Inc.
136 West Street
Suite 202
Northampton
Massachusetts 01060
USA

A catalogue record for this book
is available from the British Library

ISBN 1 84376 364 8

Printed and bound in Great Britain by MPG Books Ltd, Bodmin, Cornwall

# Contents

## PART FOUR   NEW APPLICATIONS OF TRADE THEORY

# Contributors

Mary Amiti
Economist, International Monetary Fund
Washington, DC
USA

Ian Coxhead
Professor, Department of Agricultural and Applied Economics, and
Director, Center of Southeast Asian Studies
University of Wisconsin
Madison, Wisconsin
USA

Peter B. Dixon
Professor, and Director, Centre of Policy Studies
Monash University
Melbourne
Australia

Rod Falvey
Leverhulme Professor of International Economics
Leverhulme Centre for Research on Globalisation and Economic Policy
School of Economics
University of Nottingham
UK

David Greenaway
Professor of Economics and Head of School
Director, Leverhulme Centre for Research on
Globalisation and Economic Policy
School of Economics
University of Nottingham
UK

Sisira Jayasuriya
Director, Asian Economics Centre
Department of Economics
University of Melbourne
Australia

Ronald W. Jones
Xerox Professor of Economics
Department of Economics
Rochester University
Rochester, New York
USA

Kunio Kawamata
Professor of Economics
Keio University
Tokyo
Japan

Wen Fang Liu
Assistant Professor
Department of Economics
University of Washington
Seattle, Washington
USA

Donald MacLaren
Associate Professor
Department of Economics
University of Melbourne
Australia

Steve McCorriston
Professor of Agricultural Economics
University of Exeter
UK

Mark Melatos
Lecturer
University of Sydney
Australia

Chris Milner
Professor of International Economics
Leverhulme Centre for Research on Globalisation and Economic Policy
School of Economics
University of Nottingham
UK

Maureen T. Rimmer
Senior Research Fellow
Centre of Policy Studies
Monash University
Melbourne
Australia

Roy J. Ruffin
M.D. Anderson Professor of Economics
Department of Economics
University of Houston
Houston, Texas
USA

A.G. Schweinberger
Professor of International Economics
Faculty of Economics and Statistics
University of Konstanz
Germany

Stephen J. Turnovsky
Castor Professor of Economics
Department of Economics
University of Washington
Seattle, Washington
USA

Alan Woodland
Australian Professorial Fellow and Professor of Econometrics
Department of Economics
University of Sydney
Australia

# Introduction

## Sisira Jayasuriya

These two volumes, *Trade Theory, Analytical Models and Development* and *Trade Policy Reforms and Development*, bring together papers prepared in honour of Professor Peter Lloyd (Ritchie Professor of Economics at the Department of Economics, University of Melbourne, Australia) on the occasion of his formal retirement after a distinguished career of over four decades in academia. A group of his close friends and collaborators – drawn from four continents – was present to honour him at a *Festschrift* conference held on 23–24 January 2003 at the University of Melbourne where preliminary versions of most of these chapters were presented. The chapters have been subsequently revised in the light of comments from referees and participants at the workshop.

Peter Lloyd, at present one of the most distinguished and internationally renowned Australian economists, started life – in his own words – as a 'boy from the bush' in New Zealand, completed his undergraduate and Masters at the Victoria University of Wellington in New Zealand, and did his doctoral studies at Duke University, USA. After graduation he returned to the Victoria University of Wellington to start his university career and subsequently held positions in economics departments at the Michigan State University, the Australian National University and finally, in 1983, at the University of Melbourne. In between he spent periods at various universities around the world, including a period as Visiting Professor at the National University of Singapore in the early 1980s.

The titles of the two volumes and the diversity of topics covered by the contributors reflect Peter Lloyd's core interests as a professional economist: development of rigorous theory and analytical models to understand and elucidate real-world behaviour, and the application of conclusions from theory to inform policy. Peter's own wide-ranging interests have led him to write not only on international economics, but also on production theory, welfare economics, macroeconomics, health economics, finance, economic demography, history of economic thought and mathematical economics, though his reputation in international economics perhaps tends to overshadow his important contributions to these other fields.

Peter has been – and remains – an 'old-fashioned' academic in the best sense of the term, devoted to maintaining the highest standards of academic integrity and scholarly rigour in his own work and within the profession. His research is also driven by a sense of social responsibility, in the best traditions of the classical economists. While strongly believing in 'the essentiality of theory to understanding the real world and to policy advice', Peter has consistently resisted the temptation to 'do theory for its own sake' (or, for the sake of a 'good' journal paper!). With obvious regret, in his introduction to his selected essays (*International Trade Opening and the Formation of the Global Economy*, Edward Elgar, 2002) he wrote that:

> an increasing proportion of academic writers devote their efforts to theory which is divorced from any policy advice or even any general interest in policies. There is more interest today in theory for its own sake. This is most notable in the United States but is increasingly true in Australia. Specialization in the activities of economists has produced much higher levels of skills and much inventive theorising but the profession of economics would in my view be more productive as a social instrument if closer links between theory and policy were re-established.

One consequence of this strong interest in real-world economies and policy issues has been Peter's increasing interest in international policy debates centred around the ongoing process of globalization and international economic integration. Dating from his time in Singapore in the early 1980s, he has become a leading analyst of trade and development issues in Asia. Similarly, the global trading system and the role and nature of the WTO have attracted much of his attention in recent years.

Without attempting an exhaustive survey of Peter's research output – his publications list includes 16 books, nine research monographs, 102 journal publications, and 98 book chapters (the complete list is accessible at www.economics.unimelb.edu.au/staffprofile/plloyd.htm) – it is worth briefly reviewing some of his writings to illustrate both the significance of Peter's academic contributions and his versatility. Peter Lloyd's contribution to the study of intra-industry trade is internationally recognized and demonstrates how careful examination of real-world developments paved the way for major advances in theory. His joint paper with Herbert Grubel in 1971 on 'The empirical measurement of intra-industry trade' in the *Economic Record* examined Australian trade data in detail and argued that the phenomenon of intra-industry trade was not a mere statistical artefact but a real phenomenon that demanded more attention from international trade theorists and analysts. The index presented in that paper – later known as the 'Grubel–Lloyd' index – remains to this day the most popular measure of intra-industry trade in the empirical literature. This was followed by their book *Intra-Industry Trade* (Macmillan, 1975), which documented in detail that intra-industry trade was indeed an important and increasingly significant global phenomenon in international trade. In the light of subsequent developments in international trade theory, particularly the class of models associated with the New Trade Theory pioneered by Paul Krugman and others that combine differentiated products and imperfectly competitive markets, the concluding paragraph of the 1971 paper makes interesting reading:

> Different actual cases called for diverse explanations in terms of advantages of specialization in narrow product ranges, joint production unmatched by complementarity in demand, and trade across borders in high transportation cost industries. *The explanation of other intra-industry trade flows may require consideration of product differentiation strategies in oligopolistic markets which have been neglected by most international trade theorists.* (emphasis added)

The stimulus for rigorous theorizing provided by the requirements of practical policy making is evident in the 1974 *Journal of International Economics* paper, 'A more general theory of price distortions in open economies', which attempted to derive simple policy rules that ensure welfare improvements for the realistic case of *partial* reforms to trade regimes – piecemeal tariff reforms – which raise the standard second-best problems of moving from one distorted situation to another. The paper examined the even now widely practised policies of reductions in extreme tariffs and uniform reductions in all tariff rates. Interest in piecemeal reforms and analytical approaches to dealing with welfare changes in distorted economies led to the paper with Albert Schweinberger on 'Trade expenditure functions and gains from trade' in 1988 (*Journal of International Economics*), enables normative analysis of multi-household economies with distinct preferences and endowments. The basic concept of the trade expenditure function has subsequently been applied – most notably by James Anderson and Peter Neary – to the measurement and analysis of protection in the presence of tariff and non-tariff barriers and to the impact of piecemeal reforms.

The '3 × 3 theory of customs unions' paper in the *Journal of International Economics* in 1982 surveyed, consolidated and synthesized the theoretical analysis of customs union models that extended the analysis to three countries and three commodities. This paper demonstrated how different assumptions about patterns of trade in the 3 × 3 model lead to a wide diversity of results. In subsequent work Peter has continued to work on the theoretical (and empirical) analysis issues of regional trade blocs and their policy implications. He has been particularly interested in the 'deepening' of regional trade agreements to achieve full economic integration by extending the scope of such agreements beyond removing barriers to trade at the border to also eliminate other internal barriers hindering market integration, thus enhancing market access to permit the 'law of one price' to hold is critical to achieving a fully integrated regional (or a global) economy. This interest is reflected in several of his writings on WTO and regional trade integration issues that emphasize the role of harmonization of standards, tax regimes and competition policy. Recognizing the problems posed by increasingly complicated 'rules of origin' in regional trade agreements, he has examined alternative policy measures to achieve the desired ends more efficiently – see, for example, 'Country of origin in the global economy', in *World Trade Review* (2002). Given this interest in regional and global market integration, it must be gratifying for Peter that his work has clearly had a major impact on policy discussions to move towards a fully integrated economy between New Zealand and Australia – his native and adopted countries. His 1991 study, *The Future of CER: A Single Market for Australia and New Zealand*, published by CEDA and the Institute of Policy Studies in Wellington, New Zealand, recommended an EU-style single market for the two countries, and ongoing moves to further deepen the Australia–New Zealand Closer Economic Agreement (CER) suggest that this may well become a reality in the foreseeable future.

Despite increasing involvement in policy issues in recent years, Peter has not lost his interest in making analytical models more policy relevant. This is nowhere better exemplified than in his 2002 paper 'Generalising the Stolper–Samuleson theorem: A tale of two matrices' (*Review of International Economics*) that extends the celebrated theorem on the distributional effects of relative price changes to the case of many goods and factors with diversified holding of factors. The paper shows that though diversified factor ownership by households fundamentally changes the relationships between prices and real incomes, the essential spirit of the theorem can be maintained in a much more general context. (Peter treasures a letter received from Paul Samuelson himself commending this extension of the theorem!)

What is truly remarkable is that Peter has maintained this record of consistently high research productivity while carrying a full load of teaching and, particularly in recent years, several heavy administrative responsibilities. As the Dean of the Faculty of Economics and Commerce from 1988 to 1993, he provided leadership and guidance during a difficult transitional period for both the Faculty and the University. He took a leadership role in developing Asia-oriented research in economics at the University of Melbourne and was the founding Director of the Asian Economics Centre and its predecessor, the Asian Business Centre. Peter has always been committed to teaching. Even when teaching was not compulsory, as was the case during his 14 years at the Australian National University, he maintained a regular programme of teaching. He has a well-founded reputation among students fortunate enough to have been taught by him as a brilliant and dedicated teacher, generous with his time and advice as well as sympathy and understanding – as I can attest from my own personal experience. Another facet of his character is revealed by the many co-authored publications: Peter enjoys interaction and collaboration with colleagues.

The enthusiastic response to the *Festschrift* in honour of Peter Lloyd was a reflection of the high regard and esteem in which he is held by his friends, colleagues and collaborators, both here in Australia and overseas. John Freebairn, Head of the Department of Economics in 2002, mooted the idea of holding the *Festschrift* and committed departmental resources. Jeff Borland, who took over as Head in 2003, with the administrative support of Cherie Millerick, Persefoni Gouletas and Colin Newell, ensured that the *Festschrift* activities ran smoothly. The authors, discussants and other participants at the workshop – some of whom literally travelled around the globe to be present – enabled this published tribute to Peter Lloyd to become a reality. Premachandra Athukorala, Daniel M. Bernhofen, Max Corden, Mark Crosby, Geoff Edwards, Christopher Findlay, John Freebairn, Hal Hill, Patrick Jomini, Stephen King, Jay Menon, Richard Pomfret, David Robertson, John Shannon and Peter Stemp also provided refereeing and other academic assistance. In preparing the manuscript for publication, Lee Smith provided invaluable editorial assistance at short notice.

Department of Economics
University of Melbourne
Melbourne 3010, Victoria
Australia

# PART ONE

# Real Trade Theory

# 1. Real wages and trade: insights from extreme examples

## Roy J. Ruffin and Ronald W. Jones*

The effect of international trade on wage rates within a country has been the object of much scrutiny in journal articles, conferences and the wider media. The classic theoretical observation dates back to the 1941 article by Wolfgang Stolper and Paul Samuelson wherein the effects of commercial policy or of more open trade on real wage rates were seen to depend only upon the factor intensity ranking of a nation's import-competing product with its exportables. Their theorem presupposed that productive factors had the same high degree of ability to relocate from one industrial activity to another. However, labour is often thought of as different from other productive factors, in being more mobile between sectors compared with capital or natural resources, and modelling of such an asymmetry leads naturally to the specific-factors model (Jones, 1971; Samuelson, 1971). In this context a quarter century ago Ruffin and Jones (1977) argued that there was a *presumption* that international trade would lead to real wage gains for labour, regardless of the pattern of trade. James Melvin and Robert Waschik (2001) recently questioned this result; they provided a computer-generated example wherein labour would suffer real wage losses with any kind of international trade. In response, Jones and Ruffin (2004) probed more deeply into the properties of specific-factors models to emphasize that asymmetries between sectors in labour intensity as well as in the flexibility of technology were crucial in determining how real wages would fare with changes in commodity prices brought about by international trade. Furthermore, they showed how the Melvin–Waschik challenge properly reveals how such asymmetry depends endogenously on the degree of factor substitutability in both sectors.

Simple examples often do much to reveal the essence of an argument without the need to follow the more elaborate reasoning required for the general case. This remark, we would argue, has relevance for the effect of trade on real wages. In this chapter we show how the extreme cases concerning production structure can exhibit many of the results of more elaborate reasoning. In particular, we consider cases either in which there is no possibility of factor substitution in either sector (the Leontief case of fixed coefficients), or in which each factor can independently produce commodities on its own (we call this the 'Ricardian' case). In addition, we investigate the case in which one sector is Leontief and the other is Ricardian.

## THE SIMILARITY IN PRODUCTION POSSIBILITIES

It proves convenient to begin by contrasting the production possibilities schedule appropriate to each of these extreme cases. Technology (in both cases) is linear homogeneous and we suppose that in each of two sectors capital, $K_i$, is specific to that sector whereas labour, $L$, is mobile between sectors.

The Leontief case is probably the more familiar of the two, with its right-angled isoquants illustrating that labour and capital must cooperate with each other in rigid proportions. Letting $a_{ij}$ indicate input–output coefficients, the representation of production functions is shown by (equation 1.1):

$$X_i = \text{Min}\{L_i/a_{Li}, K_i/a_{Ki}\}. \tag{1.1}$$

We assume that there is sufficient labour that either one or the other type of capital could be fully employed, but not enough labour to allow both types of capital to earn positive rents simultaneously. These assumptions are captured in the three constraint lines in Figure 1.1 as well as in the solid inner broken-line transformation schedule that disallows over-full employment of any of the three factors. The slope of the $AB$ middle section is $-a_{L1}/a_{L2}$. Only along this section will the entire labour force be employed (and labour receive a positive wage rate). Letting $p_1$ denote the price of the first commodity, with commodity 2 always serving as numeraire, consider the end points, $A$ and $B$. For positive values of $p_1$ smaller than the ratio $a_{L1}/a_{L2}$, the country produces at point $A$, with type-2 capital receiving a positive rental. Type-1 capital, by contrast, is not fully employed at this point and receives no rent. Thus all revenue received in sector 1 accrues to labour so that the nominal wage rate is shown by $p_1/a_{L1}$. If, instead, the price of the first commodity should exceed $a_{L1}/a_{L2}$, production would take place at point $B$. Now it is type-2 capital that suffers unemployment (and a zero rent), while labour and type-1 capital are fully employed. In the second sector labour receives all the revenue, so that the nominal wage rate, $w$, would stay equal to $1/a_{L2}$ even as $p_1$ increases. That is, increases in the price of the first commodity when production is at $A$ get captured entirely by workers, while at $B$ further increases in the price of the

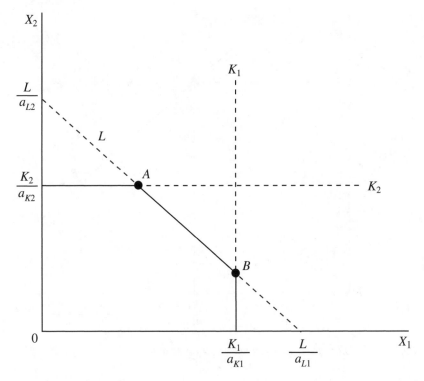

*Figure 1.1   The Leontief transformation schedule*

first commodity go only into increasing the rents earned by type-1 capital. The determination of the wage rate in the Leontief case can be summarized by equation (1.2):

$$w = \text{Min}\{p_1/a_{L1}, p_2/a_{L2}\}. \tag{1.2}$$

Intuition is aided by the fact that one of the specific capitals must always be unemployed, receiving zero rent, so that the wage rate is determined by the price in that sector, which is the sector with the lower $p_i/a_{Li}$.[1]

Figure 1.2 displays the comparable transformation schedule for the Ricardian case in which each factor can, on its own, produce a commodity – labour can produce either, but capital of each type can only produce that specific commodity. Thus the production functions are shown by equation (1.3):

$$X_i = L_i/a_{Li} + K_i/a_{Ki}. \tag{1.3}$$

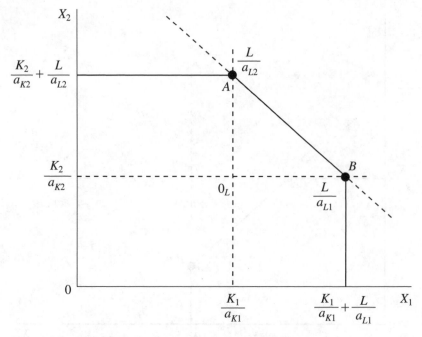

*Figure 1.2    The 'Ricardian' transformation schedule*

In Figure 1.2 an origin for labour, $0_L$, has been positioned at the intersection of the two capital constraint lines. The labour constraint line has been measured from this origin since factor outputs are additive. As a consequence, the production-possibilities schedule for the Ricardian case has a somewhat similar three-part shape as that in the Leontief case! The slope of the middle section is again given by the ratio of intensity input coefficients, $-a_{L1}/a_{L2}$. But if the (relative) price of the first commodity is lower than this ratio, so that production takes place at point $A$, each type of capital is fully employed and earns rentals, while the entire labour force is engaged in producing the second commodity. As a consequence, any increase in the price of the first commodity that keeps production at $A$ does nothing for the nominal wage rate and therefore accrues only in the form of greater rents for type-1 capital. By contrast, if $p_1$ exceeds the crucial ratio, $a_{L1}/a_{L2}$, the entire labour force is devoted to the production of the first commodity so that now the nominal wage is $p_1/a_{L1}$ and any further rise in $p_1$ would raise the wage rate by the same relative amount. (Of course the rentals on type-1 capital also increase by this same relative amount, and the return to type-2 capital would remain the same.) In the event that the relative commodity price ratio matches the slope of the labour constraint line, labour can be used in both sectors. In general for this case:

$$w = \text{Max}\{p_1/a_{L1}, p_2/a_{L2}\}. \tag{1.4}$$

Each commodity can be produced by labour alone, so that labour simply moves to the sector with the higher-valued marginal product. In the Ricardian case factor prices are determined uniquely by commodity prices, independently of factor endowments because each factor can, on its own, produce a commodity regardless of other factor supplies.[2]

The production-possibilities locus in the mixed case illustrated in Figure 1.3 has technology in sector 1 of the Ricardian type, while that in sector 2 is Leontief. Thus production of the second commodity is capped by the amount $K_2/a_{K2}$, just as in Figure 1.1, while that in the first sector would reach a maximum at point $B$ (when the relative price of the first commodity exceeds $a_{L1}/a_{L2}$) shown by the sum of $K_1/a_{K1}$ and $L/a_{L1}$, just as in Figure 1.2. For low prices of the first commodity that lock production at point $A$, small increases in $p_1$ now raise the wage rate by the same proportional amount

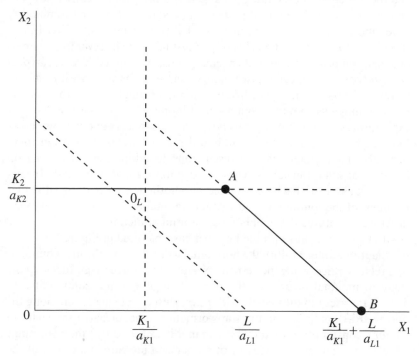

*Figure 1.3   Mixed technologies*

since some labour does produce the first commodity (on its own). This stands in contrast to the position of labour at point $A$ in Figure 1.2. Note also that such a rise in $p_1$ that keeps production at $A$ must serve to reduce rentals to type-2 capital since the wage rate increases and commodity 2's price is fixed (good 2 being the numeraire). When the price of the first commodity increases sufficiently that point $B$ is the production point, all labour produces the first commodity and, just as in Figure 1.2, the wage rate rises in proportion to $p_1$. Indeed, labour *always* benefits by an increase in commodity 1's relative price since the wage rate always equals $p_1/a_{L1}$. Wages are determined in the sector with the more flexible technology.

## REAL WAGES AND TRADE

In the general treatment found in Jones and Ruffin (2004) emphasis is placed on what we call the 'Beta' function, where $\beta_1$ represents the relative increase in the nominal wage rate given a 1 per cent increase in the price of the first commodity (with the price of the second commodity remaining constant), and the 'function' shows how $\beta_1$ changes with price. In the earlier Stolper–Samuelson model the value of $\beta_1$ would exceed unity if the first commodity were labour intensive, and be negative if it were capital intensive. In our specific-factors setting, the value of $\beta_1$ must lie in the interval from zero to one. If it is a proper fraction there emerges the possibility of a *neoclassical ambiguity* as to the effect of price changes on the *real wage*, since if $p_1$ should increase, the rise in the cost of living for labourers might exceed the increase in the nominal wage rate if commodity 1 looms especially large in labour's expenditures. As we shall see, this possibility disappears in our examples as long as labour consumes both commodities. None the less it is convenient in our subsequent diagrams and discussions to adopt the constraints on labour's consumption habits that we used in Jones and Ruffin (2004). In particular, we assumed that labour shared a homothetic taste pattern with other members of the community and, in our diagrammatic treatment, everyone's tastes were captured by a Cobb–Douglas utility function.

We start once again with the Leontief case, pictured in Figure 1.4. In the top diagram, Figure 1.4(a), the horizontal axis measures the first commodity's relative price, while the vertical axis measures three magnitudes: (i) the share in national income of the production of the first commodity, $\theta_1$. This share rises monotonically with price, with a vertical section along the downward-sloping flat of the transformation schedule;[3] (ii) the share in labour's consumption of the first commodity, $\delta_1$, and (iii) the percentage increase in the nominal wage rate of a 1 per cent increase in the price of the first commodity, $\beta_1$. Note that three alternative $\delta_1(\cdot)$ loci have been drawn.

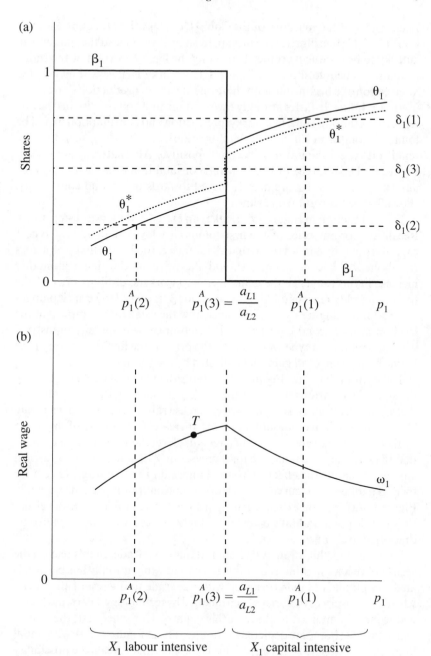

*Figure 1.4   The Leontief case*

Each is horizontal, reflective of the Cobb–Douglas utility function assumption. The $\delta_1(3)$ line illustrates a taste pattern that would lead the economy in autarky to be producing somewhere along the flat $AB$ portion of the transformation schedule shown in Figure 1.1. Autarky is always shown at the intersection of a $\delta_1$ consumption share line and the $\theta_1$ production share curve in Figure 1.4(a). If tastes strongly favoured the first commodity instead, as reflected in the $\delta_1(1)$ line, in autarky, production and consumption would be found at point $B$ in Figure 1.1, with an autarky price, $p_1^A(1)$, such that the rental on type-1 capital now becomes positive. Alternatively, point $A$ in Figure 1.1 becomes the production and consumption point, with $p_1^A(2)$ the autarky price, if tastes are heavily biased towards the second commodity, shown by the horizontal $\delta_1(2)$ line.

The $\beta_1$-function in Figure 1.4(a) takes an extreme 'downward step' form. Recall that for any price of the first commodity lower than $a_{L1}/a_{L2}$, type-1 capital is not fully employed, so that all revenue earned in the first sector goes to labour. As a consequence, should the price of the first commodity increase in this range, all the gains accrue to workers; until the price of the first commodity reaches $a_{L1}/a_{L2}$, the value for $\beta_1$ is unity. However, it plunges to zero for any higher value of $p_1$, since now the wage rate is trapped at the level set in the second industry by the fixed price of numeraire industry 2 with zero rentals on type-2 capital. As the price of the first commodity rises in this higher range, all gains get collected by the specific factor, $K_1$.

The bottom diagram, Figure 1.4(b), plots the fate of the *real wage* along the $\omega_1$ curve at various prices for the first commodity. In the lower range of these prices $\beta_1$ is unity, so that a price increase raises the nominal wage rate by a greater relative amount than the increase in the cost of living to workers. For prices above the crucial $a_{L1}/a_{L2}$ level the value of $\beta_1$ is zero, so that the real wage must decline for increases in $p_1$. There is no 'neoclassical ambiguity' about the effect of price changes on the *real* wage. Of course there is a different $\omega_1$ curve for each of the consumption patterns shown in Figure 1.4(a), but since each reaches a peak at the same $p_1^A(1)$ price level and rises to this point and falls below it for higher prices, we have simplified by drawing in only one $\omega_1$ curve.

So far nothing has been said about international trade. In this section the scenario we have in mind is that this is a country that initially has been isolated from trade and then opens up with free trade to the rest of the world, where relative prices there have been dictated by technology, tastes and factor endowments unrelated to those in this country. Consider, first, the case in which tastes at home are depicted by the $\delta_1(3)$ line in Figure 1.4(a), with initial autarky price at $p_1^A(3) = a_{L1}/a_{L2}$. This is the case that reveals the possibility emphasized by Melvin and Waschik (2001),[4] that is, labour loses by *any* trade, regardless of the pattern. Real wages are at a peak in autarky, and trading contact with the rest of the world must depress real wages. Note how this result does correspond with what might be expected because of the factor intensity ranking of exportables and import-competing goods. As already described, in the lower range of prices for the first commodity, type-1 capital is unemployed and receives zero rents. Therefore labour's distributive share in the first sector, $\theta_{L1}$, is unity. That is, the first commodity is labour-intensive in this range. However, the intensity ranking switches over for $p_1$ in the higher range since there it is the second commodity in which capital is unemployed so that $\theta_{L2}$ is unity. If the world price of the first commodity is higher than in autarky, the country exports the first commodity, which is capital-intensive, and this depresses the real wage. By contrast, if the world price of the first commodity is lower than in autarky, this country imports the first commodity, which is now labour intensive, which once again spells trouble for labour, which suffers from a fall in nominal wage rates exceeding that in the cost of living. The country always imports its labour-intensive commodity and labour always suffers from trade.

Figure 1.4(a), however, has illustrated two other alternative taste patterns for labour, and in these the possible effects of trade on real wages are not so grim. If tastes are described by the $\delta_1(1)$ line, the home country has a relatively high price for the first commodity in autarky. If the world price were even higher, real wages would be depressed by trade since the home country would export the (capital-intensive) first commodity. However, suppose the world price of the first commodity were somewhat lower. Then there is a range in which trade (with the home country now importing the first commodity) would raise the real wage rate. Indeed, if the world price settled so that real wages were shown by a point such as $T$ in Figure 1.4(b), labour would find that free trade has been beneficial, but would also note that some degree of protection for local producers of the first commodity (say to raise the domestic price to $a_{L1}/a_{L2}$) would prove to be an even better solution for workers. (Such a move would indeed maximize labour's position, since all returns to capital would vanish.) Analogous remarks could be made if local tastes had led to situation 2, with $p_1^A(2)$ the autarky price.

The two parts of Figure 1.5 illustrate how radically different the scenario is for labour in the case in which each sector possesses a Ricardian technology. The basic pattern for the $\theta_1$ and $\delta_1(\cdot)$ curves is similar to that of the Leontief case, reflecting the parallels between transformation loci for the two types of technologies. But the effect of trade on real wages is very different. In the lower range of prices for the first commodity no labour is used in that sector (that is, commodity 1 is capital-intensive, with $\theta_{L1}$ equal to zero), so that any increase in commodity 1's price leaves the nominal wage rate unchanged. Since the price increase raises labour's cost of living, real wages must decline in this range. Similarly, in the higher range of prices

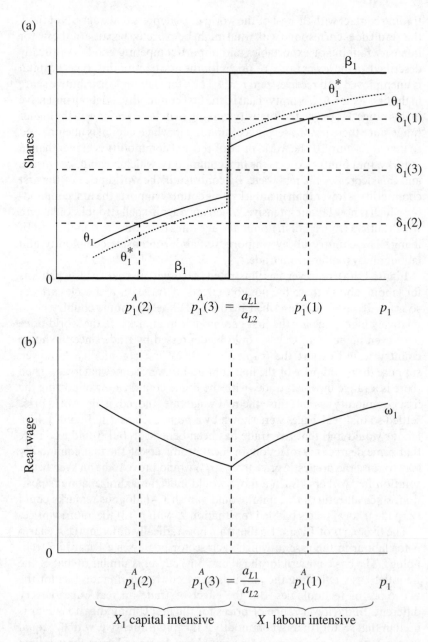

*Figure 1.5  The 'Ricardian' case*

all the labour force is employed in the first sector and thus it becomes the labour-intensive sector. Increases in $p_1$ would raise the nominal wage by the same relative amount and thus unambiguously raise the real wage. If tastes are illustrated by the $\delta_1(3)$ line, autarky price for the first commodity is $a_{L1}/a_{L2}$, and trade with the rest of the world *in either direction* must serve to increase the real wage at home. Note that in this case the home country must export its labour-intensive commodity.[5] Such a rosy picture for labour would, of course, need to be appropriately modified if the autarky price were at some other level, for example, as it would be under taste pattern $\delta_1(1)$ or $\delta_1(2)$.

Finally, we consider the case of mixed technologies in Figure 1.6, where it is assumed that the second sector is Leontief while the first sector is 'Ricardian'. The transformation schedule was illustrated in Figure 1.3, supporting the fact that the $\beta_1$ function is the horizontal line at value unity. For all positive prices of the first commodity labour on its own can produce the first commodity and the wage rate will increase in proportion to $p_1$. Commodity 1 has a very much more flexible technology than does commodity 2, and this asymmetry firmly establishes that any trade that follows from the world price for commodity 1 being higher than in autarky helps labour, while a lower price would unambiguously hurt labour.

## TWO-COUNTRY TRADE

The preceding discussion presented the home country, originally in autarky, with some arbitrary different terms of trade ruling in world markets. Instead, now we consider the possibility that the price ratio ruling in world markets is endogenously determined by the interaction between the home country and a foreign country, differing either in its factor endowment base or in its technology.

### Labour Abundance

Suppose the foreign country has a larger endowment of labour than does the home country, but shares the same technology as well as endowment of the specific capital in each sector. In Figures 1.4–1.6 this implies a different $\theta_1^*$ production share curve for the foreign country, but no change in the $\delta_1(\cdot)$ consumption lines or, most importantly, the $\beta_1$ function. In the Leontief case of Figure 1.4 in the lower range of prices for the first commodity, good 1 is labour-intensive, so that at a given price ratio the relative share of the first commodity produced is higher abroad than at home. In the higher range of prices the first commodity is capital-intensive, and

(a)

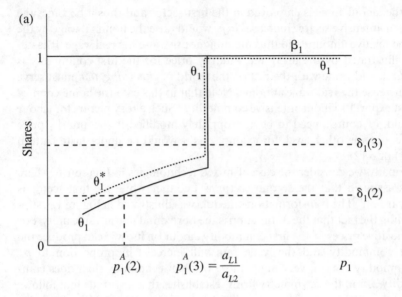

(b)

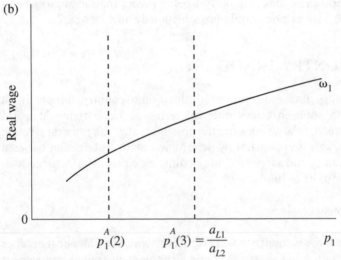

*Figure 1.6   Mixed technologies*

thus its share in the labour-abundant foreign country is lower than at home for each price. In Figure 1.4(a) the foreign $\theta_1^*$ curve is shown by the dotted curve.

Because the factor-intensity ranking in the Ricardian case of Figure 1.5(a) is reversed, so also is the shift in the foreign $\theta_1^*$ curve.[6] The first commodity is capital intensive in the lower range of prices for the first commodity, and thus the labour-abundant foreign country would, at each price, produce relatively less of the first commodity. In the higher range of prices the labour-abundant foreign country would again produce relatively more of the labour-intensive commodity at each price than does the home country, but this is now the first commodity. This supports the drawing in Figure 1.5(a) of its dotted $\theta_1^*$ curve. In the mixed technology case of Figure 1.6, in the lower range of prices for the first commodity it is labour-intensive, so that the foreign country's $\theta_1^*$ curve lies above that for the home country. In the higher range of prices both countries are specialized completely to the first commodity, so that the value of the $\theta_1$ share is unity for both.

The repositioning of the foreign country's production share curve implies that autarky prices are different from those at home. The free-trade price lies between the autarky price ratios in the two countries. Thus the pattern of trade will be determined by the difference in labour endowments. In the Leontief case if (common) tastes are shown by the $\delta_1(1)$ line, the labour-abundant foreign country must face a lower price for the first commodity with trade than in autarky, and thus must export the second commodity, which is labour-intensive. Trade will increase real wages in the foreign labour-abundant country and lower them in the home-capital-abundant country. In the event that both countries have a much stronger preference for the second commodity, the $\delta_1(2)$ case, the foreign country will find that the free-trade relative price of the first commodity is higher than in autarky and thus export this good to the home country. Once again it is the relatively labour-abundant country that finds its real wage improved by trade, and it is in the capital-abundant home country that trade has caused the real wage to deteriorate.

How different is the story in the Ricardian case of Figure 1.5? Now in the lower range of prices for the first commodity (with common tastes shown by the $\delta_1(2)$ line), its relative autarky price is higher abroad than at home, so that with trade the foreign country will import the first commodity. Once again, trade causes the real wage rate to increase in the labour-abundant foreign country (and fall at home). And a similar pattern is revealed should the common taste pattern be shown by the $\delta_1(1)$ line – the labour-abundant foreign country exports the first commodity and its labour force once again gains.

A robust result is obtained in all cases: if the world free-trade price is determined endogenously in trade between two countries sharing the same technology and endowments of specific factors but differing in the supplies of labour, and if the free-trade price differs from autarky price,[7] it is always the case that the real wage rises in the relatively labour-abundant country and falls in the other country. This is a strong result in that it holds for either type of technology (or, indeed, the mixed case of Figure 1.6). Although the actual *pattern* of trade depends on the common taste pattern, the relatively labour-abundant country always exports its labour-intensive commodity.

### Abundance in a Specific Capital

The fate of labour in each country when trade is opened up and they differ only in labour endowments is asymmetric: labour gains by trade in the labour-abundant country and loses in the labour-scarce country. Of course an analogous result would hold if both specific capitals were greater in one country by the same percentage amount, with the same labour force. Here we consider a different case, one in which the foreign country has a richer endowment of type-1 capital, but the same endowment of type-2 capital and labour as does the home country. Consider the Leontief case. In Figure 1.4(a) the $\theta_1^*$ schedule to the left of $a_{L1}/a_{L2}$ is unchanged (since $K_1$ is in excess supply in any case), while the foreign $\theta_1^*$ curve to the right gets shifted upwards. Either there is no trade (for low autarky price of the first commodity), or the labour-abundant home country exports its labour-intensive commodity and experiences an increase in its real wage for high prices of the first commodity. In the Ricardian case shown in Figure 1.5 the $\theta_1^*$ curve is shifted upwards for all prices. Although this is not shown explicitly in the diagram, it now could be the case that the autarky prices in two countries straddle the central $a_{L1}/a_{L2}$ ratio. As a consequence free trade could *lower* the real wage in *both* countries, with each country exporting its capital-intensive commodity. This is reminiscent of the older literature on factor-intensity reversals, in which free trade moves relative wages in the same direction in both countries.[8]

### Different Technologies

If two countries have different technologies, the only effect on the $\beta_1$ function will be on the position of the vertical section if labour input coefficients are not proportional between countries. In such a case the $\omega_1$ curve for the home country and foreign country reach a peak in Figure 1.4(b) or a low point in Figure 1.5(b) at different relative prices.

Suppose that autarky in each country takes place along the downward-sloping section of its transformation schedule. If both have Leontief technologies this implies that real wages will be at their maximum in autarky so that international trade at different prices harms mobile labour in *both* countries. International trade, by pushing economies towards greater specialization, lets the associated complementary (specific) factor reap the rewards at the expense of labour. By contrast, if production is exemplified by Ricardian technology in both sectors in each country, autarky will be at the point of minimum real wage rates for each country. International trade now encourages labour to specialize in the sector with the greater value of its marginal product in both countries. This case therefore merits the 'Ricardian' label.

These examples illustrate that the source of trade is important. If it is caused by differences in technology, low elasticities of substitution in production make it likely that mobile labour will suffer a loss in real wages. The other extreme is reminiscent of the standard Ricardian one-factor case, in which labour unambiguously gains with trade at prices different from those ruling in autarky, and in the specific-factors model is analogous to having infinite values for the elasticity of substitution.

## CONCLUDING REMARKS

In a specific-factors setting, with labour mobile between two sectors and capital specific to each, the effect of opening trade or of changes in the terms of trade on real wages is more complex than in the simple Stolper–Samuelson theorem wherein real wages are unambiguously harmed by more open trade if the country imports its labour-intensive product. Here we have chosen two extreme examples in which technology either exhibits the Leontief characteristic of perfect complementarity with zero substitution between factors possible or exhibits a 'Ricardian' characteristic whereby each factor on its own can produce commodities – labour in either sector and specific capital only in the sector in which it is located. Without having to pursue the formal analytical treatment required in the general case discussed in Jones and Ruffin (2004), we have none the less illustrated several important results in these examples:

1.  The impact of trade on real wages in these examples does not suffer from the 'neoclassical ambiguity' often found in the more general case, in which a price change has a less than proportionate change in the nominal wage rate, which might be outweighed by a higher consumption price weight for labour. A price change either leaves nominal wages unchanged, or moves them in the same proportion as the price change.
2.  Another consequence of dealing only with these extreme cases is that the argument put forth in Ruffin and Jones (1977) and Jones and Ruffin (2004) for a *presumption* that labour gains from free trade cannot be maintained. As those papers suggest, the presumption rests upon

the possibility that the $\beta_1$ curve for nominal wage changes might lie between the $\theta_1$ curve of production shares and the $\delta_1$ locus of consumption shares.

3.  Even if both sectors share the same extreme technology, the impact of trade on the real wage depends very much on whether the two sectors exhibit either zero or infinite substitution possibilities. If they share the Leontief rigid technology and if in autarky neither specific capital is 'binding' in the sense of being fully employed, any different terms of trade in the world economy will cause labour to suffer a deterioration in its real wage. It was a computer-generated example of this kind of result (in a less extreme case than Leontief) that was introduced by Melvin and Waschik (2001) to cast doubt on the 'presumption' about real wages argued by Ruffin and Jones (1977), that is, that labour would gain from trade. As the country trades, an improvement in its terms of trade leads to gains for the country but not to labour since the specific factor employed in the export sector captures all the increased revenues. On the other hand, if substitution possibilities in each sector allow factors independently to produce commodities with constant returns to scale (the Ricardian assumption), labour can gain in real terms regardless of the direction of trade.

4.  If we suppose that the world terms of trade are endogenously determined by trade only between two countries that share the same technology and tastes and differ only in their endowment of labour, a strong result is obtained: The labour-abundant country's labour force will, once trade is opened, experience an improvement in its real wage and whatever commodity is exported, it will be produced by relatively labour-intensive techniques. The other country's labour force suffers by trade. This result does not depend on the common value of elasticities of substitution, whether low or high. The Melvin and Waschik (2001) possibility does not arise.

5.  If, instead, the two countries have the same technology and labour force but differ in the endowment of one of the specific factors, it is possible that with trade the real wage could move in the same direction in the two countries. This was not the case if they differ only in their labour endowment. If countries differ in their technologies, trade may move real wages together or apart.

6.  In the case in which one sector exhibits Leontief rigid coefficients while in the other factors can independently produce commodities, so that sectors are extremely asymmetric in the flexibility of their technologies, labour's fate is always linked to the commodity with the more flexible technology. The real wage is monotonically and positively related to that commodity's relative price.

## NOTES

\*   The ordering of author names has been selected in order to avoid confusion with the referenced paper, Jones and Ruffin (2004), which order was itself chosen to avoid confusion with Ruffin and Jones (1977). Both authors claim equal input of the other author in all these papers, regardless of any signal sent by the alphabet.

1.   Consider the typical back-to-back diagram for determining the wage rate in the specific-factors model. In each sector the demand-for-labour curve would be horizontal at the level $p_i/a_{li}$ up to the point at which all the specific capital gets employed. It falls vertically after that. Equilibrium wages are at the level at which the vertical section of the commodity with the relatively high price intersects the horizontal section of the commodity whose relative price is lower than $a_{L1}/a_{L2}$.

2.   Ruffin (1988) examines the Heckscher–Ohlin model under this 'Ricardian' technology and finds this same property of universal factor price dependence only upon commodity prices.

3.   As $p_1$, rises, the $\theta_1$ share increases, but not as much, relatively, as does $p_1$.

4.   The case in Melvin and Waschik (2001) has elasticities of substitution equal to 0.4 in each sector. In Jones and Ruffin (2004) that corresponds to a downward-sloping $\beta_1$ function. Here we have illustrated the extreme case in which substitution elasticities in production are even lower, zero.

5.   Melvin and Washik (2001) also illustrate the case in which each sector's elasticity of substitution is unity, and with appropriate tastes labour always gains from trade. Here, of course, the elasticities of substitution are both infinite. The value of unity for the elasticity puts results more in line with the Ricardian case of Figure 1.5 than the Leontief version in Figure 1.4.

6.   In Figure 1.2 an increase in the labour endowment moves point $A$ vertically upwards and point $B$ to the right.

7.   If each country has taste pattern $\delta_1(3)$, differences in labour endowments may not alter their common autarky price ratios.

8.   For example, see the implications of free trade on factor prices in Figure 5 of Jones (1956).

## REFERENCES

Jones, Ronald W. (1956), 'Factor proportions and the Heckscher–Ohlin theorem', *Review of Economic Studies*, **24**, 1–10.

Jones, Ronald W. (1971), 'A three-factor model in theory, trade and history', in J.N. Bhagwati, R.W. Jones, R.A. Mundell and J. Vanek (eds), *Trade, Balance of Payments and Growth*, Amsterdam: North-Holland, Chapter 1.

Jones, Ronald W. and Ruffin, Roy J. (2004), 'Trade and wages: a deeper investigation', unpublished manuscript.

Melvin, James and Waschik, Robert (2001), 'The neoclassical ambiguity in the specific-factors model', *Journal of International Trade and Economic Development*, **10**, 321–37.

Ruffin, Roy J. (1988), 'The missing link: the Ricardian approach to the factor endowments theory of trade', *American Economic Review*, **78**, 759–72.

Ruffin, Roy J. and Jones, Ronald W. (1977), 'Protection and real wages: the neoclassical ambiguity', *Journal of Economic Theory*, **14**, 337–48.

Samuelson, Paul A. (1971), 'Ohlin was right', *Swedish Journal of Economics*, **73**, 365–84.

Stolper, Wolfgang and Samuelson, Paul A. (1941), 'Protection and real wages', *Review of Economic Studies*, **9**, 58–73.

# 2. The factor scarcity (abundance) hypothesis, factor mobility, and the political economy of international trade policy

A.G. Schweinberger*

## 1. INTRODUCTION

One of the most widely known and apparently accepted insights originating from the Heckscher–Ohlin model is that owners of relatively scarce factors lose and owners of relatively abundant factors gain from free international goods trade (see, for example, Dixit and Norman, 1980; Woodland, 1982; Hillman, 1989; and Freeman, 1995) or a recent book on the effects of globalization by Rodrick (1997). We refer to this insight as the factor scarcity (abundance) hypothesis.

Initially the factor scarcity (abundance) hypothesis was confined to the $2 \times 2 \times 2$ Heckscher–Ohlin model but in the 1970s and 1980s the Heckscher–Ohlin model and theorem were generalized to $n$ dimensions (see, for example, Ethier, 1984). These generalizations are undoubtedly worthwhile but they also have one major drawback: they invariably make use of the property of factor price equalization, see again Ethier (1984). This entails that normally the said method of analysis cannot readily be extended to applications of the factor scarcity (abundance) hypothesis to a sector-specific factor model.

It now seems to be generally agreed that applications of the sector-specific factor model have important political-economy messages. Even fairly recent publications make extensive use of it (see, for example, Grossman and Helpman, 1994). It therefore seems rather surprising that to date no attempt has been made to apply the factor scarcity (abundance) hypothesis to a general sector-specific factor model and relate the results to one of the most fundamental issues raised in international political economy: the changes in the distribution of income of the owners of the sector-specific factors brought about by a movement from an autarkic to a free-trade equilibrium.

The present chapter's purpose is to eliminate this gap.[1] The main political-economy appeal of the sector-specific factor model derives from the fact that it features a direct link between trading patterns and the distribution of income of the owners of the sector-specific factors.

The key question addressed in this chapter relates to the appropriate definition of relative or absolute scarcity or abundance of the sector-specific factors. A sector-specific factor may be relatively abundant or scarce using other sector-specific factors and/or the mobile factor as benchmarks for comparison. Therefore a key task is to put forward useful definitions of factor scarcity or abundance.

By useful definitions of factor scarcity or abundance we mean restrictions on the relative endowment differences (between countries) which are conflict-generating between the owners of the sector-specific factors employed in different industries. In a certain rather limited sense the chapter may be viewed as putting forward novel conditions for the formation of interest groups which lobby either for or against free international trade. But at this point a note of caution is in order. It would be presumptious to argue that this chapter can actually explain the formation of interest groups. Strictly speaking the existence of interest groups, which is fundamental to international political economy, cannot be explained in a model with perfect competition in factor and goods markets (it may, of course, be assumed, as in many standard references). We can at most claim that the chapter throws some light on necessary conditions for the existence of interest groups lobbying for or against free international trade.

Furthermore it should be noted that relating the pattern of comparative advantage to the differences in the factor endowments between countries in a sector-specific factor model is not an entirely novel task. Krugman and Obstfeld (1997) make use of differences in the endowments of the sector-specific factors to explain the pattern of comparative advantage of the USA and Japan. However, given their limited purpose, they confine themselves to a very special modelling framework. As will be seen, the analysis of the present chapter is considerably more general and also addresses different issues. Unlike Krugman and Obstfeld (1997) we allow, for example, for a limited mobility of the sector-specific factors. This enables us in section 4 to analyse the effects of the formation of 'nuggets' (see Bond et al., 2002) on the pattern of comparative advantage.

Mention should also be made of Dixit and Norman (1980). They allow (within a two-good model) for differences in the endowments with one sector-specific factor (keeping initially the endowment with the mobile factor unchanged). Their focus is on factor price equalization or at least a narrowing of the factor price differences of the mobile factor through free international trade. Their main conclusion is agnostic: there is no reason why one should argue that free international trade results in a narrowing of the factor price differences of the mobile factor.

By far the most general and comprehensive analysis of the relationship between factor endowment differences and comparative advantage can be found in Dixit and Woodland (1982). Dixit and Woodland make use of a global and a local approach. In their local analysis they focus on weak and strong output effects (from the Rybczynski matrix) which guarantee the corresponding (Heckscher–Ohlin–Samuelson) HOS effects on net exports. Dixit and Woodland obtain a number of very general and useful results but they do not address the key issue of the present chapter, that is, the effect of free trade on the distribution of income of the owners of the sector-specific factors in the light of the endowment differences of sector-specific and mobile factors between countries.

In this context the chapter looks into a somewhat neglected policy issue. Can trade policy be used to achieve a targeted redistribution of income? As is well known, the standard literature generally emphasizes the efficiency effects of free international trade. In this context one is reminded of a time-honoured exception to this general trend. Ricardo argued in favour of free trade because he felt that capitalists should gain at the expense of land-owners, because capitalists in contrast to landowners earn their income by their own efforts.

At this point it should be noted that our approach differs from the standard approach of international political economy inasmuch as the initial equilibrium is not a free trade but an autarkic equilibrium (which may be explained in terms of prohibitive tariffs or quotas). The main tenet is that in order to understand the possible emergence of lobbying groups (which behave as single actors) it is indispensable to predict the pattern of comparative advantage. Protectionist policies are not considered because they involve additional complications due to various possible distributions of tariff revenue.

The chapter is structured as follows: the key assumptions and the model are explained in Section 2. All the results hinge on the special properties of a novel Rybczynski-type matrix (the Ricardo–Viner matrix). Its properties are summarized in a lemma. Sections 3 and 4 contain all the main results. They are stated as Propositions I, II and III. The chapter concludes with a summary and suggestions for future research.

## 2.   THE MODEL AND THE ASSUMPTIONS

A key feature of international political-economy models is that certain interest groups attempt to influence the policy decisions of the government. A very important and sometimes neglected issue arises in this context.

How much information concerning the working of the economy do agents have? The standard approach in international political economy is to postulate that the owners of the sector-specific factors have enough information to calculate the effect of various policies on their real income (see, for example, Mayer, 1984), who notes that this assumption is very restrictive.

In the present chapter we make use of the following two behavioural assumptions.

## Assumption A

The owners of a sector-specific factor employed in a certain industry lobby for (against) free international trade if their country has a comparative advantage (disadvantage) in the production of a good which uses the sector-specific factor. A country is deemed to have a comparative advantage (disadvantage) in the production of a good if the autarkic price of the good is lower (higher) in this country than in the other country.

It cannot be emphasized strongly enough that Assumption A is a behavioural assumption. The key idea underlying it is that agents do not have enough information to calculate the general equilibrium effects. The implicit assumption that agents can observe autarkic prices in the home and foreign countries is entirely consistent with the assumption of perfect competition. The same cannot be said if one assumes that agents have enough information to calculate all general equilibrium effects.

Another key assumption of the whole chapter is Walrasian stability.

## Assumption B

All goods markets satisfy the Walrasian stability condition. If there is an excess demand (supply) in a market, the price rises (falls). World market equilibrium prices for all goods lie strictly between the autarkic equilibrium prices in both countries.

Assumption B is a standard assumption in a considerable part of traditional international trade theory based upon perfect competition and constant returns to scale. Another important standard assumption is that in a given industry the same production function is used in both countries. This is a very restrictive assumption. It may be relaxed. If the production functions differ only because of factor-augmenting technical progress, factor endowments have to be reinterpreted. They must be measured in efficiency rather than physical units.

The model to be formalized below is a three-industry sector-specific factor model. The choice of three industries (sectors) is deliberate. On the one hand the model is general enough to allow for, for example, coalition formation between the owners of the sector-specific factors used in two industries; on the other hand the model is simple enough to make the economic meaning of the algebraic results transparent. It can be shown that all the results of the chapter can readily be extended to any finite ($n$) dimensions. The model consists of the following three autarkic goods market equilibrium conditions:

$$x_1(p_1, p_2, p_3, K_1, K_2, K_3; L) = c_1(p_1, p_2, p_3; Y) \tag{2.1}$$

$$x_2(p_1, p_2, p_3, K_1, K_2, K_3; L) = c_2(p_1, p_2, p_3; Y) \tag{2.2}$$

$$x_3(p_1, p_2, p_3, K_1, K_2, K_3; L) = c_3(p_1, p_2, p_3; Y) \tag{2.3}$$

$$Y = p_1 x_1(\cdot) + p_2 x_2(\cdot) + p_3 x_3(\cdot), \tag{2.4}$$

where:
$x_j(\cdot), j = 1, 2, 3$ stand for the supply functions (or production graphs) of the three goods
$c_j(\cdot)$      the Marshallian (uncompensated) demand functions, $j = 1, 2, 3$ and $Y$ for the value of output and spending.

Note that it follows from Walras's law that we cannot solve for $p_1, p_2$ and $p_3$. As usual, a numeraire good has to be chosen and one equilibrium condition has to be eliminated. Equally important in writing up the model in terms of aggregate (over the households) demand functions for the three goods, we have assumed that the preferences of all households are identical and either homothetic or quasi-homothetic, see, for example, Deaton and Muellbauer (1986) for the relevant aggregation theorem.

We now define the excess supplies of the three goods as:

$$e_1 = x_1(\cdot) - c_1(\cdot) \tag{2.5}$$

$$e_2 = x_2(\cdot) - c_2(\cdot) \tag{2.6}$$

$$e_3 = x_3(\cdot) - c_3(\cdot). \tag{2.7}$$

Keeping the prices of all the goods fixed, the excess supply functions are now differentiated totally with respect to $K_1, K_2, K_3$ and $L$. The country with the endowments $K_1 + dK_1, K_2 + dK_2, K_3 + dK_3, L + dL$ is referred to as the home country. Note that $p_1 de_1 + p_2 de_2 + p_3 de_3 = 0$ follows from Walras's law. Furthermore, Assumptions A and B imply that if, for example, $de_1 > 0$, $de_2 < 0$ and $de_3 < 0$, then the home country has a comparative advantage in good 1 and a comparative disadvantage in goods 2 and 3.

Making use of a local comparative static analysis for the purpose of explaining the pattern of comparative advantage raises an important methodological issue.

The analysis can, of course, be interpreted as a strictly local analysis and the results interpreted accordingly. In this case the analysis is subject to all the standard limitations of a comparative static analysis. It is not entirely clear for which 'very small' endowment differences (between countries) it is a good enough approximation. Another more satisfactory approach is to interpret it in terms of midpoint evaluations of Taylor's expansions; see, for example, Ethier (1984). Moreover it should be noted that Dixit and Woodland (1982) also employ a strictly local (calculus) approach to analyse the relationship between factor endowment differences and the pattern of comparative advantage.

After total differentiation of (2.1), (2.2) and (2.3) with respect to $K_1$, $K_2$, $K_3$ and $L$ we make use of the following expressions to transform the system so that it becomes amenable to economic interpretation (see Appendix A for details):

$$L\frac{\partial x_1}{\partial L} = x_1 - \frac{\partial x_1}{\partial K_1}K_1 - \frac{\partial x_1}{\partial K_2}K_2 - \frac{\partial x_1}{\partial K_3}K_3 \tag{2.8}$$

$$L\frac{\partial x_2}{\partial L} = x_2 - \frac{\partial x_2}{\partial K_1}K_1 - \frac{\partial x_2}{\partial K_2}K_2 - \frac{\partial x_2}{\partial K_3}K_3 \tag{2.9}$$

$$L\frac{\partial x_3}{\partial L} = x_3 - \frac{\partial x_3}{\partial K_1}K_1 - \frac{\partial x_3}{\partial K_2}K_2 - \frac{\partial x_3}{\partial K_3}K_3 \tag{2.10}$$

$$L\frac{\partial Y}{\partial L} = Y - \frac{\partial Y}{\partial K_1}K_1 - \frac{\partial Y}{\partial K_2}K_2 - \frac{\partial Y}{\partial K_3}K_3 \tag{2.11}$$

$$\frac{\partial Y}{\partial K_1} = p_1\frac{\partial x_1}{\partial K_1} + p_2\frac{\partial x_2}{\partial K_1} + p_3\frac{\partial x_3}{\partial K_1} \tag{2.12}$$

$$\frac{\partial Y}{\partial K_2} = p_1\frac{\partial x_1}{\partial K_2} + p_2\frac{\partial x_2}{\partial K_2} + p_3\frac{\partial x_3}{\partial K_2} \tag{2.13}$$

$$\frac{\partial Y}{\partial K_3} = p_1\frac{\partial x_1}{\partial K_3} + p_2\frac{\partial x_2}{\partial K_3} + p_3\frac{\partial x_3}{\partial K_3}. \tag{2.14}$$

Expressions (2.8) to (2.11) follow from the linear homogeneity (in factor endowments) of appropriately defined national revenue functions; see, for example, Woodland (1982); expressions (2.12) to (2.14) from a total differentiation of $Y$ with respect to $K_1$, $K_2$ and $K_3$ respectively (keeping goods prices fixed). Expressions (2.8) to (2.14) are substituted into the expressions for $de_1$, $de_2$ and $de_3$ (see Appendix A). This yields:

$$de_1 = \alpha_{11} K_1 \left( \frac{dK_1}{K_1} - \frac{dL}{L} \right) + \alpha_{12} K_2 \left( \frac{dK_2}{K_2} - \frac{dL}{L} \right)$$

$$+ \alpha_{13} K_3 \left( \frac{dK_3}{K_3} - \frac{dL}{L} \right) + \left( 1 - \frac{\partial \log c_1}{\partial \log Y} \right) \frac{dL}{L} \qquad (2.15)$$

$$de_2 = \alpha_{21} K_1 \left( \frac{dK_1}{K_1} - \frac{dL}{L} \right) + \alpha_{22} K_2 \left( \frac{dK_2}{K_2} - \frac{dL}{L} \right)$$

$$+ \alpha_{23} K_3 \left( \frac{dK_3}{K_3} - \frac{dL}{L} \right) + \left( 1 - \frac{\partial \log c_2}{\partial \log Y} \right) \frac{dL}{L} \qquad (2.16)$$

$$de_3 = \alpha_{31} K_1 \left( \frac{dK_1}{K_1} - \frac{dL}{L} \right) + \alpha_{32} K_2 \left( \frac{dK_2}{K_2} - \frac{dL}{L} \right)$$

$$+ \alpha_{33} K_3 \left( \frac{dK_3}{K_3} - \frac{dL}{L} \right) + \left( 1 - \frac{\partial \log c_3}{\partial \log Y} \right) \frac{dL}{L}, \qquad (2.17)$$

where:

$$\alpha_{11} = \left( \frac{\partial c_2}{\partial Y} + \frac{\partial c_3}{\partial Y} \right) \frac{\partial x_1}{\partial K_1} - \frac{\partial c_1}{\partial Y} \left( \frac{\partial x_2}{\partial K_1} + \frac{\partial x_3}{\partial K_1} \right)$$

$$\alpha_{12} = \left( \frac{\partial c_2}{\partial Y} + \frac{\partial c_3}{\partial Y} \right) \frac{\partial x_1}{\partial K_2} - \frac{\partial c_1}{\partial Y} \left( \frac{\partial x_2}{\partial K_2} + \frac{\partial x_3}{\partial K_2} \right)$$

$$\alpha_{13} = \left( \frac{\partial c_2}{\partial Y} + \frac{\partial c_3}{\partial Y} \right) \frac{\partial x_1}{\partial K_3} - \frac{\partial c_1}{\partial Y} \left( \frac{\partial x_2}{\partial K_3} + \frac{\partial x_3}{\partial K_3} \right)$$

$$\alpha_{21} = \left( \frac{\partial c_1}{\partial Y} + \frac{\partial c_3}{\partial Y} \right) \frac{\partial x_2}{\partial K_1} - \frac{\partial c_2}{\partial Y} \left( \frac{\partial x_1}{\partial K_1} + \frac{\partial x_3}{\partial K_1} \right)$$

$$\alpha_{22} = \left( \frac{\partial c_1}{\partial Y} + \frac{\partial c_3}{\partial Y} \right) \frac{\partial x_2}{\partial K_2} - \frac{\partial c_2}{\partial Y} \left( \frac{\partial x_1}{\partial K_2} + \frac{\partial x_3}{\partial K_2} \right)$$

$$\alpha_{23} = \left( \frac{\partial c_1}{\partial Y} + \frac{\partial c_3}{\partial Y} \right) \frac{\partial x_2}{\partial K_3} - \frac{\partial c_2}{\partial Y} \left( \frac{\partial x_1}{\partial K_3} + \frac{\partial x_3}{\partial K_3} \right)$$

$$\alpha_{31} = \left( \frac{\partial c_1}{\partial Y} + \frac{\partial c_2}{\partial Y} \right) \frac{\partial x_3}{\partial K_1} - \frac{\partial c_3}{\partial Y} \left( \frac{\partial x_1}{\partial K_1} + \frac{\partial x_2}{\partial K_1} \right)$$

$$\alpha_{32} = \left( \frac{\partial c_1}{\partial Y} + \frac{\partial c_2}{\partial Y} \right) \frac{\partial x_3}{\partial K_2} - \frac{\partial c_3}{\partial Y} \left( \frac{\partial x_1}{\partial K_2} + \frac{\partial x_2}{\partial K_2} \right)$$

$$\alpha_{33} = \left(\frac{\partial c_1}{\partial Y} + \frac{\partial c_2}{\partial Y}\right)\frac{\partial x_3}{\partial K_3} - \frac{\partial c_3}{\partial Y}\left(\frac{\partial x_1}{\partial K_3} + \frac{\partial x_2}{\partial K_3}\right).$$

It should be noted that the goods are measured in units so that $p_1 = p_2 = p_3 = 1$. This facilitates the exposition. As can be seen from expressions (2.15) to (2.17), each expression for $de_j$ ($j = 1, 2, 3$) consists of two effects. There is first of all a relative factor endowment effect (represented by the first three terms) and a scale effect (represented by the last term). Not surprisingly, the scale effect vanishes if preferences are homothetic.

In order to focus on essentials we assume homothetic preferences. Note that with homothetic preferences all goods are normal in demand.

To understand that equations (2.15) to (2.17) may be interpreted as generalizations of the 'Heckscher–Ohlin effect' assume that the composite commodity theorem can be applied to goods 2 and 3 and that all the sector-specific factors become perfectly mobile. Under these conditions we have $K_1 + K_2 + K_3 = K$ and

$$\frac{\partial x_j}{\partial K_1} = \frac{\partial x_j}{\partial K_2} = \frac{\partial x_j}{\partial K_3} = \frac{\partial x_j}{\partial K} \quad j = 1, 2, 3.$$

Expression (2.15) now becomes:

$$de_1 = \left[\frac{\partial \tilde{c}_2}{\partial Y}\frac{\partial x_1}{\partial K} - \frac{\partial c_1}{\partial Y}\frac{\partial \tilde{x}_2}{\partial K}\right]K\left(\frac{dK}{K} - \frac{dL}{L}\right), \tag{2.18}$$

where:
$\tilde{c}_2$ and $\tilde{x}_2$ denote the demand and supply of the composite good made up of goods 2 and 3.

We refer to the expression in the square brackets as the Heckscher–Ohlin effect. If good 1 is capital intensive we know that $\partial x_1/\partial K > 0$ and $\partial \tilde{x}_2/\partial K < 0$. It follows that the Heckscher–Ohlin effect is positive.

An inspection of the matrix of the coefficients of: $dK_1/K_1 - dL/L$, $dK_2/K_2 - dL/L$ and $dK_3/K_3 - dL/L$ in equations (2.15) to (2.17) reveals that all the diagonal elements, that is:

$$\alpha_{11}K_1, \quad \alpha_{22}K_2 \quad \text{and} \quad \alpha_{33}K_3 \text{ are positive.}$$

The diagonal coefficients may therefore be interpreted as generalized Heckscher–Ohlin effects. The diagonal coefficients are positive because it is well known that:

$$\frac{\partial x_j}{\partial K_j} > 0 \quad \text{and} \quad \frac{\partial x_j}{\partial K_i} < 0, \quad i \neq j.$$

It is convenient to refer to the matrix of the coefficients of $dK_1/K_1 - dL/L$, $dK_2/K_2 - dL/L$ and $dK_3/K_3 - dL/L$ in equations (2.15) to (2.17) as the Ricardo–Viner matrix.

The Ricardo–Viner matrix has two important properties which can be used to derive a number of results (see the following Section 3). We have just seen that all the diagonal elements are positive. We now prove that all the off-diagonal elements must be negative.

Take any off-diagonal element, say $\alpha_{12}$. We know that $\partial x_1/\partial K_2 < 0$ but what about:

$$\frac{\partial x_2}{\partial K_2} + \frac{\partial x_3}{\partial K_2}?$$

Note that from expression (2.13) we have:

$$\frac{\partial Y}{\partial K_2} - \frac{\partial x_1}{\partial K_2} = \frac{\partial x_2}{\partial K_2} + \frac{\partial x_3}{\partial K_2}. \tag{2.19}$$

Since the marginal value product of $K_2$ is positive we know that $\partial Y/\partial K_2 > 0$ and also $\partial x_1/\partial K_2 < 0$. This implies that the right-hand side of (2.19) is positive. The same reasoning can be applied to any off-diagonal element.                                                                     Q.E.D.

The results obtained so far regarding the properties of the Ricardo–Viner matrix are now summarized in the following lemma.

**Lemma**

Consider the matrix of the coefficients of $dK_1/K_1 - dL/L$, $dK_2/K_2 - dL/L$ and $dK_3/K_3 - dL/L$ in equations (2.15) to (2.17). This matrix of coefficients is referred to as the Ricardo–Viner matrix, which has positive diagonal elements. All the off-diagonal elements are negative.

All the following results hinge on the above-mentioned sign properties of the elements of the Ricardo–Viner matrix. It should be obvious that the sign properties of the matrix can readily be generalized to $n$ dimensions.

In concluding section 2 we put forward a definition which will turn out to be useful in the derivation of results in section 3.

**Definition 1**

The Ricardo–Viner matrix is diagonally dominant with respect to good $i$ if and only if the diagonal element is larger in absolute magnitude than any off-diagonal element in the same row. The latter is the case if in each row the sum of the diagonal element and all the off-diagonal elements is positive.

The concept of diagonal dominance is well known from Arrow and Hahn (1971). The application of this concept to relate excess supplies to differences in endowments with sector-specific factors relative to the mobile factor appears to be novel. The concept captures the idea that the *own* effects of specific factor endowment differences (relative to the mobile factor) dominate the sum of all the *cross*-effects (see Arrow and Hahn, 1971, p. 233).

## 3. RESULTS IN A GENERAL SECTOR-SPECIFIC FACTOR MODEL

In this section we first show how the lemma can be applied to prove some of the results of the received literature.

Krugman and Obstfeld (1997, p. 59) put forward an interesting argument in favour of explaining trading patterns in terms of the expected effects of free international trade on the incomes of the owners of the sector-specific factors. This political-economy perspective is due to Ricardo and the discussion concerning the repeal of the Corn Laws. In this context, Krugman and Obstfeld make use of factor endowment differences in a sector-specific factor model to explain the pattern of comparative advantage between the USA and Japan. The two sector-specific factors are capital and land; the mobile factor is labour. Let Japan be the home country. Japan is assumed to have more capital and less land per worker than the USA. Let good 1 be produced by means of capital and labour (and the other good by means of land and labour).

It follows immediately that Japan must have a comparative advantage in manufactured goods and the USA in food; see equation (2.15) and the lemma. In this case we have:

$$\frac{dK_1}{K_1} > \frac{dL}{L} > \frac{dK_2}{K_2},$$

where $K_1$ is capital and $K_2$ land.

Equation (2.15) highlights the limitation of this result. Assume good 1 is food and the USA is the home country and more abundantly endowed with capital, land *and* labour, that is:

$$\frac{dK_1}{K_1} > \frac{dK_2}{K_2} > \frac{dL}{L} > 0.$$

Since we only know the signs but not the magnitudes of $\alpha_{11}K_1$ and $\alpha_{12}K_2$ we cannot predict that the USA has a comparative advantage in food.

Dixit and Norman (1980, p. 102–106) also apply a simple (two-good) sector-specific factor model to explain trading patterns in terms of differences in endowments with the sector-specific and mobile factors (between countries). However, their main purpose is to show that generally free trade does not result in a move towards an equalization of the price of the mobile factor. To this end they assume a *ceteris paribus* difference in the endowments of the two countries with the sector-specific factor in industry 1, then in industry 2 and finally the mobile factor. All their results follow directly from the properties of the Ricardo–Viner matrix and equation (2.15). Furthermore Dixit and Norman show that *ceteris paribus* differences in the endowment with the mobile factor (between countries) are compatible with an equilibrium without trade. To show this in our more general model we now form the sum of $\alpha_{11}K_1$, $\alpha_{12}K_2$ and $\alpha_{13}K_3$. From equations (2.15) to (2.17) and the definitions of $\alpha_{11}$, $\alpha_{12}$ and $\alpha_{13}$ it is straightforward to show that (see Appendix B for more detail):

$$\alpha_{11}K_1 + \alpha_{12}K_2 + \alpha_{13}K_3 = \left(\frac{\partial c_2}{\partial Y} + \frac{\partial c_3}{\partial Y}\right)c_1\left(1 - \frac{\partial \log x_1}{\partial \log L}\right)$$
$$- \frac{\partial c_1}{\partial Y}c_2\left(1 - \frac{\partial \log x_2}{\partial \log L}\right) - \frac{\partial c_1}{\partial Y}c_3\left(1 - \frac{\partial \log x_3}{\partial \log L}\right). \quad (2.20)$$

Remember that preferences are homothetic, hence:

$$\frac{\partial c_2}{\partial Y}c_1 = \frac{\partial c_1}{\partial Y}c_2 \quad \text{and} \quad \frac{\partial c_3}{\partial Y}c_1 = \frac{\partial c_1}{\partial Y}c_3. \quad (2.21)$$

Rewriting expression (2.20) in the light of (2.21) we have:

$$\frac{\partial c_2}{\partial Y}c_1\left(\frac{\partial \log x_2}{\partial \log L} - \frac{\partial \log x_1}{\partial \log L}\right) + \frac{\partial c_1}{\partial Y}c_3\left(\frac{\partial \log x_3}{\partial \log L} - \frac{\partial \log x_1}{\partial \log L}\right)$$
$$= \alpha_{11}K_1 + \alpha_{12}K_2 + \alpha_{13}K_3. \quad (2.22)$$

Setting $dK_1 = dK_2 = dK_3 = 0$ in equation (2.15) and following Dixit and Norman in assuming that:

$$\frac{\partial \log x_1}{\partial \log L} = \frac{\partial \log x_2}{\partial \log L} = \frac{\partial \log x_3}{\partial \log L}, \quad (2.23)$$

it can readily be seen from equation (2.15) that $de_1 = 0$. Furthermore it can be shown from equation (2.23) that we must also have: $de_2 = de_3 = 0$; see again Appendix B.

We now proceed to prove more general results. The purpose is to shed more light on the relationship between emerging trading patterns and the changes in the distribution of income of sector-specific factor owners as a consequence of free international trade. In adopting this focus we follow the time-honoured tradition of Ricardo in assigning to the owners of sector-specific factors a special role in political activities.

The results are formalized as Propositions I and II.

## Proposition I

Let the goods and sector-specific factors in the two countries be labelled such that:

$$\frac{dK_1}{K_1} \geq \frac{dK_2}{K_2} \geq \frac{dK_3}{K_3} \geq \cdots \geq \frac{dK_n}{K_n} \tag{2.24}$$

and Assumptions A and B hold. Then:

(a)  the owners of the sector-specific factor in industry 1 lobby in the home country in favour of free international trade if:

$$\frac{dK_1}{K_1} \geq \frac{dL}{L} \geq \frac{dK_2}{K_2} \geq \frac{dK_3}{K_3} \geq \cdots \geq \frac{dK_n}{K_n} \tag{2.25}$$

and

(b)  the owners of the sector-specific factor in industry $n$ lobby in the home country against free international trade if:

$$\frac{dK_1}{K_1} \geq \frac{dK_2}{K_2} \geq \frac{dK_3}{K_3} \geq \cdots \geq \frac{dK_{n-1}}{K_{n-1}} \geq \frac{dL}{L} > \frac{dK_n}{K_n}. \tag{2.26}$$

## Proof
Proposition I follows directly from the sign properties of the elements of the Ricardo–Viner matrix stated in the lemma. Proposition I has been stated assuming $n$ goods (and industries). The generalization of the lemma to $n$ industries should be obvious.                                              Q.E.D.

The interest of Proposition I lies in the fact that it is counterintuitive. One would probably have expected that if the home country is better endowed with the sector-specific factor in industry 1 relative to all other sector-specific factors *and* the mobile factor, then the home country should have a comparative advantage in good 1. As can be seen from expressions (2.24) and (2.25) this is not necessarily the case. The endowment differences of the mobile factor must partition the ranking of the sector-specific factor endowment differences so that one sector-specific factor is in one set and all the others in the other set.

At this point two observations are in order.

First, it is straightforward to apply Proposition I to the problem raised by Ricardo. The government can use the move to free trade to raise the income of the owners of the sector-specific factor in industry 1 or lower the income of the owners of the sector-specific factor in industry $n$ if the conditions of Proposition I are satisfied.

Second, as is well known, lobbying is not a costless activity. If we allow for the fact that lobbying makes use of factors of production as inputs, we may have the phenomenon of reversals of the pattern of comparative advantage. This interesting possibility is not pursued here because of lack of space. It is conspicuous by its absence from the received literature on international political economy.

Two useful corollaries follow from Proposition I.

### Corollary I

(a) Assume that $dL/L = 0$ and $dK_1/K_1 > 0$ but $dK_2/K_2 < 0, dK_3/K_3 < 0, \ldots, dK_n/K_n < 0$. Then it follows that the owners of the sector-specific factor in industry 1 lobby (in the home country) in favour of free international trade.

(b) Assume that $dL/L = 0$ and $dK_1/K_1 > 0, dK_2/K_2 > 0, dK_3/K_3 > 0 \ldots, dK_{n-1}/K_{n-1} > 0$ but $dK_n/K_n < 0$. Then the owners of the sector-specific factor in industry $n$ lobby (in the home country) against free international trade.

### Corollary II

Assume that the *relative* endowments with sector-specific factors in the two countries are the same. Then differences in the endowments with the mobile factor do not affect the pattern of comparative advantage if: $dK/K > dL/L > 0$ or $dL/L > dK/K > 0$, where by assumption $dK/K = dK_1/K_1 = dK_2/K_2 = dK_3/K_3 = \cdots = dK_n/K_n$.

The two corollaries follow directly from equations (2.15) to (2.17) and the lemma as well as the conditions stated in the corollaries.

Corollaries I and II state, of course, results based on special assumptions, but they highlight important analytical properties of the generalized sector-specific factor model. First, note that the results stated as Corollary I hold even without homothetic preferences. Second, Corollary II shows that as in the Heckscher–Ohlin model the *pattern* of comparative advantage depends only upon the differences (between countries) of the relative endowments with a *composite* sector-specific and the mobile factors.

We now turn to the derivation of the final result in this section. It will be obvious from equations (2.15) to (2.27) and Definition I that additional and stronger results can be obtained if we can prove that:

$$\alpha_{i1}K_1 + \alpha_{i2}K_2 + \alpha_{i3}K_3 > 0 \quad i = 1, 3. \tag{2.27}$$

If the latter is the case then the diagonal elements dominate all the off-diagonal elements.

We now proceed by stating a set of conditions which guarantee that the expressions under (2.27) are satisfied.

**Assumption C**
Let

$$\frac{\partial \log a_{K_1}}{\partial \log r_1} > \frac{\partial \log a_{K_j}}{\partial \log r_j} \frac{\beta_{K_1}}{\beta_{K_j}} \quad j = 2, \ldots, n$$

**Assumption D**
Let

$$\frac{\partial \log a_{K_n}}{\partial \log r_n} > \frac{\partial \log a_{K_j}}{\partial \log r_j} \frac{\beta_{K_n}}{\beta_{K_j}} \quad j = 1, \ldots, n-1$$

where $\beta_{K_j}$ denotes the cost share and $a_{K_j}$ the input coefficient of the sector-specific factor in industry $j$.

It is straightforward to prove that Assumption C entails that:

$$\frac{\partial \log x_j}{\partial \log L} > \frac{\partial \log x_1}{\partial \log L} \quad j = 2, \ldots, n \tag{2.28}$$

$$\frac{\partial \log x_j}{\partial \log L} > \frac{\partial \log x_n}{\partial \log L} \quad j = 1, \ldots, n-1. \tag{2.29}$$

To this end it is shown in Appendix B that:

$$\alpha_{11}K_1 + \alpha_{12}K_2 + \alpha_{13}K_3 + \alpha_{n1}K_n > 0$$

if expression (2.28) holds. Similarly

$$\alpha_{n1}K_1 + \alpha_{n2}K_2 + \alpha_{n3}K_3 + \alpha_{nn}K_n > 0$$

if expression (2.29) holds.

We are now in a position to state Proposition II.

**Proposition II**

Let the labelling of goods and sector-specific factors be such that expression (2.24) is satisfied. Then:

(a)   the owners of the sector-specific factor in industry 1 lobby in favour of free international trade if Assumptions A, B and C hold and: $dK_1/K_1 > dL/L$;

(b)   the owners of the sector-specific factor in industry $n$ lobby against free international trade if Assumptions A, B and D hold and: $dL/L > dK_n/K_n$.

**Proof**

Proposition II follows from the fact that if Assumptions C and D are satisfied, the sums of all the off-diagonal elements of the first and $n$th row of the Ricardo–Viner matrix are smaller in absolute magnitude than the respective diagonal elements.

The main message of Propositon II is straightforward. Intuitively we would expect that the home country should have a comparative advantage in good 1 if it is relatively well endowed with the sector-specific factor used in industry 1. By relatively well endowed we mean relative to all the other sector-specific factors *and* the mobile factor. Proposition I taught us that such a conjecture generally is not correct; for example, the following ranking: $dK_1/K_1 > dK_2/K_2 > dK_3/K_3, \ldots, > dK_n/K_n > dL/L$ does not yield any results making use only of Proposition I. This is due to the fact that 'cross'-effects can always be strong enough to dominate 'own'-effects. Proposition II states a set of sufficient conditions under which 'cross'-effects are never strong enough to dominate 'own'-effects (with regard to goods 1 and $n$). As can be seen from Assumptions C and D a key role in this context is played by the relative ease with which the mobile factor can be substituted for the sector-specific factor in each industry if the price of the mobile factor falls, and the price of the sector-specific factor rises.

The property of diagonal dominance is, of course, a very convenient one if we want to obtain clearcut comparative static results (see Arrow and Hahn, 1971). It plays a pivotal role in a very well-known article (see Grossman and Helpman, 1994). Grossman and Helpman proceed by ruling out all cross-effects by assumption. To this end they postulate that in one of the industries only the mobile factor is used. The output of this industry is chosen as a numeraire. Proposition II is, of course, based upon restrictive assumptions but it seems preferable to the Grossman and Helpman approach because it draws attention to a complex problem rather than assuming it away. Furthermore it yields results which are empirically testable.

## 4. FACTOR MOBILITY

Traditional trade theory features two extreme approaches to the modelling of factor mobility between industries: either all factors are assumed to be mobile between all industries or there is a sector-specific factor in each industry and only one factor is mobile between all industries (as in the sector-specific factor model). There are some exceptions in the literature (see, for example, Mussa, 1982; Grossman, 1983; Schweinberger, 1980 and 2002; or Bond et al., 2002). However, it appears that the effects of limited factor mobility on the pattern of comparative advantage have not received any attention in the literature. Our aim is to eliminate this gap. To this end we now allow for the sector-specific factors in industries 1 and 2 to be mobile between these two industries. In the terminology of Bond et al. (2002) or Jones et al. (1999) industries 1 and 2 now form a 'nugget'.

It is very straightforward to rewrite equations (2.15) to (2.17) taking into account the mobility of the (sector-specific) factors between industries 1 and 2.

$$
de_1 = \left[ \left( \frac{\partial c_2}{\partial Y} + \frac{\partial c_3}{\partial Y} \right) \frac{\partial x_1}{\partial K_{12}} - \frac{\partial c_1}{\partial Y} \left( \frac{\partial x_2}{\partial K_{12}} + \frac{\partial x_3}{\partial K_{12}} \right) \right] K_{12} \left( \frac{dK_{12}}{K_{12}} - \frac{dL}{L} \right)
$$
$$
+ \left[ \left( \frac{\partial c_2}{\partial Y} + \frac{\partial c_3}{\partial Y} \right) \frac{\partial x_1}{\partial K_3} - \frac{\partial c_1}{\partial Y} \left( \frac{\partial x_2}{\partial K_3} + \frac{\partial x_3}{\partial K_3} \right) \right] K_3 \left( \frac{dK_3}{K_3} - \frac{dL}{L} \right) \quad (2.30)
$$

$$
de_2 = \left[ \left( \frac{\partial c_1}{\partial Y} + \frac{\partial c_3}{\partial Y} \right) \frac{\partial x_2}{\partial K_{12}} - \frac{\partial c_2}{\partial Y} \left( \frac{\partial x_1}{\partial K_{12}} + \frac{\partial x_3}{\partial K_{12}} \right) \right] K_{12} \left( \frac{dK_{12}}{K_{12}} - \frac{dL}{L} \right)
$$
$$
+ \left[ \left( \frac{\partial c_1}{\partial Y} + \frac{\partial c_3}{\partial Y} \right) \frac{\partial x_2}{\partial K_3} - \frac{\partial c_2}{\partial Y} \left( \frac{\partial x_1}{\partial K_3} + \frac{\partial x_3}{\partial K_3} \right) \right] K_3 \left( \frac{dK_3}{K_3} - \frac{dL}{L} \right) \quad (2.31)
$$

$$
de_3 = \left[ \left( \frac{\partial c_1}{\partial Y} + \frac{\partial c_2}{\partial Y} \right) \frac{\partial x_3}{\partial K_{12}} - \frac{\partial c_3}{\partial Y} \left( \frac{\partial x_1}{\partial K_{12}} + \frac{\partial x_2}{\partial K_{12}} \right) \right] K_{12} \left( \frac{dK_{12}}{K_{12}} - \frac{dL}{L} \right)
$$
$$
+ \left[ \left( \frac{\partial c_1}{\partial Y} + \frac{\partial c_2}{\partial Y} \right) \frac{\partial x_3}{\partial K_3} - \frac{\partial c_3}{\partial Y} \left( \frac{\partial x_1}{\partial K_3} + \frac{\partial x_2}{\partial K_3} \right) \right] K_3 \left( \frac{dK_3}{K_3} - \frac{dL}{L} \right). \quad (2.32)
$$

The factor market equilibrium conditions are given by:

$$
a_{L_1} x_1 + a_{L_2} x_2 + a_{L_3} x_3 = L \quad (2.33)
$$

$$
a_{K_{121}} x_1 + a_{K_{122}} x_2 = K_{12} \quad (2.34)
$$

$$
a_{K_3} x_3 = K_3. \quad (2.35)
$$

Equations (2.33) to (2.35) can readily be reduced to a nugget by solving (2.35) for $x_3$ and substituting into equation (2.33). Note carefully that we have assumed that the factor endowment differences between the countries are not too big. Otherwise one of the two countries may not be in the nugget.

Equations (2.33) to (2.35) can now be used to derive the signs of: $\partial x_1 / \partial K_{12}, \partial x_2 / \partial K_{12}, \partial x_3 / \partial K_{12}, \partial x_1 / \partial K_3, \partial x_2 / \partial K_3, \partial x_3 / \partial K_3$.

As may be expected, the signs of these derivatives depend crucially upon the factor intensity of goods 1 and 2.

If we assume that good 1 is intensive in the use of the mobile factor $L$ (relative to $K_{12}$) we have:

$$\frac{\partial x_1}{\partial K_{12}} < 0, \quad \frac{\partial x_2}{\partial K_{12}} > 0, \quad \frac{\partial x_3}{\partial K_{12}} = 0 \quad \text{and} \quad (2.36)$$

$$\frac{\partial x_1}{\partial K_3} < 0, \quad \frac{\partial x_2}{\partial K_3} > 0, \quad \frac{\partial x_3}{\partial K_3} > 0. \quad (2.37)$$

If, on the other hand, we assume that good 1 is intensive in the use of $K_{12}$ (relative to $L$) then we have:

$$\frac{\partial x_1}{\partial K_{12}} > 0, \quad \frac{\partial x_2}{\partial K_{12}} < 0, \quad \frac{\partial x_3}{\partial K_{12}} = 0 \quad \text{and} \quad (2.38)$$

$$\frac{\partial x_1}{\partial K_3} > 0, \quad \frac{\partial x_2}{\partial K_3} < 0, \quad \frac{\partial x_3}{\partial K_3} > 0. \quad (2.39)$$

We are now in a position to state our final proposition.

## Proposition III

(a)  Assume that good 1 is intensive in the use of the mobile factor $L$. Then the home country has a comparative advantage in good 1 if:

$$\frac{dL}{L} > \frac{dK_{12}}{K_{12}} \quad \text{and} \quad \frac{dL}{L} > \frac{dK_3}{K_3},$$

that is, the home country is better endowed with the mobile factor $L$ than the foreign country.

(b)  Assume that good 1 is intensive in the use of the factor $K_{12}$. Then the home country has a comparative advantage in good 2 if:

$$\frac{dL}{L} > \frac{dK_{12}}{K_{12}} \quad \text{and} \quad \frac{dL}{L} > \frac{dK_3}{K_3}.$$

(c)  1.  Assume that good 1 is intensive in the mobile factor $L$. Then the home country has a comparative advantage in good 3 if:

$$a_{L2} > a_{L1}, \quad a_{K122} > a_{K121} \quad \text{and}$$

$$\frac{dK_{12}}{K_{12}} > \frac{dL}{L}, \quad \frac{dK_3}{K_3} > \frac{dL}{L}.$$

2. Assume that good 2 is intensive in the mobile factor $L$. Then the home country has a comparative advantage in good 3 if:

$$a_{L1} > a_{L2}, \quad a_{K121} > a_{K122} \quad \text{and}$$

$$\frac{dK_{12}}{K_{12}} > \frac{dL}{L}, \quad \frac{dK_3}{K_3} > \frac{dL}{L}.$$

Proposition III follows directly from equations (2.30) to (2.32) and (2.36) to (2.39).                                    Q.E.D.

It should be noted that the proposition can easily be extended to more than three industries provided that there is only one sector-specific factor and one mobile factor ($L$) in each of the additional industries.

What is the main message of Proposition III? Undoubtedly the asymmetry in the determination of the pattern of comparative advantage between goods 1 and 2 on the one hand and good 3 on the other hand. Points (a) and (b) state novel but expected results. However, the dependence of the pattern of comparative advantage of good 3 on the absolute values of the productivities of the mobile factors $L$ and $K_{12}$ in the production of goods 1 and 2 comes as a surprise. It reminds one that if we allow for mobility of factors, not only relative but also absolute productivity differences determine the trading patterns.

To conclude, we only point out that the political-economy implications of Proposition III are clearcut, as far as the owners of the factors $K_{12}$ and $L$ are concerned, because the prices of these factors are determined by the zero profitability conditions for goods 1 and 2 (along standard Stolper–Samuelson considerations).

## 5.   CONCLUSIONS AND EXTENSIONS

One of the central tasks of political economy of international trade policy is to explain the existence of interest groups lobbying either for or against free international trade. A considerable part of the received literature circumvents this central task by assuming the existence of vested interest groups making use of the well-known conflict-generating properties of changes in product prices associated with the Heckscher–Ohlin or sector-specific factor models. The present chapter is more ambitious.

It endeavours to make a case for the existence of interest groups lobbying for or against free international trade on the basis of factor endowment differences between countries. The central question raised and tentatively answered is this: under which conditions will the owners of abundant factors lobby for, and the owners of scarce factors against, free international trade? Crucial in this context is the definition of factor abundance or scarcity. Different definitions are appropriate for different models. The present approach is based upon a general version of the sector-specific factor model (see, for example, Jones, 1971 or Ruffin and Jones, 1977).

If a country is better endowed with a certain sector-specific factor (relative to the other country) using any one of the other sector-specific factors or the mobile factor as benchmarks, the said sector-specific factor owners will lobby for free international trade subject to the Assumptions A, B and C (see Proposition II). If Assumptions A, B and D hold, it can be shown that the country's scarce sector-specific factor owners will lobby against free international trade (see again Proposition II). Assumptions C and D are not required to derive the above-mentioned results concerning the lobbying behaviour of the owners of the sector-specific factors if the factor endowment differences are as shown by expressions (2.25) and (2.26), see Proposition I.

The intuition underlying these results is straightforward. If two countries are identical in every respect and preferences are homothetic except that the home country is better endowed with the sector-specific factor in industry 1, it is obvious that the home country has a comparative advantage in industry 1. This also holds if countries differ only in terms of the endowments with the sector-specific factor in industry 1 and the mobile factor. However, generally there are 'cross'-effects if the two countries differ in the endowments with all factors. The 'cross'-effects may either reinforce or counteract the 'own' effects. Proposition I states restrictions on factor endowment differences which imply that the 'cross'-effects reinforce the 'own' effects. In deriving Proposition II 'cross'-effects are allowed to counteract the 'own' effects but the stated restrictions on factor endowment differences imply that 'own' effects are stronger than 'cross'-effects.

Sections 1 to 3 of the chapter are based upon a generalized version of the sector-specific factor model. In Section 4 we allow for a limited degree of factor mobility. To be precise, the sector-specific factors used in two industries become mobile between the two industries. In the reduced form of the factor market equilibrium conditions so-called nuggets emerge (see also Schweinberger, 2002 or Bond et al., 2002). If the factor endowments of the two countries lie within the same diversification cone it is relatively easy to relate the pattern of comparative advantage to the endowment differences between the two countries.

Many extensions of these results are possible. We only point out two. First, an unemployed mobile factor (in addition to the fully employed mobile factor) may be introduced. If the unemployed mobile factor (the relevant wage is fixed at a too high level) is used in fixed proportions in the production of all goods, many of the standard properties of the sector-specific factor model survive.

Second, one may postulate that trade in final goods already takes place. Final goods are produced by means of primary factors (as in the standard sector-specific factor model) and one intermediate good. Each final goods industry also produces one intermediate good which it uses in the production of its own final good. The opening up of the country to international trade in intermediate goods will be in the interest of some sector-specific factor owners but not all of them, depending upon the pattern of comparative advantage in intermediate goods.

In this context another useful approach to the modelling of the conflict-generating effects of product price changes on the welfare of factor owners should be mentioned; see Lloyd and Schweinberger (1997). In this article the authors derive some very general results by imputing outputs to the factors owned by various (heterogeneous) households. It appears plausible that this approach might yield interesting insights into the determination of patterns of comparative advantage taking into account various patterns of factor ownership by households.

At this point, it should be mentioned that the assumption of identical preferences may be relaxed. Whether insightful comparative static results are attainable without the assumption of identical preferences (of households in different countries), however, remains to be seen. It may be conjectured that results can be obtained only at the cost of imposing fairly strong restrictions on the differences in preferences so that the effects of endowment differences on comparative advantage are not more than offset by the effects of differences in the distribution of income between the owners of factors in different countries.

In conclusion, it should be noted that the focus in this chapter has been only on one 'source' of comparative advantage: differences in the factor endowments between countries. Very recently the focus of the literature has shifted to differences in the market structure and the internal organization (corporate structure) of domestic and foreign firms in determining (*inter alia*) the comparative advantage of firms and countries; see, for example, Hillman et al. (2001).

The challenge for future research lies in integrating these two different strands of literature by modelling carefully the interaction between factor and goods markets on the one hand and the internal organization of firms and market structure on the other hand.

## NOTES

* I am grateful to an unknown referee for useful comments. The usual caveat applies, of course.
1. It should be noted that there are a number of articles which relate the pattern of commodity trade to factor endowment differences; see, for example, Dixit and Woodland (1982). This article contains interesting general results but does not address the specific issue of this chapter. Some very special results in simple models can be found in Dixit and Norman (1980, pp. 102–106) and in Krugman and Obstfeld (1997, pp. 52–3). This literature is reviewed below. On the factor scarcity (abundance) hypothesis and international political economy see also Hillman (1989).

## REFERENCES

Arrow, K.J. and Hahn, F.H. (1971), *General Competitive Analysis*, Amsterdam: North Holland.

Bond E., Jones, R. and Wang, P. (2002), 'Economic take-offs in a dynamic process of globalization', Working Paper, University of Rochester, NY, and Vanderbilt University, Nashville, TN.

Deaton, A. and Muellbauer, J. (1986), 'Economics and consumer behavior', Cambridge: Cambridge University Press.

Dixit, A. and Norman, V. (1980), 'Theory of international trade, a dual general equilibrium approach', Cambridge: Cambridge University Press, pp. 102–106.

Dixit, A. and Woodland, A. (1982), 'Factor endowments and commodity trade', *Journal of International Economics*, **13**, 201–14.

Ethier, W.J. (1984), 'Higher dimensional issues in trade theory', *Handbook of International Economics*, Vol. I, Chapter 3, Amsterdam: North-Holland.

Freeman, R. (1995), 'Are your wages set in Beijing?', *Journal of Economic Perspectives*, **9**(3), 15–32.

Grossman, G.M. (1983), 'Partially mobile capital', *Journal of International Economics*, **15**, 1–17.

Grossman, G.M. and Helpman, E. (1994), 'Protection for sale', *American Economic Review*, **84**, 833–50.

Hillman, A.L. (1994), *The Political Economy of Protection*, Chur: Harwood Academic Publishers.

Hillman, A.L., Van Long, Ngo and Soubeyan, A. (2001), 'Protection, lobbying and market structure', *Journal of International Economics*, **54**, 383–409.

Jones, R. (1971), 'A three factor model in theory, trade, and history', in Bhagwati, J.V., Jones, R.V., Mundell, R.A. and Vanek, J. (eds), *Trade, Balance of Payments and Growth*, Amsterdam: North-Holland, Ch. 1.

Jones, R., Belach, H. and Marjit, Sugata (1999), 'The three faces of factor intensities', *Journal of International Economics*, **48**, 413–20.

Krugman, P.R. and Obstfeld, M. (2003), *International Economics: Theory and Policy*, 6th edn, Addison Wesley, Boston.

Lloyd, P.J. and Schweinberger, A.G. (1997), 'Conflict generating product price changes: the imputed output approach', *European Economic Review*, **41**, 1569–87.

Mayer, W. (1984), 'Endogenous tariff formation', *American Economic Review*, **74**, 970–85.

Mussa, M. (1982), 'Imperfect factor mobility and the distribution of income', *Journal of International Economics*, **12**, 125–41.

Rodrick, D. (1997), *Has Globalisation Gone Too Far?*, Washington, DC: Institute of International Economics.

Ruffin, R. and Jones, R. (1977), 'Protection and real wages: the neoclassical ambiguity', *Journal of Economic Theory*, **14**, 337–48.

Schweinberger, A.G. (1980), 'Medium run resource allocation and short run capital specificity', *Economic Journal*, **90**, 330–40.

Schweinberger, A.G. (2002), 'Foreign aid, tariffs and nontraded private or public goods', *Journal of Development Economics*, **69**, 255–75.

Woodland, A.D. (1982), *International Trade and Resource Allocation*, Amsterdam: North-Holland.

# APPENDIX

The appendix is divided into two parts. In part A we derive equations (2.15) to (2.17) of section 2. In part B the conditions stated as Assumptions C and D are shown to imply the sector-specific factor intensity condition; see Proposition II.

## [A]

Differentiating expressions (2.5) to (2.7), see also expressions (2.1) to (2.4), we obtain:

$$de_1 = \left(\frac{\partial x_1}{\partial K_1}K_1 - \frac{\partial c_1}{\partial Y}\frac{\partial Y}{\partial K_1}K_1\right)\frac{dK_1}{K_1} + \left(\frac{\partial x_1}{\partial K_2}K_2 - \frac{\partial c_1}{\partial Y}\frac{\partial Y}{\partial K_2}K_2\right)\frac{dK_2}{K_2}$$

$$+ \left(\frac{\partial x_1}{\partial K_3}K_3 - \frac{\partial c_1}{\partial Y}\frac{\partial Y}{\partial K_3}K_3\right)\frac{dK_3}{K_3} + \left(\frac{\partial x_1}{\partial L}L - \frac{\partial c_1}{\partial Y}\frac{\partial Y}{\partial L}L\right)\frac{dL}{L} \quad (2.40)$$

$$de_2 = \left(\frac{\partial x_2}{\partial K_1}K_1 - \frac{\partial c_2}{\partial Y}\frac{\partial Y}{\partial K_1}K_1\right)\frac{dK_1}{K_1} + \left(\frac{\partial x_2}{\partial K_2}K_2 - \frac{\partial c_2}{\partial K_2}\frac{\partial Y}{\partial K_2}K_2\right)\frac{dK_2}{K_2}$$

$$+ \left(\frac{\partial x_2}{\partial K_3}K_3 - \frac{\partial c_2}{\partial Y}\frac{\partial Y}{\partial K_3}K_3\right)\frac{dK_3}{K_3} + \left(\frac{\partial x_2}{\partial L}L - \frac{\partial c_2}{\partial Y}\frac{\partial Y}{\partial L}L\right)\frac{dL}{L} \quad (2.41)$$

$$de_3 = \left(\frac{\partial x_3}{\partial K_1}K_1 - \frac{\partial c_3}{\partial Y}\frac{\partial Y}{\partial K_1}K_1\right)\frac{dK_1}{K_1} + \left(\frac{\partial x_3}{\partial K_2}K_2 - \frac{\partial c_3}{\partial K_2}\frac{\partial Y}{\partial K_2}K_2\right)\frac{dK_2}{K_2}$$

$$+ \left(\frac{\partial x_3}{\partial K_3}K_3 - \frac{\partial c_3}{\partial Y}\frac{\partial Y}{\partial K_3}K_3\right)\frac{dK_3}{K_3} + \left(\frac{\partial x_3}{\partial L}L - \frac{\partial c_3}{\partial Y}\frac{\partial Y}{\partial L}L\right)\frac{dL}{L} \quad (2.42)$$

To obtain equations (2.15) to (2.17), we substitute for $(\partial x_1/\partial L)L$, $(\partial x_2/\partial L)L$ and $(\partial x_3/\partial L)L$ expressions (2.9) to (2.10) of the text. We also substitute (2.12), (2.13) and (2.14) for $\partial Y/\partial K_1$, $\partial Y/\partial K_2$, $\partial Y/\partial K_3$. Finally we substitute (2.12), (2.13) and (2.14) into (2.11) and the resulting expression for $(\partial Y/\partial L)L$ into (2.40), (2.41) and (2.42) of the Appendix.

Collecting terms and noting that as partial derivations $c_1 = x_1$, $c_2 = x_2$ and $c_3 = x_3$ we obtain equations (2.15) to (2.17).

**[B]**

From equations (2.15) to (2.17) of the text and the definitions of the $\alpha$s we have:

$$
\alpha_{11}K_1 + \alpha_{12}K_2 + \alpha_{13}K_3 = \left[\left(\frac{\partial c_2}{\partial Y} + \frac{\partial c_3}{\partial Y}\right)\frac{\partial x_1}{\partial K_1} - \frac{\partial c_1}{\partial Y}\left(\frac{\partial x_2}{\partial K_1} + \frac{\partial x_3}{\partial K_1}\right)\right]K_1
$$

$$
+ \left[\left(\frac{\partial c_2}{\partial Y} + \frac{\partial c_3}{\partial Y}\right)\frac{\partial x_1}{\partial K_2} - \frac{\partial c_1}{\partial Y}\left(\frac{\partial x_2}{\partial K_2} + \frac{\partial x_3}{\partial K_2}\right)\right]K_2
$$

$$
+ \left[\left(\frac{\partial c_2}{\partial Y} + \frac{\partial c_3}{\partial Y}\right)\frac{\partial x_1}{\partial K_3} - \frac{\partial c_1}{\partial Y}\left(\frac{\partial x_2}{\partial K_3} + \frac{\partial x_3}{\partial K_3}\right)\right]K_3
$$

$$
= \left(\frac{\partial c_2}{\partial Y} + \frac{\partial c_3}{\partial Y}\right)\left(K_1\frac{\partial x_1}{\partial K_1} + K_2\frac{\partial x_1}{\partial K_2} + K_3\frac{\partial x_1}{\partial K_3}\right)
$$

$$
- \frac{\partial c_1}{\partial Y}\left[\left(\frac{\partial x_2}{\partial K_1}K_1 + \frac{\partial x_2}{\partial K_2}K_2 + \frac{\partial x_2}{\partial K_3}K_3\right)\right.
$$

$$
\left. + \left(\frac{\partial x_3}{\partial K_1}K_1 + \frac{\partial x_3}{\partial K_2}K_2 + \frac{\partial x_3}{\partial K_3}K_3\right)\right]
$$

Making use of expressions (2.8) to (2.10) of the text, the last expression can be rewritten as:

$$
\left(\frac{\partial c_2}{\partial Y} + \frac{\partial c_3}{\partial Y}\right)\left(x_1 - \frac{\partial x_1}{\partial L}L\right) - \frac{\partial c_1}{\partial Y}\left[\left(x_2 - \frac{\partial x_2}{\partial L}L\right) + \left(x_3 - \frac{\partial x_3}{\partial L}L\right)\right]
$$

$$
= \left(\frac{\partial c_2}{\partial Y} + \frac{\partial c_3}{\partial Y}\right)c_1\left(1 - \frac{\partial \log x_1}{\partial \log L}\right) - \frac{\partial c_1}{\partial Y}c_2\left(1 - \frac{\partial \log x_2}{\partial \log L}\right)
$$

$$
- \frac{\partial c_1}{\partial Y}c_3\left(1 - \frac{\partial \log x_3}{\partial \log L}\right)
$$

$$
= c_2\frac{\partial c_1}{\partial Y}\left(\frac{\partial \log x_2}{\partial \log L} - \frac{\partial \log x_1}{\partial \log L}\right) + c_3\frac{\partial c_1}{\partial Y}\left(\frac{\partial \log x_3}{\partial \log L} - \frac{\partial \log x_1}{\partial \log L}\right)
$$

if preferences are homothetic, because in this case expression (2.21) of the text must be satisfied.

An analogous expression for: $\alpha_{31}K_1 + \alpha_{32}K_2 + \alpha_{33}K_3$ may also be derived. We obtain:

$$\left( \frac{\partial c_1}{\partial Y} + \frac{\partial c_2}{\partial Y} \right) c_3 \left( 1 - \frac{\partial \log x_3}{\partial \log L} \right) - \frac{\partial c_3}{\partial Y} c_1 \left( 1 - \frac{\partial \log x_1}{\partial \log L} \right)$$

$$- \frac{\partial c_3}{\partial Y} c_2 \left( 1 - \frac{\partial \log x_2}{\partial \log L} \right).$$

This last expression can be simplified if preferences are homothetic. In this case we have:

$$c_3 \frac{\partial c_2}{\partial Y} \left( \frac{\partial \log x_2}{\partial \log L} - \frac{\partial \log x_3}{\partial \log L} \right) + c_1 \frac{\partial c_3}{\partial Y} \left( \frac{\partial \log x_1}{\partial \log L} - \frac{\partial \log x_3}{\partial \log L} \right)$$

PART TWO

Theory of Trade Policy

# 3. Are uniform tariffs optimal?

## Mary Amiti*

## 1. INTRODUCTION

Tariffs rates vary widely along the production chain. Most industries are characterized by escalating tariffs where tariffs are lowest on raw materials and increasing as one goes up the value chain. Dividing the value chain into first stage, semi-processed and fully processed, World Bank figures indicate that 48 out of 86 countries had escalating tariffs in their industrial products between 1994 and 2000.[1] For example, in 2000 Mauritius had an average tariff rate of 3.1 per cent on the first stage, 4 per cent on semi-processed and 44.4 per cent on the final stage. Some countries had uniform tariff rates; for example, Chile had an average tariff rate of 9 per cent on all production stages; and other countries had a mix of increasing and then decreasing tariff rates from one stage to the next. Bolivia was the only country to report, on average, de-escalating tariffs with a 10 per cent tariff rate on the first stage and semi-processed, and 9.3 per cent on final goods. Given these large disparities in tariff rates, this raises the question of how to proceed with tariff reform.

A guiding principle for tariff reform in developing countries in the 1970s and 1980s has been the 'concertina theorem', which involves reducing tariffs on those goods with the highest tariffs first (Michaely et al., 1991). This idea dates back to Meade (1955) who concluded that the welfare gains will be larger if tariffs on those goods with the highest tariffs are reduced first. This result was formalized by a number of authors, including Bertrand and Vanek (1971), Lloyd (1974) and Falvey (1988) for a small open perfectly competitive economy. However, by introducing pure intermediate inputs that are not produced domestically, López and Panagariya (1992) showed that applying the concertina theorem does not always lead to welfare improvements and may in fact be welfare-reducing. In general, taking account of vertical structures of production stages complicates the effects of trade liberalization, as demonstrated in the effective protection literature (see Corden, 1971).[2]

This chapter analyses whether uniform tariffs do in fact give rise to the highest welfare compared with either escalating or de-escalating tariffs.

We show that countries may be better off with de-escalating tariffs where tariff rates are higher on intermediate inputs and lower on final goods. The key point is that higher tariffs can encourage agglomeration of intermediate input suppliers and final goods producers in one country. With high tariffs on intermediate inputs the benefits of close proximity to final goods producers may outweigh the benefits of locating according to comparative advantage, which is more likely when the share of intermediate inputs in producing final goods is high. De-escalating tariffs yield the highest welfare when the benefits of agglomeration are very high, and this is the case when varieties of inputs and final goods have a low elasticity of substitution. The lower the substitution, the higher the value of each variety in the production of final goods and the utility of consumers. These benefits of agglomeration accrue to both countries in the form of lower prices.

We extend the previous literature by allowing all inputs to be produced domestically and abroad, rather than only having pure imported intermediate inputs as in López and Panagariya (1992), and by introducing imperfect competition. We build on the new economic geography literature to analyse piecemeal tariff reform between two countries that differ in relative factor endowments. To date, most new economic geography models have combined upstream and downstream industries into one sector within one-factor models (see Krugman and Venables, 1995). Here, we assume that the manufacturing sector comprises two distinct vertically linked industries that differ in relative factor intensities and are monopolistically competitive, as in Amiti (2005a). There are tariffs on intermediate inputs and final goods and both industries are also subject to real resource trade costs such as freight costs. Trade liberalization takes the form of symmetric tariff reductions between the two countries.

The rest of the chapter is organized as follows. Section 2 sets out the formal model. Section 3 solves for equilibrium. Section 4 presents the results on industrial location and draws out the welfare implications. Section 5 concludes.


## 2.   THE MODEL

The model has two factors of production, labour and capital; and the industries differ in factor intensities. The two factors of production are immobile between two countries that differ in terms of relative factor endowments, where country $l$ is assumed to be labour abundant and country $k$ is capital abundant. Both countries have access to the same technology; and consumers in each country have identical homothetic preferences. There are two imperfectly competitive manufacturing industries, upstream and downstream industries, that are vertically linked through an input–output structure; and a perfectly competitive 'agricultural' industry, with constant returns to scale technology, employing labour and capital.

Upstream firms produce intermediate inputs, using labour and capital, which they sell to firms in the downstream industry. Downstream firms combine intermediate inputs with labour and capital to produce final manufacturing goods, which they sell to consumers. The market structure in each of the vertically linked industries is assumed to be Chamberlinian monopolistic competition: there are many firms in both industries, each employing increasing returns to scale technology and producing differentiated goods. Each firm can choose to locate in either country and it draws on the labour and capital available in the country in which it locates.

Trade costs are modelled as tariffs and real resource costs. Tariff rates can differ between upstream and downstream firms. We include positive real resource costs throughout the analysis for two reasons. One is that production patterns are indeterminate if all trade costs are zero because the number of industries is greater than the number of factors. Two, allowing for real resource costs in transporting goods highlights that even if we can reduce tariff rates to zero we cannot reduce the cost of shipping goods between countries to zero and these real resource costs affect location.

## Utility

We present the model for country $l$ and note that symmetric equations hold for country $k$. All subscripts denote the country and superscripts the industry. The two manufacturing industries are labelled by superscripts $i = u, d$, where $u$ denotes the upstream industry and $d$ denotes the downstream industry. The aggregate utility function, $U_l$, for the representative consumer in country $l$ is Cobb–Douglas,

$$U_l = (C_l^d)^s (C_l^a)^{1-s}, \tag{3.1}$$

where $C_l^d$ is aggregate consumption of final manufactured goods and $C_l^a$ is consumption of agricultural goods. Aggregate demand for final manufactured goods can be represented by a quantity index or sub-utility function, $C_l^d$, defined as

$$C_l^d = \left[ \sum_{v=1}^{n_l^d} (c_{ll}^{dv})^{\frac{\sigma-1}{\sigma}} + \sum_{v=1}^{n_k^d} (c_{lk}^{dv})^{\frac{\sigma-1}{\sigma}} \right]^{\frac{\sigma}{\sigma-1}}. \tag{3.2}$$

We assume that consumers have Dixit–Stiglitz preferences so there is a taste for variety and each variety $v$ enters the utility function symmetrically;

preferences are separable and homothetic. The elasticity of substitution between any pair of differentiated goods $\sigma$ is assumed to be greater than one. A consumer's utility is increasing in the number of varieties. There are $n_l^d$ varieties of final goods produced in country $l$ and $n_k^d$ varieties produced in country $k$. Domestic demand in country $l$ for each variety $v$ is given by $c_{ll}^{dv}$, and demand for imported varieties from country $k$ by $c_{kl}^{dv}$. $\tau > 1$ represents the real resource cost in shipping downstream goods between the two countries.

Dual to the quantity index for final manufactured goods, the price index is

$$P_l^d = \left[ \sum_{v=1}^{n_l^d} (p_l^{dv})^{1-\sigma} + \sum_{v=1}^{n_k^d} (p_k^{dv}\tau(1 + T^d))^{1-\sigma} \right]^{\frac{1}{1-\sigma}}, \qquad (3.3)$$

where $p_l^d$ is the producer price of a variety $v$ produced in country $l$ and $p_k^d\tau(1 + T^d)$ is the price of an imported variety from country $k$ to country $l$, and $T^d \geq 0$ is an *ad valorem* tariff on final goods.

## Manufacturing

The production technology in the manufacturing sector consists of a small fixed cost of setting up a plant, $f$, to produce each variety. This gives rise to increasing returns technology; and the small size of $f$ ensures that the number of varieties produced is large enough to make oligopolistic interactions negligible.

In the downstream industry, $d$, the production function for each variety is

$$(L_l^d)^\delta (K_l^d)^{1-\delta-\mu}(C_l^u)^\mu = f + \beta x_l^d.$$

To produce output $x_l^d$, firms use labour, $L_l^d$, capital, $K_l^d$, and many varieties of intermediate inputs. These intermediate inputs enter the production function through the quantity index, $C_l^u$, which is defined analogously to $C_l^d$ in equation (3.2), with the superscript $d$ replaced with $u$. Hence, industry $u$'s output of intermediate inputs enters the production function of each downstream firm through a CES aggregator as in Ethier (1982) and Venables (1996). The share of intermediate inputs in production, $\mu$, is a key parameter in the model, representing the vertical linkages between the two industries.

Profits of each firm are given by total revenue less total costs. In the downstream industry, profit for each firm, $\pi_l^d$, is given by

$$\pi_l^d = p_l^d x_l^d - w_l^\delta r_l^{1-\delta-\mu}(P_l^u)^\mu (f + \beta x_l^d),$$

where $P_I^u$ is the price index of intermediate inputs, defined as in equation (3.3) with the superscript $d$ replaced with $u$.

In the upstream industry, $u$, the production function for each intermediate input variety is given by:[3]

$$(L_I^u)^\alpha (K_I^u)^{1-\alpha} = f + \beta x_I^u,$$

where $L_I^u$ and $K_I^u$ are the labour and capital amounts employed by each firm to produce output $x_I^u$. Profits are given by

$$\pi_I^u = p_I^u x_I^u - w_I^\alpha r_I^{1-\alpha}(f + \beta x_I^u).$$

We assume there is free entry and exit in both upstream and downstream industries, leading to zero profits.

**Agriculture**

The production function for the perfectly competitive agricultural industry is

$$X_I^a = (L_I^a)^\gamma (K_I^a)^{1-\gamma},$$

where $\gamma$ is the share of labour used in production. Agricultural goods are assumed to be freely traded,[4] with the price set equal to 1, $P^a = 1$. Then the profit function can be written as[5]

$$\pi_I^a = X_I^a - w_I^\gamma r_I^{1-\gamma} X_I^a.$$

Factor markets are assumed to be perfectly competitive and factors are fully employed.

# 3. EQUILIBRIUM

We solve for equilibrium in four steps. First, we solve the representative consumer's utility maximization problem to derive the demand for final goods. Second, we solve for each firm's profit maximization problem in each industry $i$ to derive producer prices, and downstream firms' demand for intermediate inputs. Using the free entry and exit condition, we derive the number of units each manufacturing firm must produce to cover fixed cost. Third, we determine product market clearing conditions and fourth, solve the factor market clearing conditions.

## Consumers

The representative consumer's utility-maximizing problem is solved using two-stage budgeting. In stage one the consumer allocates expenditure between manufactures and agriculture by maximizing the utility function, equation (3.1), subject to the budget constraint, which gives

$$C_l^a = (1 - s)Y_l \tag{3.4}$$

$$P_l^d C_l^d = sY_l. \tag{3.5}$$

The budget constraint is given by $Y_l = w_l L_l + r_l K_l + G_l$, where $G_l = p_k^d T^d \times c_{kl}^d n_k^d + p_k^u T^u c_{kl}^u n_k^u$ is the tariff revenue collected in country $l$, which is assumed to be distributed back to consumers. In stage two the consumer maximizes the sub-utility function, $C_l^d$ (equation 3.2), subject to the budget constraint, $sY_l$ in equation (3.5), to derive demand functions for each variety of manufactured good produced in country $l$ and each imported variety produced in country $k$, respectively:

$$c_{ll}^d = (p_l^d)^{-\sigma}(P_l^d)^{\sigma-1} s Y_l \tag{3.6}$$

$$c_{kl}^d = \tau^{1-\sigma}(1 + T^d)^{-\sigma}(p_k^d)^{-\sigma}(P_l^d)^{\sigma-1} s Y_l. \tag{3.7}$$

## Firms

Now we consider firm behaviour in the manufacturing sector and in agriculture.

### Manufacturing

In the manufacturing sector, upstream and downstream firms choose a variety and pricing so as to maximize profits, taking as given the variety choice and pricing strategy of the other firms in the industry. Each firm will produce a distinct variety since it can always do better by introducing a new product variety than by sharing in the production of an existing type. In the downstream industry, each firm maximizes profits with respect to quantity to derive producer prices:

$$\frac{\partial \pi_l^d}{\partial x_l^d} = 0 \Rightarrow p_l^d = w_l^\delta r_l^{1-\delta-\mu}(P_l^u)^\mu \frac{\beta\sigma}{\sigma - 1}.$$

This gives the usual marginal revenue equals marginal cost condition, with producer price as a constant mark-up over marginal cost. The producer price, $p_l^d$, received by a firm in country $l$ is the same whether the good is sold domestically or exported; and the tariff-inclusive price is $p^d_{lk} = p^d_l \tau (1 + T^d)$.[6] We choose units of measurement so that $\beta \sigma = \sigma - 1$, then $p^d_l = w^\delta_l r^{1-\delta-\mu}_l \times (P^u_l)^\mu$. A proportion, $\delta$, of downstream industry's revenue is spent on labour, $1-\delta-\mu$ on capital and $\mu$ on intermediate inputs. Hence total expenditure on upstream intermediate inputs is given by $e^u_l = \mu n^d_l p^d_l x^d_l$. The demand functions for each variety of intermediate input produced domestically and abroad are analogous to consumers' demand functions for final manufactured goods:

$$c^u_{ll} = (p^u_l)^{-\sigma}(P^u_l)^{\sigma-1}e^u_l \tag{3.8}$$

$$c^u_{kl} = \tau^{1-\sigma}(1 + T^u)^{-\sigma}(p^u_k)^{-\sigma}(P^u_l)^{\sigma-1}e^u_l. \tag{3.9}$$

Similarly, in the upstream industry, each firm maximizes profit with respect to quantity:

$$\frac{\partial \pi^u_l}{\partial x^u_l} = 0 \Rightarrow p^u_l = w^\alpha_l r^{1-\alpha}_l. \tag{3.10}$$

We can derive the number of varieties produced in each industry by imposing the free entry and exit condition, which leads to zero profits. This condition determines the quantity of output required to cover fixed costs. With

$$\pi^i_l = 0, \quad x^i_l = \frac{f(\sigma - 1)}{\beta}, \quad i = u,d. \tag{3.11}$$

Without loss of generality, firm size is scaled so that profits are equal to zero at size one, by setting $f = 1/\sigma$. Note that the equilibrium scale of output is independent of price and the number of firms. This is a direct consequence of Dixit–Stiglitz preferences and a constant elasticity of substitution. Then the complementary slack condition implies that at least one of the following equations must hold with equality,

$$x^i_l \leq 1, \quad n^i_l \geq 0, \quad i = u,d. \tag{3.12}$$

For example, if output in industry $i$, $x^i_l$, is less than one, then firms would earn negative profits so the equilibrium number of firms in that industry, $n^i_l$, would equal zero.

### Agriculture
In the agricultural industry, profit maximization implies price equals marginal cost.

$$1 = w_l^\gamma r_l^{1-\gamma} \tag{3.13}$$

Recall that agriculture is the numeraire good.

## Product Markets and Factor Markets

We are now ready to solve for equilibrium in the product and factor markets. Product market equilibrium requires that demand equals supply for each good in each industry,[7]

$$x_l^i = c_{ll}^i + c_{lk}^i, \quad i = u, d. \tag{3.14}$$

And the factor market clearing conditions are given by

$$L_l = \frac{1}{w_l} = [\gamma X_l^q + \alpha p_l^u n_l^u + \delta p_l^d n_l^d], \tag{3.15}$$

$$K_l = \frac{1}{r_l} = [(1-\gamma)X_l^q + (1-\alpha)p_l^u n_l^u + (1-\delta-\mu)p_l^d n_l^d]. \tag{3.16}$$

The factor market clearing conditions (equations 3.15 and 3.16) and the product market clearing conditions below (equations 3.17 and 3.18), which are derived by substituting equations (3.3, 3.6, 3.7, 3.8, 3.9, and 3.11) into (3.14), with the analogous equations for country $k$ simultaneously solve for the equilibrium number of firms in each country and factor prices.

$$
\begin{aligned}
x_l^u &= \frac{\mu n_l^d x_l^d w_l^\delta r_l^{1-\delta-\mu}}{(p_l^u)^\sigma \left[ n_l^u(p_l^u)^{1-\sigma} + n_k^u \left( p_k^u \tau(1+T^u) \right)^{1-\sigma} \right]^{\frac{\sigma-1+\mu}{\sigma-1}}} \\
&\quad + \frac{\mu n_k^d x_k^d w_k^\delta r_k^{1-\delta-\mu}}{\tau^{\sigma-1}(p_l^u(1+T^u))^\sigma \left[ n_l^u(p_l^u \tau(1+T^u))^{1-\sigma} + n_k^u(p_k^u)^{1-\sigma} \right]^{\frac{\sigma-1+\mu}{\sigma-1}}}
\end{aligned}
\tag{3.17}
$$

$$
\begin{aligned}
x_l^d &= \frac{s(w_l L_l + r_l K_l + T^d c_{kl}^d n_k^d + T^u c_{kl}^u n_k^u)}{(p_l^d)^\sigma [n_l^d(p_l^d)^{1-\sigma} + n_k^d(p_k^d \tau(1+T^d))^{1-\sigma}]} \\
&\quad + \frac{s(w_k L_k + r_k K_k + T^d c_{lk}^d n_l^d + T^u c_{lk}^u n_l^u)}{\tau^{\sigma-1}(p_l^d(1+T^d))^\sigma [n_l^d(p_l^d \tau(1+T^d))^{1-\sigma} + n_k^d(p_k^d)^{1-\sigma}]}
\end{aligned}
\tag{3.18}
$$

$$x_l^i \leq 1, \, n_l^i \geq 0, \, i = u, d.$$

These equations will form the basis for analysing the effects of trade liberalization on industrial location.

## 4. RESULTS

We consider three different cases, each with an average tariff rate of 5 per cent (i) de-escalating tariffs – 10 per cent tariff on intermediates and 0 per cent on final goods; (ii) escalating tariffs – 0 per cent tariff on intermediates and 10 per cent on final goods; (iii) uniform tariffs – 5 per cent on intermediates and final goods. The results are summarized in Table 3.1. Throughout the analysis we will assume that agricultural goods are freely traded, in order to focus our attention on the manufacturing sector. The real resource cost on shipping intermediate and final goods will be kept constant at 10 per cent, which is based on estimates in Hummels (1999).

For concreteness, we assume that the intermediate inputs are capital intensive ($\alpha = 0.1$), and final goods are labour intensive ($\delta = 0.3$).[8] The two countries are similarly sized in terms of initial factor endowments, with $L_l = 200$, $L_k = 100$, $K_l = 100$, $K_k = 200$. We discuss implications of changing these

*Table 3.1 Results*

### Labour-abundant country

| $T^u$ | $T^d$ | $sh_l^u$ | $sh_l^d$ | $w_l$ | $r_l$ | $U_l^w$ | $U_l^r$ | $U_l$ |
|-------|-------|----------|----------|-------|-------|---------|---------|--------|
| 0.10  | 0.00  | 0        | 0.00     | 0.35  | 0.71  | 2.33    | 4.66    | 931.60 |
| 0     | 0.10  | 0        | 0.44     | 0.38  | 0.65  | 2.50    | 4.23    | 923.71 |
| 0.05  | 0.05  | 0        | 0.17     | 0.36  | 0.69  | 2.41    | 4.47    | 929.63 |
| 0.00  | 0.00  | 0        | 0.41     | 0.38  | 0.66  | 2.51    | 4.31    | 931.82 |

### Capital-abundant country

| $T^u$ | $T^d$ | $sh_k^u$ | $sh_k^d$ | $w_k$ | $r_k$ | $U_k^w$ | $U_k^r$ | $U_k$ | $U_l + U_k$ |
|-------|-------|----------|----------|-------|-------|---------|---------|---------|-------------|
| 0.10  | 0.00  | 1        | 1.00     | 0.55  | 0.46  | 3.77    | 3.13    | 1003.80 | 1935.40     |
| 0     | 0.10  | 1        | 0.56     | 0.51  | 0.49  | 3.33    | 3.21    | 975.91  | 1899.62     |
| 0.05  | 0.05  | 1        | 0.83     | 0.54  | 0.47  | 3.60    | 3.14    | 989.23  | 1918.86     |
| 0     | 0.00  | 1        | 0.59     | 0.51  | 0.49  | 3.37    | 3.25    | 987.49  | 1919.31     |

*Notes*
The real resource cost, $\tau$, is set at 10 per cent in all policy experiments
$T^u$ – tariff rate on upstream goods (intermediate inputs)
$T^d$ – tariff rate on downstream goods (final goods)
$sh_l^u$ – share of upstream industry located in labour-abundant country
$sh_l^d$ – share of downstream industry located in labour-abundant country
$w_l, r_l$ – factor prices in labour-abundant country
$U_l^w$ – real returns to workers in labour-abundant country
$U_l^r$ – real returns to capitalists in labour-abundant country
$U_l$ – aggregate utility in the labour-abundant country
$U_l + U_k$ – aggregate world utility
All $k$-subscripted variables refer to the capital-abundant country

assumptions below. We assume that the factor intensity of agricultural goods is in between the final and intermediate goods ($\gamma = 0.5$). This, combined with the assumption that the share of manufactures in final consumption is less than a half ($s = 0.45$), ensures that both countries always produce agricultural goods, hence equation (3.13) always holds. This simplifies the analysis by ensuring that trade liberalization cannot lead to an increase in both factor returns within a country.[9] The large differences in factor intensities between intermediate and final goods works against agglomeration but the high share of intermediate inputs in final goods ($\mu = 0.6$) promotes agglomeration. And the low elasticity of substitution between intermediate varieties and between final goods ($\sigma = 3$) makes the benefits of agglomeration very high.

In general, firms consider two broad factors in deciding where to locate: large markets for their output (market access) and the availability of cheap inputs (production costs). In order to save on fixed costs, each firm prefers to locate in only one country. Other things equal, the preferred country is the one with the largest demand, in order to save on trade costs. Hence, downstream firms prefer to locate in a country with many consumers; whereas upstream firms prefer to locate in a country with many downstream firms since they form the market for intermediate inputs. This gives rise to a demand linkage, drawing upstream firms close to downstream firms. In turn, downstream firms benefit from being close to a large number of upstream firms due to the cost linkage: the more upstream firms in a country the lower the cost of intermediate inputs. We can see this from equation (3.3), by replacing superscript $d$ with superscript $u$ – the price index, $P_l^u$, is decreasing in the number of upstream firms.[10] This cost linkage reinforces the demand linkage, giving rise to forces for an agglomeration of all upstream and downstream firms in one country.

There are two forces working against agglomeration. One, with fixed endowments of labour and capital, demand for final goods comes from both countries, encouraging downstream firms to locate in country $k$ and country $l$. Two, given the differences in factor intensities between upstream and downstream firms, the production cost effect pulls them in opposite directions, with upstream firms drawn to the country that offers a relatively lower rental rate and downstream firms to the country that offers a relatively lower wage rate. Whether upstream and downstream firms agglomerate in one country depends on the relative strengths of the agglomeration and diversification forces, which depend on the level of trade costs on intermediate and final goods, and the size of the vertical linkages.

## Upstream Firms

The market access effect draws upstream firms to locations with a large number of downstream firms (which form the market for their output). The production cost effect draws upstream firms to countries with the lowest rental. An upstream firm locates in country $k$ if profits are higher than in country $l$, which is the case if

$$
x_k^u - x_l^u = \frac{\mu n_k^d x_k^d w_k^\delta r_k^{1-\delta-\mu} \{(p_l^u)^\sigma (1+T^u)^\sigma \tau^{\sigma-1} - (p_k^u)^\sigma\}}{\tau^{\sigma-1}(p_l^u p_k^u (1+T^u))^\sigma \left[ n_l^u (p_l^u \tau (1+T^u))^{1-\sigma} + n_k^u (p_k^u)^{1-\sigma} \right]^{\frac{\sigma-1+\mu}{\sigma-1}}}
$$
$$
+ \frac{\mu n_l^d x_l^d w_l^\delta r_l^{1-\delta-\mu} \{(p_l^u)^\sigma - (p_k^u)^\sigma (1+T^u)^\sigma \tau^{\sigma-1}\}}{\tau^{\sigma-1}(p_l^u p_k^u (1+T^u))^\sigma \left[ n_l^u (p_l^u)^{1-\sigma} + n_k^u (p_k^u \tau (1+T^u))^{1-\sigma} \right]^{\frac{\sigma-1+\mu}{\sigma-1}}} > 0.
$$

(3.19)

A sufficient condition for this to hold is that the difference in the terms in the curly brackets is positive, since all other terms are positive. Whenever the second expression is positive, then this implies the first expression is too. The second expression is positive if

$$
\left(\frac{p_l^u}{p_k^u}\right) = \left(\frac{w_l}{w_k}\right)^\alpha \left(\frac{r_l}{r_k}\right)^{1-\alpha} > \tau^{\frac{\sigma-1}{\sigma}}(1+T^u).
$$

(3.20)

Upstream firms locate in country $k$ if the production cost advantage outweighs the cost of exporting to country $l$. Note that the overall sign of equation (3.19) may still be positive even if the inequality in equation (3.20) does not hold, for example, if the number of downstream firms in country $k$ is high.

Recall that in our numerical simulations, we have assumed a very high capital intensity in the production of intermediate inputs with $\alpha = 0.1$. Consequently, in all the policy experiments considered in Table 3.1, the production cost effect arising from a relatively low rental rate in the capital-abundant country dominates the market access effect. This leads to all upstream firms locating in the capital-abundant country.

As well as affecting the location of upstream firms, import tariffs on intermediate inputs also affect the location of downstream firms, since downstream firms are drawn to locations with a large number of upstream firms. So by influencing the location of upstream firms, these tariffs also affect the location of downstream firms.

## Downstream Firms

The location of downstream firms is also influenced by trade costs on final goods. Lower tariffs on final goods make it possible for all downstream firms to locate in one country and serve the other through exports. A downstream firm locates in country $k$ if profits are higher than in country $l$,

$$x_k^d - x_l^d = \frac{sY_k\{(p_l^d)^\sigma(1+T^d)^\sigma\tau^{\sigma-1} - (p_k^d)^\sigma\}}{(p_l^d p_k^d)^\sigma(1+T^d)^\sigma\tau^{\sigma-1}[n_l^d(p_l^d\tau(1+T^d))^{1-\sigma} + n_k^d(p_k^d)^{1-\sigma}]}$$

$$+ \frac{sY_l\{(p_l^d)^\sigma - (p_k^d)^\sigma(1+T^d)^\sigma\tau^{\sigma-1}\}}{(p_l^d p_k^d)^\sigma(1+T^d)^\sigma\tau^{\sigma-1}[n_l^d(p_l^d)^{1-\sigma} + n_k^d(p_k^d\tau(1+T^d))^{1-\sigma}]} > 0.$$

$$\tag{3.21}$$

A sufficient condition for this to hold is that the difference in the terms in the curly brackets is positive, since all other terms are positive. Whenever the second expression is positive, then this implies the first expression is too. The second expression is positive if

$$\left(\frac{p_l^d}{p_k^d}\right) > \tau^{\frac{\sigma-1}{\sigma}}(1+T^d). \tag{3.22}$$

Downstream firms locate in country $k$ if the production cost advantage outweighs the cost of exporting to country $l$. Even if the second expression in equation (3.21) were negative, the overall sign may still be positive, for example, if the income in country $k$ is high. Whether the inequality in equation (3.22) holds depends on relative factor prices, the number of upstream firms and tariffs on intermediate inputs, as can be seen by

$$\left(\frac{p_l^d}{p_k^d}\right) = \left[\left(\frac{w_l}{w_k}\right)^\delta\left(\frac{r_l}{r_k}\right)^{1-\delta-\mu}\right]\left[\frac{n_l^u(p_l^u\tau(1+T^u))^{1-\sigma} + n_k^u(p_k^u)^{1-\sigma}}{n_l^u(p_l^u)^{1-\sigma} + n_k^u(p_k^u\tau(1+T^u))^{1-\sigma}}\right]^{\frac{\mu}{\sigma-1}}. \tag{3.23}$$

The first square-bracketed term represents the factor cost advantage of locating in country $l$, with labour-intensive firms putting more weight on lower relative wages. The second square-bracketed term represents the cost linkage – the more upstream firms in country $k$, the lower the price of intermediate inputs there, and the higher $\mu$ is the greater the weight on this term. Whether condition (3.21) holds or not will depend on the tariff rates on intermediate and final goods.[11]

**Trade Liberalization**

Reducing tariffs on final goods to zero while keeping tariffs on intermediates as high as 10 per cent promotes agglomeration of upstream and downstream firms in the capital-abundant country. From Table 3.1, we see that with $T^u = 10$ per cent, $T^d = 0$, the share of upstream and downstream goods produced in the labour-abundant country is zero ($sh_l^u = 0$, $sh_l^d = 0$) – the labour-abundant country only produces agriculture. High tariffs on intermediate inputs increases the benefits of upstream and downstream firms locating in one country; and low tariffs on final goods makes it possible for all downstream firms to locate in one country and export goods to the other. The lower trade costs on final goods reduces the importance of downstream firms locating in country $l$ to be close to consumers. Even though the lower relative wage rate attracts downstream firms to the labour-abundant country, the tariff of 10 per cent on intermediates makes it too costly for downstream firms to locate in the low-wage country and import intermediates.

In contrast, escalating tariffs works against agglomeration. With $T^u = 0$, $T^d = 10$ per cent, all intermediate inputs are still produced in the capital-abundant country but now the labour-abundant country produces 44 per cent of final goods. Low trade costs on intermediates means that the lower relative wage cost in the labour-abundant country draws downstream firms there and the high tariff on final goods increases the importance of downstream firms locating in both countries close to consumers. As more downstream firms locate in the labour-abundant country they bid up the relative wage rate until it no longer becomes profitable for any more downstream firms to locate there.

Interestingly, both countries are better off with the de-escalating tariffs that results in agglomeration than with escalating tariffs. The utility in the capital-abundant country is $U_k = 1003.8$ with de-escalating tariffs compared with $U_k = 975.9$ with escalating tariffs. Surprisingly, the labour-abundant country is also better off with the agglomeration in the capital-abundant country rather than producing 44 per cent of final goods. Its utility with de-escalating tariffs is $U_l = 931.6$ compared with $U_l = 923.7$ with escalating tariffs. The basic intuition is that the labour-abundant country also shares in the benefits of agglomeration through lower prices of final goods. The benefits are so high in this example because the share of intermediate input is high at $\mu = 0.6$ and the elasticity of substitution is low at $\sigma = 3$. The low elasticity of substitution makes varieties very imperfect substitutes. So the benefit of differentiated varieties in the production of final goods is very high (see equation 3.3 with the subscript $d$ replaced with $u$).

If the elasticity of substitution were higher, then the labour-abundant country might be better off without the agglomeration, that is, with escalating tariffs the aggregate world welfare could go either way. The labour-abundant country could be better off having some share of the manufacturing industry, as is the case with escalating tariffs depending on which of a number of opposing effects dominates. First, a higher share of the labour-intensive downstream industry increases the relative demand for workers bidding up the relative wage to rental ratio. Second, even though tariffs on intermediates are zero in the de-escalating example, there are still real resource costs in shipping intermediate inputs. The forgone benefits of agglomeration result in higher prices of final goods. In this example, workers have a higher wage and capitalists a lower rental in the de-escalating case. The higher goods prices without agglomeration do not offset the wage rise so workers are better off but capitalists are worse off in real terms. Here, the benefits to workers do not outweigh the costs to capitalists in the de-escalating case but with different parameter values it could go the other way around. Three, in the escalating case the labour-abundant country collects tariff revenue on imports of final goods; however, in the de-escalating case all intermediate and final goods are produced in the capital-abundant country and tariffs on final goods are zero so there is no tariff revenue.

With uniform tariff rates at 5 per cent, the labour-abundant country produces 17 per cent of final goods. Given that the capital-abundant country produces 83 per cent of final goods under uniform tariffs, there are still some gains from agglomeration so the utility with uniform tariffs is higher in both countries compared with escalating tariffs, but not as high as with de-escalating tariffs where the full benefits of agglomeration are gained. So in our example, the worst-case scenario is that of escalating tariffs.

Reducing tariffs to zero on both intermediate inputs and final goods does not result in complete specialization based on comparative advantage since there is still a 10 per cent real resource cost in shipping intermediates and final goods. At zero tariff rates, the labour-abundant country produces 41 per cent of final goods and achieves the highest utility; however, zero tariff rates lead to lower utility in the capital-abundant country compared with de-escalating tariffs that results in agglomeration. In this example, aggregate world welfare is highest with agglomeration. Lower shipping costs, $\tau$, could change this result. Recall that we maintained $\tau = 10$ per cent on intermediates and final goods to highlight that these costs would still exist even when tariffs had successfully been reduced to zero. Positive shipping costs could prevent complete specialization based on comparative advantage and differential shipping rates on intermediates and final goods can lead to different patterns of industrial location.

So far we have assumed that intermediate inputs are relatively more capital intensive. If instead intermediate inputs were labour intensive and final goods were capital intensive, there would be a stronger tendency for the agglomeration to locate in the labour-abundant country. De-escalating tariffs on the final goods would encourage more capital-intensive downstream firms to locate in the labour-abundant country to be close to the intermediate input suppliers.

The assumption of similar-sized countries ensures that the market access effect is of similar magnitude for downstream firms in both countries. However, if one country is significantly larger than the other country, this will increase its attractiveness for downstream firms. For example, if country $l$ were very large, we see from equation (3.21) that a high relative income[12] in country $l$ (a high $Y_l$ relative to $Y_k$) can change the sign of that expression and make it more profitable for downstream firms to locate in country $l$. With a higher number of downstream firms in country $l$, we see from equation (3.19) that this could also increase the profitability of upstream firms locating in country $l$, hence promoting agglomeration of upstream and downstream firms in the labour-abundant country.

## 5.  CONCLUSIONS

This chapter has shown that uniform tariffs in an imperfectly competitive world do not always yield the highest welfare. In some cases, a high tariff on intermediate inputs and low tariff on final goods can promote agglomeration of upstream and downstream firms in one country. The benefits of agglomeration give rise to lower prices of final goods, which benefit both countries. So even though the labour-abundant country can attract a higher share of the manufacturing industry with escalating or uniform tariff rates, its welfare might be higher if all the manufacturing industry were located in one country – even if the agglomeration is located in the other country. In our example, escalating tariffs, which characterize tariff structures in most countries, yields the lowest welfare in the labour-abundant and in the capital-abundant countries.

The key to the welfare gains arising from de-escalating tariffs is that location of firms is endogenous and this tariff structure could lead to agglomeration. Indeed, in our model there is free entry and exit and the fixed cost of setting up a firm is assumed to be very small. In industries that are characterized by high entry and exit costs, lower tariffs on intermediate inputs relative to final goods could give rise to higher welfare as firms benefit from cheaper intermediate inputs.

The benefits of agglomeration are likely to dominate in industries that are highly imperfectly competitive, are subject to high increasing returns to scale and produce imperfect substitutes. In our model, these characteristics were proxied by a low elasticity of substitution. It should be noted that the model presented is highly stylized and abstracts from many other important factors; for example, there could be additional benefits of agglomeration such as learning externalities but there could also be costs such as congestion and pollution. In practice, it is difficult to identify and properly measure these characteristics. However, further research along these lines could aid the tariff reform process.

## NOTES

\*   I would like to thank Caroline Freund, Will Martin, Martin Richardson, Maurice Schiff, David Tarr and participants at the *Festschrift* in honour of Peter Lloyd for valuable comments. This paper was written while the author was visiting the World Bank on sabbatical from the University of Melbourne. The author is currently with the International Monetary Fund on leave from the University of Melbourne.
1.   See www.worldbank.org/trade.
2.   Other arguments for uniform tariffs are based on political-economy grounds. See Rodrik and Panagariya (1993). There are also many arguments for non-uniform tariffs, such as terms of trade effects and profit-shifting reasons. See Tarr (2002) for a survey.
3.   For simplicity, we assume that $f$ and $\beta$ are the same in both upstream and downstream industries. Allowing them to differ changes the scale of production but does not affect the results.
4.   We assume that agricultural goods are freely traded in order to focus on manufacturing goods.
5.   The constant term in the marginal cost function is suppressed to simplify notation.
6.   In a monopolistically competitive model, segmented and integrated market solutions are equivalent.
7.   By Walras's law we do not need to specify the equilibrium condition in the agricultural sector.
8.   Note that the ratio of labour to capital coefficient is $(\delta/(1-\delta-\mu)) = 3$, so final goods are assumed to be very labour intensive compared to the other sectors.
9.   Both factor prices can increase in one country if $s > 0.5$. See Amiti (2005a).
10.  The cost linkage would also be present if the upstream industry were a Cournot oligopoly producing a homogeneous good. See Amiti (2001). In that case the larger the number of upstream firms, the lower the price of intermediate inputs due to increased competition.
11.  Note that whether the conditions in equation (3.19) and (3.20) hold will be independent of the initial distribution of firms for the parameter values in the simulations. The equilibrium outcome for each tariff combination underlying Table 3.1 is unique so the sequence of trade liberalization in these examples are irrelevant. See Amiti (2005b) for examples of path dependence.
12.  Of course, the relative size of a country not only depends on the size of endowments but also on the endogenous factor returns. But with agriculture produced in both countries, both factors within a country cannot simultaneously experience an increase, that is, an increase in $w_l$ is associated with a fall in $r_l$.

# BIBLIOGRAPHY

Amiti, Mary (2001), 'Regional specialisation and technological leapfrogging', *Journal of Regional Science*, **41** (1), 149–72.

Amiti, Mary (2005a), 'Location of vertically linked industries: agglomeration versus comparative advantage', *European Economic Review*, May, **49** (4), 809–32.

Amiti, Mary (2005b), 'How the sequence of trade liberalization affects industrial location', International Monetary Fund mimeo.

Bertrand, Trent J. and Jaroslav Vanek (1971), 'The theory of tariffs, taxes and subsidies: some aspects of the second best', *American Economic Review*, **61**, 925–31.

Buffie, Edward F. (2001), *Trade Policy in Developing Countries*, Cambridge: Cambridge University Press.

Corden, Max (1971), *The Theory of Protection*, Oxford: Oxford University Press.

Dicken, Peter (1998), *Global Shift: Transforming the World*, 3rd edn, London: Paul Chapman.

Dixit, Avinash K. and Gene M. Grossman (1982), 'Trade and protection with multistage production', *Review of Economic Studies*, **XLIX**, 583–94.

Dixit, Avinash K. and Joseph E. Stiglitz (1977), 'Monopolistic competition and optimum product diversity', *American Economic Review*, **67**, 297–308.

Ethier, W. (1982), 'National and international returns to scale in the modern theory of international trade', *American Economic Review*, **72**, 389–405.

Falvey, Rodney E. (1988), 'Tariffs, quotas and piecemeal policy reform', *Journal of International Economics*, **25**, 177–83.

Fujita Masahisa, Paul Krugman and Anthony J. Venables (1999), *The Spatial Economy: Cities, Regions and International Trade*, Cambridge, MA: MIT Press.

Helpman, Elhanan and Paul R. Krugman (1989), *Trade Policy and Market Structure*, Cambridge, MA: MIT Press, pp. 138–40.

Hummels, David (1999), 'Toward a geography of trade costs', Purdue University mimeo.

Krugman, Paul (1991), 'History versus expectations', *Quarterly Journal of Economics*, **106** (2), 651–67.

Krugman, Paul and Anthony J. Venables (1995), 'Globalization and the inequality of nations', *Quarterly Journal of Economics*, **110** (4), 857–80.

Lloyd, Peter J. (1974), 'A more general theory of price distortions in open economies', *Journal of International Economics*, **4**, 365–86.

López, Ramón and Arvind Panagariya (1992), 'On the theory of piecemeal tariff reform: the case of pure imported intermediate inputs', *American Economic Review*, **82** (3), 615–25.

Meade, J. (1955), *Trade and Welfare*, Oxford: Oxford University Press.

Michaely, Michael, Demetris Papageorgiou and Armeane Choksi (1991), *Liberalizing Foreign Trade: Lessons of Experience in the Developing World*, Oxford: Blackwell.

Michalopoulos, Constantine (1999), 'Trade policy and market access issues for developing countries: implications for the millennium round', World Bank Working Paper 2214.

Rodrik, Dani and Arvind Panagariya (1993), 'Political economy arguments for a uniform tariff', *International Economic Review*, **34** (3), 685–703.

Tarr, David G. (2002), 'Arguments for and against uniform tariffs', in Bernard Hoekman, Aaditya Mattoo and Philip English (eds), *Development, Trade, and the WTO*, Washington, DC: World Bank.

UNCTAD (1998), 'Market access: developments since the Uruguay Round, impli-
   cations, opportunities and challenges'.
Venables, Anthony J. (1996), 'Equlibrium locations of vertically linked industries',
   *International Economic Review*, **37** (2), 341–59

# 4. On the measurement of welfare changes at second-best optima

**Kunio Kawamata**

## 1. INTRODUCTION

When not all of the agents in an economy act on a common efficiency price vector (which is proportional to the vector of marginal rates of substitution whenever the latter exists), the allocation is not Pareto-optimal under the standard assumptions about the economic environment, including the convexity of preferences and technologies and the non-existence of external economies. The price distortion as described above is an unavoidable consequence of sales taxes and monopolistic pricing.

Allais (1973) and Debreu (1951), among others, defined a measure of welfare loss in a non-optimal state by the proportion of the initial resources that would be unnecessary if the distortions were completely removed (see also Kawamata, 1974). There are also related measures of loss based on the second-order derivatives of the welfare function evaluated at the initial optimal point (see Hotelling, 1938; Boiteaux, 1951; and Harberger, 1964). The relationships among these and some other measures of loss are discussed by Diewert (1981).

The chief purpose of this chapter is to evaluate the welfare change from one second-best position to another when there takes place a small change in the distortionary constraint of the model. We measure the loss by the amount of a single good, say the numeraire, that would just compensate for a one-unit change in the distortionary constraint. Clearly, the idea underlying this measure is quite similar to those of Debreu and Allais.

Diewert (1981) conjectured that the welfare loss will increase if substitutability in consumption increases. A similar result was established by Samuelson (2001) in a economic model where the representative consumer has a CES utility function and a sales tax is imposed to finance a good for public service. We will show that simple formulae for welfare changes depending on inverse substitution coefficients can be derived when losses are evaluated at second-best optimal points. The formulae for welfare changes are usually very complicated, and to simplify the results and facilitate comparisons they need to be evaluated at the first-best points in the previous work (see, for example, Corlett and Hague, 1953–54; Atkinson and Stiglitz, 1980; Diewert, 1981; and Diewert, et al., 1989).

The formulae for welfare changes at second-best optima take on somewhat different forms depending on the nature of the constraints. In the case where there is a single exogenously given *ad valorem* distortion of the Lipsey–Lancaster (1956–57) type, the measure may be expressed in terms of tax revenue and the demand and supply elasticities. If there is a constraint on the government budget as in the classical model of Ramsey (1927), extensively studied by Diamond and Mirrlees (1971) among others, it can be expressed by a dimensionless number depending only on the elasticities. Similar problems arise in international economics and public economics. We refer to Lloyd (1974) and Dixit (1975) for special features of the models. The Antonelli–Hicks–Allen transformation will help to bring out analytical similarities among the theorems that arise from various second-best problems discussed in the literature. This approach is especially useful to evaluate the welfare loss at non-Pareto-optimal points where standard duality formula for the consumption theory is not directly applicable. Early literature using the Antonelli matrix in the second-best analysis includes Lloyd (1977), Kawamata (1977) and Deaton (1981).

## 2.  PARTIAL EQUILIBRIUM ANALYSIS

Before presenting the formal model and stating general results on the welfare effects of changes in distortionary constraints, we will demonstrate the solutions of our problems in a partial equilibrium framework. Although the analysis in this section uses the notion of consumer's surplus, our formal analysis and results in the later sections do not rely on this concept.

In the standard partial equilibrium framework, let $x$ be the amount of output, and $p = p(x)$ and $q = q(x)$ be the inverse demand and supply functions with $p'(x) < 0$ and $q'(x) > 0$. Suppose that two curves intersect at a point $E$ that defines the competitive output $x(0)$ and the competitive price $p(x(0))$ (see Figure 4.1).

We are interested in evaluating the changes of the deadweight loss in three different situations. In each case, the deadweight loss is expressed as

$$L(x^*(\alpha)) = \int\limits_{x^*(\alpha)}^{x(0)} (p(x) - q(x))dx, \qquad (4.1)$$

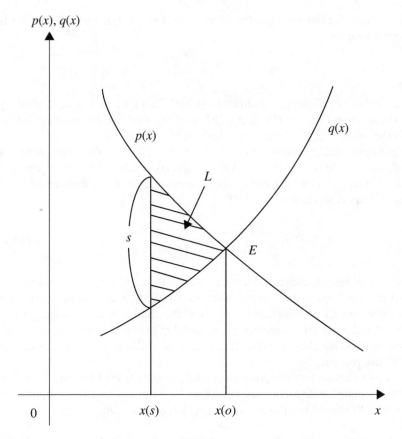

*Figure 4.1 The measure of welfare loss*

where $x(0)$ is the competitive output level and $x^* = x^*(\alpha)$ with $x^*(\alpha) < x(0)$ is the actual output level dependent on a parameter $\alpha$. Differentiating $L(x^*(\alpha))$ with respect to $\alpha$ we have

$$\frac{dL(x^*(\alpha))}{d\alpha} = \frac{-(p(x^*) - q(x^*)) \cdot dx^*}{d\alpha}. \tag{4.2}$$

In the following we will consider three particular types of distortion arising from (i) imposition of a specific tax, (ii) imposition of an *ad valorem* tax and (iii) Ramsey-type tax revenue requirement.

(i) Let the specific tax rate $s$ be given parametrically. Corresponding to each $s$ in the range $0 < s < p(0) - q(0)$ is a unique $x = x(s)$ such that $p(x) - q(x) = s$. This relation implies that $x'(s) = 1/(p' - q')$. Inserting this into (4.2), the derivative of the deadweight loss $L(x(s))$ with respect to $s$ is computed as

$$\frac{dL}{ds} = \frac{s}{(p' - q')},$$   (4.3)

where all functions are evaluated at $x(s)$. This case has been studied by Atkinson and Stiglitz (1980, pp. 367–9). Note that the dimension of $dL/ds$ is the same as that of the output level $x$.

(ii) For each *ad valorem* tax rate $t$, $0 < t < (p(0) - q(0))/q(0)$, there is a unique $x = x(t)$ such that $t = (p(x) - q(x))/q(x)$. It follows from this that $x'(t) = q/(p' - (1+t)q')$. Hence the derivative of the deadweight loss $L(x(t))$ with respect to $t$ is computed as

$$\frac{dL}{dt} = \frac{(p-q)q}{(1+t)q' - p'} = \frac{(p-q)x}{(1+t)(1/\varepsilon + 1/\eta)},$$   (4.4)

where all functions are evaluated at $x(t)$ and $1/\varepsilon$ and $1/\eta$ are the elasticities of inverse demand and supply functions (that is, $\varepsilon$ and $\eta$ are the elasticities of demand and supply functions). Thus the change in the deadweight loss is related positively to the tax revenue and negatively to the sum of inverse elasticities. We also note that the dimension of $dL/dt$ is the same as that of the tax revenue.

(iii) Suppose that the government has to raise a fixed amount $R > 0$ of tax revenue by distortionary taxation. This implies that the output level $x = x(R)$ should be chosen so that $(p(x) - q(x))x = R$.

This solution exists if $R$ is given to be not greater than the maximum of the tax revenue function. But there remains a complication in this case due to the fact that there may be more than one solution to the above equation. Disregarding abnormal situations, we shall confine ourselves to the range of $R$ (and $x$) where tax revenue is increasing in $x$ (see Samuelson, 2001 for a comment on the declining branch of the tax burden curve).

Thus let $x > 0$ be the output level where the local maximum of the tax revenue function is attained closest to the competitive output $x(0)$, and $\underline{R} > 0$ be the corresponding tax revenue. In the interval $[\underline{x}, x(0)]$ tax revenue is a decreasing function of $x$ and we have $x'(R) = 1/((p - q) + (p' - q')x)$. The derivative of the deadweight loss $L(x(R))$ with respect to $R$ $(0 < R < \underline{R})$ is now computed as

$$\frac{dL}{dR} = \frac{-(p-q)}{(p-q)+(p'-q')x} = \frac{t}{1/\varepsilon(1+t)+1/\eta - t},$$   (4.5)

where functions are evaluated at $x(R)$. Notice that the sum of the first two terms in the denominator represents the elasticities of 'price-wedge function' $p - q$ and that the whole expression is independent of the units of the output level and the two prices.

It turns out that we can define a measure of welfare (which does not rely on the concept of consumer's surplus) so that similar, simple formulae can be derived for the general second-best models that have appeared in the literature. Theorem 1 in Section 4 generalizes the above formula (4.4) for the problem of Lipsey and Lancaster (1956–57) with an *a priori* specified *ad valorem* distortion. Theorem 2 in Section 5 does the same to formula (4.3) for the similar problem with a specific distortion. The formula corresponding to (4.5) will be obtained for the classical problem of Ramsey (1927) with a tax revenue constraint. We shall also examine the conditions under which the measure (as expressed by one of the above formulae) would faithfully reflect the true changes in the welfare (utilities of the consumer).


## 3.  BASIC ASSUMPTIONS

We will consider a closed economy. Let $x = (x_1, \ldots, x_n)$ be the production vector and $\omega = (\omega_1, \ldots, \omega_n)$ the vector of initial endowment of commodities. The amounts of consumption may then be expressed as $x + \omega$.

For expository convenience we suppose that there is a representative consumer and the production technology of the whole economy is given. We assume that the utility of the consumer can be expressed by a real valued function

$$z = f(x + \omega), \tag{4.6}$$

and the production technology by

$$g(x) = 0, \tag{4.7}$$

another real valued function. It is implicit in this formulation that there is no distortion within the production sector (and consumption sector). Only the inter-sectoral distortion will be considered in this chapter.

We suppose that $f$ and $g$ have continuous partial derivatives up to the second order, to be denoted as $f_i = \partial f/\partial x_i$ and $f_{ij} = \partial^2 f/\partial x_j\, \partial x_i$ and so on. It is assumed that

$$f_i \geq 0, \quad g_i \leq 0 \quad (i = 1, 2, \ldots, n) \tag{4.8}$$

with strict inequality holding for $i = 1$ and $n$. It is also assumed that $f$ is a strictly quasi-concave function and $g$ a strictly quasi-convex function.

Let us denote the consumer's (resp. producer's) marginal rate of substitution of commodity $i$ for commodity $n$ by $P^i(x)$ (resp. $Q^i(x)$):

$$P^i(x) = f_i(x)/f_n(x) \quad (i = 1, 2, \ldots, n)$$

$$Q^i(x) = g_i(x)/g_n(x) \quad (i = 1, 2, \ldots, n). \tag{4.9}$$

Let $i$, $j$ and $n$ be the indices of three different commodities, with $n$ being used as numeraire. According to Hicks and Allen (1934), commodity $i$ is a substitute for (resp. a complement to) $j$ if $P^i(x)$ is reduced (resp. increased) when $j$ is substituted for the numeraire in such a way as to leave the consumer at the same utility level as before. Formally, commodity $i$ is a substitute for or complement to commodity $j$ depending on whether

$$a_{ij}(x) = P^i_j(x) - P^j(x)P^i_n(x) \tag{4.10}$$

is negative or positive (where $P^i_j(x)$ denotes the partial derivative of $P^i(x)$ with respect to the $j$th argument). The first term of (4.10) measures how $P^i(x)$ (the marginal rate of substitution of commodity $i$ for commodity $n$) changes due to the change in the consumption of commodity $j$ and the second term measures the compensating change in the amount of the numeraire good to keep the consumer in the same utility level. It is clear that the second term vanishes if the utility function is linear in $x_n$, (that is if $u(x_1, \ldots, x_n)$ may be written as $v(x_1, x_2, \ldots, x_{n-1}) + x_n$). It is known that the Hicks–Allen definition of substitutability coincides with the Slutzky–Hicks definition for the three-commodity case. It is known that the Hicks–Allen definition of substitutability coincides with the Slutzky–Hicks definition for the three-commodity case.

It will be assumed that the Antonelli matrix $A = (a_{ij})$ $(i, j = 1, 2, \ldots, n - 1)$ is symmetric and negative definite. It is known (see Samuelson, 1950 and Katzner, 1970) that $A$ is the inverse of Slutzky–Hicks substitution matrix of the first $n - 1$ commodities and so the above conditions on $A$ hold, in particular, if the Slutzky matrix is symmetric and negative definite.

For the producer we shall similarly define

$$b_{ij}(x) = Q^i_j(x) - Q^j(x)Q^i_n(x) \tag{4.11}$$

and assume that $i$ is symmetric and positive definite. In the case where production technology is linear, $B = (b_{ij})$ is a 0 matrix.


# 4.   *AD VALOREM* DISTORTION AND WELFARE LOSS

Although we have analysed the specific distortion first and then *ad valorem* distortion in Section 2, we will reverse the order in the following analysis.

The *ad valorem* case is studied in this section and the specific case is studied in the next section. This is due to expository convenience; once the *ad valorem* case is studied, key equations for the specific case may be written with minor changes but not the other way round.

Let us assume that there is a given *ad valorem* distortion $t \neq 0$ between commodities 1 and $n$. The situation typically arises when the $n$th commodity is untaxable and used as numeraire and an *ad valorem* tax is imposed on commodity 1. By definition, $t_1$ must satisfy

$$P^1(x + \omega) = (1 + t_1)Q^1(x) \qquad (4.12)$$

at the final allocation. For definiteness we shall assume that $t_1$ is positive.

Following Lipsey and Lancaster (1956–57), we consider the problem of maximizing the objective function $f$ with respect to $(x_1, \ldots, x_n)$ subject to the production and institutional constraints (4.7) and (4.12). It is convenient to denote the optimal *ad valorem* distortion by $t_i$. By definition $t_i$ satisfies

$$P^i(x + \omega) = (1 + t_i)Q^i(x), \quad (i \in I) \qquad (4.13)$$

where the functions are evaluated at the second-best optimal and $I$ is the set of indices such that $Q^i(x) \neq 0$ (that is, $g_i \neq 0$). We will assume that $I = \{1, 2, \ldots, n - 1\}$ in the following discussion (see Remarks 1 (iv)).

Expressing the Lagrangean of the problem as

$$z = f(x + \omega) - \alpha g(x) + \beta(P^1(x + \omega) - (1 + t_1)Q^1(x)), \qquad (4.14)$$

we obtain the following first-order conditions:

$$z_r = f_r(x + \omega) - \alpha g_r(x) + \beta(P^1_r(x + \omega) - (1 + t_1)Q^1_r(x)) = 0$$
$$(r = 1, 2, \ldots, n). \qquad (4.15)$$

In view of definitions (4.9), we may express them in the following matrix form:

$$\begin{pmatrix} Q^r & P^1_r - (1 + t_1)Q^1_r \\ 1 & P^1_n - (1 + t_1)Q^1_n \end{pmatrix} \begin{pmatrix} \alpha g_n \\ \beta \end{pmatrix} = \begin{pmatrix} P^r \\ 1 \end{pmatrix} f_n.$$
$$(r = 1, 2, \ldots, n - 1) \qquad (4.16)$$

Let $\Delta(r)$, where $r$ range from 2 to $n(r = 1, 2, \ldots, n - 1)$, denote the $2 \times 2$ matrix in (4.16). This is expressed as

$$\Delta(r) = \begin{vmatrix} Q^r & P_r^1 \\ 1 & P_n^1 \end{vmatrix} - (1 + t_1) \begin{vmatrix} Q^r & Q_r^1 \\ 1 & Q_n^1 \end{vmatrix}$$

$$= (1 + t_1)b_{1r} - a_{1r} - (P^r - Q^r)P_n^1. \tag{4.17}$$

In particular, we have

$$\Delta(1) = (1 + t_1)b_{11} - a_{11} - t_1 Q^1 P_n^1, \tag{4.18}$$

or alternatively,

$$\Delta(1) = (1 + t_1)b_{11} - (a_{11} + t_1 P_1^1)/(1 + t_1). \tag{4.19}$$

It is convenient to summarize some of the implications of our analysis before we proceed.

**Remarks 1**

(i) We have $P_1^1 = (f_1 f_{n1} - f_n f_{11})/(f_n)^2$ and $P_n^1 = (f_n f_{1n} - f_1 f_{nn})/(f_n)^2$, by definition. If there are only two commodities 1 and $n$, the condition $P_1^1 < 0$ (resp. $P_n^1 > 0$) implies that commodity $n$ (resp. commodity 1) is *normal* in the sense that the income term of the corresponding Slutzky equation is positive, or that the income consumption curve (Hicks, 1946, pp. 27–8) between the two commodities slopes upward and to the right. Similar implications hold even when there are more than two commodities so long as the consumption of commodities other than 1 and $n$ (resp. 1) is *normal* against commodity 1 (resp. $n$) if $P_1^1 < 0$ (resp. $P_n^1 > 0$).

(ii) It can readily be shown that

$$a_{11} = - \begin{vmatrix} 0 & f_1 & f_n \\ f_1 & f_{11} & f_{1n} \\ f_n & f_{n1} & f_{nn} \end{vmatrix} /(f_n)^3,$$

that is, negative under our assumptions. Hence we must have either $P_1^1 < 0$ or $P_n^1 > 0$. Similarly, our assumption that $b_{11} > 0$ implies that either $Q_1^1 > 0$ or $Q_n^1 < 0$.

(iii) From (2.19) and Remark (i), it follows that $\Delta(1) > 0$ whenever $P_1^1 < 0$, that is, whenever commodity $n$ is normal against commodity 1.

(iv) It is possible to show (although the result will not be needed for the main discussion) that the optimal *ad valorem* distortion $t_i$ $(i \in I)$ of the problem may be expressed as

$$\frac{t_i}{t_1} = \frac{a_{1i} - (1 + t_1)b_{1i}}{a_{11} - (1 + t_1)b_{11}} \cdot \frac{Q'}{Q^i} \tag{4.20}$$

(see Kawamata, 1977, equation (15)). Hence $t_1 > 0$ implies $t_1 > t_i > 0$ if commodity $i$ $(i \in I)$ is a substitute for 1 when $n$ is used as numeraire (see Kawamata, 1977). Using the above formula we can immediately infer that

$$\Delta(r) = \frac{a_{1r} - (1 + t_1)b_{1r}}{a_{11} - (1 + t_1)b_{11}} \cdot \Delta(1) , \quad (r \in I). \tag{4.21}$$

Assume that commodity $n$ is normal against commodity 1. Then $\Delta(1)$ is positive and so from (4.19) we find that

$$\beta = \frac{-t_1 Q^1 f_n}{\Delta(1)} \tag{4.22}$$

is negative.

We now proceed to study the welfare effect of changes in the initial endowment $\omega_i$ and the given distortion $t_1$. Our solution vector $x$ determined by (4.7), (4.9), (4.12) and (4.15) is now considered to be a vector of functions of these two parameters which can be found by applying the implicit function theorem.

We first differentiate (4.14) with respect to $\omega_i$, remembering that $\alpha$ and $\beta$ as well as $x$ are continuously differentiable functions of $\omega_i$ in the neighbourhood of the original second-best state. We can thus evaluate the marginal utility of $\omega_i$ at the second-best allocation as

$$\frac{\partial z}{\partial \omega_i} = \sum_{r=1}^{n} z_r \frac{\partial x_r}{\partial \omega_i} + f_i - \beta P_i^1$$

$$= f_i - \beta P_i^1, \quad (i = 1, 2, \ldots, n), \tag{4.23}$$

using (4.15). Since $\beta < 0$ we infer that the 'social' marginal utility of $\omega_i$ is greater than 'private' marginal utility if and only if $\omega_i$ raises $P^1$.

**Proposition 1**

If commodity $n$ is normal against commodity 1, then $\partial z / \partial \omega_i$ is greater than or smaller than $f_i = \partial f / \partial \omega_i$ depending on whether $P_i^1$ is negative or positive. In particular, $\partial z / \partial \omega_1 < f_1$ and $\partial z / \partial \omega_n > f_n$.

From (4.18), (4.22) and (4.23) it is easy to derive

$$\frac{\partial z}{\partial \omega_n} = \frac{(a_{11} - (1 + t_1)b_{11})f_n}{-\Delta(1)},$$ (4.24)

a result which will be used in a moment. A similar result for $\partial z/\partial \omega_i$ follows from (4.20).

We next consider the effect of a change in $t_1$, remembering that $x$, $\alpha$ and $\beta$ are functions of $t_1$ and obtain

$$\frac{\partial z}{\partial t_i} = \sum_{r=1}^{n} z_r \frac{\partial x_r}{\partial t_1} + \beta Q^1$$

$$= \beta Q^1$$

$$= -(P^1 - Q^1)Q^1 f_n/\Delta(1),$$ (4.25)

using (4.15) and (4.22).

We define the inverse elasticity of demand $\varepsilon_i^-$ and that of supply $\eta_i^-$ by

$$\varepsilon_i^- = -a_{ii} x_i / P^i$$ (4.26)

and

$$\eta_i^- = b_{ii} x_i / Q^i$$ (4.27)

for each $i = 1, 2, \ldots, n - 1$ such that $P^i \neq 0$ and $Q^i \neq 0$.

Given an *ad valorem* distortion $t_1 > 0$, we measure the economic loss due to a marginal change in $t_1$ by the amount of $\omega_n$ that would just compensate for it. Our first theorem states that the loss that accompanies the change can be evaluated in terms of the revenue from the distortion (tax revenue) and the sum of inverse demand and inverse supply elasticities. Roughly, this means that welfare loss increases with effective tax revenue and decreases with the sum of the inverse demand and supply elasticities.

**Theorem 1**

Suppose that commodity $n$ is normal against 1 (that is, $P_1^1 < 0$) and that the *ad valorem* distortion is at a level $t_1 > 0$. Then the rate of change of $\omega_n$ that would just compensate for a marginal change in $t_1$ is given by $(P^1 - Q^1)x_1/(1 + t_1)(\varepsilon_i^- + \eta_i^-)$.

**Proof**
By (4.24) and (4.25) we have

$$\left. \frac{\partial \omega_n}{\partial t_1} \right|_{z:\,\text{const}} = -\frac{\partial z}{\partial t_1} \Big/ \frac{\partial z}{\partial \omega_n}$$

$$= \frac{-(P^1 - Q^1)Q^1}{a_{11} - (1 + t_1)b_{11}}$$

$$= \frac{(P^1 - Q^1)x_1}{(1 + t_1)(\varepsilon_i^- + \eta_i^-)}, \tag{4.28}$$

as was to be shown.

**Remarks 2**

Using the fact that the Antonelli matrix is the inverse of the $(n - 1) \times (n - 1)$ Slutzky matrix of the first $(n - 1)$ goods, it is possible to express the inverse elasticities in terms of the ordinary elasticities. For the three-commodity case, this is especially simple if the utility function is of form $U(X, Y) + Z$. Denoting ordinary elasticities of demand as $\varepsilon_{XX}(p, q) = -pX_p/X$, $\varepsilon_{XY}(p, q) = -qX_q/X$ and so on and inverse elasticities of demand as $\varepsilon_{XX}^-(X, Y) = -XP_X/P$, $\varepsilon_{XY}^-(X, Y) = -XP_Y/Q$ and so on, we have $\varepsilon_{XX}^- = \varepsilon_{YY}/\Delta$, $\varepsilon_{XY}^- = -\varepsilon_{YX}/\Delta$, $\varepsilon_{YX}^- = -\varepsilon_{XY}/\Delta$ and $\varepsilon_{YY}^- = \varepsilon_{XX}/\Delta$, where $\Delta = \varepsilon_{XX} \varepsilon_{YY} - \varepsilon_{YX} \varepsilon_{XY}$.

## 5. SPECIFIC DISTORTION AND WELFARE LOSS

In this section we consider the case where a specific distortion of a given rate $s_1 > 0$ is imposed on commodity 1 in terms of commodity $n$. The requirement is as in the case of *ad valorem* distortions. The previous condition (4.12) must now be replaced by

$$P^1(x + \omega) - Q^1(x) = s_1 \tag{4.29}$$

Our problem now is to maximize the objective function (1) with respect to $(x_1, \ldots, x_n)$ subject to the constraints (4.7) and (4.29). Let us write the Lagrangean of the problem as

$$z = f(x + \omega) - \alpha g(x) - \beta(P^1(x + \omega) - Q^1(x) - s_1). \tag{4.30}$$

We then obtain the first-order conditions

$$z_r = f_r(x + \omega) - \alpha g_r(x) - \beta(P_r^i(x + \omega) - Q_r^i(x)) = 0, \quad (r = 1, 2, \ldots, n). \tag{4.31}$$

This is of the same form as (4.15) for $t_1 = 0$. Hence (4.19) must hold for $t_1 = 0$. Therefore the last expression of (4.17) now reduces to

$$\Delta(r) = b_{1r} - a_{ir} - s_r P_n^1 \quad (r = 1, 2, \ldots, n - 1), \tag{4.32}$$

where $s_r$ is the specific distortion defined by

$$s_r = P^r(x + \omega) - Q^r(x), \quad (r = 1, 2, \ldots, n-1). \tag{4.33}$$

In particular, we have

$$\Delta(1) = b_{11} - a_{11} - s_1 P_1^1, \tag{4.34}$$

or alternatively,

$$\Delta(1) = b_{11} - (Q^1 a_{11} + s_1 P_1^1)/P^1. \tag{4.35}$$

**Remarks 3**

(i) From (4.34), it is clear that $\Delta(1)$ is positive if commodity $n$ is normal against commodity 1 (that is, if $P_1^1 < 0$).

(ii) It is possible to show using the first-order conditions that the optimal distortion $s_i$ ($i = 1, 2, \ldots, n$) of the present problem can be expressed as

$$s_i = (a_{1i} - b_{1i})s_1/(a_{11} - b_{11}) \tag{4.36}$$

(see Kawamata, 1977, equation (18)). It therefore follows that

$$\Delta(r) = (a_{1r} - b_{1r})/(a_{11} - b_{11})\Delta(1), \quad (r = 2, 3, \ldots, n-1). \tag{4.37}$$

Assume that commodity $n$ is normal against commodity 1. Then, $\Delta(1)$ is positive and so we may express $\beta$ as

$$\beta = -s_1 f_n/\Delta(1) \tag{4.38}$$

using (4.19) for $t_1 = 0$.

The welfare effect of a change in $\omega_i$ may be evaluated as

$$\frac{\partial z}{\partial \omega_i} = f_i - \beta P_i^1, \quad (i = 1, 2, \ldots, n) \tag{4.39}$$

in the same way as we derived (4.23). Since $\beta < 0$ under our assumption, *Proposition 1 is true for the specific case also.*

We note also that for $i = n$ (4.39) may be written as

$$\frac{\partial z}{\partial \omega_n} = \frac{(b_{11} - a_{11})f_n}{\Delta(1)} \tag{4.40}$$

using (4.45). On the other hand, the welfare effect of a change in $s_1$ may be evaluated as

$$\frac{\partial z}{\partial s_1} = \beta = \frac{-s_1 f_n}{\Delta(1)} \tag{4.41}$$

in the same way as we derived (4.25).

We now state:

**Theorem 2**

Suppose that commodity $n$ is normal against 1 (that is, $P_1^1 < 0$), and that the specific distortion (tax rate) is at a level $s_1 > 0$. The rate of change of $\omega_n$ that would just compensate for a marginal change in $s_1$ is given by $s_1/(b_{11} - a_{11})$.

**Proof**
By (4.40) and (4.41) we have

$$\left. \frac{\partial \omega_n}{\partial s_i} \right|_{z:\text{const}} = -\frac{\partial z}{\partial s_i} \Big/ \frac{\partial z}{\partial \omega_n}$$

$$= \frac{s_1}{b_{11} - a_{11}} \tag{4.42}$$

as was to be shown.

## 6.   RAMSEY'S PROBLEM

In this section we consider the situation in which the government raises a fixed amount of revenue by means of distortionary taxation. The government's problem is to maximize the object function

$$z = f(x + \omega) \tag{4.43}$$

with respect to $(x_1, \ldots, x_n)$ subject to the production technology constraint

$$g(x) = 0, \tag{4.44}$$

and the revenue restriction

$$\sum_{i=1}^{n-1} (P^i(x + \omega) - Q^i(x))x_i = R, \tag{4.45}$$

where $R \geq 0$ is the exogenously specified amount of taxation revenue to be raised. Commodity $n$ is assumed to be untaxable. We suppose that $R \geq 0$ is such that the set of feasible allocations (namely, $x$ which satisfies (4.7) and (4.40) is not empty).

This problem was first studied in the classical paper by Ramsey (1927) and has been modified and extended by other economists. Major contributions in related fields are listed in Atkinson and Stiglitz (1980) and Sheshinski (1986). See also Baumol et al. (1982). Our primary concern here is to examine the sensitivity of welfare to the changes in $R$ and $\omega_n$ (the initial endowment of commodity $n$).

We write the Lagrangean of the problem as

$$z = f(x + \omega) - \alpha g(x) + \beta \left( \sum_{i=1}^{n-1} (P^i(x + \omega) - Q^i(x))x_i - R \right) \quad (4.46)$$

and derive the following first-order conditions:

$$z_r = f_r(x + \omega) - \alpha g_r(x) + \beta \left( \sum_{i=1}^{n-1} (P_r^i(x + \omega) - Q_r^i(x))x_i \right.$$

$$- P^r(x + \omega) - Q^r(x) = 0 \bigg)$$

$$(r = 1, 2, \ldots, n) \quad (4.47)$$

This may be expressed in matrix form as

$$\begin{vmatrix} P^1 & Q^1 & \sum_i (P_1^i - Q_1^i)x_i + (P^1 - Q^1) \\ P^r & Q^r & \sum_i (P_r^i - Q_r^i)x_i + (P^r - Q^r) \\ 1 & 1 & \sum_i (P_n^i - Q_n^i)x_i \end{vmatrix} \begin{pmatrix} -f_n \\ \alpha g_n \\ \beta \end{pmatrix} = 0$$

$$(r = 2, 3, \ldots, n - 1), \quad (4.48)$$

where each summation $i$ runs from 1 to $n - 1$.

This implies that, for each $r$, the determinant of the $3 \times 3$ matrix on the left-hand side is zero; hence we have

$$\begin{vmatrix} P^1 & Q^1 & \sum_i (a_{i1} - b_{i1})x_i \\ P^r & Q^r & \sum_i (a_{ir} - b_{ir})x_i \\ 1 & 1 & 0 \end{vmatrix} = 0 \quad (4.49)$$

Denoting the optimal *ad valorem* tax rate by $t_r$ ($r = 2, \ldots, n - 1$), we have

$$t_r Q^r \sum_{i=1}^{n-1} (a_{i1} - b_{i1}) x_i = t_1 Q^1 \sum_{i=1}^{n-1} (a_{ir} - b_{ir}) x_i$$
$$(r = 2, \ldots, n - 1). \tag{4.50}$$

Hence

$$\theta = \sum_{i=1}^{n-1} (a_{ir} - b_{ir}) x_i / t_r Q^r \tag{4.51}$$

is independent of $r$.

**Lemma 1**

If $R > 0$, then $\theta < 0$

**Proof**

$$R\theta = \sum_{r=1}^{n-1} t_r Q^r x^r \theta$$
$$= x'(A - B)x, \tag{4.52}$$

where $A$ (resp. $B$) is the Antonelli matrix for consumption (resp. production). Since $A$ is negative definite and $B$ is positive definite, the result follows.

A direct consequence of the above analysis is the following *n*-commodity version of Ramsey's formula originally stated in this form for one commodity case:

**Theorem 3**

An optimal tax rule for Ramsey's problem is given by

$$t_r = -\left( \sum_{i=1}^{n-1} \varepsilon_{ir}^- + \sum_{i=1}^{n-1} \eta_{ir}^- \right) \Big/ \left( \theta + \sum_{i=1}^{n-1} \varepsilon_{ir}^- \right)$$
$$(r = 1, 2, \ldots, n - 1) \tag{4.53}$$

where $\varepsilon_{ir}^-$ and $\eta_{ir}^-$ are inverse demand and supply elasticities defined by $\varepsilon_{ir}^- = -a_{ir} x_i / P^r$ and $\eta_{ir}^- = b_{ir} x_i / Q^r$ ($i, r = 1, 2, \ldots, n > 1$).

**Proof**

In view of (4.51) and the definition of inverse elasticities we can write

$$\theta = -\left(\sum_i (1 + t_r)\varepsilon_{ir}^- + \sum_i \eta_{ir}^-\right)/t_r.$$

We only need to solve for $t_r$ to obtain the desired formula.

We next proceed to express $\beta$ in terms of $x$. For this we rewrite (4.48) in the following way:

$$\begin{pmatrix} Q^r & \sum_i (P_r^i - Q_r^i)x_i + (P^r - Q^r) \\ 1 & \sum_i (P_n^i - Q_n^i)x_i \end{pmatrix}\begin{pmatrix} \alpha g_n \\ \beta \end{pmatrix} = \begin{pmatrix} P^r \\ 1 \end{pmatrix} f_n$$

$$(r = 2, 3, \ldots, n - 1). \tag{4.54}$$

For each $r = 1, 2, \ldots, n - 1$, let $\Delta(r)$ be the determinant of the $2 \times 2$ matrix on the left-hand side of (4.54). Then we have

$$\Delta(r) = -\sum_i (P_r^i - P^r P_n^i)x_i + \sum_i (Q_r^i - Q^r Q_n^i)x^i - (P^r - Q^r)\left(1 + \sum_i P_n^i x_i\right)$$

$$= \sum_i (b_{ir} - a_{ir})x_i - (P^r - Q^r)\left(1 + \sum_i P_n^i x_i\right)$$

$$= -t_r Q^r\left(\theta + 1 + \sum_i P_n^i x_i\right) \tag{4.55}$$

using (4.51).

Now if $\theta + 1 + \sum_i P_n^i x_i$ is non-zero, $\Delta(r)$ is non-zero (see the Remark below). Hence from (4.54) we can solve for $\beta$ as

$$\beta = \frac{-(P^r - Q^r)f_n}{\Delta(r)}$$

$$= \frac{f_n}{\theta + 1 + \sum_i P_n^i x_i}. \tag{4.56}$$

This Lagrange multiplier shows how welfare changes in response to a change in $R$. Indeed, by differentiating (4.46) with respect to $R$ and using (4.47) we have

$$\frac{\partial z}{\partial R} = \sum_r z_r \frac{\partial x_r}{\partial R} + \beta$$

$$= \beta, \tag{4.57}$$

where the summation $r$ runs from 1 to $n$.

This shows that $\beta$ and $\partial z/\partial R$ have the same sign. As in the one-commodity case (see Section 2 example (iii)), however, the tax revenue may exhibit rather complicated behaviour as a function of the amount of consumption $x$ or as a function of initial endowment, $\omega$. Disregarding abnormal situations, we shall confine ourselves to the range of $R$ (and $x$) where the constraint is effective in the sense that $\partial z/\partial R < 0$. This means that we consider the part where the Laffer curve is decreasing.

## Remarks 4

If $R = 0$, the allocation that is realized is Pareto-optimal (where $P^i = Q^i$ for $i = 1, 2, \ldots, n-1$). We can show that if $R$ is close to zero (and hence the resulting allocation is close to a Pareto-optimal one in the regular case), the constraint is actually effective. Indeed using Lemma 1 we have

$$R\left(\theta + 1 + \sum_i P^i_n x_i\right) = x'(A - B)x + (P - Q)'x\left(1 + \sum_i P^i_n x_i\right),$$

where $P = (P^1, \ldots, P^{n-1})$ and $(Q^1, \ldots, Q^{n-1})$.

In the above equation the first term on the right-hand side is negative and the second term is zero at the Pareto-optimal point. Hence by continuity if $R > 0$ is sufficiently small then $\theta + 1 + \sum_i P^i_n x_i < 0$, and $\partial z/\partial R = \beta < 0$.

We next analyse the effect of a change in $\omega_i$. Differentiating (4.46) with respect to $\omega_i$ and using (4.47) and (4.56) we obtain

$$\frac{\partial z}{\partial \omega_i} = \sum_r z_r \frac{\partial x_r}{\partial \omega_i} + f_i - \beta \sum_r P^r_i x^r$$

$$= f_i - \beta \sum_r P^r_i x^r, \quad (i = 1, 2, \ldots, n), \tag{4.58}$$

where the summation $i$ runs from 1 to $n$.

In view of (4.56) it then follows that

$$\frac{\partial z}{\partial \omega_n} = \frac{(\theta + 1)f_n}{\theta + 1 + \sum_i P^i_n x_i}$$

$$= \beta(\theta + 1). \tag{4.59}$$

The above analysis implies a result that corresponds to Proposition 1 in Section 4.

## Proposition 2

If all of the non-numeraire goods are normal against the numeraire good $n$, then $\partial z/\partial \omega_n > f_n$; that is, the social utility of the commodity $n$ is greater than its private marginal utility.

### Proof
Notice that $\beta$ is negative by the previous argument and that $P_n^i$ is positive if commodity $i$ is normal against commodity $n$, since Remark 1(i) applies for commodities $i$ and $n$ as well as for commodities 1 and $n$. The proof of the proposition is then obvious from (4.58).

We now proceed to measure the welfare loss that would result from a small increase in $R$ by the amount of $\omega_n$ that would just compensate for the initial change. The next theorem asserts that this loss can be expressed in terms of the inverse demand and supply elasticities.

## Theorem 4

If $R > 0$ the rate of change in $\omega_n$ that would just compensate for a marginal change in $R$ is given by

$$-1/(\theta + 1) = t_r / \left( \sum_{i=1}^{n} (1 + t_r)\varepsilon_{ir}^- + \sum_{i=1}^{n} \eta_{ir}^- - t_r \right), \quad (r = 2, 3, \ldots, n-1).$$

If $R$ is sufficiently small (so that the constraint is effective), and all of the non-numeraire consumption goods are normal against the numeraire good then the above measure is positive.

### Proof
By (4.57) and (4.59), we have

$$\left. \frac{\partial \omega_n}{\partial R} \right|_{z\,:\,\text{const}} = \frac{\partial z}{\partial R} / \frac{\partial z}{\partial \omega_n}$$

$$= -1/(\theta + 1).$$

Hence the first part of the theorem follows from the relation in the proof of Ramsey's formula. The second part of the theorem is clear from

Lemma 2 and the assumption that $P_n^i > 0$ and $x_i \geq 0$ for any non-numeraire consumption good $i$.

We note that the above measure reduces to formula (4.5) in Section 2 when $n = 1$. It clearly indicates how inverse elasticities affect the welfare loss.

## 7. CONCLUSION

We have provided a formula for the welfare change arising from a change in a distortion when all other distortions are adjusted second-best optimally. We measured the welfare loss in a non-optimal state by the amount of the numeraire that would just compensate for a one-unit change in the given distortion.

We have evaluated the welfare loss in three different situations: first, when the original distortion is a specific distortion; second, when it is an *ad valorem* distortion; and third, where there is Ramsey-type revenue constraint. Our analysis confirms the conjecture by Diewert (1981) that welfare loss will increase if substitutability in consumption increases. This also supports a similar view expressed by Samuelson (2001) for a public-good economy. Similar formulae could be obtained for cases when several distortions are exogenously given. But the corresponding formula would become very complicated unless exogenously given distortions are chosen (second-best) optimally in some senses.

The formula for the welfare loss for each case is expressed in terms of inverse elasticities of Antonelli matrices. The result may be expressed using ordinally demand and supply elasticities. The expression takes on a simple form in the three commodity case with a quasi-linear utility function (see Remark 2). To our knowledge, there has not been a general study of sensitivity of welfare changes, apart from that near the first-best point. We hope that the present study gives information about the strength of various price distinctions from the viewpoint of welfare loss.

## REFERENCES

Allais, M. (1973), 'La théorie générale des surplus et l'apport fondamental de Vifredo Pareto', *Revue d'Economie Politique*, **83**, 1044–97. An English translation appeared as 'The general theory of surplus and Pareto's fundamental contributions', in *Convegno Internazionale Vilfredo Pareto*, Rome: Accademia Nazionale dei Lincei, 1975, pp. 109–63.

Antonelli, G.B. (1886), *Sulla Teoria Matematica della Economia Politica*, Pisa: nella Tipografia del Folchetto (privately published). An English translation appeared as 'On the mathematical theory of political economy', in J.S. Chipman, L. Hurwicz,

M.K. Richter and H. Sonnenschein (eds) (1971), *Preferences, Utility, and Demand*, New York: Harcourt Brace Jovanovich.

Atkinson, A.B. and J.E. Stiglitz (1980), *Lectures on Public Economics*, New York: McGraw-Hill.

Baumol, W.J., J.C. Panzar and R.D. Willing (1982), *Contestable Market and the Theory of Industry Structure*, New York: Harcourt Brace Jovanovich.

Boiteux, M. (1951), 'Le "revenu distruable" et les pertes economiques', *Econometrica*, **19**, 112–33.

Corlett, W.J. and D.C. Hague (1953–54), 'Complementarity and excess burden of taxation', *Review of Economic Studies*, **21**, 21–30.

Deaton, Angus (1981), 'Optimal taxes and the structure of preference', *Econometrica*, **49**, 1245–60.

Debreu, G. (1951), 'The coefficient of resource utilization', *Econometrica*, **19**, 273–92.

Diamond, P.A. and J.A. Mirrlees (1971), 'Optimal taxation and public production II: Tax rules', *American Economic Review*, **61**, 261–78.

Diewert, W.E. (1981), 'The measurement of deadweight loss revisited', *Econometrica*, **49**, 1225–44.

Diewert, W.E., A.H. Turunen-Red and A.D. Woodland (1989), 'Productivity and Pareto improving changes in taxes and tariffs', *Review of Economic Studies*, **56**, 199–216.

Dixit, A.K. (1975), 'Welfare effects of tax and price changes', *Journal of Public Economics*, **4**, 103–23.

Harberger, A.C. (1964), 'The measurement of waste', *American Economic Review*, **54**, 58–76.

Hicks, J.R. (1946), *Value and Capital*, 2nd edn, Oxford: Clarendon Press.

Hicks, J.R. and R.G.D. Allen (1934), 'A reconsideration of the theory of value', *Econometrica*, **1**, 52–75, 196–219.

Hotelling, H. (1938), 'The general welfare in relation to problems of taxation and of railway and utility rates', *Econometrica*, **6**, 242–69.

Katzner, D.W. (1970), *Static Demand Theory*, London: Macmillan.

Kawamata, K. (1974), 'Price distortion and potential welfare', *Econometrica*, **42**, 435–60.

Kawamata, K. (1977), 'Price distortion and the second best optimum', *Review of Economic Studies*, **44**, 23–9.

Lipsey, R.G. and K.J. Lancaster (1956–57), 'The general theory of second best optimum', *Review of Economic Studies*, **24**, 11–32.

Lloyd, P.J. (1974), 'A more general theory of price distortion in open economies', *Journal of International Economics*, **4**, 365–86.

Lloyd, P.J. (1977), 'Optimal revenue taxes with some unalterable taxes and distribution effects', *Australian Economic Papers*, 86–96.

Ramsey, F. (1927), 'A contribution to the theory of taxation', *Economic Journal*, **37**, 47–61.

Samuelson, P.A. (1950), 'The problem of integrability in utility theory', *Economica*, NS **17**, 355–85.

Samuelson, P.A. (2001), 'One way to measure how much second best "second best" is', in Takashi Negishi et al. (eds), *Economic Theory, Dynamics and Markets – Essays in Honor of Ryuzo Sato*, Boston, MA: Kluwer Academic Publishers.

Sheshinski, E. (1986), 'Positive second-best theory: a brief survey of the theory of Ramsey pricing', in K.J. Arrow and M.D. Intriligator (eds), *Handbook of Mathematical Economics*, volume 3, Amsterdam: North-Holland.

# 5. Pareto-optimal customs unions with transfers

## Mark Melatos and Alan Woodland[*]

## 1. INTRODUCTION

A customs union constitutes a trade agreement or contract in which members commit to: (i) zero tariffs on intra-union trade, (ii) common external tariffs rates on trade with non-members, (iii) a formula for distributing common external tariffs revenue amongst members and (iv) a criterion for the determination of the common external tariffs. While the first two elements have received considerable attention in the literature, the latter two elements have not. As a result, little is known about how asymmetric customs union members select the common external tariffs and how they choose to share the common external tariff revenue among themselves. It is clear, however, that these decisions are closely related. The choice of common external tariff rates bears upon the customs union's total tariff revenue, which must then be shared among members according to some mutually agreed set of transfers.

This chapter is motivated by the fact that despite being observed, intra-union transfers have attracted surprisingly little attention in the customs union literature. Indeed, transfers play an important role in the most developed customs union of all – the European Union (EU). While the EU's budget is tiny relative to the overall size of its member economies, concern over the financing of transfers and their allocation among members has proven to be a vexing issue. Almost immediately following its accession to the European Community in 1973, the United Kingdom (UK) complained about the relatively large net contributions it was required to make.[1] This imbalance was corrected in 1984 with EU members agreeing to reduce the UK's contributions by two-thirds and to make up the shortfall themselves. In March 1998, Germany, the Netherlands, Austria and Sweden indicated that they too now considered their net contributions to be excessive 'relative to their prosperity'.[2]

The possibility of transfers has often been acknowledged and sometimes even assumed in analytical work. Yet, even in those cases in which transfers play a role, there has been little attempt to investigate their impact on customs union behaviour. In Kemp and Wan's (1976) seminal contribution, lump sum transfers among union members are used to sustain the proposition that a Pareto-improving customs union always exists. These transfers provide the mechanism by which the gains from policy coordination may be shared among partners.[3] Kemp and Wan, however, did not explicitly model the disposition of tariff revenues and, therefore, did not address the issue of what form the associated transfers will take.[4] Similarly, the allocation of common external tariffs revenue is not directly addressed by Gatsios and Karp (1991), who nevertheless argue that a customs union member's desire to delegate (to its partner) authority over the choice of common external tariffs may persist even if intra-union transfers are permitted. In the present chapter, transfer choice by customs union members is modeled explicitly.

While a number of studies do model international transfers explicitly, the underlying revenue-sharing rules are invariably chosen exogenously and in a somewhat *ad hoc* manner. Kowalczyk and Sjostrom (1994, 2000), for example, calculate the exact value of international side payments that are required to induce countries to cooperate under global free trade. They do not, however, examine the role of transfers in customs union formation. Kowalczyk and Sjostrom (1994, 2000) derive explicit formulae for transfers based, respectively, on the Shapley value and a transfer mechanism of the form analysed by Grinols (1981). In each case, no justification (aside from simplicity) is provided for why the particular payoff vector assumed (e.g., the Shapley value) is likely to be chosen under global free trade. One of the main objectives of the present chapter is to motivate intra-union transfer choice by endogenizing the underlying revenue-sharing rule.

In a large number of studies, the exogenously imposed rule for sharing common external tariffs revenue among customs union members rules out the possibility of intra-union transfers altogether. Studies by Perroni and Whalley (2000), Abrego et al. (2003) and Kose and Riezman (2002), among many others following in the spirit of Riezman (1985), fall into this category. These papers assume a very special distribution of common external tariffs revenue. Each customs union member retains all tariff revenue raised at their border with the rest of the world. Beyond an appeal to simplicity, the literature provides no justification for this choice of sharing rule despite the fact that the intra-union transfer mechanism it implies (i.e., no transfers) is inconsistent with the observed experience of the EU. Moreover, *a priori* it would appear that such a sharing rule would be unlikely to attract broad support among customs union members and could, therefore, prove difficult to implement. This is especially likely if some members are natural 'gateways' for foreign goods entering the union, and so attract a disproportionately large share of union imports from non-members. In this case, such members are also likely to gain a disproportionately large share of common external tariffs revenue. This has proven to be an issue in the EU where the superior port facilities of countries such as the Netherlands make them natural gateways for foreign imports entering the Union.

Recently, Syropoulos (2003) has investigated the implications for customs union formation of a number of different sharing rules. These include the 'population rule' (common external tariffs revenue distributed in proportion to each member's share of the total population of the customs union), the 'consumption rule' (common external tariffs revenue distributed in proportion to each member's share of total customs union consumption) and the 'import absorption rule' (common external tariffs revenue distributed in proportion to each member's share of total customs union imports from non-members). While all these rules and their associated transfer mechanisms sound plausible and are highlighted because they are historically relevant, the fact remains that they are imposed exogenously. Hence, there is no guarantee that they will be chosen by union members if, for example, other rules exist that Pareto-dominate them. To be fair, Syropoulos (2003) is primarily interested in understanding the relationship between these particular sharing rules and the union's choice of common external tariffs. While this is a crucial question in its own right, it does not shed light on the equally important issue of which underlying sharing rule and associated transfer mechanism customs union members should select. This latter question is the central focus of this chapter.

Closest in spirit to this chapter is the work of Burbidge et al. (1997), who provide a rigorous analysis of transfers as they pertain to the formation of customs unions. They show that, in the presence of intra-union transfers, the grand coalition may be unsustainable as an equilibrium if more than two states exist. If there are only two countries, however, global free trade is the unique outcome. In Burbidge et al. (1997), union members first choose optimal tax rates and then share aggregate consumption according to a cooperative bargaining solution. The present chapter describes a different game in which union members simultaneously choose tariffs and transfers optimally. Nevertheless, the important point in Burbidge et al. (1997), which is also at the heart of the present chapter, is that customs union members can choose from a menu of different rules for sharing the common external tariffs revenue raised.

In Melatos and Woodland (2003), the modeling of common external tariffs choice was undertaken using a Paretian welfare principle. The present chapter argues that the problem of how customs union members choose to share common external tariffs revenue among themselves can be similarly modeled. Given the close relationship identified above between common external tariffs choice and the sharing of this revenue among members, the primary concern of this chapter is with the criteria chosen for the determination of both. In particular, attention focuses on how the introduction of lump sum transfers of income between members influences the set of Pareto-optimal customs unions.

To facilitate the analysis, a model of a customs union is developed that deals with all four characteristics described at the outset. The axiomatic bases for the model are that unanimity is required to reach agreement. A country only agrees to join a union if it yields higher utility than the alternatives available to it. Prospective members consider all possible Pareto-optimal (from the point of view of the union) utility outcomes from the proposed union. In this way, countries decide whether to join the union and, if so, choose among the set of outcomes by a bargaining process. The consideration of all possible Pareto-optimal outcomes for union members avoids the potential difficulties associated with the arbitrary choice of common external tariffs and transfer rules implicit in the literature.

The model is expressed as a three-stage game. At the first stage, countries decide whether to join the union and, if so, choose the weights to be used in the social welfare function employed to determine the common external tariffs and intra-union transfers. That is, they are deciding upon the nature of the union contract. This contract restricts the choices of the common external tariffs and the allocation of tariff revenue to those that yield Pareto-efficient outcomes at the final stage of the game. At the second stage of the game, the common external tariffs and intra-union transfers and the tariffs levied by non-member countries are simultaneously determined as a Nash equilibrium to a policy game. The final stage establishes the competitive equilibrium for the world economy, given the countries' tariff and transfer policy choices. The modeling approach taken provides a basis for endogenously choosing the rule for sharing of the union's common external tariff revenue among members.

Following the development of the model of a customs union with intra-union transfers in section 2, the role played by transfers in determining the nature of Pareto-optimal customs unions is investigated in section 3 using numerical simulation techniques. The focus is on the position and shape of the utility possibilities frontiers obtained under various assumptions regarding intra-union transfers. Section 4 then examines various revenue-sharing rules that have been used in the literature to determine their welfare implications. Conclusions then follow.

## 2.   THE CUSTOMS UNION MODEL

The theoretical framework presented in this section closely follows that
introduced in Melatos and Woodland (2003). In that paper, a model of a
customs union was developed in which the union members chose the
common external tariff vector to obtain a conditional Pareto-optimal
outcome – optimal for the members of the customs union, compared to
these members' utility outcomes under a unilateral (stand-alone) tariff-
setting game equilibrium. Indeed, there it was argued that custom union
members would only choose common external tariff vectors that yielded
such a conditional Pareto-optimal outcome. However, Melatos and
Woodland (2003) do not permit lump sum transfers between customs
union members, each member receiving exactly the common external tariff
revenue collected at its border. The role of the present chapter is, primarily, to allow for intra-union transfers of the common external tariff
revenue and to draw out the implications arising when such transfers are
allowed.[5]

### 2.1   Framework and Assumptions

World trade is modeled within a general equilibrium framework. The
world economy comprises many countries (denoted by the set $I$) trading in
many goods (denoted by the set $J$). Each nation comprises a production
sector, consumption sector and a government. The world price vector for
traded goods is denoted $p^w$, while $t^i$ is the vector of *ad valorem* tariff rates
levied by country $i$.[6] Domestic price vectors are denoted as $p^i$. The relationship between world and domestic prices and the *ad valorem* tariff
vector may be expressed as $p^i = \rho(p^w, t^i)$, where element $j$ of vector $\rho(p, t^i)$
is $\rho_j(p, t^i) = p_j^w(1 + t_j^i)$.
    In each nation $i \in I$, the net outputs are chosen to maximize net revenue,
yielding the net revenue function $R(p^i)$ and the net supply functions
$y^i = Y^i(p^i)$. The consumption sector of nation $i \in I$ comprises one representative consumer who chooses a consumption vector $c^i$ to maximize
a utility function defined over consumption subject to the budget constraint, taking domestic prices $p^i$ and income $m^i$ as given, yielding the
consumer demand functions $c^i = \varphi^i(p^i, m^i)$. National income, $m^i$, takes the
form

$$m^i = p^{iT} y^i + T^i, \quad i \in I, \tag{5.1}$$

where $T^i$ is the tariff revenue distributed to country $i$ in a lump sum form.

The specification of tariff revenue depends upon whether the country is a member of the customs union. For countries that are not members of the customs union (denoted by the index set $I^N$), tariff revenue is given by

$$T^i = (p^i - p^w)^T(c^i - y^i) = \sum_{j \in I} t^i_j p^w_j (c^i_j - y^i_j), \quad i \in I^N. \tag{5.2}$$

The variables endogenous to country $i$ are determined by the exogenous variables, which comprise the world price vector $p^w$ and the tariff vector $t^i$. Thus, for these countries the consumption demand vector for country $i$ may be written as $c^i = C^i(p^w, t^i)$, $i \in I^N$. The indirect utility function and the vector of net export functions can similarly be written in the form $u^i = V^i(p^w, t^i)$ and $X^i(p^w, t^i)$, $i \in I^N$.

For countries that are members of the customs union (denoted by the index set $I^U$), tariff revenue depends upon the tariff revenue collected by the union and upon the rule established by the union for its allocation amongst union members. The tariff revenue collected by the union depends upon the vector of union trade with the rest of the world and the common external tariff chosen by the union and may be expressed as $T^U = (p^U - p^w)^T \Sigma_{i \in I^U}(c^i - y^i)$, where $p^U = \rho(p^w, t^U)$ is the internal union price vector common to all member countries. The union allocates its tariff revenue to union members according to the rule $T^i = \alpha^i T^U$, where $\alpha^i$ is the proportion of customs union tariff revenue allocated to country $i$. If these proportions are restricted to be non-negative, only transfers of the customs union's tariff revenue are possible. If proportions are allowed to be negative or greater than unity, transfers beyond the union's tariff revenue are possible.[7]

For the customs union, the optimal consumption and tariff revenue allocation conditions may be combined as

$$c^i = \varphi^i(p^U, R^i(p^U) + T^i), \quad i \in I^U \tag{5.3}$$

$$T^i = \alpha^i \left[ (p^U - p^w)^T \sum_{k \in I^U}(c^k - Y^k(p^U)) \right], \quad i \in I^U, \tag{5.4}$$

where $p^U = \rho(p^w, t^U)$. These equations may be simultaneously solved for the members' consumption vectors $c^i$ and tariff revenue allocations $T^i$ as functions of the world price vector $p^w$, the customs union's common external tariff vector $t^U$ and the vector of revenue allocation shares $\alpha = (\alpha^i, i \in I^U)$. The other endogenous variables within the customs union can then be expressed in terms of $p^w$, $t^U$ and $\alpha$. Thus, the consumption demand vector for member country $i$ may be written as $c^i = C^i(p^w, t^U, \alpha)$, $i \in I^U$, the utility functions as $u^i = V^i(p^w, t^U, \alpha)$, $i \in I^U$ and the vector of net exports as $X^i(p^w, t^U, \alpha)$.

The determination of the share terms, $\alpha^i$, is an important issue. As mentioned in section 1, some of the rules for the determination of these shares used in the customs union literature include the population, consumption and import-absorption rules. There are three approaches that can be undertaken. First, the shares may be determined exogenously by defining the underlying sharing rule over exogenous variables in the model; for example, if common external tariff revenue is assumed to be shared among union members on the basis of their initial endowments or population. Second, the underlying sharing rule may be expressed in terms of endogenous variables within the union and so, ultimately, upon world prices and the common external tariffs. An example is where the common external tariff revenue is shared among union members in proportion to their share of the total volume of goods imported into the union from non-members (the import-absorption rule). In this case, each share depends on the net exports of union members, which themselves depend on world prices and tariffs, including the union's common external tariff. Accordingly, the endogenous shares may be written as $\alpha^i(p^w, t^U)$. In the above, this expression may be used to eliminate $\alpha$ and so all of the union's endogenous variables, such as utility and net exports, can be expressed as functions of $(p^w, t^U)$ alone.

In the present chapter, we suggest and use a third approach whereby the tariff revenue allocation shares are chosen optimally. In this case, the shares $\alpha^i$ are treated as variables, their chosen values to be determined below. By allowing the shares to be determined as variables, the external tariff revenue can be allocated among members in any way. Moreover, by permitting shares to be non-negative, the model allows countries to receive transfers of any size (e.g., more than the custom union's tariff revenue).

## 2.2 The Structure of the Game

The behavioral model is structured as a three-stage non-cooperative game with perfect and complete information. In the first stage, the members decide whether to form a customs union and, if so, how to structure it by determining weights in a social welfare function using a Paretian principle. In the second stage, all policy instruments are determined as a Nash equilibrium in a policy game played between the customs union and the non-member countries. The final stage of the game determines the equilibrium prices to clear markets. The game is solved backwards to obtain a subgame perfect Nash equilibrium.

### 2.2.1 Trading equilibrium (stage 3)

Stage 3 of the game is the determination of the competitive equilibrium for the world economy, given tariff choices made by all countries and the revenue share decision made by union members at stage 2. In equilibrium, the market for each good clears and so the world market equilibrium conditions may be expressed as

$$\sum_{i \in I^N} X^i(p^w, t^i) + \sum_{i \in I^U} X^i(p^w, t^U, \alpha) = 0, \tag{5.5}$$

using the national net export functions $X^i(\cdot)$ defined above. These market equilibrium conditions determine solutions for world prices in terms of tariffs and the parameters of the model, that is, $p^w = p^w(t^1, \ldots, t^M, \alpha)$, where $t^i = t^U, i \in I^U$.[8]

### 2.2.2  Tariff and transfer setting (stage 2)

In this model, a group of countries form a customs union with a common external tariff vector and internal transfers while other countries stand alone and choose their own tariff vectors. We look for a Nash equilibrium in tariffs and common external tariff revenue shares.

For countries that are not members of the customs union, the vector of trade taxes levied is given by

$$t^i = \arg\max_{t^i} V^i(p^w(t^1, \ldots, t^M, \alpha), t^i), \quad i \in I^N, \tag{5.6}$$

where country $i$ assumes that *all* other tariffs and the revenue shares of customs union members are fixed. That is, equation (5.6) represents country $i$'s tariff reaction function, $R^i(t^1, \ldots, t^M, \alpha) = 0$. As is well known, each national tariff vector may be normalized without loss of generality, for example, by setting one of the tariff rates equal to zero.

The determination of the customs union's common external tariff vector and its vector of revenue shares, $\alpha$, is more complex since the union has to operate on behalf of its members and they may disagree on the levels of tariff rates and revenue shares that are appropriate.[9] Given this potential range of views, a criterion for choosing the union's common external tariffs and revenue shares is required. It is assumed that rational union members will consider all possible common external tariff and revenue share vectors that yield a utility point for union members that is on the utility possibilities frontier, given the tariff choices by all other countries. Points on the utility possibilities frontier may be obtained as a solution to the problem of maximizing a linear combination of the members' utility functions. That is, these points may be obtained by maximizing the union's social welfare function.

Accordingly, the union is assumed to choose the common external tariff vector to maximize union welfare, which is measured using an appropriately defined social welfare function. The union's social welfare function is assumed to be a linear combination of member indirect utilities, that is, $W^U = \Sigma_{i \in I^U} d_i V^i(p^w, t^U, \alpha)$, where $d_i$ is the weight given to country $i$'s level of utility. Changing the weights, $d_i$, affects the union's social welfare function; the greater the value of $d_i$, the greater the importance of country $i$ in the union's social welfare function. The weights may be normalized; without loss of generality, they are restricted to be on the unit sphere $D \equiv \{d : \Sigma_{i \in I^U} d_i^2 = 1\}$.

The welfare maximization problem may be expressed formally as

$$\max_{t^U, \alpha} \left\{ \sum_{i \in I^U} d_i V^i(p^w(t^1, \ldots, t^M, \alpha), t^U, \alpha) : t^i = t^U, i \in I^U, \alpha \in S \right\}, \quad i \in I^U, \text{(5.7)}$$

where $S \equiv \{\alpha : \Sigma_{i \in I^U} \alpha^i = 1\}$ is the set of feasible proportions. In solving this problem, the union takes the tariff vectors for all other countries as given. The first-order necessary conditions for a solution for $t^U$ and $\alpha$ to this problem may be written implicitly as $R^T(t^U, t^N, \alpha; d) = 0$ and $R^A(t^U, t^N, \alpha; d) = 0$ respectively, where $d = (d_i, i \in I^U)$ is the vector of weights in the union's social welfare function and $t^N = (t^i, i \in I^N)$ is a vector of all other countries' tariffs. These constitute the union's reaction functions for its common external tariffs and tariff revenue shares in implicit form. Since the common external tariff vector and the tariff revenue share vector are functions of the weights, $d$, changing the weights in the social welfare function generally alters the union's choice of the common external tariffs and tariff revenue shares.

The Nash equilibrium for the tariff game engaged in by the customs union and countries in the rest of the world is the solution to the system of implicit reaction functions

$$R^T(t^U, t^N, \alpha; d) = 0$$
$$R^A(t^U, t^N, \alpha; d) = 0$$
$$R^i(t^1, \ldots, t^M, \alpha) = 0, \quad i \in I^N, \text{(5.8)}$$

where $t^i = t^U$ for $i \in I^U$ and $t^N = (t^i, i \in I^N)$. The solution to system (5.8) yields the equilibrium tariff vectors (the common external tariff and revenue share vectors, respectively $t^U$ and $\alpha$ for the union, and the vector of all non-members' tariffs $t^N$) as functions of the vector of welfare weights, $d$. Thus, these variables may be expressed as $t^U(d)$, $t^i(d)$, $i \in I^N$ and $\alpha(d)$.

Stages 2 and 3 of the game thus determine all tariff rates, union member revenue shares, world prices and national utility levels as functions of the weights of the union's social welfare function.

### 2.2.3  Formation of the union (stage 1)

Having obtained equilibrium tariffs, revenue shares and world prices, attention can now turn to the first stage of the game in which union members determine the design of the customs union contract by choosing the weights, $d$, in the union's social welfare function. Notice that equilibrium tariffs, tariff allocation shares and prices are all functions of the union social welfare function weights, $d$. Hence, the welfare of every country, whether or not it is a member of the customs union, is also a function of $d$, that is, $u^i = U^i(d)$, $i \in I$.

Let the union's social welfare function weights vary over the unit sphere $D$ (defined above). For all possible $d \in D$, the equilibrium utilities of each member can be plotted to trace out the union's utility possibilities frontier, $F(D)$. Not all choices of $d \in D$ will yield utility vectors that are Pareto-optimal for the union, but a subset of weights will yield utility vectors for union members that are Pareto-optimal. This set of weights is denoted by $D^O$. The resulting Pareto-optimal utility possibilities frontier is denoted by $F^O = F(D^O)$.

The customs union model specified here is based upon several behavioral assumptions or axioms, which are discussed in detail in Melatos and Woodland (2003). These assumptions are that (i) unanimity is required to form a customs union, (ii) given that a customs union is to be formed, union members will choose among utility outcomes that are Pareto-optimal for the union, and (iii) a country will not join a customs union that yields a utility outcome that is Pareto inferior to the unilateral tariff setting (stand-alone) utility outcome.

In interpreting these axioms, it is important to note that the issue is whether a particular customs union is to be formed and, if so, how the common external tariff is to be set and how the common external tariff revenue is to be distributed among members. It is implicitly assumed that no other customs unions can arise. Within this context, the axioms above provide the basis for identifying the set of feasible outcomes. The utility possibility set for the union members indicates the set of all utility points that a customs union can deliver, each point in the set corresponding to a particular choice of a union social welfare function. Only Pareto-efficient points on the utility possibilities frontier will be considered by a union that requires unanimity of choice and so this Pareto-efficient set defines the set of efficient contracts for the union. This Pareto-efficient set then has to be compared to the utility outcome from the unilateral tariff setting (stand-alone) equilibrium to determine whether the union will occur. If it does, bargaining between the union members can determine the particular outcome on the Pareto-optimal frontier.

### 2.2.4 Extension to allow for two policy agencies

In the above model, it was assumed that the customs union chose its common external tariff rates and the tariff revenue allocation shares to maximize a social welfare function with weight vector $d$. The resulting choices of tariff rates and allocation shares are intricately linked through the choice of weight vector $d$. Here, we relax this assumption by allowing the two sets of policy instruments (tariffs and transfers) to be chosen independently by two different policy agencies, each maximizing a social welfare function but with (possibly) different weights.

First, consider the tariff policy agency. This agency chooses the common external tariff by solving

$$t^U(t^N, \alpha; d) = \arg \max_{t^U} \left\{ \sum_{i \in I^U} d_i V^i(p^w(t^1, \ldots, t^M, \alpha), t^U, \alpha) : t^i = t^U, i \in I^U \right\},$$

(5.9)

where $d$ is the vector of weights (elements $d_i$, $i \in I^U$) in the union's social welfare function. This agency takes the tariff revenue share vector $\alpha$ and the foreign tariffs $t^N$ as given.

Second, the transfer agency chooses the tariff revenue share vector by solving

$$\alpha(t^N, t^U; e) = \arg \max_{\alpha} \left\{ \sum_{i \in I^U} e_i V^i(p^w(t^1, \ldots, t^M, \alpha), t^U, \alpha) : t^i = t^U, \right.$$

$$\left. i \in I^U, \alpha \in S \right\},$$

(5.10)

where $e$ is the vector of weights (elements $e_i$, $i \in I^U$) in the union's social welfare function. This agency takes the common external tariff vector $t^U$ and the foreign tariffs $t^N$ as given.

For each choice of the two sets of weights, $d$ and $e$, there will be an equilibrium solution for the union's common external tariffs and transfer shares, the tariffs of non-members and world prices. This equilibrium implies utilities $u^i = U^i(d, e)$, $i \in I$. By independently varying the two sets of weights, $d$ and $e$, over the unit sphere a set of utility points is generated. The boundary of the resulting set of utilities for union members constitutes the union's utility possibilities frontier (UPF).

The previous model is clearly a special case of the one just presented, obtained by restricting the choices of weights to satisfy the equality $d = e$.

By relaxing this restriction, the present model opens up policy formation and yields Pareto-superior utility outcomes along the 'grand' utilities possibilities frontier.

## 2.3   Simulation Model

The general theoretical framework discussed above is numerically simulated to illustrate the nature of the utility possibilities frontier when union members choose common external tariff rates and the sharing rule for disposition of the tariff revenue raised from imports into the union. For simplicity, this simulation model assumes three countries that trade in three goods. Further, countries 1 and 2 wish to form a customs union $CU(1, 2)$, while country 3 is the sole non-member.

It is further assumed that countries comprise one representative agent whose preferences are defined, for country $i$, by the constant elasticity of substitution utility function defined in terms of the elasticity of substitution parameter $\sigma_i$ (with $\sigma_i > 0$ and $\sigma_i \neq 1$) and the positive distribution parameters $\gamma_j^i$. The parameters chosen for the numerical simulation example are such that countries 2 and 3 have approximately Cobb–Douglas preferences ($\sigma_2 = \sigma_3 = 0.99$), while the distribution parameters are the same in each country and are product neutral, taking values $\gamma_j^i = 1/3, \forall i, j$. The examples will be distinguished by different values for the elasticity of substitution in country 1. There is no production in the simulation model, each country having a fixed endowment of each of the three goods. The endowment distribution, presented in Table 5.1, is symmetric in that each country is endowed with 1 unit of its export good and 0.1 units of the commodities it imports. Thus, in this example, endowments are symmetrically distributed over countries thus effectively neutralizing endowment effects.

Within this model specification, it is assumed that the Meade trade pattern, in which only country $i$ exports good $i$, applies. Country 3 sets tariffs on the imports of goods 1 and 2 from the union members but does not tax its exports. The union members, countries 1 and 2, impose zero tariffs on imports of goods 1 and 2 from each other so that there is free trade within the customs union. The customs union imposes a common

*Table 5.1   Endowment distribution*

|            | Good 1 | Good 2 | Good 3 |
|------------|--------|--------|--------|
| Country 1  | 1.0    | 0.1    | 0.1    |
| Country 2  | 0.1    | 1.0    | 0.1    |
| Country 3  | 0.1    | 0.1    | 1.0    |

external tariff on imports of good 3 from country 3 and does not impose taxes on exports of goods 2 and 3 to country 3.

In accordance with the theoretical model specified above, the customs union chooses the common external tariff and the tariff revenue share vector that maximizes the union's social welfare function, which is a linear function of the member country's utility functions. The vector of weights, which constitutes a point on the unit circle, is denoted as $(d_1, d_2) = (\cos\theta, \sin\theta)$ with $\theta \in [0, 360]$ being the angle between the vector of weights and the utility axis for country 1. The parameter $\theta$ constitutes a convenient measure of the degree of influence exercised by each customs union partner in common external tariff and transfer choice.[10] In the model with two policy agents, the vector of welfare weights that determines the allocation of union common external tariff revenue among members is defined as $(e_1, e_2) = (\cos\psi, \sin\psi)$ with $\psi \in [0, 360]$.

# 3.   DESIGNING THE CUSTOMS UNION CONTRACT

In the remainder of the chapter, the general theoretical framework discussed above is numerically simulated to illustrate the nature of the utility possibilities frontier when union members choose common external tariff rates and the sharing rule for disposition of the tariff revenue. The model is first simulated in the absence of optimal intra-union transfers, as in Melatos and Woodland (2003). It is demonstrated that there are potential welfare outcomes that Pareto-dominate the unilateral tariff setting (UTS) equilibrium but that cannot be attained by a customs union characterized by a sharing rule that precludes optimal intra-union transfers. Next, the model is simulated in the presence of optimal transfers between customs union members. Of interest is whether any of the Pareto-efficient outcomes identified as being unattainable in the absence of optimal transfers can now be reached by a customs union characterized by 'appropriately' chosen common external tariffs and an 'appropriately' chosen revenue-sharing rule.

In the following simulations, we distinguish between two policy specifications. The first, labeled 'no-discretionary-transfers', corresponds to a policy whereby each country receives a transfer from the customs union exactly equal to the tariff revenue collected at that country's border with the rest of the world. That is, no transfers beyond (or below) national tariff revenue accruals occur. In the simulation model, the Meade trade pattern holds and implies that the Syropoulos's import-absorption rule is being used to allocate the common external tariff revenue. The second policy specification, hereafter labeled 'discretionary-transfer', frees the revenue allocation shares from this rule and allows them to be determined optimally (in the sense of maximizing social welfare).

## 3.1 The Importance of Transfers

Consider Figures 5.1 and 5.2 in which $\sigma_1 = 0.5$ and 2 respectively. In each case, the point labeled UTS identifies the unilateral tariff-setting Nash equilibrium in which all three countries stand alone and levy optimal tariffs on imports. The no-discretionary-transfers UPF traces out the locus of potential welfare outcomes for countries 1 and 2 when they agree to form a union, $CU(1, 2)$, and country 3 is excluded. Each point on this locus corresponds to a different rule for choosing the union's common external tariffs. In other words, each point is associated with a distinct choice of weights (i.e., a $\theta$) in the customs union's social welfare function. Along the no-discretionary-transfers UPF, each member is assumed to keep all the common external tariffs revenue it collects on imports from country 3. Therefore, along this curve, discretionary intraunion transfers between countries 1 and 2 are prohibited.

In contrast, the discretionary-transfer UPF traces out the locus of potential member welfare outcomes associated with $CU(1, 2)$ when intra-union transfers are permitted. Along this curve, each point corresponds to a different criterion for determining, not only the common external tariffs, but

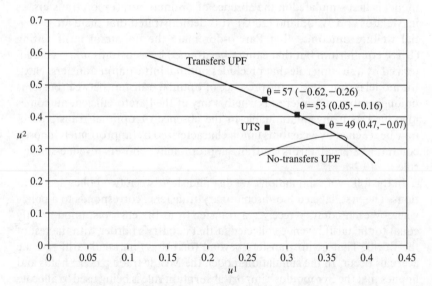

*Figure 5.1    Utility possibilities frontiers for CU(1, 2) with and without discretionary transfers when $\sigma_1 = 0.5$*

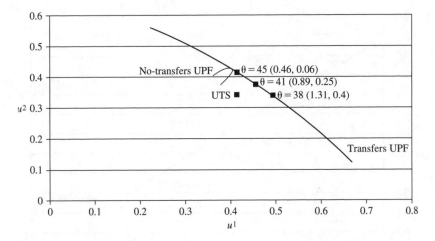

*Figure 5.2    Utility possibilities frontiers for CU(1, 2) with and without discretionary transfers when $\sigma_1 = 2$*

also how the revenue so raised is to be distributed among members (transfers indicated in parentheses). Moving along the transfer UPF in the direction of increasing $\theta$ implies a higher weighting for country 2's utility in the customs union's social welfare function. Effectively, as $\theta$ increases, country 2 exercises greater influence over the union's choice of common external tariffs as well as the magnitude and direction of intra-union transfers.

Figures 5.1 and 5.2 provide the impetus for the following proposition regarding the role of transfers in customs union formation.

**Proposition 1**   Discretionary transfers are often (although not always) necessary to ensure the formation of a customs union.

In both figures, no part of the no-transfers UPF encroaches into the north-east quadrant emanating from UTS. In Figure 5.1 ($\sigma_1 = 0.5$), the entire no-discretionary-transfers UPF lies to the south-east of UTS. Thus, country 2 refuses to join any $CU(1, 2)$ in which the underlying rule for sharing common external tariffs revenue implies zero intra-union discretionary transfers. In Figure 5.2 ($\sigma_1 = 2$), the no-discretionary-transfers UPF lies to the north-west of UTS. In this case, country 1 refuses to join any $CU(1, 2)$ in which transfers are precluded. Thus, in these examples, a rational customs union would not be formed without discretionary transfers. On the other hand, the optimal transfers UPF does include a segment in the quadrant north-east of UTS, implying that $CU(1, 2)$ would form if discretionary transfers were permitted. Indeed, in both figures, the set of

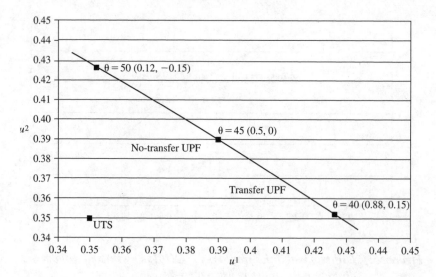

*Figure 5.3    Utility possibilities frontiers for CU(1, 2) with and without
discretionary transfers when $\sigma_1 = 0.99$*

customs unions, $CU(1, 2)$, that Pareto-dominate the UTS equilibrium
involve discretionary lump-sum transfers between members.

While in Figures 5.1 and 5.2 discretionary transfers are necessary for
the formation of $CU(1, 2)$, this need not always be the case. Consider,
for example, Figure 5.3, in which $\sigma_1 = 0.99$. In this example, the initial UTS
point is Pareto-dominated both by customs unions in which discretionary
transfers do take place and by unions in which they are absent. Since
$\sigma_1 = 0.99$ in this example, all countries (in particular, countries 1 and 2) are
symmetrically identical and consequently the no-discretionary-transfers
UPF collapses to a single point – countries 1 and 2 select the same common
external tariffs regardless of the choice of social welfare function parameter, $\theta$. As can be seen from Figure 5.3, this point Pareto-dominates the
UTS welfare outcome from the point of view of the union's members. At
the same time, Figure 5.3 reveals that other Pareto-preferred $CU(1, 2)$s exist
in which discretionary intra-union transfers play a role.

Together, Figures 5.1, 5.2 and 5.3 also suggest the following conjecture.

**Conjecture 1**  Intra-union discretionary transfers are required to guarantee the formation of a customs union when members are 'sufficiently'
asymmetric.

This observation is confirmed by Table 5.2, which summarizes the results
obtained by varying $\sigma_1$ while keeping $\sigma_2 = \sigma_3 = 0.99$ and maintaining the

*Table 5.2   Country 1 elasticities of substitution for which intra-union transfers are necessary for the formation of CU(1, 2)*

| $\sigma_1$ | Transfers necessary for CU formation? | Direction of transfer |
|---|---|---|
| $\sigma_1 \leq 0.7$ | Yes | $1 \rightarrow 2$ |
| $0.6 \leq \sigma_1 \leq 1.6$ | No | $1 \rightarrow 2$ or $2 \rightarrow 1$ |
| $\sigma_1 \geq 1.7$ | Yes | $2 \rightarrow 1$ |

same endowment distribution described earlier. Table 5.2 shows that intra-union transfers are necessary for customs union formation when one member's preferences are 'sufficiently' inelastic relative to those of its partner. The recipient of the transfer is the member whose preferences are characterized by a relatively high elasticity of substitution. When member preferences are 'sufficiently' similar, the UTS equilibrium is Pareto-dominated both by some customs unions that involve discretionary transfers and some that do not. In such cases, discretionary transfers in the Pareto-efficient set may flow to either the less or more elastic member, depending on the weights placed on each member's utility in the union's social welfare function.

Finally, in every simulation undertaken at least some part of the discretionary-transfers UPF was found to Pareto-dominate the UTS. As shown by Figures 5.1 and 5.2, the same could not be said for customs unions in which such transfers were prohibited. The suggestion arising from this analysis is that a customs union characterized by discretionary transfers between members can always be found that makes both members better off relative to the initial UTS equilibrium. However, this suggestion is not generally valid. In particular, this result contrasts with the example provided by Richardson (1995) in which both members of the customs union are worse off than at the UTS equilibrium. Indeed, Richardson points out (p. 702) that, in his example, it is not possible to find a common external tariff rate and an internal transfer that are mutually welfare improving for members compared to the UTS.

## 3.2   Financing Transfers

Having demonstrated the importance of discretionary transfers in the design of the customs union contract, the issue of how such transfers ought to be financed is now addressed. In particular, members must decide whether discretionary transfers should be financed purely from common external tariffs revenue or from other sources as well.

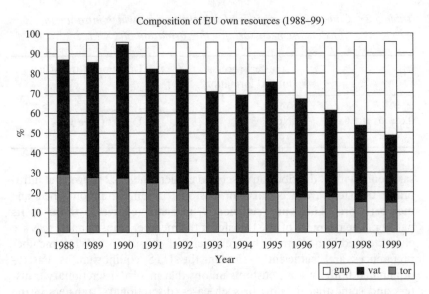

*Note:*  Transfers have been financed by a combination of levies on member GNP, the VAT
base, and 'traditional own resources' (CET revenue).

*Figure 5.4   The composition of transfer funding in the European Union,*
*1988–99*

In the European Union, the mixture of financing instruments has
evolved over time. At present, the contributions of EU member governments comprise a mixture of: common external tariffs and agricultural
duties revenue (the so-called 'traditional own resources') collected by
members at their borders with the rest of the world; a value-added-tax
(VAT) levy which represents a proportion of each state's annual indirect
taxation revenue; and a levy based on each member's GNP. Figure 5.4
shows how the relative importance of these contributions (measured as a
proportion of EU budget revenue) has changed over the period 1988–99.
Revenue from traditional own resources ('TOR' in the figure) and the VAT
resource has almost halved over this time. Simultaneously, contributions
based on GNP have risen over five fold.

The EU experience emphatically suggests that the financing of transfers
is an issue of great concern to customs union members. The UK's
displeasure, soon after accession, with its proportionately high VAT contributions has already been mentioned. Recently, the poorer EU members,
Greece, Spain and Portugal among them, have begun to push for greater
progressivity in EU contributions; that is, an expanded role for the GNP
levy.

The model used throughout this chapter abstracts from domestic taxation. In this framework, the only sources of finance available to members are common external tariffs revenue and the taxation of national endowments (i.e., a GNP levy). Returning to Figures 5.1–5.3, note that the transfer to country 1, expressed as a share of total common external tariffs revenue (i.e., $\alpha^1$), is provided in brackets (first number) along with the actual *discretionary* transfer to country 1 (second number).[11] Thus, in Figure 5.1, for example, the $CU(1, 2)$ contract characterized by $\theta = 53$ sees country 1 get 5 percent of the union's total common external tariffs revenue net of transfers and country 2 get 95 percent, with country 1 paying a transfer to country 2 of 0.16. In this case, the two countries share the union's tariff revenue, but not in proportion to their national tariff revenue accruals; discretionary transfers are used.

If more weight is placed on country 2's utility in the union's social welfare function (say $\theta = 57$), then country 1 transfers an amount of national income equal to 62 percent of the union's total common external tariff revenue to the customs union and country 2 gets 162 percent. The actual size of this discretionary transfer from country 1 to country 2 is 0.26. As evidenced by the negative share term, $\alpha^1 = -0.62$, this amount is more than the common external tariffs revenue collected by country 1 at its border with the rest of the world. Conversely, country 2 keeps all the common external tariffs revenue it has collected and gains the additional 0.26 from country 1.

An additional instructive example is given by Figure 5.3. In this case, where union members are identically symmetric, a choice of union social welfare function characterized by $\theta = 45$ yields the no-discretionary-transfer outcome exactly. At this point, each member receives 50 percent of the union's total common external tariffs revenue and there are no discretionary transfers. When $\theta = 45$, each member collects an identical amount of common external tariffs revenue at their border with country 3. Thus, each member automatically has half of the union's common external tariffs revenue and so there is no need for any discretionary transfers between them.

The preceding discussion suggests two observations *apropos* the financing of intra-union transfers. A discussion of these follows.

**Proposition 2**  A Pareto-optimal customs union may imply that one member pays a discretionary transfer in excess of the common external tariffs revenue it has collected.

In Figures 5.1 and 5.2, the Pareto-optimal set of discretionary-transfer-augmented customs unions consists of some $CU(1, 2)$s in which such transfers are less than the amount of common external tariffs revenue collected by the payer (e.g., $\theta = 41$ in Figure 5.2) and some $CU(1, 2)$s in which

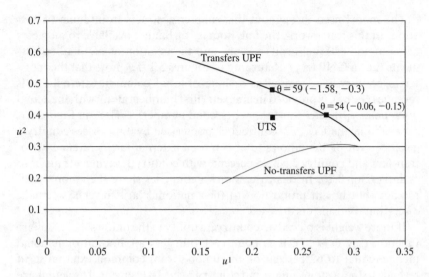

*Figure 5.5    Utility possibilities frontiers for CU(1, 2) with and without discretionary transfers when $\sigma_1 = 0.2$*

the size of the transfer exceeds the payer's external tariffs revenue (e.g., $\theta =$ 38 in Figure 5.2). In the latter case, the discretionary transfer is being financed out of the payer's (i.e., country 2's) GNP.

**Conjecture 2**    Customs unions in which one member is required to make a discretionary transfer that exceeds the amount of common external tariffs revenue it has collected are more likely to arise when the union members are 'sufficiently' asymmetric.

This is best seen by comparing Figure 5.3 with Figure 5.5, which illustrates the case $\sigma_1 = 0.2$. In the identically symmetric case the transfers that characterize the Pareto-optimal customs unions are always smaller than the common external tariffs revenue collected by the payer. On the other hand, in Figure 5.5, when country 1's preferences are significantly more inelastic than its partner's, the chosen transfers in the Pareto-efficient set are, without exception, greater than the common external tariffs revenue collected by the payer, in this case country 1.

The above observations are consistent with the European Union's experience described above. EU membership, by any measure, has become increasingly asymmetric as it has expanded. In light of the simulations undertaken here, it is, therefore, not surprising that pressure has built for its transfer program to be financed increasingly from sources other than common external tariffs revenue. The accession of poorer Eastern European transition economies to the EU is likely to exacerbate the trend towards increased financing of EU transfers through the GNP levy.

An important lesson from this section is that theoretical work should allow for the possibility of transfers differing from a member's accrued common external tariffs revenue, that is, allow for discretionary transfers. Imposing constraints on the magnitude of transfers may result in plausible customs union contracts being overlooked.

### 3.3 The Nature of the Pareto-efficient Set

As described above, customs unions either permit or do not permit discretionary transfers. Here, we consider the possibility that they can choose a mixture of these two policy specifications. According to this approach, the customs union would choose the policy specification that put the final utility outcome on the envelope of the two separate policy specified utility possibilities frontiers that is north-east of (Pareto-dominates) the stand alone utility point UTS.

All the cases presented thus far (Figures 5.1–5.3) have the common feature that this envelope frontier is downward sloping from left to right. This is due to the shape of the discretionary-transfer UPF and that either (i) no part of the no-discretionary-transfer UPF Pareto-dominates the UTS (in the asymmetric cases) or (ii) the no-discretionary-transfer UPF corresponds exactly to a point on the discretionary-transfer UPF (as in the identically symmetric case $\sigma_1 = 0.99$).

However, for numerous cases in which countries 1 and 2 are similar but not identically symmetric, the shape of the envelope Pareto-efficient set is more complicated. This can be clearly seen from Figure 5.6, which illustrates the case $\sigma_1 = 0.8$. In this case, significant portions of both the discretionary-transfer and no-discretionary-transfer UPFs Pareto-dominate the initial UTS point. Thus, numerous $CU(1, 2)$s both with and without discretionary transfers are plausible. Figure 5.7 magnifies the area in Figure 5.6 around which the individual UPFs intersect. Note that the envelope Pareto-efficient set (indicated by the thick curve) is discontinuous, jumping from the discretionary-transfer UPF to the no-discretionary-transfer UPF and back again. One interpretation of this situation is that prospective union members may bargain over whether transfers should be part of the customs union contract and then, in light of this decision, bargain over their degree of influence in common external tariffs and transfer choice.

The fact that the no-discretionary-transfer UPF intersects the discretionary transfer UPF and Pareto-dominates the latter over some segment perhaps needs explanation. The reason is that each policy specification

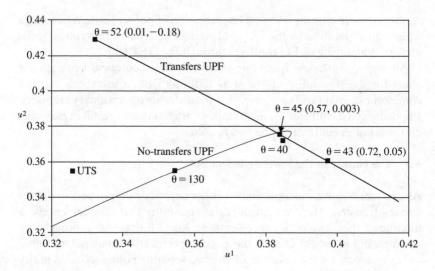

*Figure 5.6   Utility possibilities frontiers for CU(1, 2) with and without discretionary transfers when $\sigma_1 = 0.8$*

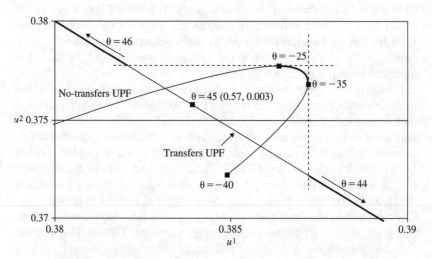

*Note:*   The Pareto-optimal set, the boundary of which is bolded, jumps between the discretionary-transfers and no-discretionary-transfers UPFs.

*Figure 5.7   Discontinuous Pareto-optimal set for CU(1, 2) when $\sigma_1 = 0.8$*

presents a particular offer surface, which is exploited by the rest of the world (here country 3) through optimal tariff choices. In the case where there are no discretionary transfers, the rest of the world takes the union's common external tariff as given and, implicitly, also takes the endogenous revenue-sharing rule as given. In the case of discretionary transfers, the rest of the world bases their tariff responses upon the union's common external tariff and, implicitly, the given revenue shares vector. Different responses by the rest of the world to these different offer surfaces yield different utility outcomes. There is no presumption that the utility outcomes from one policy specification will Pareto-dominate the outcomes from the other specification.

### 3.4 The Optimal Mix of Tariff and Transfer Policies

In the previous section, it was demonstrated that discretionary transfers play a crucial role in the design of the customs union contract. However, the usefulness of such transfers as a policy instrument for union members was not fully exploited. This was because the simulations undertaken assumed implicitly that union members based their choice of transfers and common external tariffs on a single criterion: namely, a single union social welfare function parameterized by $\theta$. Giving customs union members the opportunity to base their external tariff and transfer choices on different criteria, and so arming them with an extra degree of policy freedom, may improve their potential welfare outcomes.

In subsection 2.2.4, the model was extended to allow customs union members to select common external tariffs and transfers on the basis of different objectives. One interpretation of this modeling approach is that tariff and transfer choice are controlled by independent supranational policy-making institutions competing against one another in pursuit of different (and potentially conflicting) objectives. The special case in which these objectives coincide corresponds to the analysis studied in preceding sections of this chapter – effectively, a single policy maker controls common external tariffs and transfer choice.

This section demonstrates, by way of example, that allowing common external tariff and transfer choice on the basis of competing criteria can improve the welfare of customs union members over the situation in which a single criterion is used. As pointed out in subsection 2.2.4, there are now two $CU(1, 2)$ social welfare functions – one for common external tariffs choice and one for transfer determination. Thus, for each choice of transfer rule, $\psi$, varying the common external tariffs choice rule, $\theta$, produces UPFs like the no-transfer UPFs illustrated previously.[12] In turn, each point along these UPFs corresponds to a different $\theta$ in the range [0, 360]. Within this framework, the Pareto-optimal set of transfer-augmented $CU(1, 2)$s,

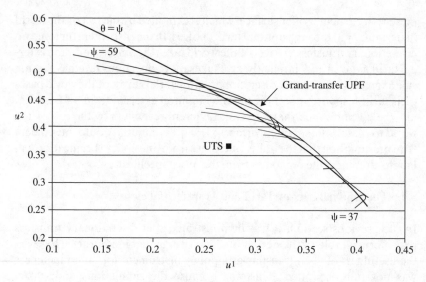

*Note:*    The Pareto-optimal set is constructed as the envelope of the $CU(1, 2)$ UPFs
corresponding to each choice of transfer rule, $\psi$.

*Figure 5.8*    *Pareto-optimal set of $CU(1, 2)$s when $\sigma_1 = 0.5$ and common*
*external tariffs and transfers choices are made on the basis of*
*distinct objectives*

henceforth termed the 'grand transfer UPF,' is the envelope of all the
discretionary-transfer UPFs.

Figure 5.8 illustrates the grand transfer UPF for the case $\sigma_1 = 0.5$. For
comparison, the single-objective (i.e., $\theta = \psi$) transfer UPF is also included.
Remember from section 3.1 that when $\sigma_1 = 0.5$, discretionary transfers are
necessary to ensure the formation of $CU(1, 2)$.

Figure 5.8 clearly shows that the grand-transfer UPF Pareto-dominates
its single-objective counterpart in the region north-east of the unilateral
tariff setting Nash equilibrium, UTS.[13] Thus, in this region, any choice of
$CU(1, 2)$ that implicitly assumes $\theta = \psi$ is Pareto-dominated by at least one
$CU(1, 2)$ in the dual-objective framework. This result is not surprising given
that, as mentioned at the outset, the former implies an additional degree of
policy freedom for union members. For our purposes, the relevance of the
grand-transfer UPF is that customs union members, if they are already at
a point on this locus, cannot redesign their union contract to achieve a
mutual welfare improvement. In this sense, therefore, the grand-transfer
UPF is the 'true' Pareto-optimal set of $CU(1, 2)$ contracts that prospective

members should consider when bargaining over the design of the union in the first stage of the game.

## 4. ALTERNATIVE REVENUE-SHARING RULES

In this section, a number of sharing rules that have been used in the literature are analysed to determine whether they are Pareto-optimal and, therefore, plausible. The sharing rules investigated include those based on members' import-absorption, consumption and population. The existing literature has tended to use these intuitively attractive rules as the basis on which customs union members will share common external tariff revenue. Invariably, however, the choice of sharing rule is not justified theoretically. Syropoulos (2003), for example, investigates these rules because they are 'historically relevant' and 'have formed the basis for much of the theoretical literatures on endogenous trade policies and preferential trading agreements.' The task of this section, therefore, is to investigate the welfare consequence of alternative common external tariff revenue-sharing rules. It is demonstrated that the use of these sharing rules may result in Pareto-inferior customs union contracts being considered or, conversely, plausible agreements being overlooked.

The main lesson of this section is that no one sharing rule is likely to be appropriate in every situation, that is, for every combination of model parameters. Rather, customs union members in bargaining over the design of the union contract will consider all possible common external tariffs revenue-sharing rules just as they consider all possible ways in which to select the common external tariff rates (Melatos and Woodland, 2003). In fact, union members will consider the entire menu of external tariff and transfer combinations that yield Pareto-efficient utility outcomes in the process of designing their customs union contract.

### 4.1 The Import-absorption Rule

Under the import-absorption rule, as described by Syropoulos (2003), common external tariff revenue is distributed in proportion to each member's share of total customs union imports from non-members. If a member imports nothing from outside the union, then they receive a zero share of the common external tariffs revenue raised. In the context of the simulation model employed throughout this chapter, if countries 1 and 2 decide to form $CU(1, 2)$, they agree to share external tariffs revenue according to their relative imports of good 3.

In the simulation model, the import-absorption rule implies that there will be no intra-union discretionary transfers of income. Implementing this sharing rule, therefore, yields the no-discretionary-transfers $CU(1, 2)$ contracts discussed in earlier sections, such as those illustrated in Figures 5.1 and 5.6.

In section 3.1 it was argued that intra-union transfers are necessary to support a customs union when its members are 'sufficiently' asymmetric. For example, in the case $\sigma_1 = 0.5$ and $\sigma_1 = 2$ (illustrated in Figures 5.1 and 5.2), exogenously assuming the import-absorption rule reproduces the no-discretionary-transfers UPF. That is, any customs union contract based on this rule could not form as one of the members would prefer to stand alone. Furthermore, as is clear from both Figures 5.1 and 5.2, numerous $CU(1, 2)$ contracts exist that Pareto-dominate the UTS, but every one of these is characterized by an alternative sharing rule.

Of course, Pareto-optimal $CU(1, 2)$ contracts characterized by the import-absorption rule can and do exist; for example, when $\sigma_1 = 0.8$ (illustrated in Figures 5.6 and 5.7). However, in order to attain these efficient contracts while sharing common external tariffs revenue according to the import-absorption rule, the common external tariff rates (i.e., the weights in the union's social welfare function) must be chosen very carefully, that is, $-35 < \theta < -25$.

## 4.2   The Consumption and Population Rules

Common external tariffs revenue may also be distributed among union members based on their consumptions or endowments. These rules have feature, not only in the literature, but also in practice (Syropoulos, 2003). Under the consumption rule, common external tariffs revenue is allocated in proportion to each member's share of total customs union consumption. In the simulations undertaken in this chapter, it has been assumed that member preferences are identical and homothetic. Therefore, as pointed out by Syropoulos (2003), in this very special situation the consumption rule is equivalent to one in which external tariffs revenue is shared among members in proportion to their GDPs.

The population rule, meanwhile, requires that common external tariffs revenue be distributed in proportion to each member's share of the union's total population. In the simulated model presented above there was no production. Rather, countries were assumed to be endowed with a fixed (and positive) amount of each good. In the following discussion, therefore, the population rule is reinterpreted such that common external tariffs revenue is shared among members in proportion to their initial endowment of a particular good. Since in the simulations above union members have been

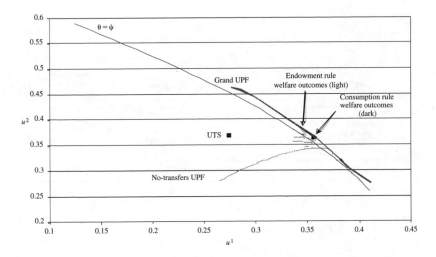

*Figure 5.9  Comparison of CU(1, 2) welfare outcomes, under the consumption, endowment and import-absorption revenue sharing rules, for the case $\sigma_1 = 0.5$*

assumed, for simplicity, to be symmetric in endowments, then this rule implies that each member gets an equal share of the total revenue raised from common external tariffs.

Consider Figure 5.9 illustrating the case $\sigma_1 = 0.5$. This example is chosen because it provides a stark example of how seemingly plausible transfer rules may be implausible in practice, in the sense that they yield utility outcomes that are not Pareto efficient. Figure 5.9 plots the welfare outcomes under the population and endowment rules. The relevant area is magnified in Figure 5.10, in which the bracketed numbers identify the ($\psi$; $\theta$) combinations that correspond to the consumption and endowment rules. The grand UPF drawn is that derived from enveloping the UPFs in Figure 5.8. Finally, as pointed out above, the no-discretionary-transfers UPF coincides with the import-absorption rule.

Inspection of Figures 5.9 and 5.10 reveals that:

1. No $CU(1, 2)$ contract that implements the consumption rule Pareto-dominates the UTS equilibrium.
2. Some $CU(1, 2)$ contracts that implement the endowment rule Pareto-dominate the UTS point.
3. No $CU(1, 2)$ contract implementing either the consumption or endowment sharing rules lies on the grand UPF.

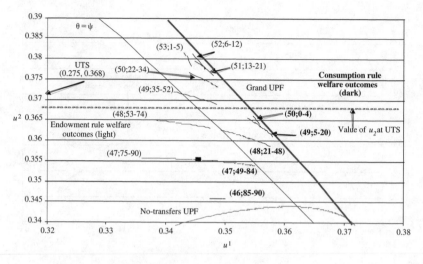

*Note:*   The numbers in parentheses identify the ($\psi$; $\theta$) combinations that correspond to
          each rule. The UTS equilibrium lies (off the figure) at ($u^1$, $u^2$) = (0.275, 0.368).

*Figure 5.10*   *Comparison of CU(1, 2) welfare outcomes, under the
                consumption, endowment and import-absorption revenue-
                sharing rules, for the case $\sigma_1 = 0.5$*

4.  The import-absorption rule (the no-discretionary-transfers UPF)
    yields some $CU(1, 2)$s on the Pareto-optimal frontier. However, these
    do not Pareto-dominate the UTS.
5.  The consumption and endowment rules yield identical member welfare
    outcomes when $\psi = 47$ and $\theta \in [75, 84]$.[14]

These observations imply that, in some cases, Pareto-efficient customs
unions necessarily require the implementation of discretionary transfer
mechanisms that are not based on the underlying import-absorption, consumption or endowment-sharing rules often assumed in the literature and
employed in practice.

Of course, these results are for the very special case in which $\sigma_1 = 0.5$
and, therefore, may not hold for alternative choices of the model parameters. However, the purpose of this section has been to show that adoption
of seemingly intuitive sharing rules may not always be appropriate in practice. For this reason, therefore, it is argued that the only robust approach to
modeling the design of the customs union contract is to consider all Pareto-
efficient outcomes.

## 5.  CONCLUSION

This chapter has addressed the issue of how customs union members agree to share among themselves the revenue raised from the imposition of common external tariffs on imports into the union. This issue has received relatively little attention in the literature, as has the closely related problem of how customs union members select the common external tariff rates. Nevertheless, the recent experience of the European Union suggests that countries seriously consider these issues in evaluating their membership of a customs union. While this chapter has focused on the common external tariff revenue allocation (transfer) problem, the modeling approach adopted has endogenized the relationship between the choice of common external tariffs and the sharing of the revenue so raised.

The importance of transfers was demonstrated by showing that, in some cases, discretionary transfers are necessary for the formation of a customs union, such as when prospective members are asymmetric. The issue of financing was also shown to play an important role in the design of the customs union contract. In particular, it was shown that a customs union may have to be supported, as a matter of necessity, by a transfer mechanism that requires one member to contribute more than it has collected in common external tariff revenue. In this case, the excess was financed from the taxation of endowments, a requirement reminiscent of the EU's GNP levy.

The provision of an additional degree of policy freedom to customs union members was used as a tool to derive the Pareto-efficient (i.e., plausible) set of customs unions. It was argued that countries will choose the union contract from this set. The issue of which of these contracts is actually chosen was not resolved. This is an important open question that is left for future research. Having derived the set of plausible customs union contracts, the performance of some popular sharing rules was evaluated against the criterion of Pareto efficiency. It was found that situations can easily arise in which intuitively appealing sharing formulae, such as the consumption and population rules, do not yield Pareto-optimal utility outcomes. In this spirit, the last section of the chapter counseled that caution should be exercised when such revenue-sharing rules are used in theoretical work.

## NOTES

*    The authors wish to thank an anonymous referee for helpful comments. All remaining errors are our own. Woodland gratefully acknowledges the financial support of the Australian Research Council. Melatos wishes to acknowledge the financial support of the Ronald Henderson Research Foundation as well as an Australian Postgraduate Award.

The authors thank the Department of Economics at the University of Bristol (Woodland) and the Economic Policy Research Unit at the University of Copenhagen (Melatos) for their hospitality during the completion of this chapter.

1. This imbalance was due to the proportionately high call on its value-added-tax (VAT) revenue as well as the low Common Agricultural Policy receipts attracted by its relatively small rural sector.
2. See the European Commission (1998) for more detail.
3. Dixit and Norman (1980, pp. 192–4) show, under suitable assumptions, that the transfer mechanism may be replaced by a set of domestic commodity taxes to effect a welfare gain.
4. Grinols (1981) provides an explicit formula for the required transfers in the Kemp–Wan model.
5. Note that coalition formation is not the focus of this chapter. The Pareto-optimal utility outcomes for customs union members in the model considered below dominate the utility outcomes for the stand-alone situation. Whether or not these utility outcomes are also Pareto efficient with respect to alternative trading arrangements (including customs unions involving other countries) can readily be determined, but this is outside the scope of the current study. The issue of coalition formation is taken up by Melatos and Woodland (2004).
6. In general, taxes on trade may involve import duties or subsidies and export taxes or subsidies. We follow the convenient convention of using the term 'tariffs' to refer to all of these cases. Throughout this chapter, the terms 'trade tax' and 'tariff' will be used interchangeably.
7. In this case, we then have to introduce an explicit restriction that national income must be positive after the transfers.
8. By Walras's law, one of these market equilibrium conditions is redundant and may be ignored and, by their homogeneity in prices, one world price may be designated the numeraire and normalized to unity.
9. In special cases, the union members will agree upon the choice of the CET rates. An example is where the members are symmetrically identical.
10. At $\theta = 0$ the weight vector is $(d_1, d_2) = (1, 0)$ and so only country 1's utility has any value to the union; at $\theta = 90$ the weight vector is $(d_1, d_2) = (0, 1)$ and so the union chooses the common external tariff and intra-union transfers to maximize its own utility function; for other values of $\theta$ both countries' utility functions are taken into account.
11. For country $i$, the share term is defined as follows: $\alpha^i = (CETREV^i + b^i)/TOTCETREV$, where $CETREV^i$ is the common external tariffs revenue raised by country $i$ at its border with the rest of the world; $b^i$ represents the discretionary lump-sum transfer to country $i$; and $TOTCETREV^i$ is the customs union's total common external tariffs revenue. Note also that $\Sigma_{i \in I^U} \alpha^i = 1$.
12. The angle of weights $e$ in the social welfare function for transfer choice is $\psi$.
13. As drawn, the grand UPF is incomplete; it is drawn in the figure as the envelope of $\psi$-constant UPFs only from $\psi = 37$ to $\psi = 59$. The complete UPF lies north-east of the single-objective UPF.
14. This can be seen by examining the $\psi = 47$ curve in Figure 5.10. The dark dot on this curve corresponds to $\theta = 75$; this is where the endowment rule UPF (the lighter curve) ends. The point where the light and dark curves meet is $\theta = 84$. Thus, in the range $\theta \in (75, 84)$ both the consumption and endowment rules overlap.

# REFERENCES

Abrego, L., Riezman, R. and Whalley, J. (2003), 'How often are propositions on the effects of customs unions theoretical curiosa and when should they guide policy?', NBER Working Papers 8304. (Revision of earlier version entitled

'Propositions on the effects of regional trade agreements: blending theory and numerical simulation,' 1999.)

Burbidge, J., De Pater, J., Myers, G. and Sengupta, A. (1997), 'A coalition-formation approach to equilibrium federations in trading blocs', *American Economic Review*, **87**, 940–56.

Dixit, A.K. and Norman, V. (1980), *Theory of International Trade*, Cambridge: Cambridge University Press.

European Commission (1998), *Financing the European Union: Commission Report on the Operation of the Own Resources System*, Brussels: European Commission.

Gatsios, K. and Karp, L. (1991), 'Delegation games in customs unions', *Review of Economic Studies*, **58**, 391–7.

Grinols, E.L. (1981), 'An extension of the Kemp–Wan theorem on the formation of customs unions', *Journal of International Economics*, **11**, 259–66.

Kemp, M.C. and Wan Jr, H.Y. (1976), 'An elementary proposition concerning the formation of customs unions,' *Journal of International Economics*, **6** (1), 95–7.

Kose, M.A. and Riezman, R. (2002), 'Small countries and preferential trade agreements: how severe is the innocent bystander problem?', *Pacific Economic Review*, **7** (2), 279–304.

Kowalczyk, C. and Sjostrom, T. (1994), 'Bringing GATT into the core', *Economica*, **61**, 301–17.

Kowalczyk, C. and Sjostrom, T. (2000), 'Trade and transfers, GATT and the core', *Economics Letters*, **66** (2), 163–9.

Melatos, M. and Woodland, A.D. (2003), 'Pareto optimal delegation in customs unions,' unpublished paper, University of Sydney.

Melatos, M. and Woodland, A.D. (2004), 'Endogenous trade bloc formation in an asymmetric world,' unpublished paper, University of Sydney.

Perroni, C. and Whalley, J. (2000), 'The new regionalism: trade liberalization or insurance?', *Canadian Journal of Economics*, **33** (1), 1–24.

Richardson, M. (1995), 'On the interpretation of the Kemp/Wan theorem', *Oxford Economic Papers*, **47**, 696–703.

Riezman, R. (1985), 'Customs unions and the core', *Journal of International Economics*, **19** (3–4), 355–65.

Syropoulos, C. (2003), 'Rules for the disposition of tariff revenues and the determination of common external tariffs in customs unions', *Journal of International Economics*, **60** (2), 387–416.

# PART THREE

# Trade and Market Structure

# 6. Endogenous mergers and tariffs in an integrated market*

**Rod Falvey**

## 1. INTRODUCTION

The objective of this chapter is to explore the effects of tariffs on the profitability and global welfare consequences of mergers in open economies. The general reduction in trade barriers in the last few decades has brought the international aspects of domestic competition policies into greater prominence, and there now exists a significant literature dealing with mergers between firms located in different political jurisdictions.[1] Two questions have been of particular interest. First, what type of merger activity, if any, has been encouraged by this general process of trade liberalization? Answering this question involves assessing the effects of trade policy on the profitability of mergers to their potential participants. But given that mergers are regulated in most states, a second element must also be considered. Are competition authorities likely to view mergers more or less favourably in a more open economy? Answering this question involves consideration of the effects of trade policy on the welfare costs and benefits of mergers.

The success of international agreements constraining the ability of governments to use trade policies because of their undesirable beggar-thy-neighbour consequences has raised concern that some governments may be tempted to substitute other policies, competition policy in particular, with similar outcomes (Lloyd and Sampson, 1995). Should trade agreements be complemented by agreements on, or 'harmonization' of, competition policies, and what form should such agreements take (Lloyd, 1998)? This concern prompted research investigating the links between competition policy and trade policy, where the latter is broadly defined to include import and export taxes and subsidies, and domestic production subsidies. Because this literature focuses on the welfare effects of mergers, the competition policy decision is typically modelled, for simplicity, as the choice of the number of identical domestic firms.[2]

Where the decision by firms to merge has been the focus of analysis, it is typically modelled as motivated either by fixed cost savings or variable cost rationalization. Salant et al. (1983) have shown that identical Cournot-competing firms with constant marginal costs have no incentive to merge in a closed market, unless the participants collectively have a large share of the market pre-merger, or the merger saves on fixed costs.[3] But small tariffs are likely to have rather a limited impact where the incentive to merge is to avoid fixed costs,[4] and so the natural focus in this chapter is on mergers motivated by rationalization of production.[5] The simplest way to introduce inter-firm efficiency and size differences is to suppose firms have different technologies, reflected in different (constant) marginal costs. In this context, Lahiri and Ono (1988) have shown that the exit of the most inefficient firm can be welfare improving. A merger with a more efficient firm is one mechanism through which this might occur, as long as the merger is also profitable to the participants. Head and Ries (1997), for example, use this model to investigate the potential conflicts that arise between national competition authorities if the effects of mergers spill over national borders.[6]

In most of this literature, only a few of the potential mergers are considered, and they tend to be chosen exogenously. More recently some consideration has been devoted to examining the full constellation of merger possibilities, in order to predict which mergers are likely to be proposed in which circumstances. Horn and Persson (2001) have established some general results on 'endogenous mergers' under both fixed cost saving and variable cost rationalization motives. We draw on the latter below.

Investigations of the effects of trade policy on mergers motivated by variable cost rationalization are relatively scarce. Long and Vousden (1995) consider the effects of unilateral and bilateral trade liberalization on the incentives for an exogenously chosen merger in a world composed of two countries with symmetric segmented markets. They characterize potential mergers in terms of the differences in the pre-merger marginal costs of the participants. For any given tariff only a range of cost differences generates profitable mergers, and this range shifts with changes in the tariff. They find that a unilateral tariff reduction will increase the profitability of mergers with small cost differences (mergers which 'primarily concentrate on market power', in their terms). In contrast bilateral tariff cuts will increase the profitability of mergers with larger cost differences (mergers which 'primarily reduce costs'). Horn and Persson (1999) consider equilibrium ownership structures in a model where international mergers can avoid trade costs. They assume two identical countries with segmented markets, each with two identical owners of an asset in fixed supply that can be used to produce a homogeneous good. They then show that international (rather than domestic) mergers are more likely when trade costs are low, and that this result holds when mergers generate either fixed cost savings or variable cost synergies.

This chapter extends these results by considering the implications of tariffs for both the profitability and global welfare consequences of endogenous mergers, in an integrated international market, where countries and firms are not necessarily identical. We employ a simple model of the market for a single homogeneous product, in which firms are Cournot competitors and differ in their levels of efficiency. Demand is linear and firms have constant marginal costs. This structure allows for relatively simple solutions, where the effects of discrete changes in the number of firms (mergers) on profits and welfare can be considered. The impact of a small tariff change on these effects can then be derived. Horn and Persson (2001) discuss the relative merits of the various approaches to endogenizing mergers. Here we adapt the approach of Barros (1998), who considers a market with three potential participants and shows that merger outcomes depend on technology differences, which are assumed to be constant.[7] Assuming that merger to monopoly is precluded, he finds that if the technology difference is small there are no mergers. For intermediate technology differences the least and most efficient firms merge. For large technology differences, the two most efficient firms merge.[8] We retain the assumption of three firms, as this allows the full range of outcomes of interest,[9] but we allow variable technology differences, and hence generate a wider range of outcomes, particularly with respect to welfare.

We begin by considering the global economy in free trade, in Section 2, in order to illustrate the conditions for the merger to be privately profitable and socially desirable, before introducing the tariff. Which mergers will be proposed, if any, depends on relative firm efficiencies as reflected in relative firm outputs were they all to produce. Whether a merger would be approved by the global competition authority[10] depends on the relative size (market share) of the less efficient merger partner. In general any merger likely to be approved will be proposed. Section 3 considers the effects of a tariff by one (the home) country on the profitability of mergers, and their global welfare effects, when the world market is integrated. How firms are affected by the tariff depends on whether they are located inside or outside the protected market. This allows a range of cases to be considered. Because the tariff 'distorts' the market, its implications for the welfare consequences of the merger are not confined to its effects on the market share of the less efficient merger partner. The final section presents a summary and conclusions.

## 2. THE FREE TRADE ECONOMY[11]

Consider a world economy in which there are three (potential) producers of a homogeneous product. Each firm ($j$) has constant unit costs ($c_j$) and no fixed costs. Unit costs differ across firms, and firms are ordered so that

$k > j$ implies $c_k > c_j$. Competition in this market is assumed to be Cournot. There are two countries, home and foreign (whose variables are denoted with an asterisk), with demands respectively of

$$D = A - p \quad \text{and} \quad D^* = A^* - p^*, \tag{6.1}$$

where $A$ and $A^*$ are positive constants, and $p$ and $p^*$ prices. In this section we assume free trade and no transport costs, implying that firms in this integrated market face world demand

$$\bar{D} = D + D^* = A + A^* - 2\bar{p}. \tag{6.1'}$$

Each producing firm $j$ therefore chooses its output $(x_j)$ to maximize $\pi_j = [\bar{p} - c_j]x_j$, taking $d\bar{p}/dx_j = -1$. Solving the first-order conditions for optimal firm output, summing these to obtain total output $(\bar{X})$, and then substituting in (6.1'), gives the equilibrium values:

$$\bar{p} = \frac{A + A^* + C}{2[n + 1]}; \quad \bar{x}_j = 2[\bar{p} - c_j]; \quad \pi_j = 2[\bar{p} - c_j]^2 = \bar{x}_j^2/2, \tag{6.2}$$

where $C = \Sigma_{j \in N} c_j$, and $n$ is the number and $N$ the set of producing firms.

When two firms in this market ($k$ and $j$) 'merge', they become a single decision-making unit. Given that the merger itself has no effect on the technology of the participants, cost minimization by the new merged firm implies the abandonment of firm $k$'s (relatively inefficient) technology, and the new market equilibrium is simply that which obtains with the closure of firm $k$.[12] Total output falls, the market price rises, the profits of the remaining firms rise and consumer surplus falls.[13] Consumers lose from the merger, and non-participating producers gain. The incentive to merge is the additional profits that may accrue to the merged firm as a result of the higher price. The shift to the new post-merger equilibrium (where $\Delta y$ denotes the change in variable $y$ as a consequence of the merger) has

$$\Delta \bar{p} = \frac{\bar{x}_k}{6}; \quad \Delta x_h = \frac{\bar{x}_k}{3}, \ h \neq k; \quad \Delta \bar{D} = \Delta \bar{X} = -\frac{\bar{x}_k}{3} \tag{6.4}$$

The closure of firm $k$ results in an increase in the output of each of the remaining firms. Given our assumptions of linearity and constant marginal costs, their outputs rise by the same absolute amount, which is one third of the closing firm's original output. Since only two firms remain, total output falls (by $\bar{x}_k/3$), and price rises (by $\bar{x}_k/6$).

The change in profits of continuing firm $h$ is the increased profits on its original output plus the profits from its increased output. This can be rearranged into three terms – a transfer from consumers, who are paying a higher price for the firm's output, a transfer of profits from the closing firm, and the increased profit resulting from the greater efficiency of this firm relative to the closing firm. Only the last term represents a social gain. Substituting from (6.4),

$$\Delta \pi_h = \frac{\bar{x}_k}{6}\left[ 2\bar{x}_h + \frac{\bar{x}_k}{3}\right] > 0 \tag{6.5}$$

This merger will have been profitable for the participants only if the increase in profits to firm $j$ exceeds the lost profits of the closed firm. Substituting from (6.5), this gain is

$$G(j, k) = \Delta \pi_j - \pi_k = \frac{\bar{x}_k}{18}[6\bar{x}_j - 8\bar{x}_k] \tag{6.6}$$

Equation (6.6) provides a condition on relative firm sizes (or relative shares of output) for a profitable merger. Given $\bar{x}_k$, and the number of firms, the larger the initial output of the continuing partner the more likely the merger is to yield a net gain.

In his analysis of endogenous mergers in this type of market, Barros (1998) notes that there are two general conditions that the distribution of profits of the merged firm must satisfy in equilibrium. First, there are participation constraints that limit the possible payoffs to the two partners. Consider again a merger between firms $j$ and $k$. Let $\pi^{jk}$ denote the total profits of the merged firm, and $\pi_j^{jk}$ denote the 'payoff' to partner $j$ (so that $\pi^{jk} = \pi_j^{jk} + \pi_k^{jk}$). Then the participation constraint for this merger requires that

$$\pi^{jk} - \pi_k \geq \pi_j^{jk} \geq \pi_j \tag{6.7}$$

The left side of this inequality indicates the largest payoff that can be made to partner $j$ (that is, the remainder after partner $k$ is paid exactly what it would receive if there were no merger), while the right side indicates the minimum payoff to partner $j$ (that is, what it would receive if there were no merger). Satisfying these participation constraints requires that the merger be profitable (that is, $\pi^{jk} \geq \pi_j + \pi_k$). Second, there are the stability constraints, which recognize that each merger partner may have the option of merging with the outside firm ($h$). These conditions require

$$\pi_j^{jk} \geq \pi^{jh} - \pi_h^{jk} \equiv o_j^{jk} \quad \text{and} \quad \pi_k^{jk} \geq \pi^{kh} - \pi_h^{jk} \equiv o_k^{jk}, \tag{6.8}$$

that is, the payoffs to each partner be no less than the maximum offer that the outside firm $h$ would be willing to make for their participation in the alternative merger.[14]

We can now use these constraints to determine the conditions under which different mergers may occur. With three firms there are, in principle, three possible mergers. But since $\pi^{13} > \pi^{23} = \pi_2^{13}$, it is always more profitable for the smallest firm to combine with the largest firm rather than with the intermediate firm,[15] and the intermediate firm would always prefer the $\{1,3\}$ merger. Hence the potential mergers are $\{1,3\}$ and $\{1,2\}$ – that is, firms 2 and 3 are 'bidding' over a possible merger with 1. When both mergers are profitable, we follow Barros in assuming that the one with the largest internal gain (taking account of the gains from being an outside firm) will occur. Thus merger $\{1,2\}(\{1,3\})$ occurs if

$$\pi^{12} - [\pi_1 + \pi_2^{13}] > (<) \, \pi^{13} - [\pi_1 + \pi_3^{12}].$$

This ranking corresponds to that based on outside offers, since the maximum outside offer each of the smaller firms will make to 1 are, respectively,

$$o_1^{12} = \pi^{12} - \pi_2^{13} > 0 \quad \text{and} \quad o_1^{13} = \pi^{13} - \pi_3^{12} > 0.$$

Which of these is the greater depends on relative outputs, but since

$$o_1^{12} - o_1^{13} = \pi^{12} - \pi^{13} - \frac{8}{18}\left[ (\bar{x}_2)^2 - (\bar{x}_3)^2 \right] = \frac{[\bar{x}_2 - \bar{x}_3]}{18}\{6\bar{x}_1 - 7[\bar{x}_2 + \bar{x}_3]\},$$

$$(6.9)$$

there will be cases where firm 3 makes the larger outside offer to 1, even though merger $\{1,3\}$ is not the most profitable (that is, $\pi^{12} > \pi^{13}$).[16]

The profitability conditions can be obtained from equation (6.6). Merger $\{1,2\}$ is profitable if $6\bar{x}_1 \geq 8\bar{x}_2$, while merger $\{1,3\}$ is profitable if $6\bar{x}_1 \geq 8\bar{x}_3$. If the former is profitable, so is the latter. Consideration of the participation and stability constraints then leads to the following outcomes depending on the distribution of firm sizes:

1. If $6\bar{x}_1 \leq 8\bar{x}_3$, then no merger is profitable and all three firms produce;
2. If $8\bar{x}_3 < 6\bar{x}_1 \leq 8\bar{x}_2$, then merger $\{1,3\}$ would be proposed, since it is the only profitable merger;
3. If $8\bar{x}_2 \leq 6\bar{x}_1$, then both mergers $\{1,2\}$ and $\{1,3\}$ are profitable, and which is proposed depends on the stability conditions;

(a) if $6\bar{x}_1 < 7[\bar{x}_2 + \bar{x}_3]$, then merger {1,3} is proposed; while
(b) if $6\bar{x}_1 > 7[\bar{x}_2 + \bar{x}_3]$, then merger {1,2} is proposed.

Corresponding to each of these cases will be a distribution of the profits of any merged firm between the partners (that is, specific values of $\pi_j^{jk}$ and so on). This distribution should reflect the outside opportunities of the partners, but is otherwise indeterminate.

These outcomes are illustrated in Figure 6.1a. Given the size of the largest firm $(x_1)$, the requirement that $x_1 \geq x_2 \geq x_3$ constrains the range of feasible outputs for the other firms to the triangle $OQx_1$. The combinations of relative outputs (reflecting relative costs) that give rise to each of the cases are shown by the labelled areas. For example, if all outputs are sufficiently similar (region 1) no merger will be proposed; while if firm 1 is much larger than the others (region 3b) both mergers will be profitable, but merger {1,2} will be proposed.

**Welfare Effects**

Total benefits $(\tilde{W})$ from this market are the sum of consumer surplus (CS) and total profits ($\Pi$):

$$\tilde{W} = CS + \sum_j \pi_j = \frac{D^2}{2} + \frac{D^{*2}}{2} + \frac{1}{2} \sum_{j \in N} x_j^2 \qquad (6.10)$$

The change in consumer surplus in any country as a consequence of the merger has two components, both negative. There is a transfer from consumers to firms as a result of the price rise, and a consumption deadweight loss. In examining the welfare effects of mergers it is useful to express equilibrium demands as functions of total output $(\bar{X})$. From (6.1′) we have that $\bar{p} = [A + A^* - \bar{X}]/2$, and therefore we can write

$$D = \frac{A - A^* + \bar{X}}{2} \quad \text{and} \quad D^* = \frac{A^* - A + \bar{X}}{2}. \qquad (6.11)$$

If we let $\bar{X}_m$ denote aggregate output after the merger, then the changes in consumer surplus in the two countries can be written as

$$\Delta CS = \frac{[\bar{X}_m - \bar{X}]}{4} \left\{ A - A^* + \frac{[\bar{X}_m + \bar{X}]}{2} \right\}; \quad \text{and}$$

$$\Delta CS^* = \frac{[\bar{X}_m - \bar{X}]}{4} \left\{ A^* - A + \frac{[\bar{X}_m + \bar{X}]}{2} \right\}.$$

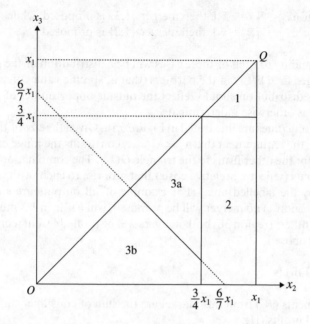

*Figure 6.1a    Merger preferences in free trade*

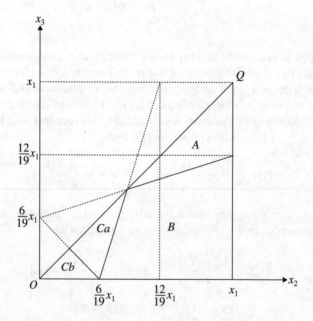

*Figure 6.1b    Merger approvals in free trade*

The change in global consumer surplus is then

$$\Delta C\tilde{S} = \frac{[\bar{X}_m - \bar{X}]}{4}[\bar{X}_m + \bar{X}] < 0 \qquad (6.12)$$

and is negative since each merger results in a reduction in total output. The larger the output of the closing firm the larger the consumer surplus loss.

A positive gain to the merging firms is sufficient for total profits to rise since the outside firm's profits always increase. The overall change in profits has three components. There is the transfer from consumers, who are paying a higher price, and an efficiency gain from redistributing output to lower-cost firms. Both of these are positive. But there is also the lost profit on the discontinued output.

The change in total welfare then reflects the balance between the consumption deadweight loss and the lost profits on the one hand and the efficiency gain on the other. Thus for merger {1,3} we find, using (6.12), (6.15) and (6.6), that

$$\Delta C\tilde{S}(1, 3) = -\frac{\bar{x}_3}{12}\left\{2[\bar{x}_1 + \bar{x}_2] + \frac{5}{6}\bar{x}_3\right\} \quad \text{and}$$

$$\Delta\Pi(1, 3) = \frac{\bar{x}_3}{18}\{6[\bar{x}_1 + \bar{x}_2] - 7\bar{x}_3\}.$$

Combining these, we have

$$\Delta\tilde{W}(1, 3) = \frac{\bar{x}_3}{36}[6\bar{X} - 25\bar{x}_3]. \qquad (6.13)$$

Equation (6.13) provides a global competition authority with a simple condition for welfare improvement that depends only on the share of the closing firm. As Lahiri and Ono (1988) have pointed out, the elimination of a minor firm has two opposing effects on welfare in an oligopoly with different technologies. It improves average efficiency, yet at the same time creates a less competitive market structure. Provided the market share of the minor firm is not too large, net welfare can increase as a consequence of its closure.

The corresponding expressions for merger {1,2} show that this merger will raise welfare if $\bar{x}_2/\bar{X} < 6/25$. Clearly if merger {1,2} raises welfare, so does {1,3}. Since

$$\Delta\tilde{W}(1, 2) - \Delta\tilde{W}(1, 3) = \frac{[\bar{x}_2 - \bar{x}_3]}{36}[25\bar{x}_1 - 19\bar{X}], \qquad (6.14)$$

we conclude that merger {1,2} will yield a higher welfare change than merger {1,3} if the most efficient firm is sufficiently large (that is, $\bar{x}_1/\bar{X} > 19/25$), in which case both mergers are welfare improving.

These outcomes are illustrated in Figure 6.1b. No merger would be approved in area $A$. In area $B$, merger $\{1,3\}$ would be approved,[17] but $\{1,2]$ would not be. In area $Ca$ either merger would be welfare improving, but merger $\{1,3\}$ would give the greater welfare improvement.[18] In area $Cb$, either merger is welfare improving, but merger $\{1,2\}$ yields the larger welfare gain.

The conditions for a global welfare improvement can be combined with the conditions for merger profitability and stability to derive the circumstances under which mergers will be proposed and approved. We assume, as seems reasonable, that a proposal is a precondition for approval, and that the competition authority is not in a position to 'force' mergers.

In case (1), no merger is proposed if $6\bar{x}_1 \leq 8\bar{x}_3$; in case (2), merger $\{1,3\}$ is proposed when $8\bar{x}_3 < 6\bar{x}_1 < 8\bar{x}_2$ and approved if $25\bar{x}_3 < 6\bar{X}$, that is, if $19\bar{x}_3 < 6[\bar{x}_1 + \bar{x}_2]$. Note that this merger will not be approved if it is just on the margin of profitability (that is, $6\bar{x}_1 \approx 8\bar{x}_3$); in case (3), both mergers are profitable, and

(a) $\{1,3\}$ is proposed if $8\bar{x}_2 < 6\bar{x}_1 < 7[\bar{x}_2 + \bar{x}_3]$ and approved if $19\bar{x}_3 < 6[\bar{x}_1 + \bar{x}_2]$. Note that this merger will be approved at the upper margin (i.e., $6\bar{x}_1 \approx 7[\bar{x}_2 + \bar{x}_3]$); while

(b) $\{1,2\}$ is proposed if $8\bar{x}_2 < 6\bar{x}_1$ and $7[\bar{x}_2 + \bar{x}_3] < 6\bar{x}_1$; and approved if $19\bar{x}_2 < 6[\bar{x}_1 + \bar{x}_3]$.

Two points are worth noting, in particular. First, all mergers that would be approved would be profitable.[19] Second, there is a range of outputs[20] where merger $\{1,2\}$ would be proposed, but merger $\{1,3\}$ would lead to a higher welfare improvement. Whether a global competition authority could or should be able to reject one welfare-improving merger on the grounds that an alternative, and also profitable, merger would raise welfare even further is an interesting policy issue.

## 3.   TARIFFS AND MERGERS

The aim of this section is to investigate the effects of tariffs on the incentives for and welfare consequences of the mergers considered above. We now construct the market equilibrium assuming a small specific tariff of $t$ per unit is imposed by the home country, that we assume will continue to be an importer after any mergers. We continue to deal with an integrated world market, where there are no transport costs and costless arbitrage between markets is possible. Arbitrage activities will occur if the deviation in prices in the two markets ever exceeds the relevant tariff (that is, if $p > p* + t$, or $p* > p$). A tariff will therefore affect the equilibrium in both markets.[21]

The determination of the market equilibrium is modelled as a two-stage game. In the first stage, firms determine their sales in each market, taking each others' sales as given. In the second stage, arbitrage activity occurs if the first-stage decisions generate a price differential between the two markets that exceeds the relevant tariff. The activities of profit-seeking private arbitrageurs will generate a volume of arbitrage $(R)$ that ensures that $p - p^* \leq t$.

Let $h_j$, $f_j$ $(h_j^*, f_j^*)$ denote the sales of home (foreign) firm $j$ in the home and foreign markets respectively, and let $N$ and $N^*$ be the sets of home and foreign firms. Market clearing in the second stage then requires that

$$p = A - [H + H^*] - R; \quad p^* = A^* - [F + F^*] + R, \qquad (6.15)$$

where $H = \Sigma_{j \in N} h_j$ and so on. The non-profitability of further arbitrage in equilibrium (that is, $p = p^* + t$) implies that

$$R = \frac{A - A^* + [F + F^*] - [H + H^*] - t}{2} \qquad (6.16)$$

In the first stage, the $j$th home firm's optimization problem, taking account of the possibility of arbitrage activity in the second stage, is:

$$\max_{h_j, f_j} \pi_j = [p - c_j]h_j + [p^* - c_j]f_j,$$

where $p$, $p^*$ and $R$ are as determined by (6.15) and (6.16). Each firm takes the outputs of other firms as given, but recognizes the implications of its own choices for (future) arbitrage activity. The first-order conditions for this problem are:

$$h_j \geq 0; \frac{\partial \pi_j}{\partial h_j} \leq 0; h_j\frac{\partial \pi_j}{\partial h_j} = 0 \quad \text{and} \quad f_j \geq 0; \frac{\partial \pi_j}{\partial f_j} \leq 0; f_j\frac{\partial \pi_j}{\partial f_j} = 0. \quad (6.17)$$

As long as the tariff is below that which eliminates arbitrage, we have:

$$\frac{\partial \pi_j}{\partial h_j} = [p - c_j] - \left[\frac{h_j + f_j}{2}\right]; \quad \text{and} \quad \frac{\partial \pi_j}{\partial f_j} = [p^* - c_j] - \left[\frac{h_j + f_j}{2}\right].$$

Since $p = p^* + t > p^*$, the solution to (6.17) is $h_j = 2[p - c_j], f_j = 0$, with $\pi_j = h_j^2/2$.

The corresponding optimization problem for the $j$th foreign firm,

$$\max_{h_j^*, f_j^*} \pi_j^* = [p - t - c_j^*]h_j^* + [p^* - c_j^*]f_j^*,$$

yields equivalent first-order conditions, with

$$\frac{\partial \pi_j^*}{\partial h_j^*} = [p - t - c_j^*] - \left[\frac{h_j^* + f_j^*}{2}\right]; \quad \text{and} \quad \frac{\partial \pi_j^*}{\partial f_j^*} = [p^* - c_j^*] - \left[\frac{h_j^* + f_j^*}{2}\right].$$

Since $p - t = p^*$, these two conditions are identical, giving solution

$$h_j^* + f_j^* = x_j^* = 2[p^* - c_j^*], \quad \text{and} \quad \pi_j^* = \frac{[x_j^*]^2}{2}.$$

Thus profit maximization yields an equilibrium that has home firms selling only in the home market, while foreign firms are indifferent as to where they sell (in the absence of transport costs).

In addition to changing total outputs, the tariff also shifts the distribution of any given output between demands in the two markets. In place of (6.11) we now have

$$D = \frac{A - A^* - t + \bar{X}}{2} \quad \text{and} \quad D^* = \frac{A^* - A + t + \bar{X}}{2}. \tag{6.18}$$

The tariff tends to reduce consumption in the tariff-imposing country and raise it in the exporting country.

The implications of the tariff for equilibrium prices and mergers will depend on where firms are located. To illustrate the possibilities we consider four alternative allocations of firms between countries, each of which is consistent with the home country being a net importer both in free trade and after any merger.

## (A)  All Firms are Located in the Exporting Country

In this case there are no domestic firms to protect, but the tariff could be imposed for revenue-raising or terms-of-trade reasons. The equilibrium prices under the tariff are given by $p = \bar{p} + 7t/8$ and $p^* = \bar{p} - t/8$, where $\bar{p}$ is the 'free-trade' price determined above. In the absence of a domestic supply, the main impact of the tariff is to raise the price in the importing country. The output of firm $j$ is given by $x_j = 2[p^* - c_j] = \bar{x}_j - t/4$, where $\bar{x}_j$ denotes the free-trade output of the firm.[22] Each firm's total sales fall by the same absolute amount as a result of the tariff.

The implications of the tariff for proposed mergers then follow directly – that is,

1.  no merger is proposed if $6\bar{x}_1 + 0.5t \leq 8\bar{x}_3$;
2.  merger {1,3} is the only profitable merger if $8\bar{x}_3 < 6\bar{x}_1 + 0.5t < 8\bar{x}_2$;

3. (a) both mergers are profitable, and {1,3} is proposed if $8\bar{x}_2 < 6\bar{x}_1 + 0.5t$ and $6\bar{x}_1 + 2t < 7[\bar{x}_2 + \bar{x}_3]$

   (b) both mergers are profitable, and {1,2} is proposed if $8\bar{x}_2 < 6\bar{x}_1 + 0.5t$ and $6\bar{x}_1 + 2t > 7[\bar{x}_2 + \bar{x}_3]$.

Since firms' outputs are reduced in the same amount by the tariff, the accompanying fall in profits is proportionately larger the smaller is the firm. This increases the likelihood that either merger will be profitable, and therefore that some merger will be proposed (as shown by case 1). These changes in relative outputs imply corresponding changes in relative outside offers when both mergers are profitable, that make merger {1,2} more likely to be preferred at the margin, as shown by case 3. Although the profits of merged firm {1,2} fall by more than the profits of merged firm {1,3}, the profits of outside firm 2 from merger {1,3} also fall by more than the profits of outside firm 3 from merger {1,2}. The net result of these changes is that 2 becomes relatively more interested in participating in a merger. These outcomes are illustrated by the shifts of the boundary lines in Figure 6.2a. The no-merger area (1) contracts. The areas where {1,3} is profitable (2+3a+3b) and where {1,2} is profitable (3a+3b) both expand. But the areas where {1,3} is proposed (2 and 3a) contracts, while the areas where {1,2} is proposed (3b) expand.

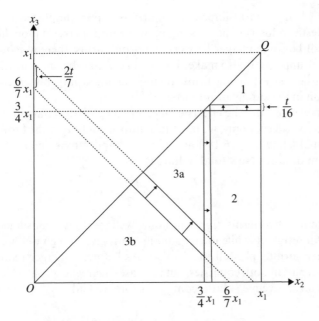

*Figure 6.2a    Case (A) merger preferences*

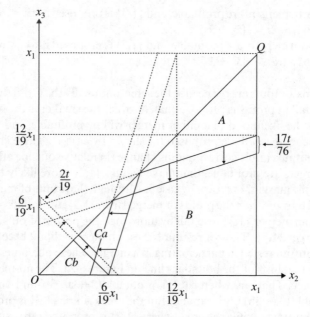

*Figure 6.2b    Case (A) merger approvals*

Thus when the tariff-imposing country is a 'pure' importer (that is, has no domestic industry), the imposition of the tariff makes it more likely that there will be some merger between exporting firms, thereby reducing the supply of imports. It also makes it more likely that this merger will involve the two largest exporting firms, thereby giving a larger merger-induced reduction in the supply of imports.

When we consider the effects of mergers on global welfare in this tariff-distorted world economy, we must take into account that the tariff has distributional (shown by (6.18)) and revenue implications, in addition to its effects on outputs. Now total welfare is

$$\tilde{W} = \frac{D^2}{2} + tD + \frac{D^{*2}}{2} + \Pi.$$

Here the first two terms represent home welfare (home consumer surplus plus tariff revenue), while the remaining terms give foreign welfare (foreign consumer surplus plus all the profits). As before, a merger reduces consumer surplus in both countries, but increases aggregate profits. Now it also reduces tariff revenue.[23] Proceeding as before we find

$$\Delta \tilde{W} = \frac{[X_m - X]}{4} \{X_m + X + 2t\} + \Pi_m - \Pi \tag{6.19}$$

The direct effect of the tariff (that is, other than through its indirect effects on outputs, and hence also profits) is to increase the absolute value of the first (negative) term.

To proceed further we need to consider specific mergers. Under merger {1,3}, equation (6.19) becomes

$$\Delta \tilde{W}(1, 3) = \frac{x_3}{36}[6X - 25x_3 - 6t] \qquad (6.20)$$

Before we can compare this with (6.13), we need to take into account the influence of the tariff on outputs, which gives

$$\Delta \tilde{W}(1, 3) = \frac{x_3}{36}\left[6\bar{X} - 25\bar{x}_3 - \frac{17t}{4}\right] \qquad (6.21)$$

For this merger to generate a welfare gain in the presence of the tariff would require that the smaller partner have an even smaller share of the market in free trade. The tariff therefore makes this merger less likely to be approved by a global competition authority. This is not the outcome one would have expected based only on consideration of the (indirect) effects of the tariff on relative outputs. The tariff reduces the market share of the smallest firm, which would tend to render this merger more likely to be welfare improving. However, the direct effects of the tariff on aggregate welfare (through redistributing demand and generating revenue) lead to additional adverse welfare effects of the merger (as shown in (6.20)), and these latter consequences dominate in the aggregate.

The welfare implications of merger {1,2} follow analogously. Thus both mergers are less likely to be approved in general under the tariff. Comparing their relative welfare effects, we find that

$$\Delta \tilde{W}(1, 2) - \Delta \tilde{W}(1, 3) = \frac{[\bar{x}_2 - \bar{x}_3]}{36}[25\bar{x}_1 - 19\bar{X} + 2t]$$

Thus merger {1,2} gives the larger welfare gain for a wider market share of firm 1.

These outcomes are shown in Figure 6.2b. Area *A*, where neither merger would raise welfare, is larger under the tariff. The areas where merger {1,3} would raise welfare (*B*+*Ca*+*Cb*) and the areas where merger {1,2} would raise welfare (*Ca*+*Cb*) both contract as a result of the tariff. However if both mergers are welfare improving the likelihood that {1,2} is preferred is increased (area *Cb* expands).

## (B)   The Smallest Firm is Located in the Importing Country

An issue of interest here is whether the tariff 'protects' domestic output, not only in the sense of raising the domestic firm's output (and profits) when it operates, but also in the sense of making it less likely to be 'merged' with a foreign firm. Equilibrium prices under the tariff are given by $p = \bar{p} + 5t/8$ and $p^* = \bar{p} - 3t/8$, and outputs for the home and foreign firms, respectively, by $h_3 = \bar{x}_3 + 5t/4$ and $x_j = \bar{x}_j - 3t/4$ $(j=1, 2)$.[24] The home firm's output (and profits) rise as a result of the tariff; the foreign firms' outputs (and profits) fall.

The implications of the tariff for proposed mergers are again straight-forward:

1.   no merger is proposed if $6\bar{x}_1 - 14.5t \leq 8\bar{x}_3$;
2.   merger $\{1,3\}$ is the only profitable merger if $8\bar{x}_3 < 6\bar{x}_1 - 14.5t < 8\bar{x}_2 - 16t$;
3.   (a) both mergers are profitable, and $\{1,3\}$ is proposed if $8\bar{x}_2 < 6\bar{x}_1 + 1.5t$ and $6\bar{x}_1 - 8t < 7[\bar{x}_2 + \bar{x}_3]$
     (b) both mergers are profitable, and $\{1,2\}$ is proposed if $8\bar{x}_2 < 6\bar{x}_1 + 1.5t$ and $6\bar{x}_1 - 8t > 7[\bar{x}_2 + \bar{x}_3]$.

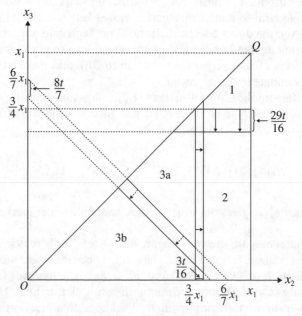

*Figure 6.3a   Case (B) merger preferences*

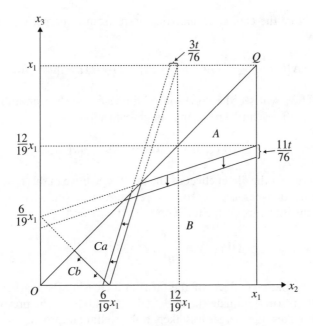

*Figure 6.3b   Case (B) merger approvals*

The likelihood that some merger is proposed falls (area 1 expands in Figure 6.3a), and we now have the possibility that merger {1,2} is profitable while merger {1,3} is not.[25] The likelihood that merger {1,3} alone is profitable contracts (case 2), while the likelihood that both mergers are profitable expands (case 3). An interesting feature is that the likelihood that merger {1,3} is preferred when both mergers are profitable (case 3a) has increased. Both merged firms have lower profits, and the gain to outside firm 2 from merger {1,3} falls, while the gain to outside firm 3 from merger {1,2} rises. This would tend to suggest that firm 3 would become relatively less interested in a merger; however, the fall in profits to merged firm {1,2} is sufficiently large that firm 3 makes a relatively stronger offer at the margin.

Does the tariff 'protect' the domestic output from disappearing in a merger? The answer may well be negative. While the likelihood of merger {1,3} is reduced at the margin where it is the only profitable merger, it is increased at the margin where both are profitable (that is, in Figure 6.3a, 2 contracts but 3a expands).

The welfare effects of mergers in this case follow fairly directly from (A), except that the change in the domestic output of the tariff-imposing country has an impact on the implications of the merger for tariff revenue. Now the change in global welfare from a merger can be represented by

$$\Delta \tilde{W} = \frac{[X_m - X]}{4} \{X_m + X + 2t\} + \Pi_m - \Pi - t[h_3^m - h_3].$$

Merger {1,3} will see the cessation of domestic production and hence a boost to tariff revenue. The change in global welfare is

$$\Delta \tilde{W}(1, 3) = \frac{h_3}{36}[6X - 25h_3 + 30t] \qquad (6.22)$$

We observe that the direct effect of the tariff is positive in this case, because of the boost this merger gives to tariff revenue. However, once we take into account the influence of the tariff on outputs, we find

$$\Delta \tilde{W}(1, 3) = \frac{h_3}{36}\left[ 6\tilde{X} - 25\tilde{x}_3 - \frac{11t}{4} \right] \qquad (6.23)$$

Overall, the indirect effects of the tariff in increasing the market share of the smallest firm dominate the direct effects, and, as in the previous case, the tariff makes this merger less likely to be welfare improving.

The alternative merger will raise domestic production and hence have a negative impact on tariff revenue. The change in global welfare is given by

$$\Delta \tilde{W}(1, 2) = \frac{x_2}{36}[6X - 25x_2 - 18t];$$

the direct effect of the tariff is negative. Once we take into account its indirect effects through the outputs (reducing the pre-merger share of firm 2 in particular), we find

$$\Delta \tilde{W}(1, 2) = \frac{x_2}{36}\left[ 6\tilde{X} - 25\tilde{x}_2 - \frac{3t}{4} \right].$$

This merger is also less likely to be welfare improving. Thus both mergers are less likely to be approved in general under the tariff, as shown by the contraction in areas $B + Ca + Cb$ and $Ca + Cb$ in Figure 6.3b. Comparing the relative welfare effects of the two mergers under the tariff when both are welfare improving is less straightforward in this case because the outputs of the two alternative merger partners do not change by the same magnitude. However, one can show that the (free-trade) output combinations that would give each merger the same welfare change in free trade would give a relatively lower welfare gain from {1,2} under the tariff. Thus the likelihood of merger {1,2} being preferred is reduced by the tariff.

## (C)  The Intermediate Firm is Located in the Importing Country

This case is very similar to (B), with firm 2 behind the tariff wall rather than firm 3. Equilibrium prices are as in (B), with firm 2's output increasing. The implications of for proposed mergers are:

1. no merger is proposed if $6\bar{x}_1 + 1.5t \leq 8\bar{x}_3$;
2. merger $\{1,3\}$ is the only profitable merger if $8\bar{x}_3 < 6\bar{x}_1 + 1.5t < 8\bar{x}_2 + 16t$;
3. (a) both mergers are profitable, and $\{1,3\}$ is proposed if $8\bar{x}_2 < 6\bar{x}_1 - 14.5t$ and $6\bar{x}_1 - 8t < 7[\bar{x}_2 + \bar{x}_3]$
   (b) both mergers are profitable, and $\{1,2\}$ is proposed if $8\bar{x}_2 < 6\bar{x}_1 - 14.5t$ and $6\bar{x}_1 - 8t > 7[\bar{x}_2 + \bar{x}_3]$.

Considering profitability alone, the area where merger $\{1,3\}$ is profitable expands, while the area where merger $\{1,2\}$ is profitable contracts. The merger between the two exporting firms is more likely under the tariff $(2 + 3a$ expands in Figure 6.4a), while the merger involving the import-competing firm is less likely (3b contracts).

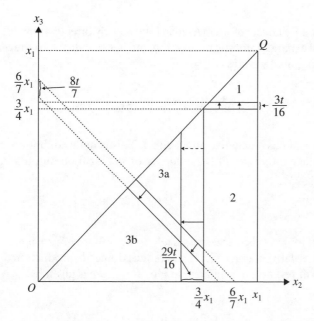

*Figure 6.4a   Case (C) merger preferences*

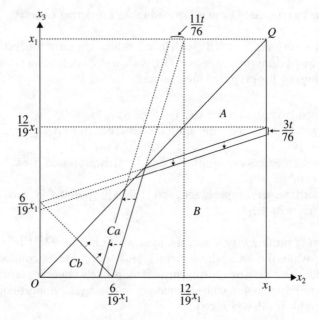

*Figure 6.4b   Case (C) merger approvals*

The welfare effects of mergers also follow fairly directly from (B). Merger {1,3} will expand domestic production and hence reduce tariff revenue. The change in global welfare is

$$\Delta \tilde{W}(1, 3) = \frac{x_3}{36}[6X - 25x_3 - 18t]$$

and the tariff has a negative direct effect. This is reduced, but not reversed, once we take into account the influence of the tariff on outputs

$$\Delta \tilde{W}(1, 3) = \frac{x_3}{36}\left[6\tilde{X} - 25\tilde{x}_3 - \frac{3t}{4}\right].$$

The tariff makes this merger less likely to be welfare improving.

The alternative merger {1,2}, will reduce domestic production and hence boost tariff revenue. The change in global welfare is given by

$$\Delta \tilde{W}(1, 2) = \frac{h_2}{36}[6X - 25h_2 + 30t];$$

the direct effect is positive, but once we take into account the indirect effects we find

$$\Delta \tilde{W}(1, 2) = \frac{h_2}{36} \left[ 6\bar{X} - 25\bar{x}_2 - \frac{11t}{4} \right].$$

Thus both mergers are less likely to be welfare improving under the tariff. Comparing the relative welfare effects of the two mergers under the tariff is complicated for the same reasons as in case (B). However, one can show that the (free-trade) output combinations that would give each merger the same welfare change in free trade would give a relatively higher welfare gain from {1,2} under the tariff. Thus the likelihood of merger {1,2} being preferred is raised by the tariff (area Cb expands in Figure 6.4b).

## (D)   Only the Largest Firm is Exporting

The issue of interest here is the effects of the tariff on the relative 'protection' given to the two firms located in the tariff-imposing country. Equilibrium prices and outputs are $p = \bar{p} + 3t/8$ and $p^* = \bar{p} - 5t/8$, $h_j = \bar{x}_j + 3t/4 (j = 2, 3)$ and $x_1 = \bar{x}_1 - 5t/4$.[26] The implications of the tariff for proposed mergers are:

1. no merger is proposed if $6\bar{x}_1 - 13.5t \le 8\bar{x}_3$;
2. merger {1,3} is the only profitable merger if $8\bar{x}_3 < 6\bar{x}_1 - 13.5t < 8\bar{x}_2$;
3. (a) both mergers are profitable, and {1,3} is proposed if $8\bar{x}_2 < 6\bar{x}_1 - 13.5t$ and $6\bar{x}_1 - 18t < 7[\bar{x}_2 + \bar{x}_3]$
   (b) both mergers are profitable, and {1,2} is proposed if $8\bar{x}_2 > 6\bar{x}_1 - 13.5t$ and $6\bar{x}_1 - 18t > 7[\bar{x}_2 + \bar{x}_3]$.

The outputs of both domestic firms are increased in the same amount by the tariff. This reduces the profitability of both mergers at the margin (cases 1 and 3), making the likelihood that some merger is proposed lower (area 1 expands in Figure 6.5a). Moreover, the likelihood that {1,2} is the preferred merger (area 3b) falls. This time the tariff reduces the profits of both merged firms, and increases the gains from being the outsider to both firms 2 and 3. But the fall in profits is larger for merged firm {1,2} and the gain from being the outsider increases more for firm 2. Thus firm 2 is relatively less interested in participating in a merger. Because of this effect, we can conclude that while a merger is less likely, the likelihood that merger {1,3} is proposed may rise or fall as a result of the tariff (areas 2+3a may expand or contract in Figure 6.5a).

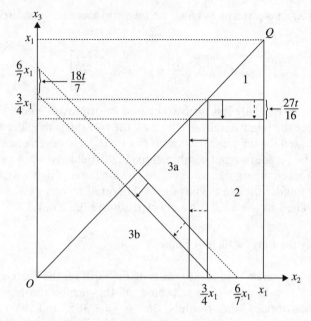

*Figure 6.5a    Case (D) merger preferences*

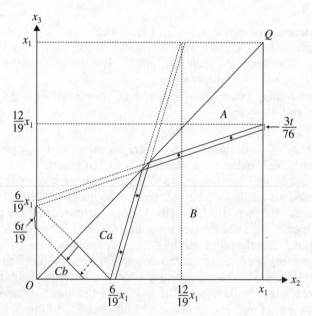

*Figure 6.5b    Case (D) merger approvals*

The global welfare effects of mergers require only slight modification to previous cases. Now

$$\Delta \tilde{W} = \frac{[X_m - X]}{4}\{X_m + X + 2t\} + \Pi_m - \Pi - t\{[h_2^m + h_3^m] - [h_2 + h_3]\}.$$

Either merger sees one home firm cease production, which tends to raise tariff revenue. The welfare effects of merger {1,3} are

$$\Delta \tilde{W}(1,3) = \frac{h_3}{36}[6X - 25h_3 + 18t],$$

which again reflects a positive direct effect of the tariff, which is reduced, but in this case not reversed, by the indirect effect, since

$$\Delta \tilde{W}(1, 3) = \frac{h_3}{36}\left[6\bar{X} - 25\bar{x}_3 + \frac{3t}{4}\right].$$

The tariff makes this merger more likely to be welfare improving (area $B + Ca + Cb$ expands in Figure 6.5b). The benefits of reducing the tariff-distorted domestic output outweigh the costs of removing a larger share of output from the market. Analogous arguments and results apply for merger {1,2}. It also is more likely to be welfare improving (area $Ca + Cb$ expands).

Comparing the relative welfare changes of the two mergers is relatively straightforward since both alternative closing partners are affected symmetrically. Thus

$$\Delta \tilde{W}(1, 2) - \Delta \tilde{W}(1, 3) = \frac{[\bar{x}_2 - \bar{x}_3]}{36}[25\bar{x}_1 - 19\bar{X} - 6t]$$

Compared with free trade, merger {1,2} is less likely to give a larger welfare gain (area $Cb$ contracts). Hence we conclude that merger {1,3} is more likely to be preferred.

The relevant features of the results for all of these cases are presented in Table 6.1 and are summarized in the next section.

## 4. CONCLUSIONS

This chapter set out to investigate the implications of tariffs for endogenous mergers in an integrated world economy. A simple partial equilibrium model of Cournot oligopolists with different technologies was used to illustrate issues. Conditions for each merger to be profitable to participants and

*Table 6.1  Summary of outcomes*

|  | Home firms | | | |
|---|---|---|---|---|
|  | None (A) | Firm 3 (B) | Firm 2 (C) | Firms 2 and 3 (D) |
| Profitability: | | | | |
| Merger {1,3} | More likely | Less likely | More likely | Less likely |
| Merger {1,2} | More likely | More likely | Less likely | Less likely |
| Proposed: | | | | |
| Merger {1,3} | Less likely | ? | More likely | ? |
| Merger {1,2} | More likely | Less likely | Less likely | Less likely |
| Welfare gain: | | | | |
| Merger {1,3} | Less likely | Less likely | Less likely | More likely |
| Merger {1,2} | Less likely | Less likely | Less likely | More likely |
| Preferred: | | | | |
| Merger {1,3} | Less likely | ? | Less likely | More likely |
| Merger {1,2} | More likely | Less likely | More likely | Less likely |

stable to offers from the outside firm were derived in the free-trade equilibrium. Conditions under which a global competition authority would approve each merger, and when it would prefer one merger over another, were also derived for this case.

The model was then extended to include a tariff. If one (the importing) country had a small tariff in place, its firms found it profitable to sell only in their home market, and the firms in the other (exporting) country received the same (net) price wherever they sold. We then looked at the effects of the tariff on merger proposals and approvals in four cases, which captured the range of possible outcomes in this model. The tariff introduces a further distortion into an already distorted (by imperfect competition) market, and introduced a revenue term into the welfare calculations. While the influence of the tariff on merger proposals could be determined straightforwardly from its influence on firm outputs, the tariff had additional (direct) effects on the welfare consequences of any merger.

Are mergers more likely to occur in the tariff-distorted global economy? This depends on where the least efficient firm is located. A merger is less likely if this firm is protected by the tariff, and more likely if it is not. So, at this margin, the tariff 'protects' an inefficient import-competing firm, both in terms of increasing its output while producing and of reducing the likelihood that it will close down through merger (the profits of the owners are increased in each case of course). Conversely the tariff 'harms' an inefficient exporting firm by reducing its output when producing and raising the probability that it will close down through merger.

How does the tariff affect which merger is likely to be proposed? From the table we see that the answer depends on whether the tariff has a 'protective' role. Merger {1,2} is less likely to be proposed as long as at least one firm is located in the protected market, and in these circumstances there is a (weak) presumption that merger {1,3} is more likely to be proposed. The opposite is true when all firms are exporting.

How is a global competition authority likely to respond? Considering mergers individually, the competition authority is less likely to approve either merger under the tariff, unless there is more than one import-competing firm. This reflects the direct effects of the distortion created by the tariff. The tariff reduces total output in all cases except where the majority of firms are behind the tariff wall, and in that case the expansion of total output comes at the expense of the output of the most efficient firm. Considering mergers together, there is a (weak) presumption that the merger that closes the least efficient firm is more likely to be preferred if that firm is protected by the tariff, and less likely to be preferred otherwise. The merger that closes the intermediate firm is less likely to be preferred where the least efficient firm is protected, and more likely to be preferred otherwise.

While this tells us about the impact of the merger on global welfare, it is important to note that in practice merger (dis)approvals are determined by national competition authorities and not by a global authority. It is reasonable to expect that national authorities will be primarily concerned with the effects of any proposed merger on national welfare. A merger that raises global welfare must improve the national welfare of at least one of the two countries, but not necessarily both. The distribution of national welfare depends on the distribution of demand, the location of firm ownership and the distribution of the gains from mergers between the merging parties. These are topics for future investigation.

## NOTES

* Paper prepared for a *Festschrift* in honour of Peter Lloyd, Melbourne, January 2003. I thank the discussant and participants at the *Festschrift* for comments and suggestions. I also thank Stephen King, Geoff Reed, Hylke Vandenbussche and participants in the workshop on 'The Impact of European Competition Policy on the Evolution of Market Structure and Firm Growth' at Leuven, the ETSG Conference in Rotterdam and a seminar at the University of Leicester for comments on earlier versions. Financial support from The Leverhulme Trust under Programme Grant F 114/BF is gratefully acknowledged. Revised August 2003.
1. See Horn and Levinsohn (1997) and WTO Annual Report 1997 for reviews of the literature investigating the links between trade policy and competition policy.

2.  In the standard 'cross-hauling' trade model, increasing the number of domestic firms is both import-substituting and export-promoting (Bliss, 1996), and competition policy choices are then influenced by the range of trade policy options available and the sequences in which policy decisions are made. Where countries have symmetric exporting and import-competing interests in the same sector, Horn and Levinsohn (1997) show that there is no unambiguous answer to the question of whether increased foreign competition will lead governments to choose more or less domestic competition. They are able to rank the optimal numbers of firms for a variety of policy-constrained cases, and find that these rankings are broadly similar for tariff and export subsidy policies. A clearer picture emerges in less symmetric cases: for example the Brander–Spencer profit-shifting model (Rysman, 1999) or the interactions between the importing and the exporting governments in a single market (Cowan, 1989). Richardson (1999) considers the advantages of harmonization of competition policies, where different governments place different weights on the welfare of their producers and consumers in computing national welfare.

3.  This analysis has been extended to non-Cournot behaviour and non-linear demand. See, for example, Deneckere and Davidson (1985), Kwoka (1989) and Fauli-Oller (1997). If a merger is proposed it can be assumed to be profitable to its participants, and so Farrell and Shapiro (1990) focus on its effects on non-participants ('external effects'). Their work has been extended to a multicountry context by Barros and Cabral (1994), who derive conditions on the output shares of participants and non-participants sufficient for the external effects of the merger to be positive.

4.  Gaudet and Kanouni (2000) consider the incentive that different levels of the tariff provide for a fixed cost saving domestic merger. The main impact arises when the tariff is large enough to influence the number of foreign competitors in the market.

5.  Perry and Porter (1985) introduce an explicit link between marginal cost and firm size through a tangible asset, assumed to be in fixed supply to the industry, whose quantity in the hands of a firm determines its unit costs. Then the merged firm has more of the asset and therefore lower costs. This approach has also been extended to a multi-country context. See Horn and Levinsohn (1997), for example. Kabiraj and Chaudhuri (1999) compare the relative profitability and welfare effects of national and cross-border mergers, and show that there exists a range of merger efficiency gains for which a cross-border merger would lead to higher domestic welfare than a national merger.

6.  They consider both fixed cost saving and variable cost rationalization motivations for mergers and relate the potential conflicts to the international distribution of consumption and ownership of firms.

7.  The marginal cost of firm $j$ is $c_1 + [j-1]\Delta$, where $c_1$ is the marginal cost of the most efficient firm, and $\Delta$ is the technology difference.

8.  This outcome is generalized in Corollary 3 in Horn and Persson (2001).

9.  And may not even be that limiting in view of Proposition 2 in Horn and Persson (2001) which establishes, under not particularly restrictive conditions, that a duopoly is the equilibrium ownership structure when monopoly is precluded.

10. We confine attention to the global welfare effects of these mergers, thereby avoiding modelling of the division of the gains from the merger between the participants. But as we note in the conclusions, in practice it is national competition authorities that approve or disapprove mergers, and their decisions are likely to be based on the merger's effects on national welfare.

11. A general version of the model in this section (with exogenous mergers) is discussed in more detail in Falvey (1998).

12. Note that by assuming a fixed number of firms we intend to preclude the divisionalization process whereby firms may gain by splitting into separate identical production decision-making units. Were divisionalization possible, the merged firm might then increase its total profits by operating as two or more units, particularly if all had access to the technology of the more efficient partner. See Ziss (2001). In common with much of the literature in this area, we take the initial number of firms and their technologies as given. Such would be the case, for example, if the technology in this industry were

patentable, the existing firms held all the patents and there was little prospect of any firm inventing a viable new technology.

13. Farrell and Shapiro (1990) provide the conditions for output to fall under more general assumptions.

14. Note that the stability condition uses $\pi_h^{jk} > \pi_h$, reflecting that the outside firm is always better off from a merger.

15. $G(1, 3) - G(2, 3) = [\bar{x}_3/3][\bar{x}_1 - \bar{x}_2] > 0$.

16. This outcome also follows from Proposition 2 in Horn and Persson (2001) which establishes, in this case, that the producing firms in equilibrium will be those that maximize total industry profits. One can readily show that total profits when only firms 1 and 2 produce are equal to total profits when only firms 1 and 3 produce if initially $6\bar{x}_1 = 7[\bar{x}_2 + \bar{x}_3]$.

17. Here $\bar{x}_3 < 6\bar{X}/25$, which can be written as $\bar{x}_3 < 6[\bar{x}_1 + \bar{x}_2]/19$.

18. Here $\bar{x}_3 < 6[\bar{x}_1 + \bar{x}_2]/19$ and $\bar{x}_2 < 6[\bar{x}_1 + \bar{x}_3]/19$ but $25\bar{x}_1 < 19\bar{X}$.

19. If $19\bar{x}_3 < 6[\bar{x}_1 + \bar{x}_2]$, then $8\bar{x}_3 < 6\bar{x}_1$, and if $19\bar{x}_2 < 6[\bar{x}_1 + \bar{x}_3]$, then $8\bar{x}_2 < 6\bar{x}_1$.

20. That is, $7[\bar{x}_2 + \bar{x}_3] < 6\bar{x}_1 < 19[\bar{x}_2 + \bar{x}_3]$.

21. Our assumptions of linear demand and a specific tariff considerably simplify the analysis that follows. Collie (1998) shows that a specific or *ad valorem* tariff has an (indirect) demand-induced rationalization effect on production as it moves the industry up its demand curve, thereby making demand flatter (steeper) if demand is concave (convex). This affects both domestic and foreign firms, with output of the *j*th firm increasing by more than the average if demand is concave (convex) and it is larger (smaller) than average. *Ad valorem* tariffs also have a direct rationalization effect by making the foreign firms' perceived demand curves flatter. This does not affect domestic firms.

22. Note that the discussion below assumes that $t < 4\bar{x}_3$, so that all firms will produce in the absence of a merger.

23. One can show that the loss due to the fall in tariff revenue more than exceeds the 'benefit' that the tariff has given by reducing the consumer surplus loss from the merger.

24. In order to keep all firms producing in the absence of the merger, we assume that $t < 4\bar{x}_2/3$. We also assume that $t < c_3 - c_1$ (or equivalently that $t < \bar{x}_3 - \bar{x}_1$), so that, if merger {1,3} occurs, the merged firm does not face a 'tariff-jumping' incentive to continue production using firm 3's technology for the home market.

25. If the tariff has made firm 3 larger than firm 2 and $8x_2 < 6x_1 < 8h_3$. This requires that all outputs are quite similar in free trade, so that $8\bar{x}_2 < 6\bar{x}_1 - 1.5t < 8\bar{x}_3 + 16t$.

26. Note that in this case the tariff raises world output. Again we assume that $t < \bar{x}_2 - \bar{x}_1$, so that either merger sees the domestic partner cease production.

# REFERENCES

Barros, P.P. (1998), 'Endogenous mergers and size asymmetry of merger participants', *Economic Letters*, **60** (1), 113–19.

Barros, P.P. and Cabral, L. (1994), 'Merger policy in open economies', *European Economic Review*, **38**, 1041–55.

Bliss, C. (1996), 'Trade and competition control', in J.N. Bhagwati and R.E. Hudec (eds), *Fair Trade and Harmonization*, vol. 1, Cambridge, MA: The MIT Press.

Collie, D.R. (1998), 'Tariffs and subsidies under asymmetric oligopoly: *ad valorem* versus specific instruments', Cardiff Business School Discussion Paper 98–111.

Cowan, S.G.B. (1989), 'Trade and competition policies for oligopolies', *Weltwirtschaftliches Archiv*, **125**, 464–83.

Deneckere, R. and Davidson, C. (1985), 'Incentives to form coalitions with Bertrand Competition', *Rand Journal of Economics*, **16**, 473–86.

146     *Trade and market structure*

Falvey, R.E. (1998), 'Mergers in open economies', *The World Economy*, **21** (8), 1061–76.

Farrell, J. and Shapiro, C. (1990), 'Horizontal mergers: An equilibrium analysis', *American Economic Review*, **80** (1), 107–26.

Fauli-Oller, R. (1997), 'On merger profitability in a Cournot setting', *Economics Letters*, **54**, 75–9.

Gaudet, G. and Kanouni, R. (2004), 'Trade liberalisation and the profitability of domestic mergers', *Review of International Economics*, **12** (3), 353–8.

Head, K. and Ries, J. (1997), 'International mergers and welfare under de-centralised competition policy', *Canadian Journal of Economics*, **30** (4b), 1104–23.

Horn, H. and Levinsohn, J. (1997), 'Merger policies and trade liberalization', RSIE Discussion Paper No. 420, University of Michigan.

Horn, H. and Persson, L. (1999), 'The equilibrium ownership of an international oligopoly', CEPR Discussion Paper 2302.

Horn, H. and Persson, L. (2001), 'Endogenous mergers in concentrated markets', *International Journal of Industrial Organisation*, **19**, 1213–44.

Kabiraj, T. and Chaudhuri, M. (1999), 'On the welfare analysis of a cross-border merger', *The Journal of International Trade and Economic Development*, **8** (2), 195–207.

Kwoka, J.E. (1989), 'The private profitability of horizontal mergers with non-Cournot and maverick behaviour', *International Journal of Industrial Organisation*, **7**, 403–11.

Lahiri, S. and Ono, Y. (1988), 'Helping minor firms reduces welfare', *Economic Journal*, **98**, 1199–202.

Lloyd, P.J. (1998), 'Multilateral rules for international competition law?', *The World Economy*, **21** (8), 1129–49.

Lloyd, P.J. and Sampson, G. (1995), 'Competition and trade policy: identifying the issues after the Uruguay Round', *The World Economy*, **18** (5), 681–705.

Long, N.V. and Vousden, N. (1995), 'The effects of trade liberalisation on cost-reducing horizontal mergers', *Review of International Economics*, **3** (2), 141–55.

Perry, M.K. and Porter, R.H. (1985), 'Oligopoly and the incentive for horizontal merger', *American Economic Review*, **75** (1), 219–27.

Richardson, M. (1999), 'Trade and competition policies: Concordia Discors?', *Oxford Economic Papers*, **51** (4), 649–64.

Rysman, M. (1999), 'Competition Policy as Strategic Trade', mimeo, University of Wisconsin.

Salant, S., Switzer, S. and Reynolds, R. (1983), 'Losses from horizontal merger: the effects of an exogenous change in industry structure on Cournot–Nash equilibrium', *Quarterly Journal of Economics*, **98** (2), 185–99.

World Trade Organization (1997), *Annual Report*, Geneva.

Ziss, S. (2001), 'Horizontal mergers and delegation', *International Journal of Industrial Organisation*, **19**, 471–92.

# 7. What have we learned from a generation's research on intra-industry trade?*

**David Greenaway and Chris Milner**

## 1. INTRODUCTION

Peter Lloyd has enjoyed a long and distinguished career, during which he has made a great many contributions to the international economics literature. Moreover, his contributions have been to theory, empirical analysis and policy evaluation. In deciding upon an appropriate topic for a *Festschrift* in his honour, one is therefore potentially spoiled for choice. But for us, the choice was straightforward: intra-industry trade. We chose this for two reasons. First, despite the fact that in terms of number of publications, Peter's contributions on this subject are relatively modest (four articles, three chapters, two edited volumes and one book),[1] their impact and especially that of the book (Grubel and Lloyd, 1975) has been enormous. So much so in fact that intra-industry trade (IIT) would be the first topic that comes to mind for most of us when we think of Peter's work. Grubel and Lloyd (1975) is his most widely cited work, not only because it develops the famous Grubel and Lloyd index, but also because it was the first systematic and comprehensive analysis of IIT and because it was the stimulus to a large number of young scholars to work in the area. That is the second reason why the topic is a natural for us, we were among those (then) young researchers who were stimulated by the book to develop a research agenda from it.

Since the publication of Grubel and Lloyd (1975) an entire generation's work has been completed. In this chapter we will take the book as our starting point and evaluate the development of this literature around three themes – measurement, explanation and policy – which essentially map onto the three substantive parts of the volume. For each theme we will aim to set out 'what we have learned' as well as commenting as appropriate, where the literature is headed. These three themes comprise Sections 2 through 4, while Section 5 concludes.[2]

## 2.  THE MEASUREMENT OF INTRA-INDUSTRY TRADE

In some respects, measurement may seem like the wrong starting point. As economists, we generally start with theory, then when we think we have something to explain, take it to the data. But it is actually quite a sensible place to start, because the entire literature started with 'measurement'. Essentially the IIT research programme was initiated by several papers probing for the effects of the establishment of the (then) European Economic Community on trade patterns, most notably Drèze (1961), Verdoorn (1960) and Balassa (1965). Standard customs union theory as articulated by Viner (1950) predicted increased inter-industry specialization and, in its wake, serious adjustment frictions. What the early documentation pointed to, however, was in fact increased intra-industry specialization. This surprising discovery had two effects. First, it led to the prediction (first set out in Balassa, 1965) that adjustment to European integration would be smoother than expected, because frictions associated with reallocating resources within as opposed to between industries would be less. This so-called 'smooth adjustment' hypothesis has enjoyed remarkable longevity and we will return to it in Section 4. The other effect was to stimulate further research into the extent of IIT, which in turn stimulated work on its measurement. Peter Lloyd's first and ultimately most lasting contribution to the literature was on measurement, with the development of the Grubel and Lloyd index, set out in Grubel and Lloyd (1971, 1975).

At its most basic, the Grubel and Lloyd (GL) index can be written as:

$$B_j = \frac{(X_j + M_j) - |X_j - M_j|}{(X_j + M_j)}$$

or

$$B_j = 1 - \frac{|X_j - M_j|}{(X_j + M_j)}.$$

In other words, for a given industry $j$, the index measures the extent to which exports and imports are matched, relative to total trade in the commodity grouping in question. Clearly $B_j$ lies in the interval of zero to one: in the case of the latter all trade is intra-industry, whilst at its lower bound there is no IIT.[3]

This index, or to be more accurate, what it purported to measure, was far from being uncontroversial, as Lloyd (2002) reminds us. The two main issues were categorical aggregation and adjustment for aggregate payments imbalance. We do not propose to spend any time on the latter as we have never regarded it as a very substantive issue. In essence it refers to the argument that when aggregate goods trade is unbalanced, IIT indices will be biased downwards. Grubel and Lloyd (1975) suggested a 'correction' for aggregate trade imbalance, as have Aquino (1978) and Bergstrand (1983). Quite apart from the technical shortcomings of particular corrections, we argued some time ago that there were no strong *a priori* arguments for adjustment since at the end of the day we have no *ex ante* knowledge of what constitutes a particular set of 'equilibrium' transactions. At a given point in time the balance of transactions across industries is presumably fashioned largely by underlying drivers of comparative advantage (see Greenaway and Milner, 1981).

Categorical aggregation on the other hand is much more fundamental and goes to the very heart of what the GL index (and of course variants thereof) actually measures. The core of the issue is how well statistical classifications map on to industries. Most researchers tend to equate an industry with the third digit of the SITC or equivalent. Some critics, most notably Finger (1975) and Rayment (1976) have argued that at this level of aggregation, there is greater variability in factor ratios within than between (third-digit) industries. Indeed, Finger (1975) went so far as to assert that this problem was so fundamental as to render measured IIT largely a 'statistical artifact'.

There is no doubt that at any chosen level of aggregation there will be some measurement error because of the inexact mapping of statistical categories onto groups of activities with similar factor ratios that we can think of as industries. But as Greenaway and Milner (1983) demonstrated using UK data, there are relatively straightforward adjustments that one can make to the GL index to give one greater confidence that what one is looking at is trade in similar products rather than vagaries of a particular aggregation system. Moreover, the fact that the GL index is still being routinely used a generation later tells its own story (Evenett and Keller, 2001 and Brülhart and Elliott, 2002 being a couple of recent examples). Besides this, the literature has moved on in other ways, most notably in respect of the measurement of marginal intra-industry trade (MIIT) in disentangling horizontal and vertical intra-industry trade (HIIT and VIIT) and in constructing indices of international trade and production.

The limitations of using changes in the standard GL index to capture the dynamics of changes in IIT is widely recognized. The first attempt to construct an index of MIIT is Hamilton and Kneist (1991). They argued that for purposes of evaluating the adjustment consequences of trade expansion it was important to focus on how IIT changes at the margin. They offered an index that effectively calculated the proportion of the changes in exports

or imports that is matched. Although there are several shortcomings associated with the Hamilton–Kneist index as set out in Greenaway et al.
(1994b) and Brülhart (1994) (both of which offer alternatives), their fundamental insight is an important one – if we are interested in adjustment,
appropriate measures of MIIT are essential. A number of recent studies
have incorporated MIIT indices, including Brülhart and Elliott (2002),
albeit with mixed results. Work is ongoing on this issue and a recent paper
by Lovely and Nelson (2002) is the first to look carefully at the theoretical
underpinnings to MIIT indices and their link to labour market adjustment.

The standard definition of IIT is the simultaneous import and export of
differentiated products. But of course products can be differentiated horizontally (different varieties of a given good) and vertically (different qual-
ities of a given variety). Moreover, as we shall see in the next section, theory
has developed to provide underpinnings to trade in both types. But the GL
index aggregates both and if their determinants vary, as indeed they do,
that can result in measurement error. In recognition of this, over the last
decade extensions of the GL index have been developed and applied by
Abd-el-Rahman (1991) and Greenaway et al. (1994a, 1995), which disen-
tangled HIIT and VIIT. Starting from the presumption that differences in
quality are reflected in differences in price, they use unit value data to separate the two. This particular method is now being extensively applied.
Among other things it is facilitating a shift in emphasis in empirical work
away from estimation towards testing.[4]

The development of measures of HIIT and VIIT is a nice example of feed-
back from theory to measurement. Another example of this is the more
recent development of a measure of extended intra-industry trade by
Greenaway et al. (2001). It has been recognized that arm's-length IIT and
cross-border production may be complements rather than substitutes. That
being so, the simple GL measure misses an important aspect of the globalization of production. To provide a more complete picture, Greenaway et al.
(2001) propose a measure which has three components: the two-way
exchange of international trade in goods; two-way exchange of international
production; two-way exchange of international trade for international production. The first component is obviously IIT; the second cross-border
affiliate sales and the third, the interaction between trade and affiliate sales.
Independently Hummels et al. (2001) have developed a measure with a
similar purpose in mind. The principal constraint to the wider application of
these measures is data on affiliate production. As these data improve,
however, one can expect to see them more widely deployed.

What can we conclude about work on measurement since Grubel and
Lloyd (1975)? The first point to make is that it was relatively slow to take
off, in part because of the preoccupation with explanation in general and

theoretical explanation in particular; and in part because IIT was controversial. Over the last ten years, however, a great deal of work has been done. As a consequence the starting point when looking at data on IIT is no longer 'does IIT exist?' but 'what kind of IIT are we looking at?', which is our second conclusion. Third, as a consequence of having a richer menu of measures, empirical analysis has progressed from a literature that was essentially about estimation to one that is increasingly about testing. The final conclusion is that almost all of the useful and usable new measures build upon the GL index. None are radical departures. So, in a very fundamental sense, the GL index remains the bedrock to the measurement of IIT.

## 3. EXPLANATION OF INTRA-INDUSTRY TRADE

I use the term 'explanation' to encompass both theoretical modelling geared to generating insights about the determinants of IIT and econometric evaluation of those models.

### Theoretical Modelling

Grubel and Lloyd (1975) was very influential in stimulating theoretical work, as Leamer (1994, p. 68) acknowledges:

> the extensive amount of intra-industry trade catalogued by Grubel and Lloyd (1975) . . . is also regarded as a blow against the generality of the H–O model and is at least partly responsible for the large theoretical literature on models with increasing returns to scale and monopolistic competition. Other than these . . . (that is, IIT and the Leontief paradox), beliefs about the sources of international comparative advantage have not been greatly affected by any observations.

Grubel and Lloyd (1975) did not ignore theory; far from it. In fact they discussed three different categories of explanation: functionally homogeneous products; differentiated products and economies of scale; and technology, product cycles and foreign processing. For a long time the first of these was widely thought of as a catch-all for idiosyncratic drivers of trade, with some justification, though the recent literature on trade costs emphasizes these factors. The second and third stimulated enormous literatures.

Grubel and Lloyd's (1975) discussion of product differentiation and scale economies was important in that many of the key insights underpinned by subsequent theoretical work are there to be found. The theoretical work that it stimulated developed rapidly with early key contributions from Krugman (1979), Lancaster (1980), Falvey (1981) and Brander (1981). Krugman picked up on a specific technical innovation, Dixit–Stiglitz preferences, and applied them in an open-economy setting. In this model consumers have a love of variety and want to benefit from every variety available, which generates an aggregate demand for goods of varying specification. If a single firm produces a single variety and there is free entry, there will be a large number of varieties, but decreasing costs ensure that that number is finite. Even two identical economies will have an incentive to trade, with gains deriving from the exchange of scale economies. Lancaster (1980) starts from the more plausible, but more difficult-to-model assumption that consumers have preferred varieties and want more of their preferred variety rather than some of all varieties. So long as consumers have different preferences, we still have an aggregate demand for goods of varying specifications and with free entry and decreasing costs, there are still incentives to engage in and gains from trade.

Falvey (1981) is really quite different to Krugman (1979) and Lancaster (1980). Whereas the last two relied upon imperfect competition, Falvey does not. Moreover, his consumers are interested in vertically rather than horizontally differentiated products, demand for which is determined by relative income. Quality is determined by relative capital intensity, products with a higher capital–labour ratio being of a higher quality. If countries have different factor endowments, the relatively capital-abundant country will export high-quality products while the relatively labour-abundant country will export lower-quality products. For obvious reasons this is sometimes referred to a neo-Heckscher–Ohlin model.

All of the foregoing are 'large-numbers' models; Brander (1981) was the first to model 'small numbers' of firms. His was a duopoly model with the two firms playing a Cournot game. He succeeded in demonstrating that even identical firms producing a homogeneous product could engage in cross-hauling. Moreover, although resources are used up in this cross-hauling, it could still be socially beneficial as a consequence of pro-competition effects.

These four papers were very influential in underpinning the intuition in Grubel and Lloyd (1975). In terms of the determinants of trade they demonstrated that scale economies may be an important driver, that trade may be stimulated by strategic interaction and that differences in factor endowments might stimulate trade in vertically differentiated goods rather than just inter-industry trade. With the exception of Falvey (1981), however, these models told us nothing about the direction of trade. With regard to the gains from trade, these early models showed formally the role of gains from greater product variety, the exchange of scale economies and pro-competitive effects. They stimulated an enormous literature, among the highlights of which are Helpman and Krugman (1985), which effectively signed off the general equilibrium framework for simultaneously determining

Heckscher–Ohlin trade and trade in horizontally differentiated goods; Krugman (1979) which extends the Dixit–Stiglitz 'trick' to bring trade costs and location into the picture, and Davis (1995), which re-focused attention on trade in vertically differentiated commodities.

Grubel and Lloyd's third class of 'models' was focused on technology, product cycles and foreign processing. This essentially started from the technology gap and product cycle models. This work was the precursor to large literatures on changing comparative advantage and the relationship between FDI and trade and more recently on links between trade and the international fragmentation of production. It is now widely recognized and documented that globalization has encouraged outsourcing and the international fragmentation of production, with a consequent increase in trade in intermediates. In turn this has stimulated considerable interest on the part of theorists to integrate fragmentation into trade models (for example, Deardorff, 2001). As reported earlier, it also motivated the search for measures of extended IIT.

## Econometric Analysis

Econometric analysis is one area of the literature where Grubel and Lloyd (1975) is essentially silent, or perhaps more accurately, muted. In the final part of the text they speculate on tests of intra-industry trade, but do not report on any studies, for the simple reason that there were none! What most people regard as the first systematic analysis of the determinants of IIT was in fact published in the same year as Grubel and Lloyd, namely Pagoulatos and Sorensen (1975). Things have changed, partly because of Grubel and Lloyd, partly because of the rapid developments in theory we have reviewed. The latter provided applied economists with a road map that did not exist beforehand.

Econometric analysis of IIT did expand quite rapidly with a proliferation of country-specific and multi-country studies in the late 1970s and 1980s. These were largely cross-section, they were largely concerned with estimation rather than testing, and results were rather inconsistent, especially where cross-industry variables were concerned. Cross-country variables were more robust. Indeed, as Torstensson (1996) demonstrated very effectively using extreme bounds analysis, results were also generally rather fragile.

There seem to be a number of factors behind these outcomes. First, although the proliferation of theory did yield testable predictions, aggregate measures of IIT did not offer opportunities to discriminate between the predictions of alternative theories. As a consequence, most empirical models were essentially *ad hoc* and geared to coefficient estimation. Second, most information took the form of highly aggregated, industry-specific and country-specific data. Not only did this increase the likelihood of errors in measurement; it also placed natural limits on what could and could not be divined from the data.

In the mid- to late 1990s there was a revival of interest in econometric analyses of IIT. In part this was data driven, with a growing availability of micro-level data. In part it was also driven by refinements in the measurement of IIT (as discussed earlier) that have facilitated a change in strategy away from coefficient estimation towards testing specific theories. Thus, for example, Hummels and Levinsohn (1995) use time-series data to test simultaneously for H–O and monopolistic competition factors while Greenaway et al. (1994a, 1995) use disaggregated data to test models predicting horizontal and vertical IIT. Work is now beginning to use firm-level data to evaluate not only the determinants of trade patterns, but also firm-level adjustment to changes in trading arrangements.

So here too the literature has moved on from searching for correlations to testing models. In the process we have learned more about the determinants of IIT and also how to search for any determinants more effectively.

## 4.  POLICY ASPECTS OF INTRA-INDUSTRY TRADE

One of the main purposes of theorizing about the determinants of trade and testing theories is to inform policy. This is no less true of IIT than of other areas. In the case of IIT, the literature has essentially focused on three (related) questions. First, are the gains from trade different to those associated with Heckscher–Ohlin trade? Second, do we need to revise our thinking regarding the impact of intervention in markets dominated by trade in differentiated products? Third, when trade expands, is adjustment smoother in an environment characterized by IIT as compared to inter-industry trade?

We have already alluded to gains from trade. With IIT there exist additional potential sources of gain – increased variety, the exchange of scale economies and pro-competition effects. Moreover, there has been some formal modelling of these potential gains, for example Krugman (1981). This is an area where empirical analysis has progressed considerably following the important paper by Cox and Harris (1985). What they did was to build a CGE model of Canadian trade, incorporating decreasing costs. The most important finding from this was that once you allowed for scale economies, the gains from trade were larger, by an order of magnitude, than the gains computed by 'adding up triangles'. This has stimulated a large literature across a large number of countries that essentially confirms this finding. Moreover, the work has manifestly influenced the policy debate on issues such as the European Union's Single Market programme, NAFTA (North American Free Trade Agreement) and APEC (Asia Pacific Economic Cooperation).

By contrast, the issue of adjustment to trade expansion has remained under-researched, which is superficially surprising, since the initial stimulus to the study of IIT was motivated by the intuition that adjustment would bring fewer frictions if trade flows were largely IIT. The reasons for limited progress are not hard to find: dynamic adjustment paths are not straightforward to model; most economists instinctively think of adjustment costs as the price we pay for change, and the evidence we have suggests that they are small relative to the present value of the gains from trade (see Matusz and Tarr, 2000). But it remains an interesting issue to probe. As argued above, the early literature emphasizing greater factor intensity differentials within than between industries seemed to contradict the smooth adjustment hypothesis (for example, Finger, 1975; Rayment, 1976). More recently however, Lundberg and Hansson (1986) and Elliott et al. (2000) have reported evidence of greater homogeneity within than between industries. There is also evidence that the costs of unemployment in terms of forsaken wages and lower expected lifetime earnings is higher in inter- than intra-industry adjustment (Haynes et al., 2000). Nevertheless, this may not constitute a convincing basis for presuming, as some analysts do, that marginal IIT indicators merely measure the degree of disruptive trade.

The area of the policy-related literature that stimulated the largest volume of work was that on the effects of intervention. This post-dates Grubel and Lloyd and indeed the initial work on models of trade and monopolistic competition. Perhaps the most important early contribution here was Krugman's (1984) paper on import protection as export promotion. This certainly excited academic attention because it appeared to be a new second-best argument for intervention, even if it sounded a little like the old infant-industry case and even if it avoided any welfare analysis (demonstrating only that with decreasing costs, segmented markets and Cournot competition, an import tariff could result in export expansion, but that would not necessarily make the home country better off). It goes without saying that the argument excited even more interest on the part of lobbies and policy makers ever on the lookout for new justifications or intervention!

This literature grew rapidly, with some focus on what happens when you introduce tariffs (or subsides) in a monopolistic competition framework but with most attention being paid to small-number cases where strategic trade policy seemed possible. Brander and Spencer (1984) is the best-known paper here, showing how under certain conditions an export subsidy can shift rents from foreign producers and leave the home economy better off. There have been a number of very good surveys of this literature, including Corden (1991). What have we learned from it? Two things essentially, neither very surprising. First, results tend to be very model specific and very sensitive to initial conditions. Second, as a consequence of this, there are 'no new general principles and certainly no new paradigm . . .' (Corden, 1991, p. 286).

## 5.   CONCLUSIONS

This chapter did not set out to survey the literature on IIT as such. Rather its objective was to take the pioneering work of Peter Lloyd (and Herbert Grubel) on IIT and evaluate both how the scientific agenda has moved on and what we have learned in the process.

Peter Lloyd may not view Grubel and Lloyd (1975) as his most original nor his most substantive piece of work, but I suspect it has been his most influential. In the evolution of work on the determinants of trade patterns the book is an important one. It brought together emerging work on the identification of what seemed to be a novel phenomenon at the time and a phenomenon which did not appear to be consistent with the predictions of the standard explanation of international trade, the H–O theorem. In that respect it was a much-needed synthesis. However, it went further in providing the most extensive documentation of the phenomenon available to that point. But, in addition, it set an agenda for future work. Grubel and Lloyd (1975) offered explanations. Those explanations were unashamedly informal but in common with other important agenda-setting volumes in international trade where explanation was also informal (in the sense of being non-mathematical) like Viner (1950), Meade (1955) and Corden (1974) it was very intuitive and replete with ideas for others to follow up. And that is exactly what happened. IIT has been one of the liveliest areas of research in international trade for a generation and we have learned quite a lot from the literature.

First, it is fair to say that some of the initial hostility that greeted work on IIT 25 years ago was triggered by it being seen as a competitor and threat to the dominant paradigm, the Heckscher–Ohlin model. A generation later we have learned that classical and neoclassical explanations of the determinants of trade and modern explanations, many of which rely upon imperfect competition and which result in IIT, are complements rather than substitutes. We now have robust and general models where trade in homogeneous and differentiated products are simultaneously determined.

Second, a generation ago many viewed measured IIT as a 'statistical artifact'. Rather than being something real and in need of explanation, it was a by-product of data aggregation systems. Categorical aggregation is undoubtedly a real problem. But a generation later we have developed metrics that allow us to disentangle aggregation influences more intelligently to give us greater confidence in what we are documenting.

Third, when Grubel and Lloyd wrote their book no theory or theories of IIT had been taken to the data systematically and early work was essentially targeted at searching for correlations between particular features of industrial structure or country characteristics and IIT indices. The development of theory and measurement combined with the growing availability of micro data has facilitated a step change in econometric analysis and a migration from estimations to testing. As a consequence we have learned more about the determinants of IIT.

Fourth, we have learned that although the determinants of IIT may be different from the determinants of inter-industry trade, we do not need to dramatically revise our thinking on the welfare aspects of international trade. There are additional possible sources of benefit that we are now more certain of but there are few new arguments for sacrificing these to protect particular groups in society.

# NOTES

*  Paper for the *Festschrift* Conference for Peter Lloyd, University of Melbourne, 23–24 January, 2003. This draft March 2003. The authors gratefully acknowledge financial support from The Leverhulme Trust under Programme Grant F114/BF.
1.  The articles are: Grubel and Lloyd (1971), Lloyd (1989), Lloyd (1994) and Greenaway et al. (2001); the chapters, Grubel and Lloyd (1979), Lloyd (1989) and Greenaway et al. (2001); the edited volumes, Lloyd and Hyun Lee (2002) and Grubel and Lloyd (2003) and the book Grubel and Lloyd (1975).
2.  The authors have been involved with two earlier syntheses and reviews of the literature, namely Greenaway and Milner (1987) and Greenaway and Torstensson (1997). Although this chapter does not directly draw upon either, it has been influenced by both and the contributions of the late Johan Torstensson are gratefully acknowledged.
3.  There are commentators who prefer to distinguish between one-way and two-way trade (for example, Fontagne and Freudenberg 2002) rather than the share of trade overlap in an industry's gross trade. The GL index has however the attractive attribute of providing a decomposition which helps to reconcile traditional trade theory explanations of net trade and new trade theories of overlapping trade.
4.  The second-best nature of their approach, even when decomposing IIT across all industries must be acknowledged. Recent work by Nielson and Luthje (2002) points to some instability of the decomposition across countries in particular. The proliferation of firm level datasets should lead to further refinements in decomposition.

# BIBLIOGRAPHY

Abd-el-Rahman, K. (1991), 'Firms' competitive and national comparative advantages as joint determinants of trade composition', *Weltwirtschaftliches Archiv*, **127** (1), 83–97.

Aquino, A. (1978), 'Intra-industry trade and intra-industry specialisation as concurrent sources of international trade in manufactures', *Weltwirtschaftliches Archiv*, **114**, 275–95.

Balassa, B. (1965), *European Economic Integration*, Amsterdam: North-Holland.

Bergstrand, J.H. (1983), 'Measurement and determinants of intra-industry international trade', in P.K. Mathew Tharakan (ed.), *Intra-Industry Trade: Empirical and Methodological Aspects*, Amsterdam: North-Holland, pp. 201–53.

Brander, J.A. (1981), 'Intra-industry trade in identical commodities', *Journal of International Economics*, **11**, 1–14.

Brander, J. and Spencer, B. (1984), 'Trade warfare: tariffs and cartels', *Journal of International Economics*, **16**, 227–42.

Brülhart, M. (1994), 'Marginal intra-industry trade: measurement and the relevance for the pattern of industrial adjustment', *Weltwirtschaftliches Archiv*, **130**, 600–613.

Brülhart, M. and Elliott, R. (2002), 'Labour market effects of intra-industry trade: evidence for the UK', *Weltwirtschaftliches Archiv*, **138**, 207–28.

Corden, W.M. (1974), *Trade Policy and Economic Welfare*, Oxford: Oxford University Press.

Corden, W.M. (1991), 'Strategic Trade Policy' in D. Greenaway, M. Bleaney and I. Stewart (eds), *Companion to Contemporary Economic Thought*, London: Routledge.

Cox, D.R. and Harris, R. (1985), 'Trade liberalisation and industrial organisation: Some estimates for Canada', *Journal of Political Economy*, **93**, 115–45.

Davis, D.R. (1995), 'Intra-industry trade: A Heckscher–Ohlin–Ricardo approach', *Journal of International Economics*, **39**, 201–26.

Deardorff, A. (2001), 'Fragmentation in simple trade models', *North American Journal of Economics and Finance*, **12**, 121–37.

Dixit, A.K. and Stiglitz, J.E. (1997), 'Monopolistic competition and optimum product diversity', *American Economic Review*, **67**, 297–308.

Drèze, J. (1961), 'Les exportations intra-C.E.E. en 1958 et la position Belge', *Recherches Economiques de Louvain*, **27**, 717–38.

Elliott, R., Greenaway, D. and Hine, R.C. (2000), 'Tests for factor homogeneity and industry classification', *Weltwirschaflliches Archiv*, **135**, 355–71.

Evenett, S. and Keller, W. (2001), 'On theories explaining the success of the gravity model', *Journal of Political Economy*, **110**, 281–316.

Falvey, R.E. (1981), 'Commercial policy and intra-industry trade', *Journal of International Economics*, **11**, 495–511.

Finger, J.M. (1975), 'Trade overlap and intra-industry trade', *Economics Inquiry*, **13**, 581–9.

Greenaway, D. and Milner, C.R. (1981), 'Trade imbalance effects and the measurement of intra-industry trade', *Weltwirtschaftliches Archiv*, **117**, 756–62.

Greenaway, David and Milner, Chris R. (1983), 'On the measurement of intra-industry trade', *The Economic Journal*, **93**, 900–908.

Greenaway, David and Milner, Chris R. (1984), 'A cross section analysis of intra-industry trade in the U.K.', *European Economics Review*, **25**, 319–44.

Greenaway, David and Milner, Chris R. (1986), *The Economics of Intra-Industry-Trade*, Oxford: Blackwell.

Greenaway, D., Hine, R. and Milner, C. (1994a), 'Country-specific factors and the pattern of horizontal and vertical intra-industry trade in the UK', *Weltwirtschaftliches Archiv*, **130**, 77–100.

Greenaway, D., Hine, R. Milner, C. and Elliot, R. (1994b), 'Adjustment and the measurement of marginal intra-industry trade', *Weltwirtschaftliches Archiv*, **130**, 418–27.

Greenaway, D., Hine, R. and Milner, C. (1995), 'Vertical and horizontal intra-industry trade: a cross-industry analysis for the United Kingdom', *Economic Journal*, **105**, 1505–19.

Greenaway, D., Lloyd, P.J. and Milner, C.R. (2001), 'New concepts and measures of the globalisation of production', *Economic Letters*, **73**, 57–64.

Grubel, H.G. and Lloyd, P.J. (1971), 'The empirical measurement of intra-industry trade', *Economic Record*, **47**, 494–517.

Grubel, Herbert G. and Lloyd, P.J. (1975), *Intra-Industry Trade: The Theory and Measurement of International Trade in Differentiated Products*, London: Macmillan.

Hamilton, C. and Kniest, P. (1991), 'Trade liberalisation, structural adjustment and intra-industry trade', *Weltwirtschaftliches Archiv*, **127**, 356–67.

Haynes, M., Upward, R. and Wright, P. (2000), 'Smooth and sticky adjustment: A comparative analysis of the US and UK', *Review of International Economics*, **8**, 517–32.

Helpman, E. and Krugman, P. (1985), *Market Structure and Foreign Trade*, Brighton: Harvester Wheatsheaf.

Hummels, D. and Levinsohn, J. (1995), 'Monopolistic competition and international trade: reconsidering the evidence', *Quarterly Journal of Economics*, **110**, 799–836.

Hummels, D., Ishii, J. and Yi, K. (2001), 'The nature and growth of vertical specialisation in world trade', *Journal of International Economics*, **54**, 75–96.

Krugman, Paul R. (1979), 'Increasing returns, monopolistic competition and international trade', *Journal of International Economics*, **9**, 469–79.

Krugman, Paul R. (1981), 'Intra-industry specialisation and the gains from trade', *Journal of Political Economy*, **89**, 959–73.

Krugman, Paul R. (1984), 'Import protection as export promotion: international competition in the presence of oligopoly and economies of scale', in Henryk Kierzkowski (ed.), *Monopolistic Competition and International Trade*, Oxford: Oxford University Press, pp. 180–93.

Lancaster, Kelvin J. (1980), 'Intra-industry trade under perfect monopolistic competition', *Journal of International Economics*, **10**, 151–75.

Leamer, E.E. (1994), 'Testing trade theory', in D. Greenaway and L.A. Winters (eds), *Surveys in International Trade*, Oxford: Blackwell.

Lloyd, P.J. (2002), 'Controversies concerning intra-industry trade', in P.J. Lloyd and H.H. Lee (eds), *Frontiers of Research in Intra-Industry Trade*, Basingstoke: Palgrave Macmillan.

Lovely, M.E. and Nelson, D.R. (2002), 'Intra-industry trade as an indicator of labour market adjustment', *Weltwirtschaftliches Archiv*, **138**, 179–206.

Lundberg, L. and Hansson, P. (1986), 'Intra-industry trade and its consequences for adjustments', in D. Greenaway and P.K.M. Tharakan (eds), *Imperfect Competition and International Trade*, Brighton: Wheatsheaf.

Matusz, S. and Tarr, D. (2000), 'Adjusting to trade policy reform', in A. Krueger (ed.), *Economic policy Reform: The Second Stage*, Chicago: University of Chicago Press.

Meade, J.E. (1955), '*Trade and Welfare*, Oxford: Oxford University Press.

Pagoulatos, E. and Sorensen, R. (1975) 'Two-way international trade: an econometric analysis', *Weltwirtschaftliches Archiv*, Vol. III, pp. 454–65.

Rayment, P.R. (1976), 'The homogeneity of manufacturing industries with respect to factor intensity', *Oxford Bulletin of Economics and Statistics*, **38**, 203–209.

Torstensson, J. (1996), 'Determinants of intra-industry trade: a sensitivity analysis', *Oxford Bulletin of Economics and Statistics*, **58**, 507–24.

Verdoorn, P.J. (1960), 'The intra-bloc trade of Benelux', in E.A.G. Robinson (ed.) *Economic Consequences in the Size of Nations*, London: Macmillan.

Viner, J. (1950), *The Customs Union Issues*, New York: Carnegie Endowment.

# 8. Reforming trade-distorting state trading enterprises[*]

## Steve McCorriston and Donald MacLaren

## 1. INTRODUCTION

State trading enterprises (STEs) are an important and controversial feature of several markets for internationally traded goods and services. While state trading enterprises were recognized in GATT 1947 (Article XVII:3) as a possible source of trade distortions because of their potentially anti-competitive effects, it is only relatively recently that state trading has emerged as a substantive issue in the context of the GATT and the World Trade Organization (WTO) (Hoekman and Low, 1998). The principal explanations for this emergence are perhaps three-fold. First, STEs are to be found largely in sectors which, until 1995, lay largely outside the application of the Articles of GATT 1947, namely, those of services and agriculture. Second, there are a number of transition economies where STEs are pervasive and which are becoming members, or which are applying to become members, of the WTO.[1] And third, STEs appear anachronistic and contrary to the general trend towards competition policy and reduced government involvement in markets, both domestic and international.

During the Uruguay Round negotiations, Article XVII of GATT 1947 was discussed with a view to making it more effective as a constraint on the activities of STEs rather than with a view to re-drafting it.[2] The main deficiency in that Article was that it had not provided a definition of an STE and, as a consequence, STEs that should have been notified to the GATT were not (Davey, 1998, p. 29). Hence there was no way of knowing whether their activities were consistent with the requirement of 'commercial considerations' (Article XVII:1(b)). That weakness was partially remedied through the following working definition of an STE which was provided in an Understanding on the Interpretation of Article XVII of GATT 1994: 'Governmental and non-governmental enterprises, including marketing boards, which have been granted exclusive or special rights or privileges, including statutory or constitutional powers, in the exercise of which they influence through their purchases or sales the level or direction of imports or exports' (WTO, 1995, p. 25).

As is clear from this definition, it is not ownership of the entity that matters for it to qualify as an STE but the nature of its exclusivity. However, the adequacy of this definition has been questioned by Petersmann (1998, p. 86), who has argued that it is a narrower definition than that provided in Article XVII:1(a) and reflects a concern by negotiators about establishing guidelines for notification requirements, the purpose of which is to ensure that STEs are operating in a way that is consistent with 'commercial considerations'. However, it is not at all obvious what the expression 'commercial considerations' means for an STE the objective of which is something other than profit maximization. His basic point was that Article XVII should apply to all STEs, not just to those involved in international trade, as well as to those which operate in a competitive market structure.

The particular economic issues raised by STEs in the services sector are different from those in the goods sector (Mattoo, 1998). In the former, the main issue is monopoly control over essential facilities (infrastructure); in the latter, it is the ability of STEs to manipulate prices through segmenting markets, through cross-subsidizing between markets and through price equalization and price pooling.[3] Of the STEs that have been notified to the WTO since 1995, approximately 70 per cent occur in the agricultural sector (OECD, 2001).[4] In this sector, the grains and dairy industries are the most important in which STEs occur and the most common form of STE is the producer marketing board.

In the agricultural sector STEs are often used by developed countries to achieve a number of 'non-economic' objectives. These include: 'fair' prices for farmers which, their proponents argue, cannot be realized when the firms to which farmers sell have oligopsony power or when farmers' cooperatives fail because of the free-rider problem; the stabilization of farm-gate prices; the raising of farm-gate prices; and, in the case of importing countries, security of supply. In developing and transition economies, STEs in the agricultural sector are often used to achieve 'fair' and stable prices for food consumers and to countervail the marketing power of multinational companies. In these economies, STEs may also exist as a revenue-raising device because, otherwise, the tax base is slim. Their management of exports and imports is conducted in such a way as to acquire revenue for the exchequer. In these three types of economies (developed, developing and transitional), it is argued by the proponents of STEs that they can achieve, *inter alia*, economies of scale and scope in marketing, the securing of beneficial long-term contracts for both importing and exporting countries, the extraction of price premiums in export market segments, and security of supply for importing countries.[5] The critics of STEs argue that many of their alleged economic benefits can be obtained through private firms (see Productivity Commission, 2000). In addition, it has been argued that STEs over-service their exports and thereby reduce the net revenues that they return to their producers (see Carter et al., 1998 for an analysis of the Canadian Wheat Board which, they conclude, does over-service). It is also a common criticism that STEs have higher administration costs than commercial firms and that they stifle innovation. Thus, the objectives of STEs and their consequent effects on domestic markets (national welfare) and on international trade will vary across developed and developing/transition countries, but these effects are notoriously difficult to measure.[6]

Despite the non-economic and, apparently, market-corrective objectives of STEs listed above, not all commentary on STEs in agriculture is supportive of their current GATT-legal status. Two principal concerns have been expressed, both of which are based on the belief that STEs violate the GATT rules for 'fair trading'. The first concern is that exporting STEs have the potential to circumvent the bindings placed on the use of export subsidies by the WTO Agreement on Agriculture (Articles 8–10). The second concern is that importing STEs have the ability to create a price wedge between the domestic and international price which exceeds the tariff binding, as well as having the potential to discriminate amongst sources of imports, in violation of Article I of the GATT, and national treatment, in violation of Article III.[7]

As a consequence of these concerns, STEs have become an important item on the agenda of the agricultural negotiations currently taking place in the WTO.[8] The issue of what to do with those which trade internationally in agricultural products is perhaps the only agricultural issue on which the European Union, Japan and the USA are in agreement. For this reason alone, their trade effects deserve to be better understood. The EU has stated that it is prepared to negotiate on the use of export subsidies in international agricultural trade so long as all instruments that affect export competitiveness, for example, export credits and STEs, are also negotiable (WTO, 2000c). In that submission, it was stated (p. 3) that '[t]he EC proposes that in respect of the operation of State Trading Enterprises (STEs), cross-subsidisation, price-pooling and other unfair trade practices in exports be abolished. To that effect the operation of STEs should be subject to mandatory notification with regard to acquisition costs and export pricing'. Japan has proposed, somewhat asymmetrically, that only exporting STEs should be disciplined, because they distort international markets, but importing STEs should not be, because, it is claimed, they affect only the internal market (WTO, 2000d). The most comprehensive proposal has been presented by the USA. In 2000, the proposal for exporting STEs was, *inter alia*, an 'end to exclusive export rights to ensure private sector competition in markets controlled by single-desk exporters' (WTO, 2000a, p. 3). That position has been elaborated in the most recent US proposal (USDA, 2002, p. 4). It was stated there that 'Members shall not restrict the right of any interested entity to export, or to purchase for export, agricultural products.'[9]

The Cairns Group, which has made wide-ranging proposals on the 'three pillars' of market access, domestic support and export competition, has been silent on the issue of STEs. Of course, Australia, Canada and, until recently, New Zealand, have been long-time users of STEs. No doubt they would prefer to decide on the basis of domestic considerations alone whether or not their STEs should continue to be accorded exclusive or special rights or privileges, rather than being obliged to trade off these rights for negotiating gains elsewhere, for example, an agreement to ban the use of export subsidies which the Group has proposed (WTO, 2000b and 2002). Although the proposals from the Cairns Group have made no mention of STEs, the MERCOSUR (Southern Cone) countries plus Chile and Colombia have objected to the way in which they are handled within the GATT and in their proposal have commented '[i]t is a cause for concern that under the pretext that some form of agricultural production and trading management is needed, monopolistic enterprises interfere in the free operation of the market, in ways which are contrary to WTO rules and disciplines' (WTO, 2001, p. 1). However, there is a group of developing countries (Small Island Developing States) that are hesitant to agree to wholesale changes being made in the WTO to STEs. For example, Mauritius has argued that '[o]ne should caution against the advent, in particular situations, of unhealthy cartelization and restrictive business practices resulting from strong disciplines for STEs' (WTO, 2000e, p. 1).

The purpose in this chapter is limited to measuring the trade-distorting effect of an exporting STE with exclusive rights to be the sole domestic and export trader.[10,11] It must be stressed that the STE acts as a marketing agency and that producers do not export directly through a producer cooperative. The debates about the relative efficiency of STEs and whether they pass a public interest test of improving national welfare relative to a situation in which they are not present are ignored. The counterfactual benchmark against which this distortion is defined is one in which the STE no longer has single-desk status but has to compete in its domestic and export markets with a small number of domestic, commercial firms.[12] In the process of deregulating the state trading monopoly, private firms are allowed to enter and compete in the domestic market, not just with respect to export sales but also for domestic sales and procurement of the raw agricultural material. It is assumed to be unlikely that exclusive rights would be retained for sales in the domestic market. This benchmark, which is best described as being imperfectly competitive, is consistent with the US proposal for the reform of exporting STEs, that is, an ending of exclusive rights to export. In this benchmark, the STE continues to satisfy the definition of an STE used in Article XVII but not in the 'working definition'. The commercial firms and the STE in the home country compete in the world market with a given number of profit-maximizing firms from the foreign country. The benchmark is defined in this way because it is not known what market structure in the home country will replace the single desk once its exclusive rights have been removed. From the benchmark, the export volumes of the home and the foreign countries are determined and the volume from the home country is then compared with exports when the single desk is in place. The question can then be answered: what export subsidy would need to be made available in the deregulated environment (the benchmark) to reproduce the trade volume of the home country when the STE has single-desk status? The size of this subsidy equivalent of the STE is a measure of the trade distortion caused by the single-desk STE, but a distortion the magnitude of which depends upon the specification of the benchmark. In this regard, we also consider a different benchmark which captures an alternative form of deregulation. As noted above, the one we focus on is where the STE loses its exclusive rights and now competes with commercial firms; the alternative is where the STE no longer exists and is replaced by commercial firms. As we show, the implied effect of an exporting STE depends significantly on the nature of the deregulation process that may occur. While a comprehensive welfare analysis of deregulation is of interest to economists and perhaps to officials involved with competition policy, in the context of the proposed reform of STEs in the WTO negotiations it is really only market access and export competition that concerns trade negotiators (Bagwell and Staiger, 2000). In the remainder of the chapter, the focus is exclusively on the positive analysis of export competition.

The structure of the chapter is as follows. Section 1 is a selective review of the extant literature which provides some background on alternative approaches that have been used to explore the trade effects of STEs. Section 2 presents a partial equilibrium, three-region model which is based on the models of Brander and Krugman (1983) and of Thursby (1988). The home country has an STE with exclusive rights to trade in its domestic and export markets. The two other regions are a foreign exporting region which has a fixed number of firms, and a perfectly competitive rest-of-the-world importing region. Section 3 defines the benchmark for the home country. In the benchmark, the government has removed the STE's exclusive rights and it now has to compete in each market with a given number of commercial firms. In Section 4 the trade-distorting effect of the STE is measured through a calibrated simulation model. The data used to calibrate the parameters of the linear demand and supply functions come from the Canadian and USA's domestic and export markets for wheat. By altering the number of firms in the home and foreign countries, the size of the subsidy required in the benchmark to reproduce the export volume of the STE with exclusive rights is measured. We also consider the implied trade-distorting effect in the alternative benchmark where the STE is privatized. The implications of these results are discussed in the context of the US proposal in the Section 5, and conclusions are drawn.

## 2. BACKGROUND

STEs exist in a variety of forms, they pursue a large number of different objectives and they do so in a number of different ways.[13] This variety makes it difficult to provide a definitive analysis of their trade-distorting effects, if any, because such effects will vary from market to market depending upon the types, objectives and functions of the STEs to be found there, and on whether or not the STE has some international market power. The effects will also depend upon the counterfactual chosen against which to measure the distortion.

Lloyd (1982) analysed STEs from the standpoint of the assignment problem, that is, as the choice of the best policy instrument to achieve a given 'non-economic' objective. Viewed in this way, an STE can be interpreted as an alternative to other trade policy instruments such as trade taxes, and its ranking relative to these other instruments can then be determined by measuring the welfare effects of each within the set of possible instruments available. The benchmark used was that of perfectly competitive domestic and international markets. Lloyd went on to argue that STEs can be seen as equivalent or quasi-equivalent to trade taxes and to suggest reasons why governments may prefer them to such taxes.[14] Such reasons included the invisibility of their decision-making processes and their flexibility when compared with tariffs and import quotas in achieving a given objective. While these are two of the alleged advantages accruing to the country using an STE, they are also the alleged consequent economic disadvantage accruing to the country's trading partners. It is these disadvantages, referred to as 'unfair trading practices', which have produced the reactions by the EU, Japan and the USA to STEs.

Alston and Gray (2000) adopted Lloyd's insight when they calculated the transfer efficiency of an STE as compared with a targeted export subsidy. Using a simulation model calibrated to the Canadian wheat market, they were able to calculate the welfare effects of these two alternative instruments and thus their transfer efficiencies, where transfer efficiency refers to the dollar amount transferred to Canadian wheat growers per dollar of economic cost incurred in effecting the transfer. They also undertook some sensitivity analysis on the effects of the degree of oligopsony and oligopoly power. The conclusions drawn were sensitive to the assumptions made, but under some assumptions, and especially when market segmentation and price discrimination were allowed, it was found that the Canadian Wheat Board had higher transfer efficiency than an export subsidy programme.

McCalla and Schmitz (1982) were among the first to consider the international grains market as a mixed oligopoly, that is, a market structure in which private firms and STEs compete. They showed, using geometry, that such a structure would produce different conclusions about trade flows and prices than a model in which only firms had market power and behaved as profit maximizers. They concluded that, in order properly to analyse how world markets for grains operate, a better understanding is required of STEs.

Hamilton and Stiegert (2002) interpreted an STE as a pre-commitment device by a government in a model of strategic profit-shifting. Focusing on the Canadian Wheat Board's pricing policy for durum wheat as an example, they were unable to reject the hypothesis that the CWB was used as a disguized form of profit-shifting. The pricing policy strategy used by the Board is to give growers of durum wheat an initial price at planting time and to use that price as a basis for its later export sales of the crop. Then, if the realized sale price exceeds the initial price, the difference, less marketing costs, is returned to growers. However, there are no doubt other explanations for the Board's pricing behaviour which do not involve strategic behaviour of the profit-shifting kind hypothesized.

Thursby (1988) captured some stylized facts of the international wheat market in a three-country model. Two countries export to a third-country market. One exporting country has a profit-maximizing single exporter, the other an STE which maximizes returns to growers. In both countries there is domestic consumption. Her specification was motivated by some unrealistic features of models of rent-shifting when they are used in markets for agricultural products, for example, profit-maximizing firms produce a good and sell it directly to consumers abroad and there is no domestic consumption. Her objective was to determine optimal government intervention in the form of consumption, production and trade taxes in each exporting country given their differences in market structure and where the firms are marketing firms. In the rent-shifting literature it had been concluded initially that an export subsidy was an optimal policy. Thursby found that this conclusion could continue to hold for the country with the private monopolist, but in the country with a regulated STE, an export tax was optimal. Regulation in this instance means ensuring that the STE prices domestically where the inverse demand function intersects the supply function of the input. However, she found that if a domestic consumption tax/subsidy could be used with a trade policy, then the objective function of the marketing agent was irrelevant to the choice of instrument.

The approach used in the remainder of this chapter incorporates the notion of subsidy equivalent explored by Lloyd and the mixed oligopoly structure of McCalla and Schmitz. However, in what follows the marketing entities behave strategically as Cournot competitors. Governments do not appear here as behaving strategically, as they do in Thursby's model or in the rent-shifting model of Hamilton and Stiegert. The only role for government in the home country is to specify the objective function of the STE and to define its exclusive rights. The governments in the foreign country and in the importing country have no role.

## 3.  EXPORTS BY AN STE WITH EXCLUSIVE RIGHTS

The STE is assumed to have exclusive rights to procure the raw material in the home country and to sell it in both the home country and world market. It is assumed that the STE has an objective function which is not profit maximization but the maximization of returns to growers. This is the stated objective of both the Australian and Canadian Wheat Boards but, as noted above, STEs have a variety of objectives and this is but one, although an important, possibility.[15] In the foreign country, there are a given number, $m$, of commercial firms which are assumed to maximize profits from sales in their domestic market and the world market. The product produced in the home and the foreign countries is differentiated in the world market. The STE and the $m$ firms compete in the world market on the basis of quantities exported, that is, they are modelled as Cournot competitors of a differentiated product.

Let the objective function, $R$, of the STE be:

$$R = p_d(y^{STE}) \cdot y^{STE} + p_w(x^{STE} + X) \cdot x^{STE} - \int_0^{y^{STE} + x^{STE}} p_s d(y^{STE} + x^{STE}). \quad (8.1)$$

In common with many papers in both the agricultural trade literature and the industrial organization literature, linear functional forms have been chosen here and are used in the simulations presented below. The functions are as follows. The home country's domestic inverse demand function is $p_d(y^{STE}) = a - by^{STE}$, where $y^{STE}$ is the quantity sold by the STE in the domestic market. The inverse demand function in the world market facing the home country's exports is $p_w(x^{STE} + X) = a_1^w - b_1^w x^{STE} - \gamma X$, where $x^{STE}$ is the STE's export volume. $X$ is the export volume to the world market of the $m$ firms located in the foreign country. Recalling that the good exported by each country is differentiated, then $b_1^w \neq \gamma$. The STE purchases the raw material from the farm sector in the home country and is assumed to have no other costs.[16] The inverse supply function facing it is upward sloping and is given by $p_s = f + k(y^{STE} + x^{STE})$. This specification is realistic and, moreover, ensures that the domestic and export markets are interdependent.

In the foreign country each of the $m$ firms is assumed to maximize profits, $\Pi$. Let the objective function of the ith firm be:

$$\Pi_i = P_d(Y) \cdot Y_i + P_w(x^{STE} + X) \cdot X_i - P_s(Y + X) \cdot (Y_i + X_i) \quad (8.2)$$

The domestic inverse demand function is $P_d(Y) = A - BY$, where $Y = \sum_{i=1}^{m} Y_i = mY_i$ is the volume of domestic sales. The inverse demand function facing the ith foreign firm on the world market is $P_w(x^{STE} + X) = a_2^w - b_2^w X - \gamma x^{STE}$, where $X = \sum_{i=1}^{m} X_i = mX_i$ and $b_2^w \neq \gamma$. The inverse supply function of the input is $P_s = F + K(Y + X)$.

There are four first-order conditions, namely,

$$\frac{\partial R}{\partial y^{STE}} = \frac{\partial R}{\partial x^{STE}} = \frac{\partial \Pi_i}{\partial Y_i} = \frac{\partial \Pi_i}{\partial X_i} = 0.$$

It is assumed that the second-order conditions for a maximum hold in each case. Setting each partial derivative equal to 0 and rearranging, gives the following equations:

$$y^{STE} = \frac{(a-f) - kx^{STE}}{(2b+k)} \quad (8.3)$$

$$x^{STE} = \frac{(a_1^w - f) - ky^{STE} - \gamma X}{(2b_1^w + k)} \quad (8.4)$$

$$Y_i = \frac{(A-F) - K(m+1)X_i}{(B+K)(m+1)} \quad (8.5)$$

$$X_i = \frac{(a_2^w - F) - K(m+1)Y_i - \gamma x^{STE}}{(m+1)(b_2^w + K)} \quad (8.6)$$

For the purposes of the numerical simulation presented below, these four equations, together with the identities $Y = mY_i$ and $X = \sum_{i=1}^{m} X_i = mX_i$, are rearranged as the system of linear equations:

$$
\begin{bmatrix}
1 & \dfrac{k}{(2b+k)} & 0 & 0 & 0 & 0 \\[2ex]
\dfrac{k}{(2b_1^w+k)} & 1 & 0 & 0 & 0 & \dfrac{\gamma}{(2b_1^w+k)} \\[2ex]
0 & 0 & 1 & 0 & \dfrac{K}{(B+K)} & 0 \\[2ex]
0 & 0 & -m & 1 & 0 & 0 \\[2ex]
0 & \dfrac{\gamma}{(b_2^w+K)(m+1)} & \dfrac{K}{(b_2^w+K)} & 0 & 1 & 0 \\[2ex]
0 & 0 & 0 & 0 & -m & 1
\end{bmatrix}
$$

$$
\times
\begin{bmatrix}
y^{STE} \\
x^{STE} \\
Y_i \\
Y \\
X_i \\
X
\end{bmatrix}
=
\begin{bmatrix}
\dfrac{(a-f)}{(2b+k)} \\[2ex]
\dfrac{(a_1^w-f)}{(2b_1^w+k)} \\[2ex]
\dfrac{(A-F)}{(B+K)(m+1)} \\[2ex]
0 \\[2ex]
\dfrac{(a_2^w-F)}{(b_2^w+K)(m+1)} \\[2ex]
0
\end{bmatrix}
\tag{8.7}
$$

The two variables of interest are the volume of exports from the home country when exporting is conducted exclusively through the STE, $x^{STE}$, and exports from the foreign country, $X$. The calibrated simulation model permits a value to be found for $x^{STE}$ and for $X$. When the STE is deregulated, the market structure in the home country and in the world market will alter but it will not change in the foreign country because $m$ is assumed to be exogenous.

## 4. THE BENCHMARK

When the STE loses its exclusive rights or privileges, the market structure in the home country becomes one of mixed oligopoly and oligopsony while the world market remains characterized as a mixed oligopoly. It is assumed that $n$ commercial firms will now operate in the home country and will compete with the STE. The commercial firms are assumed to maximize short-run profit while the STE continues to maximize producer surplus. The *n* firms compete with the STE for raw material from the home country's domestic farm sector. The STE will be prepared to offer a higher price to the farm sector than will the commercial firms because its objective function is the maximization of returns to growers, not profit maximization. This competition moderates the ability of the commercial firms to exploit their oligopsonistic power and results in a higher level of purchases and sales than would be the case if there were no STE, but in a lower level of output than if the STE had exclusive rights. Hence the trade volumes will differ between these three cases as will the subsidy equivalent of the STE.

Let the profit function of the ith firm in the home country be:

$$\pi_i = p_d(y + y^{STE}) \cdot y_i + p_w(x + x^{STE} + X) \cdot x_i$$
$$- p_s(y + x + y^{STE} + x^{STE}) \cdot (y_i + x_i),$$

where *y* is domestic sales of the *n* commercial firms and *x* is their total exports. Then the two first-order conditions are:

$$y_i = \frac{(a - f) - (b + k)y^{STE} - k(n + 1)x_i - kx^{STE}}{(n + 1)(b + k)} \tag{8.8}$$

and

$$x_i = \frac{(a_1^w - f + s^e) - (b_1^w + k)x^{STE} - k(n + 1)y_i - ky^{STE} - \gamma X}{(n + 1)(b_1^w + k)}. \tag{8.9}$$

The appearance of the term $s^e$ in equation (8.9) reflects the specific export subsidy that would be required to equalize the exports from the home country in this benchmark with those when the STE has exclusive rights (equation (8.4)). Of course, in practice this term is not present. The subsidy equivalent of the single-desk STE will be positive if this STE exports more than does the benchmark, that is, the *n* commercial firms plus the STE without single-desk status. On the other hand, if the exclusive STE exports less than does the benchmark, then its subsidy equivalent will be negative and it acts like an export tax.

Equations (8.1) and (8.2) need to be modified to reflect the competition now faced by the STE. The STE's objective function becomes:

$$R = p_d(y + y^{STE}) \cdot y^{STE} + p_w(x + x^{STE} + X) \cdot x^{STE} - \int_0^q p_s d(q),$$

where $q = y^{STE} + x^{STE} + x + y$, with first-order conditions given by:

$$y^{STE} = \frac{(a-f) - n(b+k)y_i - knx_i - kx^{STE}}{(2b+k)} \tag{8.3'}$$

and

$$x^{STE} = \frac{(a_1^w - f) - n(b_1^w + k)x_i - kny_i - ky^{STE} - \gamma X}{(2b_1^w + k)}. \tag{8.4'}$$

In the foreign country, the $m$ firms continue to maximize profit. Equation (8.5) remains unchanged but the last term in the numerator of equation (8.6) needs to be revised to reflect exports from the $n$ commercial firms in the home country as well as from the STE. Hence, that term becomes $-\gamma(x^{STE} + x)$. Combining equations (8.3'), (8.4'), (8.5) and (8.6 as revised) with equations (8.8) and (8.9), noting that total exports from the foreign country remain as $X = mX_i$, and that exports from the home country are now given by $x^T = x^{STE} + \sum_{i=1}^{n} x_i = x^{STE} + nx_i$, the benchmark model can be written as the system of equations:

$$
\begin{bmatrix}
1 & \frac{1}{(n+1)} & 0 & \frac{k}{(b+k)} & \frac{k}{(n+1)(b+k)} & 0 & 0 & 0 & 0 & 0 \\[2ex]
\frac{n(b+k)}{(2b+k)} & 1 & 0 & \frac{nk}{(2b+k)} & \frac{k}{(2b+k)} & 0 & 0 & 0 & 0 & 0 \\[2ex]
-n & -1 & 1 & 0 & 0 & 0 & 0 & 0 & 0 & 0 \\[2ex]
\frac{k}{(b_1^w+k)} & \frac{k}{(n+1)(b_1^w+k)} & 0 & 1 & \frac{1}{(n+1)} & 0 & 0 & 0 & 0 & \frac{\gamma}{(n+1)(b_1^w+k)} \\[2ex]
\frac{nk}{(2b_1^w+k)} & \frac{k}{(2b_1^w+k)} & 0 & \frac{n(b_1^w+k)}{(2b_1^w+k)} & 1 & 0 & 0 & 0 & 0 & \frac{\gamma}{(2b_1^w+k)} \\[2ex]
0 & 0 & 0 & -n & -1 & 1 & 0 & 0 & 0 & 0 \\[2ex]
0 & 0 & 0 & 0 & 0 & 0 & 1 & 0 & \frac{K}{(B+K)} & 0 \\[2ex]
0 & 0 & 0 & 0 & 0 & 0 & -m & 1 & 0 & 0 \\[2ex]
0 & 0 & 0 & \frac{n\gamma}{(m+1)(b_2^w+K)} & \frac{\gamma}{(m+1)(b_2^w+K)} & 0 & \frac{K}{(b_2^w+K)} & 0 & 1 & 0 \\[2ex]
0 & 0 & 0 & 0 & 0 & 0 & 0 & 0 & -m & 1
\end{bmatrix}
$$

$$
\times
\begin{bmatrix}
y_i \\
y^{STE} \\
y^T \\
x_i \\
x^{STE} \\
x^T \\
Y_i \\
Y \\
X_i \\
X
\end{bmatrix}
=
\begin{bmatrix}
\dfrac{(a-f)}{(n+1)(b+k)} \\[2ex]
\dfrac{(a-f)}{(n+1)(b+k)} \\[2ex]
0 \\[2ex]
\dfrac{(a_1^w-f)}{(n+1)(b_1^w+k)} + \dfrac{s^e}{(n+1)(b_1^w+k)} \\[2ex]
\dfrac{(a_1^w-f)}{(2b_1^w+k)} \\[2ex]
0 \\[2ex]
\dfrac{(A-F)}{(m+1)(B+K)} \\[2ex]
0 \\[2ex]
\dfrac{(a_2^w-F)}{(m+1)(b_2^w+K)} \\[2ex]
0
\end{bmatrix}
\tag{8.10}
$$

The volume of total exports from the home country, $x^T$, as defined in equation (8.10), now needs to be compared with the value of exports ($x^{STE}$) obtained in equation (8.7) in order to gauge the size of the trade distortion caused by the STE with exclusive rights. It is unlikely that these export volumes will be equal because the market structure in the home country differs between the single-desk STE and the benchmark cases. It is now possible to solve for the specific export subsidy, $s^e$, which would cause total exports in the benchmark to equal those in the single-desk STE case. To measure the size and sign of this export subsidy, a calibrated numerical simulation model was constructed.

## 5. THE SIMULATION MODEL

In international markets for agricultural products, wheat is an important commodity, with Canada and the USA being the major exporters. The other three exporters are Argentina (commercial firms), Australia (STE) and the European Union (commercial firms).[17] Hence the international wheat market can be characterized as a mixed oligopoly. Exports from Canada are controlled by the Canadian Wheat Board (CWB), which also controls the bulk of domestic sales. Exports from, and domestic sales in, the USA are undertaken by commercial firms.[18] These two countries,

Canada and the USA, provide the empirical counterparts to home and foreign, respectively, used in the theory sections above.

Export prices were calculated as unit export values from the export values and volumes data published by the Food and Agriculture Organization (FAO). For the USA, the farm-gate price and the domestic price (at Kansas) were obtained from the Foreign Agriculture Service (FAS) of the US Department of Agriculture. For Canada, the farm-gate price was obtained from the OECD data which are used to calculate the Producer Support Estimate (PSE) and the domestic price is the price at St Lawrence (FAS). A summary of these data is shown in Table 8.1. The considerable differences in prices between the two countries at the same level in the marketing chain should be noted.

In order to construct the calibrated simulation model, the relevant data for wheat for Canada and the USA were used to estimate the intercepts and slopes of the linear inverse demand and supply functions, given external estimates of the price elasticities of these functions. The external demand estimates used were those provided by Alston and Gray, namely, −2.54 for each country. The price elasticity of farm product supply was set at 1.0 for each country. The substitution elasticity between Canadian and US wheat in the world market was set at 3. The parameters of the export demand equations for each country were less straightforward to derive because of the assumption that wheat from each country is differentiated in the world market. However, Dixit (1988) has provided a method for dealing with this case. Export volumes and prices were used together with an estimate of the price elasticity of demand in the world market and an estimate of the elasticity of substitution between the two products. This calibration exercise provided estimates of the parameters $a_1^w$, $a_2^w$, $b_1^w$, $b_2^w$, $a$, $A$, $b$, $B$, $k$, $K$ and $\gamma$, which appear in equations (8.7) and (8.10).

Table 8.1   *Price and quantity data for calibration, 2000*

|                                      | USA    | Canada | Source[a]    |
|--------------------------------------|--------|--------|--------------|
| Domestic farm price (US$/tonne)      | 94     | 85     | A&G and FAO  |
| Domestic price (US$/tonne)           | 113    | 149    | A&G and FAO  |
| Export price (US$/tonne)             | 122    | 133    | A&G and FAO  |
| Domestic sales ($10^6$ tonnes)       | 32.927 | 8.032  | A&G and FAO  |
| Exports ($10^6$ tonnes)              | 27.830 | 18.772 | A&G and FAO  |

*Note:*
[a]  A&G refers to Alston and Gray (2000) as the data source. FAO is the Food and Agriculture Organization, available at http://www.fao.org.

*Table 8.2   Subsidy equivalent of the STE*

| $m = 20$, world $\eta^d = -20$ | |
| --- | --- |
| $n$ | $s^e$ (US$/t) |
| 1 | 24.5 |
| 2 | 22.4 |
| 3 | 20.8 |
| 4 | 19.4 |
| 5 | 18.3 |
| 10 | 14.6 |
| 20 | 11.4 |

The estimates of the parameters were substituted into equation (8.7) and a numerical value for the exports of the single-desk STE obtained. Similarly, a value for exports in the benchmark (equation (8.10)) was obtained for a given value of $n$ and of $m$. Given these two values for exports, the second of which is also a function of the specific export subsidy, it was possible to solve for the level of the export subsidy, $s^e$, which equates them. The estimates obtained are provided in Table 8.2 for a given number of foreign firms, $m = 20$, and for a given value of the price elasticity of demand in the world market, $\eta^d = -20$.

It would be expected that as the number of firms in the benchmark increases and it becomes more competitive, total exports from the home country would increase, thus reducing the gap between the lower level of exports in the benchmark and those in the single-desk case. Recall that while the single-desk STE does not exploit its monopsony power and, hence, buys and sells more of the product, the $n$ commercial firms will try to exploit their oligopsony power by restricting purchases and sales but are constrained by the STE from doing so fully. The increasing level of exports, as $n$ increases, should be revealed in a fall in the subsidy equivalent of the STE. As is evident from Table 8.2, this is the observed outcome. Hence it may be concluded that the STE does act as equivalent to an export subsidy because, given the parameter values, the subsidy is positive.

A limited amount of sensitivity analysis was undertaken. First, suppose that the number of firms in the foreign country had been 5 or 10 rather than the 20 assumed above and that the number in the home country was 5. The effect of the size of $m$ on the size of the export subsidy is such that $s^e = $ US$18.2/t at $m = 5$ and US$18.3/t at $m = 10$ as compared with US$18.3 at $m = 20$ (Table 8.2). It would appear that the subsidy equivalent of the STE is almost entirely insensitive to the number of firms in the foreign country. The reason for the relative insensitivity to $m$ is due to the elasticity of the world demand function. Since this is relatively elastic, the mark-up is small and so will be the response of the mark-up to a change in the number of foreign firms. This outcome is in contrast with that with respect to the number of firms in the home country (Table 8.2).

Second, suppose that wheat from the two countries is homogeneous, that is, $b_1^w = b_2^w = \gamma = b^w$. The effect of this assumption on the size of the export subsidy is shown in Table 8.3. If the home country's and the foreign country's wheat were assumed to be homogeneous, then the trade-distorting effect of the STE is greater than it is in the differentiated products case (Table 8.2). This outcome arises because with the two sources of wheat being very close substitutes, an export subsidy (implicit or explicit) from one country will capture a higher share of the world market from its competitor. Hence the subsidy equivalent is larger, the more homogeneous the commodity from alternative sources.

Third, suppose that the home country government chose to remove the STE altogether, rather than just to deregulate it. The effects of this more drastic change in the competitive structure of the marketing of the home country's wheat are shown in Table 8.4. Comparing the subsidy equivalents in Tables 8.2 and 8.4 for given values of $n$, it is clear that, when compared with the new benchmark in which there is no STE (Table 8.4), the trade-distorting effects of the exclusive STE are quite different at small values for $n$ from those of the STE which competes with $n$ domestic firms (Table 8.2). The intuition in this case is that if the STE is replaced with a small-number commercial oligopoly, the trade distortion created by the STE would be greater than it was when compared with the original benchmark. The commercial oligopoly would now be able fully to exploit its buying power, reduce its purchases from the level that would prevail in the mixed oligopoly/oligopsony case and thus reduce exports further from those in the original benchmark. As $n$ increases, oligopsony power is weakened, purchases

*Table 8.3  Subsidy equivalent with homogeneous wheat*

| $m = 20$, world $\eta^d = -20$ | |
|---|---|
| $n$ | $s^e$ (US$/t) |
| 1 | 27.3 |
| 2 | 24.8 |
| 3 | 22.8 |
| 4 | 21.3 |
| 5 | 20.0 |
| 10 | 16.1 |
| 20 | 12.8 |

*Table 8.4   Subsidy equivalent for the home country
with no STE*

| $m = 20$, world $\eta^d = -20$ | |
|---|---|
| $n$ | $s^e$ (US\$/t) |
| 1 | 84.7 |
| 2 | 45.3 |
| 3 | 32.2 |
| 4 | 25.7 |
| 5 | 21.7 |
| 10 | 13.9 |
| 20 | 9.9 |

from the farm sector rise and so too do exports, and the export subsidy
equivalent should fall. This convergence is illustrated by the subsidy equivalents being \$9.9 (Table 8.4) and \$11.4 (Table 8.2), respectively, when $n = 20$.
However, in both benchmarks, commercial firms still export less than does
the single-desk STE; $s^e$ remains positive.[19]

## 6.   DISCUSSION AND CONCLUSIONS

State trading remains a feature of certain international markets despite the
substantial amount of deregulation which has occurred in recent years.
Although STEs have been recognized in the GATT since its inception, the
way in which some types of STE pursue their objectives sits uneasily with
the market-based premises which guide the formulation of the rules gov-
erning international trade. In particular, it is not easy to understand how
entities that are not pursuing profit maximization can act in a way that is
consistent with 'commercial considerations'.

STEs remain common and important in the agricultural sector. Disquiet
about their potential to circumvent elements of the WTO Agreement on
Agriculture, in particular violating the constraints on export subsidies and
tariff bindings, has led to several proposals designed to discipline and curtail
their activities by insisting on greater transparency of their commercial
undertakings. These proposals have been submitted to the agriculture
negotiations currently under way in the WTO. Essentially, and unusually,
common ground has been found on an agricultural issue between the EU,
Japan and the USA, namely, the need to discipline exporting STEs.

The purpose in this chapter has been to explore the position of STEs in
the GATT/WTO and to evaluate the specific proposal made by the USA

which is designed to alter the effects on international trade of STEs exporting agricultural products. A three-region model was developed which allowed expressions for exports from the home country to be developed in two situations. The first situation, or *status quo*, involved a single-desk STE exporting to a third-country market in competition with differentiated exports from commercial firms in a foreign country. The second situation was one in which the STE lost its exclusive rights to sell in the domestic and export markets. Using a calibrated simulation model, it was shown that the home country exports more when using a single-desk STE than it does when using a mixture of the STE and commercial firms. Hence the STE does act as an implicit export subsidy and distorts trade, to the detriment of the foreign country.[20] However, the extent to which trade is distorted depends upon the number of firms which enter the home country upon deregulation of the STE. When that number is small, the subsidy equivalent of the STE is high; but when that number is large, the trade-distorting effects of the STE are much reduced.

There are two overall conclusions to this chapter. First, and of most direct relevance to the current WTO negotiations, STEs have the potential to distort trade and, therefore, they are a legitimate issue for negotiation along with other more obvious trade policy instruments. What has not been explored are the welfare effects in the home country, the foreign country and the importing region, although it is clear from the positive implicit export subsidy which the STE represents, that the signs of the welfare changes will differ among the various participants. On balance, the overall welfare gains may well be illusory when compared with those achieved against the often-assumed benchmark of perfect competition. Second, the implied trade-distorting effect depends on how competitive the post-STE market becomes and the nature of the deregulation that may occur if the eradication of exclusive rights of STEs is successfully negotiated in the WTO. As shown in the discussion above, the trade-distorting effect of single-desk STEs is much more significant when compared with a benchmark in which they were to be completely removed (say through privatization) than if they were allowed to remain but to compete with commercial firms.

## NOTES

\*   Presented at the *Festschrift* in honour of Peter J. Lloyd, The University of Melbourne, 23 and 24 January 2003. Revised June 2003.
1.   Hoekman and Kostecki (2001) summarize the experience in the GATT of admitting the centrally planned countries of Eastern Europe.
2.   Croome (1995, pp. 217–18) provides a brief history of the negotiations on STEs in the Uruguay Round.

3.  Price equalization occurs when producers receive an average of the differentiated prices obtained from sales by the STE in different market segments. Price pooling occurs when producers receive a price which is averaged across all producers in a given time period (Sieper, 1982, p. 39).

4.  Revised rules for notifications of STEs to the WTO Working Party on STEs and the introduction of counter-notification and reviews were innovations to emerge from the Uruguay Round (Croome, 1995, p. 87).

5.  For a discussion of the several objectives of the STEs that have been notified to the WTO Working Group on STEs, see OECD (2001). For an analysis of these and other object-ives thought to be achievable by exporting STEs, see the Productivity Commission (2000).

6.  In the review of the export arrangements for Australian wheat it was concluded, *inter alia*, that '[b]ecause of uncertainty about the magnitude of these three key effects ('single-desk price premiums', innovation in marketing, and grain supply chain costs), there is also some uncertainty about whether there are or are not net benefits to Australian wheat-growers and to the Australian community from the WMA [Wheat Marketing Act 1989]' (Irving et al., 2000, p. 7).

7.  These are two major concerns but there are others, for example, their role in adminis-tering tariff rate quotas. See OECD (2001) and Abbott (2002) for a description and analysis.

8.  These negotiations were mandated by Article 20 of the WTO Agreement on Agriculture but, since the Doha Ministerial Meeting of November 2001, they have become part of the single undertaking, that is, the Doha Round.

9.  A second point dealt with the financing arrangements between the STE and the govern-ment, for example, underwriting, and the third point related to information to be pro-vided annually to the Committee on Agriculture, for example, acquisition costs and export prices on a transaction-specific basis (p. 2).

10. The consequences for international trade of importing STEs is not analysed here, but see McCorriston and MacLaren (2002a).

11. This type of STE is typified by the Canadian Wheat Board and, before 1989, by the Australian Wheat Board (AWB). Since 1989, the AWB has had to compete in the domes-tic market for wheat both as a buyer and as a seller. However, it continues to retain its rights as the sole exporter. A similar arrangement exists for exports of Australian sugar, for which the Queensland Sugar Corporation is the sole exporter.

12. For the purposes of analysis we ignore the possibility that multinational firms may operate as buyers in both the home and the foreign country once the STE loses its special rights. Moreover, because of the import restrictions which are so common for agricul-tural products, we assume that firms in the home country do not import the product from the foreign country, and vice versa.

13. See OECD (2001) for a description of them.

14. The exact definition of each of these terms is to be found in Lloyd (1982, p. 125). In summary they are as follows. One instrument is equivalent to another if it replicates the market outcome of the other. Quasi-equivalence occurs when one instrument reproduces the same value of a variable or subset of variables as another instrument. Important in these definitions are the concepts of existence (of a value for an instrument) and unique-ness (of its value).

15. McCorriston and MacLaren (2002b) specified a general weighted objective function and derived expressions of the export subsidy equivalent of the STE in order to explore the effects on trade of alternative weighting schemes on consumers, producers and taxpayers.

16. Recall that the issue of the relative marketing costs of an STE and commercial firms is not an aspect of the debate about STEs being pursued here.

17. There is some dispute about whether the EU exports wheat in such a way that it should nominate to the WTO its procedure as an STE. Exports of wheat from the EU normally receive an export subsidy. The amount of the subsidy is decided by the appropriate commodity management committee in the European Commission and is defined for

specific destinations and for specific periods of time. For a discussion and a case that the EU's system of intervention buying and export restitutions, taken in its totality, constitutes as STE, see Rude and Annand (2002).

18. During the period 1985–95, the US Export Enhancement Program (a targeted export subsidy programme) was active in international wheat markets. In 1995, the Commodity Credit Corporation (the CCC is a government agency) was notified to the WTO as an STE, even although it was not directly involved in trade. With the suspension of EEP for wheat, notification also ceased, although other export subsidy programmes continue through the CCC. This example, together with that of the EU (see note 17), illustrates Petersmann's argument (see above) that, under Article XVII:1(a), any state enterprise is covered, not just those granted exclusivity with respect to trade, as occurs in the working definition.

19. It would have been possible to alter the model to reflect the position of the Australian Wheat Board, which competes in the domestic market with a commercial oligopoly but has sole rights to export. Such a simulation was not conducted but, from the intuition developed from equations (8.7) and (8.10), it is possible to conclude that the AWB would represent a smaller export subsidy equivalent, *ceteris paribus*, than a single-desk STE because of its weaker ability to price-discriminate.

20. We have shown elsewhere (McCorriston and MacLaren, 2002c) that if the foreign country uses an explicit export subsidy and the home country has an STE, then the gains to the foreign country from a reduction in, or the removal of, its export subsidy are less than they would be in a situation in which the home country has no STE. This result lends support to the negotiating position on export competition adopted by the EU in the Doha Round.

# REFERENCES

Abbott, P.C. (2002), 'Tariff rate quotas: failed market access instruments?', *European Review of Agricultural Economics*, **29**, 109–30.

Alston, J.M. and Gray, R. (2000), 'State trading versus export subsidies: the case of Canadian wheat', *Journal of Agricultural and Resource Economics*, **25**, 51–67.

Bagwell, K. and Staiger, R.W. (2000), 'GATT-Think', NBER Working Paper, No. 8005.

Brander, J.A. and Krugman, P. (1983), 'A reciprocal dumping model of international trade', *Journal of International Economics*, **15**, 313–23.

Carter, C.A., Loyns, R.M.A. and Berwald, D. (1998), 'Domestic costs of statutory marketing boards: the case of the Canadian Wheat Board', *American Journal of Agricultural Economics*, **80**, 313–24.

Croome, J. (1995), *Reshaping the World Trading System: A History of the Uruguay Round*, Geneva: World Trade Organization.

Davey, W.J. (1998), 'Article XVII GATT: An overview', in T. Cottier and P.C. Mavriodis (eds), *State Trading in the 21st Century*, Ann Arbor, MI: Michigan University Press, pp. 17–36.

Dixit, A.D. (1988), 'Optimal trade and industrial policies for the US automobile industry', in R. Feenstra (ed.), *Empirical Methods for International Trade*, Cambridge, MA: MIT Press, pp. 141–65.

Food and Agriculture Organisation (FAO). Statistical Databases. Available at: http://www.fao.org.

Hamilton, S.F. and Stiegert, K.W. (2002), 'An empirical test of the rent-shifting hypothesis: the case of state trading enterprises', *Journal of International Economics*, **58**, 135–57.

Hoekman, B.M. and Low, P. (1998), 'State trading: rule making alternatives for entities with exclusive rights', in T. Cottier and P.C. Mavriodis (eds), *State Trading in the 21ˢᵗ Century*, Ann Arbor, MI: Michigan University Press, pp. 327–44.

Hoekman, B.M. and Kostecki, M.M. (2001), *The Political Economy of the World Trading System*, 2nd edn, Oxford: Oxford University Press.

Irving, M., Arney, J. and Lindner, R. (2000), *National Competition Policy Review of the Wheat Marketing Act 1989*, Canberra.

Lloyd, P. (1982), 'State trading and the theory of international trade', in M.M. Kostecki (ed.), *State Trading in International Markets*, London: Macmillan, pp. 117–41.

Mattoo, A. (1998), 'Dealing with monopolies and state trading enterprises: WTO rules for goods and services', in T. Cottier and P.C. Mavriodis (eds), *State Trading in the 21ˢᵗ Century*, Ann Arbor, MI: Michigan University Press, pp. 37–70.

McCalla, A.F. and Schmitz, A. (1982), 'State trading in grain', in M.M. Kostecki (ed.), *State Trading in International Markets*, London: Macmillan, pp. 55–77.

McCorriston, S. and MacLaren, D. (2002a), 'The trade distorting impact of state trading enterprises in importing countries', mimeo, University of Exeter.

McCorriston, S. and MacLaren, D. (2002b), 'Do state trading exporters distort trade?', mimeo, University of Exeter.

McCorriston, S. and MacLaren, D. (2002c), 'Perspectives on the state trading issue in the WTO negotiations', *European Review of Agricultural Economics*, **29**, 131–54.

OECD (2001), *State Trading Enterprises in Agriculture*, Paris: Organization for Economic Cooperation and Development (OECD).

Petersmann, E.-U. (1998), 'GATT law on state trading enterprises: critical evaluation of Article XVII and proposals for reform', in T. Cottier and P.C. Mavriodis (eds), *State Trading in the 21ˢᵗ Century*, Ann Arbor, MI: Michigan University Press, pp. 71–96.

Productivity Commission (2000), 'Single-desk marketing: assessing the economic arguments', Staff Research Paper, Canberra: AusInfo.

Rude, J. and Annand, M. (2002), 'European Union grain export practices: do they constitute a state trading enterprise?', *The Estey Centre Journal of International Law and Trade Policy*, **3** (2), 176–202.

Sieper, E. (1982), *Rationalising Rustic Regulation*, Sydney: Centre for Independent Studies.

Thursby, M. (1988), 'Strategic models, market structure and state trading', in R. Baldwin (ed.), *Trade Policy Issues and Empirical Analysis*, Chicago, IL: University of Chicago Press, pp. 79–105.

United States Department of Agriculture (USDA) (2002), Actual language of US WTO Agriculture Proposal presented in Geneva, http://www.fas.usda.gov/itp/wto/actual.htm.

WTO (1995), *The Results of the Uruguay Round of Multilateral Trade Negotiations: The Legal Texts*, Geneva: World Trade Organization.

WTO (2000a), Proposal for Comprehensive Long-Term Agricultural Trade Reform, Submission from the United States, G/AG/NG/W/15, Geneva, 15 June.

WTO (2000b), WTO Negotiations on Agriculture: Cairns Group Negotiating Proposal – Export Competition, G/AG/NG/W/11, Geneva, 16 June.

WTO (2000c), EC Comprehensive Negotiating Proposal, G/AG/NG/W/90, Geneva, 14 December.

WTO (2000d), Negotiating Proposal by Japan On WTO Agricultural Negotiations, G/AG/NG/W/91, Geneva, 21 December.

WTO (2000e), WTO Negotiations on Agriculture: Negotiating Proposal by Mauritius, G/AG/NG/W/96, Geneva, 28 December.

WTO (2001), State Trading Enterprises, Proposal by Argentina, Brazil, Paraguay and Uruguay (MERCOSUR), Chile and Colombia, G/AG/NG/W/104, Geneva, 23 January.

WTO (2002), Cairns Group: Export Competition (further commitments), Negotiating Proposal on Export Competition, http://www.cairnsgroup.org/ proposals/ export_competition_fc.pdf.

PART FOUR


New Applications of Trade Theory

# 9. Consumption and production externalities in a small open economy with accumulating capital*

**Stephen J. Turnovsky and Wen Fang Liu**

## 1. INTRODUCTION

The role of distortions in international economies was an early interest of Peter Lloyd during the period that he and one of the present authors (Stephen Turnovsky) were colleagues at the Australian National University. Distortions may manifest themselves in diverse ways and Peter's research focused on the role of taxes and subsidies; see Lloyd (1973, 1974). Recently there has been a surge of interest in the effects of distortions arising through the presence of externalities. At issue here is the failure of agents to recognize their individual contributions to the collective economic environment, which in turn influences their own behaviour. Indeed, externalities are an integral aspect of a modern interdependent economy. The fact that households interact with one another makes it inevitable that their choices will influence one another directly, in addition to any impact that may occur through the marketplace. Economists are, of course, well aware of this phenomenon and the role of externalities has been widely studied in a variety of contexts.

Externalities can be usefully categorized as being consumption externalities, on the one hand, and production externalities, on the other. Consumption externalities have been extensively studied in the context of models of 'jealousy' and 'keeping up with the Joneses'. For example, Abel (1990) and Gali (1994) studied the effects of consumption externalities on asset pricing and the equity premium, while Ljungqvist and Uhlig (2000) analysed the impact of consumption externalities on the effect of short-run macroeconomic stabilization policy. Dupor and Liu (2003) defined alternative forms of consumption externalities and explored their relationship with equilibrium overconsumption. These models are all either pure consumption models that take output as given, or alternatively, assume a simple production technology in which labour is the only productive input.

Production externalities provided the cornerstone of endogenous growth models pioneered by Romer (1986). The key feature of this literature is that although the individual firm's capital stock may be subject to diminishing marginal physical product, the presence of an aggregate production externality enhances its productivity to such a degree that in equilibrium the economy is capable of sustaining a steady growth rate. The externality may be due to the presence of the aggregate capital stock, which serves as a proxy for technology or knowledge, as in Romer's original contribution, or it may be due to productive government expenditure, as in Barro (1990) and Turnovsky (1996).

The question of how these two types of externalities affect the performance of a growing economy is important. To what extent do they introduce distortions into the capital accumulation process, and if so, what are the appropriate corrective policy responses? The existing analyses of this issue have been restricted to closed economies, both in the context of the endogenous growth model and the Ramsey model. A well-known characteristic of the Romer model is that a positive production externality has been shown to lead to overconsumption and to suboptimally low growth. Carroll et al. (1997) introduce what they call comparison utility into an AK growth model, according to which individuals care about current consumption compared to some reference measure based on past consumption (either the agent's own or the economy-wide average), but do not address efficiency issues.[1] Fisher and Hof (2000) introduce a consumption externality ('conspicuous consumption') into a simple Ramsey model having fixed labour supply. Liu and Turnovsky (2005) present a more comprehensive analysis, considering both forms of externalities simultaneously, thereby allowing for their interaction. In addition, they consider both the Ramsey and the endogenous growth model and contrast the impacts of externalities in the two cases.

The fact that the role of externalities has not been addressed in international models of capital accumulation is a serious shortcoming for at least two reasons. First, the types of considerations that have led to their study in closed economies are just as important in an open economy, and perhaps even more so. Anecdotal evidence suggests that the consumption of imported goods (often perceived as luxury goods) in small economies is likely to arouse more jealousy than does domestic consumption. Second, the fact that agents may have access to an international financial market increases the possible ways they may respond to externalities (as well as other disturbances). In this chapter we introduce both consumption and production externalities into a stationary Ramsey model of a small open economy that accumulates capital and has access to an international financial market.[2] Indeed, as we shall show, the response of such an economy to externalities can be significantly different from what it would be in a closed economy.

Our results take the form of a series of propositions summarizing how the externalities influence the growth process, and proposing fiscal policies to correct for the distortions they may create. One general conclusion is that the importance of consumption externalities depends crucially upon whether or not labour supply is endogenous. If it is fixed, then consumption externalities have no impact on any aspect of the steady state of the economy. Moreover, nor will they have any effect on the transitional path, a result that in general does not obtain in a closed economy.

When labour is supplied elastically, a positive consumption externality leads to long-run capital and labour supply that are too low relative to their respective optima, while the economy over-accumulates traded bonds. These distortions can be easily corrected by an appropriate time-varying subsidy to consumption.

Production externalities always generate long-run distortions, irrespective of whether labour is fixed. Thus a positive production externality leads to a suboptimally low capital stock with an over-accumulation of traded bonds. This may lead to either overconsumption or underconsumption, and in either case the distortion can be corrected by an appropriate subsidy to capital. The two types of externalities will interact if and only if labour supply is endogenous. Thus, for example, with elastic labour supply, a production externality will, through its impact on the marginal product of private capital, affect the productivity of labour, and thus the leisure–consumption trade-off, thereby influencing the potency of the consumption externality on long-run consumption.

The rest of the chapter proceeds as follows. Section 2 begins by defining the two types of externalities and then introduces them into a basic one-good model of a small open economy, having access to a perfect world capital market. The macrodynamic equilibria for both the decentralized and centrally planned economies are then derived. Section 3 compares the effects of the externalities on the steady-state equilibria, while Section 4 analyses their dynamic effects in a simple case. Section 5 derives the tax policies that enable the decentralized economy to replicate the first-best optimum. Section 6 introduces a second (imported) consumption good, enabling the consumption externality to be associated with either the domestic or foreign good. The presence of a consumption externality associated with imports introduces a potential new role for tariffs, as a simple direct mechanism for eliminating the distortions that these externalities may create. Section 7 concludes, while some technical details are relegated to the Appendix.

## 2.   THE ANALYTICAL FRAMEWORK

We begin by considering a generic model of a small open economy that produces and consumes a single traded commodity.

**Preferences, Technology and Externalities**

Consider a small open economy populated by $N$ infinitely lived identical households, where $N$ remains constant through time. Let $x$ be the consumption of the representative household, $L$ be the labour input supplied by the household, and $X$ be the average per capita consumption, $X = \Sigma x/N$. Following Abel (1990) and Gali (1994), we assume the utility function of the typical household depends not only on its own consumption, $x$, and leisure, $l \equiv 1 - L$, but also on the average per capita consumption level, $X$: $U(x, X, l) \equiv U(x, X, 1 - L)$. We denote the marginal utility of private consumption, per capita aggregate consumption, and leisure by $U_x$, $U_X$ and $U_l$, respectively. We assume that agents derive positive marginal utility from their own consumption and leisure, that is, $U_x > 0$, $U_l > 0$. In addition, the utility function is concave in these two quantities, and we assume further, $U_{xl} \geq 0$, so that the marginal utility of private consumption increases with leisure.

The key issue concerns the externalities imposed by aggregate consumption on the well-being of the individual household. In considering the externality it is useful to contrast two different ways it may impinge on the agent. First, it may impact in a purely passive way, simply raising or lowering the welfare of the household, without necessarily generating any response in behaviour. Thus, following Dupor and Liu (2003), we may say that the household feels either jealous ($U_X < 0$) or admiring ($U_X > 0$) when other people's consumption increases. Second, the externality may induce some kind of direct response by the household, as a consequence of the interaction of aggregate consumption with other arguments in the household's utility function. This is often referred to as 'keeping up with the Joneses', for which different formulations can be found. Thus, for example, Gali (1994), in a model abstracting from labour supply, describes it in terms of the cross partial derivative $U_{xX}(x, X)/U_x(x, X) > 0$. However, this definition is not invariant with respect to the ordinal utility measure. For this reason, using a model with endogenous labour supply, Dupor and Liu (2003) specify it in terms of the effect of the average per capita consumption on the household's marginal rate of substitution between his own consumption and leisure.[3]

It is clear that the first type of externality is necessary for the existence of the second, but not vice versa.[4] Dupor and Liu (2003) documented that while jealousy and admiration are important for equilibrium overconsumption and underconsumption, keeping up with, or running away from, the Joneses are important for asset pricing. In our model, we show that with elastic labour supply, jealousy and admiration are the crucial factors in determining the qualitative long-run effects of consumption externalities. Whether the preferences exhibit keeping up with, or running away from, the Joneses is reflected in the magnitudes of the over- or underconsumption, as well as the speed of convergence.

We shall impose the following restrictions on the consumption externalities:

(i)   $U_x + U_X > 0$
(ii)  $U_{xx} + U_{xX} < 0$
(iii) $U_{lx} + U_{lX} \geq 0$

In effect these conditions assert that either the externality augments the direct effect, or, if it is offsetting, it is dominated by the direct effect. Thus, for example, if an individual along with the entire economy receives an additional unit of consumption, any negative effect due to jealousy ($U_X < 0$) is dominated by the direct positive effect of having more consumption.[5] These three conditions impose restrictions on the strength of these external consumption effects.

The agent has a production technology that is homogeneous of degree one in the private inputs, capital $k$ and labour $L$, with both factors having the usual positive, but diminishing, marginal physical product. This latter property, together with the homogeneity, implies the further restriction $F_{kL} > 0$. In addition, output also depends on the average (or aggregate) stock of capital, denoted by $K = \Sigma k/N$. Thus the overall production function is $F(k, K, L)$, where $F_k(k, K, L)$ denotes the marginal product of private capital, and $F_K(k, K, L)$ the marginal product of the public capital.

Analogous to consumption, at issue is the nature of the externality as specified by $F_K$. In the case that the average capital stock serves as a proxy for knowledge, as in Romer (1986, 1989), we assume $F_K > 0$ so that the aggregate capital stock generates a positive production externality. However, $F_K < 0$ may arise in a circumstance in which production depends upon a publicly provided input that is subject to some degree of congestion; see, for example, Eicher and Turnovsky (2000).[6]

As for consumption, we impose the following restrictions on the externality:

(i)   $F_k + F_K > 0$
(ii)  $F_{kk} + F_{kK} \leq 0$
(iii) $F_{Lk} + F_{LK} \geq 0$

Analogously, these conditions assert that either the externality reinforces the direct effect, or alternatively if it is offsetting, for example, if it is due to congestion, it is dominated by the direct effect. Thus, even if an increase in aggregate capital were to reduce the productivity of labour, when it occurs in conjunction with an increase in the individual's capital stock, labour productivity increases.

### Macrodynamic Equilibrium: Decentralized Economy

For our purposes, we can consolidate the consumption and production sector into a representative consumer–producer, as in Turnovsky (1997, ch. 3). The agent accumulates physical capital, with the expenditure on a given rate of investment, $\dot{k} = I$, being an increasing function of the rate of investment, as represented by the convex function $C(I)$, $C' > 0$, $C'' > 0$, where by choice of units we assume $C(0) = 0$, $C'(0) = 1$.[7] Capital does not depreciate. The agent may also accumulate bonds $b$, that are traded in the international financial market and pay an exogenous constant (real) world interest rate $r$.

The representative consumer–producer's decision is to choose his leisure, $l \equiv 1 - L$, consumption, $x$, and rates of accumulation of capital, $\dot{k}$, and traded bonds, $\dot{b}$, to maximize the concave utility function (where the rate of time discount $\beta$ is constant)

$$\int_0^\infty U(x, X, 1 - L)e^{-\beta t}dt, \tag{9.1a}$$

subject to the accumulation equations

$$\dot{b} = F(k, K, L) - x - C(I) + rb \tag{9.1b}$$
$$\dot{k} = I \tag{9.1c}$$

and initial conditions $k(0) = k_0$, $b(0) = b_0$.

We should emphasize at the outset that we will be focusing on symmetric equilibrium paths which, with all households being identical, are characterized by $x = X$, $k = K$, $b = B$, where analogously, $B = \Sigma b/N$. We will be evaluating the various derivatives at such a point. Thus, for example, $U_x(X, X, L) = \partial U(x, X, L)/\partial x|_{x=X}$ and likewise for the other derivatives.

Letting asterisks denote the equilibrium, a symmetric equilibrium is described by the equations (where in the symmetric equilibrium $k = K$, $b = B$, $x = X$)

$$U_x(X^*, X^*, 1 - L^*) = \bar{\lambda}^* \tag{9.2a}$$

$$U_l(X^*, X^*, 1 - L^*) = \bar{\lambda}^* F_L(K^*, K^*, L^*) \qquad (9.2b)$$

$$C'(I^*) = q^* \qquad (9.2c)$$

$$\dot{\lambda}^* = 0, \text{ i.e. } \lambda^* = \bar{\lambda}^* \qquad (9.2d)$$

$$\frac{F_k(K^*, K^*, L^*)}{q^*} + \frac{\dot{q}^*}{q^*} = r \qquad (9.2e)$$

$$\dot{K}^* = I^* \qquad (9.2f)$$

$$\dot{B}^* = F(K^*, K^*, L^*) - X^* - C(I^*) + rB^* \qquad (9.2g)$$

where $\lambda^*$ denotes the private shadow value of wealth in terms of traded bonds and $q^*$ is the market price of capital, together with the transversality conditions

$$\lim_{t \to \infty} \bar{\lambda}^* B^* e^{-rt} = \lim_{t \to \infty} q^* K^* e^{-rt} = 0. \qquad (9.2h)$$

These types of conditions are standard and have been discussed extensively elsewhere; see, for example, Turnovsky (1997). Equation (9.2a) equates the marginal utility of consumption to the shadow value of capital, while equation (9.2b) equates the marginal utility of leisure to the marginal utility of income forgone when leisure is increased by one unit. Equation (9.2c) determines the rate of investment by equating the marginal cost of an additional unit of capital to its shadow value. Equation (9.2d) is a consequence of the arbitrage condition equating the return on consumption to the constant return on traded bonds. With $r$, $\beta$ being constant through time, this implies that the marginal utility of wealth and therefore consumption will rise or fall indefinitely unless $r = \beta$ – a condition that we impose – in which case the marginal utility of wealth, $\lambda^*$, is constant through time. The final three equations describe the dynamics. Equation (9.2e) equates the rate of return on capital to the rate of return on traded debt, while (9.2f) describes the rate of capital accumulation in equilibrium. Finally, (9.2g) specifies balance of payments equilibrium. It asserts that the economy's current account equals the trade balance plus the balance on capital account. The agent's transversality condition on bonds also ensures that the nation remains intertemporally solvent.

Given $\bar{\lambda}^*$, equations (9.2) describe an autonomous dynamic system that can be solved in the following way. First, from equations (9.2a) and (9.2b) we may solve for $X^*$ and $L^*$ in terms of $K^*$ and $\bar{\lambda}^*$, while from (9.2c) we can solve for $I$ as a function of $q^*$. Next, substituting for these expressions into (9.2e) and (9.2f), we obtain an autonomous subsystem describing the dynamics of the capital stock and its shadow value, or the internal dynamics of the economy. Finally, substituting the solution for $K^*$ and $q^*$ into

(9.2g) yields the dynamics of the current account, or the external dynamics of the economy. All this is conditional on the given constant value of $\bar{\lambda}^*$, the value of which is obtained by solving (9.2g) and imposing the transversality condition, in (9.2h). An important consequence of the small economy having unrestricted access to the world capital market, and the resulting constancy of $\bar{\lambda}^*$, is that the steady state is dependent upon the initial stocks of assets, $K_0$, $B_0$; see Sen and Turnovsky (1989), Turnovsky (1997).

Performing this procedure, the linearized equilibrium dynamics of the decentralized economy can be described by the following:

$$K^*(t) - \bar{K}^* = (K_0^* - \bar{K}^*)e^{\mu^* t} \tag{9.3a}$$

$$q^*(t) - \bar{q}^* = \frac{\mu^*}{I'(\bar{q}^*)}(K^*(t) - \bar{K}^*) \tag{9.3b}$$

where bars denote steady-state values (to be determined in Section 3 below) and $\mu^* < 0$ is the unique stable eigenvalue and is the solution to the characteristic equation

$$\mu^{*2} - r\mu^* + I'[F_{kk}(\bar{K}^*, \bar{K}^*, \bar{L}^*) + F_{kK}(\bar{K}^*, \bar{K}^*, \bar{L}^*)$$
$$+ F_{kL}(\bar{K}^*, \bar{K}^*, \bar{L}^*)\partial L^*/\partial K^*] = 0 \tag{9.3c}$$

This solution reflects the well-known saddle-point property of the small open economy; see Turnovsky (1997).

Recall that the consumption externality associated with keeping up with the Joneses involves the cross partial derivatives, $U_{xX}$. This effect is incorporated in the term $\partial L^* / \partial K^*$, (computed from (9.2a) and (9.2b)), and thus influences the speed of convergence. Substituting (9.3a) and (9.3b) into (9.2g) and linearizing, the corresponding time path for traded bonds is given by[8]

$$B^*(t) - \bar{B}^*$$
$$= \left[\frac{F_k(\bar{K}^*, \bar{K}^*, \bar{L}^*) + F_K(\bar{K}^*, \bar{K}^*, \bar{L}^*) + F_L(\bar{K}^*, \bar{K}^*, \bar{L}^*)L_K^* - \mu^*}{\mu^* - r}\right]$$
$$\times (K^*(t) - \bar{K}^*). \tag{9.3d}$$

**Macrodynamic Equilibrium: Centrally Planned Economy**

In deriving his private optimum, the individual householder fails to internalize the externalities present in both consumption and production. As a consequence the consumption, capital and debt in a symmetric equilibrium may diverge from the socially optimal levels. To derive the optimal allocation of the economy, we consider a social planner who, in maximizing the objective (9.1a) subject to the resource constraints facing the economy, namely the accumulation equation and the current account balance, takes both externalities into account.

The corresponding macroeconomic equilibrium, denoted by tildes, comprises

$$U_x(\tilde{X}, \tilde{X}, 1 - \tilde{L}) + U_X(\tilde{X}, \tilde{X}, 1 - \tilde{L}) = \bar{\tilde{\lambda}} \tag{9.4a}$$

$$U_l(\tilde{X}, \tilde{X}, 1 - \tilde{L}) = \bar{\tilde{\lambda}} F_L(\tilde{K}, \tilde{K}, \tilde{L}) \tag{9.4b}$$

$$C'(\tilde{I}) = \tilde{q} \tag{9.4c}$$

$$\dot{\tilde{\lambda}} = 0, \text{ i.e. } \tilde{\lambda} = \bar{\tilde{\lambda}} \tag{9.4d}$$

$$\frac{F_k(\tilde{K}, \tilde{K}, \tilde{L}) + F_K(\tilde{K}, \tilde{K}, \tilde{L})}{\tilde{q}} + \frac{\dot{\tilde{q}}}{\tilde{q}} = r \tag{9.4e}$$

$$\dot{\tilde{K}} = \tilde{I} \tag{9.4f}$$

$$\dot{\tilde{B}} = F(\tilde{K}, \tilde{K}, \tilde{L}) - \tilde{X} - C(\tilde{I}) + r\tilde{B} \tag{9.4g}$$

and the transversality conditions

$$\lim_{t \to \infty} \bar{\tilde{\lambda}} \tilde{B} e^{-rt} = \lim_{t \to \infty} \tilde{q} \tilde{K} e^{-rt} = 0, \tag{9.4h}$$

where $\tilde{\lambda}$ and $\tilde{q}$ denote the social shadow values of wealth and capital in terms of traded bonds, respectively. The structure of (9.4) parallels that of (9.2). The key differences are between (9.2a) and (9.4a), where the latter reflects the consumption externality, and between (9.2e) and (9.4e), the latter reflecting the production externality.

These in turn are reflected in the optimal equilibrium dynamics, which can be described by the following:

$$\tilde{K}(t) - \bar{\tilde{K}} = (\tilde{K}_0 - \bar{\tilde{K}})e^{\tilde{\mu}t} \tag{9.5a}$$

$$\tilde{q}(t) - \bar{\tilde{q}} = \frac{\tilde{\mu}}{I'(\bar{\tilde{q}})}(\tilde{K}(t) - \bar{\tilde{K}}) \tag{9.5b}$$

(where bars denote steady-state values) and $\tilde{\mu} < 0$ is the solution to the characteristic equation

$$\tilde{\mu}^2 - r\tilde{\mu} + I'[F_{kk}(\bar{\tilde{K}}, \bar{\tilde{K}}, \bar{\tilde{L}}) + 2F_{kK}(\bar{\tilde{K}}, \bar{\tilde{K}}, \bar{\tilde{L}}) + F_{KK}(\bar{\tilde{K}}, \bar{\tilde{K}}, \bar{\tilde{L}})$$
$$+ (F_{kL}(\bar{\tilde{K}}, \bar{\tilde{K}}, \bar{\tilde{L}}) + F_{KL}(\bar{\tilde{K}}, \bar{\tilde{K}}, \bar{\tilde{L}}))\partial \tilde{L}/\partial \tilde{K}] = 0. \tag{9.5c}$$

The corresponding time path for traded bonds is given by

$$\tilde{B}(t) - \bar{\tilde{B}} = \left[ \frac{F_k(\bar{\tilde{K}}, \bar{\tilde{K}}, \bar{\tilde{L}}) + F_K(\bar{\tilde{K}}, \bar{\tilde{K}}, \bar{\tilde{L}}) + F_L(\bar{\tilde{K}}, \bar{\tilde{K}}, \bar{\tilde{L}})\tilde{L}_K - \tilde{\mu}}{\tilde{\mu} - r} \right] (\tilde{K}(t) - \bar{\tilde{K}}).$$

(9.5d)

Finally, many models treat labour as being supplied inelastically, in which case the first-order conditions for the labour/leisure decision (equations 9.2b and 9.4b) do not apply, but the remaining equations are unchanged. As we shall now see, whether labour is supplied inelastically or not is crucial for the role played by consumption externalities.

## 3. COMPARISON OF STEADY-STATE EQUILIBRIA

We begin by considering the long-term consequences of the two externalities, focusing on the steady-state equilibria. Steady state is reached when $\dot{q} = \dot{K} = \dot{B} = 0$, so that the accumulation of both capital and traded bonds ceases, and the price of capital is constant. Given our choice of units, this implies that the steady-state price of capital $\bar{q} = 1$ in both the decentralized and centrally planned economies. For notational simplicity, in this section we drop the bars we have been using to identify steady states.

**Inelastic Labour Supply**

We focus first on the case where labour is supplied inelastically. For the decentralized economy, the steady-state equilibrium satisfies

$$U_x(X^*, X^*) = \bar{\lambda}^*,$$

(9.6a)

$$F_k(K^*, K^*) = r,$$

(9.6b)

$$F(K^*, K^*) + rB^* = X^*$$

(9.6c)

together with

$$B_0 - B^* = \left[ \frac{F_k(K^*, K^*) + F_K(K^*, K^*) - \mu^*}{\mu^* - r} \right](K_0 - K^*),$$

(9.6d)

where

$$\mu^{*2} - r\mu^* + I'[F_{kk}(K^*, K^*) + F_{kK}(K^*, K^*)] = 0.$$

(9.6e)

With $q^* = 1$, in steady-state equilibrium, the private marginal product of capital equals the world interest rate (equation 9.6b), which determines the equilibrium capital $K^*$. Given $K^*$, the intertemporal solvency condition (9.6d) will determine the equilibrium stock of foreign assets owned or owed. With no steady-state investment, the amount of output available for domestic consumption then equals the amount of domestic output plus the earning from abroad, given in (9.6c).

The steady-state optimality conditions in the centrally planned economy are

$$U_x(\tilde{X}, \tilde{X}) + U_X(\tilde{X}, \tilde{X}) = \tilde{\bar{\lambda}}, \qquad (9.7a)$$

$$F_k(\tilde{K}, \tilde{K}) + F_K(\tilde{K}, \tilde{K}) = r, \qquad (9.7b)$$

$$F(\tilde{K}, \tilde{K}) + r\tilde{B} = \tilde{X}, \qquad (9.7c)$$

together with

$$B_0 - \tilde{B} = \left[ \frac{F_k(\tilde{K}, \tilde{K}) + F_K(\tilde{K}, \tilde{K}) - \tilde{\mu}}{\tilde{\mu} - r} \right] (K_0 - \tilde{K}), \qquad (9.7d)$$

where[9]

$$\tilde{\mu}^2 - r\tilde{\mu} + I'[F_{kk}(\tilde{K}, \tilde{K}) + 2F_{kK}(\tilde{K}, \tilde{K}) + F_{KK}(\tilde{K}, \tilde{K})] = 0. \qquad (9.7e)$$

The comparison of the steady states of the two economies is conducted by linearizing (9.6) about the socially optimal level defined in (9.7). Using (9.7b) we see that in the optimal allocation, (9.7d), simplifies to

$$B_0 - \tilde{B} = -(K_0 - \tilde{K}). \qquad (9.7d')$$

That is, every unit of capital that is accumulated throughout the transition is exactly offset by a reduction in the holding of foreign assets, so that the steady-state stock of wealth remains unchanged from its initial value.

In the Appendix, we show that to the first order (9.6d) is approximately

$$B_0 - B^* = -(K_0 - K^*) \qquad (9.6d')$$

and subtracting (9.6d') from (9.7d') we obtain

$$B^* - \tilde{B} = -(K^* - \tilde{K}) \qquad (9.8)$$

so that (9.8) implies that the deviation in the capital stock is exactly offset (to a linear approximation) by an equal deviation in the stock of bonds, leaving total wealth unchanged.

Because the representative household does not take account of the production externalities of capital, the equilibrium capital stock in the decentralized economy will be non-optimal. Linearizing (9.6b) about (9.7b), we obtain the approximation

$$K^* - \tilde{K} = \frac{F_K(\tilde{K}, \tilde{K})}{F_{kk}(\tilde{K}, \tilde{K}) + F_{kK}(\tilde{K}, \tilde{K})} \equiv \frac{\tilde{F}_K}{\tilde{F}_{kk} + \tilde{F}_{kK}}, \tag{9.9}$$

from which we see that the equilibrium level of capital differs from its socially optimal level if and only if $\tilde{F}_K$ is not zero. Now, linearizing (9.6c) about (9.7c) and using (9.7b) yields

$$X^* - \tilde{X} = (\tilde{F}_k + \tilde{F}_K)(K^* - \tilde{K}) + r(B^* - \tilde{B})$$
$$= r(K^* - \tilde{K}) + r(B^* - \tilde{B}) = 0 \tag{9.10}$$

With the equilibrium return to capital being exactly equal to the interest rate, any excess income from having too much capital, and therefore too much output, is exactly offset by an identical shortfall in income from the corresponding suboptimally low holding of traded bonds. Long-run personal income and consumption are therefore unaffected by the production externality. We may summarize these results with

**Proposition 1**   Consider a small open economy with inelastic labour supply in which there is a positive production externality, $(F_K > 0)$. In such an economy the steady-state equilibrium capital stock is below its optimal level $(K^* < \tilde{K})$, while its stock of bonds is correspondingly above its optimal level $(B^* > \tilde{B})$, leaving overall wealth and consumption unaffected. These relative sizes are reversed if the production externality is negative, $(F_K < 0)$. Consumption externalities have no effect on the steady-state equilibrium.

The effect of the production externality on capital and production remains identical to that in a closed economy. However, the consequences for consumption are fundamentally different. In a closed economy the underaccumulation of capital, and therefore the underproduction of output, leads to underconsumption.[10] In the present open economy the underaccumulation of capital causes an over-accumulation of foreign bonds, leaving overall income and consumption at its socially optimal level. As in the closed economy, consumption externalities play no role in determining the steady state, either directly or through their interaction with production externalities. This is because the steady-state capital stock, and therefore consumption, is determined by the production technology alone. With exogenous labour supply, consumption externalities, which impact through the labour–consumption trade-off, have no channel to affect steady-state output.

## Limitations of Linearization

It is important to emphasize that the expressions we have derived for the deviations between the equilibrium quantities in the decentralized economy and the socially optimal quantities have been obtained by linearizing the decentralized equilibrium about the centrally planned equilibrium. They are therefore first-order approximations only. While it is possible to compute second-order expansions of the equilibrium (9.6) about (9.7), this still would not necessarily yield a valid second-order, and therefore more accurate, approximation. This is because the intertemporal budget constraints (9.6d) and (9.7d), which are crucial components of the steady state, are themselves obtained by solving a linear approximation to the underlying dynamics. They therefore represent only a first-order approximation. Thus given that at least one of the underlying equilibrium relationships is only a linear approximation, we are unable to derive anything more accurate than a first-order approximation.

Nevertheless, it is instructive to consider the formal consequences of, instead, linearizing the optimal levels of the centrally planned economy about the decentralized equilibrium. The point can be illustrated by restricting ourselves to the case of an inelastic labour supply, although it applies to the more general case as well.

First, linearizing (9.7b) about (9.6b) yields

$$
\begin{aligned}
\tilde{K} - K^* &= -\frac{F_K(K^*, K^*)}{F_{kk}(K^*, K^*) + 2F_{kK}(K^*, K^*) + F_{KK}(K^*, K^*)} \\
&\equiv -\frac{F_K^*}{F_{kk}^* + 2F_{kK}^* + F_{KK}^*},
\end{aligned}
\tag{9.9'}
$$

the sign of which depends upon $F_K^*$.[11] As long as $F_K$ has a uniform sign, as we assume, then both (9.9) and (9.9') yield the same qualitative implications for $K^* - \tilde{K}$. Next, linearizing (9.7d) about (9.6d) yields

$$
\tilde{B} - B^* = -(\tilde{K} - K^*)
\tag{9.8}
$$

and finally, linearizing (9.7c) about (9.6c) and using (9.6b) and (9.8) yields

$$
\begin{aligned}
\tilde{X} - X^* &= (F_k^* + F_K^*)(\tilde{K} - K^*) + r(\tilde{B} - B^*) \\
&= F_K^*(\tilde{K} - K^*)
\end{aligned}
\tag{9.10'}
$$

Comparing (9.10) with (9.10′) yields an apparent contradiction. When we linearize around the centrally planned equilibrium we draw the conclusion, stated in Proposition 1, that consumption is unaffected by the production externality. Combining (9.9′) and (9.10′), we find that unless $F_K^* = 0$, $\tilde{X} > X^*$, implying underconsumption, irrespective of the sign of $F_K^*$. The issue can be readily resolved by observing (9.9′) and realizing that the right-hand side of (9.10′) is in fact a second-order term. Thus, to first order (9.10′) is zero, consistent with (9.10).

In most applications, whether one linearizes about point A or point B does not affect the qualitative implications, as long as the derivative of the function being linearized has the same sign at the two points. Indeed, this turns out to be the case as we extend the model in subsequent sections. But in this particular example, imposing the equilibrium conditions implies that the relevant derivative evaluated at the centrally planned equilibrium is zero, and that is the source of the apparent inconsistency. Clearly, this argues for working with second-order approximations, a position that has been argued by others in other contexts; see, for example, Judd (1998). Unfortunately, this does not seem to be tractable in this instance for the reason stated earlier that one of the intertemporal solvency conditions, crucial to the steady state, is itself derived from a linearized approximation to the underlying dynamics.

## Elastic Labour Supply

With endogenous labour supply, the steady state symmetric equilibrium in the decentralized economy is characterized by the following conditions:

$$U_x(X^*, X^*, 1 - L^*) = \bar{\lambda}^* \tag{9.11a}$$

$$U_l(X^*, X^*, 1 - L^*) = \bar{\lambda}^* F_L(K^*, K^*, L^*) \tag{9.11b}$$

$$F_k(K^*, K^*, L^*) = r \tag{9.11c}$$

$$F(K^*, K^*, L^*) + rB^* = X^*, \tag{9.11d}$$

together with

$$B_0 - B^*$$
$$= \left[ \frac{F_k(K^*, K^*, L^*) + F_K(K^*, K^*, L^*) + F_L(K^*, K^*, L^*)\partial L^*/\partial K^* - \partial X^*/\partial K^* - \mu^*}{\mu^* - r} \right]$$
$$\times (K_0 - K^*), \tag{9.11e}$$

where

$$\mu^{*2} - r\mu^* + I'[F_{kk}(K^*, K^*, L^*) + F_{kK}(K^*, K^*, L^*) + F_{kL}\partial L^*/\partial K^*] = 0$$

and the partial derivatives $\partial L^*/\partial K^*$, $\partial X^*/\partial K^*$ are computed from (9.7a) and (9.7b).

The steady-state optimality conditions for the planner's problem are

$$U_x(\tilde{X}, \tilde{X}, 1 - \tilde{L}) + U_{X'}(\tilde{X}, \tilde{X}, 1 - \tilde{L}) = \tilde{\lambda}, \tag{9.12a}$$

$$U_l(\tilde{X}, \tilde{X}, 1 - \tilde{L}) = \tilde{\lambda}F_L(\tilde{K}, \tilde{K}, \tilde{L}) \tag{9.12b}$$

$$F_k(\tilde{K}, \tilde{K}, \tilde{L}) + F_K(\tilde{K}, \tilde{K}, \tilde{L}) = r, \tag{9.12c}$$

$$F(\tilde{K}, \tilde{K}, \tilde{L}) + r\tilde{B} = \tilde{X}, \tag{9.12d}$$

together with

$$B_0 - \tilde{B} = \left[ \frac{F_k(\tilde{K}, \tilde{K}, \tilde{L}) + F_K(\tilde{K}, \tilde{K}, \tilde{L}) + F_L(\tilde{K}, \tilde{K}, \tilde{L})\partial \tilde{L}/\partial \tilde{K} - \partial \tilde{X}/\partial \tilde{K} - \tilde{\mu}}{\tilde{\mu} - r} \right]$$
$$\times (K_0 - \tilde{K}), \tag{9.12e}$$

where

$$\tilde{\mu}^2 - r\tilde{\mu} + I'[F_{kk}(\tilde{K}, \tilde{K}, \tilde{L}) + 2F_{kK}(\tilde{K}, \tilde{K}, \tilde{L}) + F_{KK}(\tilde{K}, \tilde{K}, \tilde{L})$$
$$+ [\tilde{F}_{kL} + \tilde{F}_{KL}]\partial \tilde{L}/\partial \tilde{K}] = 0$$

and the partial derivatives $\partial \tilde{L}/\partial \tilde{K}$, $\partial \tilde{X}/\partial \tilde{K}$ are computed from (9.12a) and (9.12b).

As in the case of fixed labour supply, (9.11e) and (9.12e) are the same to the first order of approximation. Using (9.12c), we can approximate these equations by

$$B_0 - \tilde{B} = -[1 + \theta](K_0 - \tilde{K}); \quad B_0 - B^* = -[1 + \theta](K_0 - K^*),$$

where

$$\theta \equiv \frac{-F_L \partial \tilde{L}/\partial \tilde{K} + \partial \tilde{X}/\partial \tilde{K}}{\tilde{\mu} - r} > 0.$$

An increase in the stock of capital will therefore be more than offset by a long-run reduction in foreign bonds, leading to an overall reduction in wealth; see Turnovsky (1997, ch. 3). Because of the endogenous labour supply decision, consumption externalities will now also affect the steady state. This is because they affect the marginal valuation of consumption, which in turn changes the optimal utility value of the marginal product of labour. Therefore, consumption distortion results in labour distortion, and thus creates production inefficiency.

To compare the steady-state equilibrium with the optimal steady-state allocation, we apply Taylor expansions to equations (9.11a)–(9.11e) around the optimal steady state $(\tilde{C}, \tilde{K}, \tilde{L}, \tilde{\lambda}, \tilde{B})$ defined in (9.12a)–(9.12e). From the results reported in the Appendix we observe the following. The coefficient of $U_X$ in equations (9A.7b) and (9A.7c) is negative, while for (9A.7d) it is positive, and for (9A.7a) it is ambiguous. As a result, admiration ($U_X > 0$) implies that steady-state equilibrium capital and labour input are both too low, while the stock of foreign assets is too high; consumption is ambiguous. Similarly, the coefficients of $F_K$ in equations (9A.7b) and (9A.7c) are negative, while the coefficient of $F_K$ in (9A.7d) is positive. A positive production externality from capital therefore leads to too little employment, too small a long-run capital stock and too much foreign lending. The effect of the production externality on consumption is ambiguous. This leads to the following proposition relating the actual and socially optimal equilibria in the presence of consumption and production externalities.

**Proposition 2**   In a small open economy with endogenous labour supply, the steady state equilibrium has the following properties. In the case of a positive consumption externality ($U_X > 0$), or if the production technology exhibits a positive aggregate capital externality ($F_K > 0$), the equilibrium capital stock and labour supply are both less than their respective long-run optimal values, while the stock of traded bonds is too high ($K^* < \tilde{K}$, $L^* < \tilde{L}$, $B^* > \tilde{B}$). Consumption may be either above or below its long-run optimum. In the case of a negative consumption (jealousy) or a negative production externality these relationships are reversed.

***Proof***   *See the Appendix.*

To understand these results in more depth, we first consider the effect of a consumption externality. The first-order condition in the household's maximization problem requires the marginal rate of substitution between consumption and leisure to equal the marginal product of labour. In the case of consumption admiration, equilibrium consumption is undervalued. Leisure is therefore overvalued, resulting in equilibrium leisure being too high, or equivalently, labour supply being too low, relative to the social optimum. Because capital and labour are complements, $F_{kL} \geq 0$, and since in the steady state the marginal product of capital is equal to $r$, a lower equilibrium labour input implies a suboptimally low equilibrium capital stock. With $\theta > 0$, this leads to a larger over-accumulation of foreign bonds, leading to an overall over-accumulation of wealth. The undervaluation of consumption causes equilibrium consumption to be suboptimally low, while the over-accumulation of wealth has the opposite effect. The net effect on consumption thus depends upon which effect prevails. The argument is reversed if preferences exhibit jealousy. From the expressions for the deviations of the decentralized equilibrium from the optimum provided in the Appendix (equations 9A.7), it is seen that consumption externalities due to keeping up with the Joneses are reflected in the magnitudes of the long-run deviations.

In the case of a positive production externality the private agent under-values the marginal product of capital. Since the marginal product of capital is diminishing, and the steady state requires the marginal product of capital to equal $r$, less capital is needed in the decentralized economy as compared to the socially optimal economy to achieve the equilibrium condition on the marginal product of capital. The reduction in capital is more than offset by the larger stock of foreign bonds, so that overall wealth rises. The production externality thus generates two effects on labour supply and consumption. First, because capital and labour are complements in production, the reduction in capital will reduce the marginal product of labour and thus reduce labour input in production, thereby reducing output and the amount available for consumption. Second, the accompanying higher flow of income from foreign lending raises consumption and the marginal utility of leisure, causing labour supply to fall further. These two effects are both negative and therefore reinforcing in so far as labour supply is concerned, while their impacts on consumption are offsetting.

Some aspects of these results contrast quite sharply with those obtained in a closed economy; see Liu and Turnovsky (2003). The difference arises from the fact that the absence of foreign debt in the closed economy means that adjustments that may be borne by external capital flows in the open economy must be accommodated by internal consumption flows in the closed economy. Thus, for example, without the possibility of capital flows, the presence of positive production externalities in a closed economy leads to unambiguously lower consumption, raising its marginal utility. This leads to a positive effect on labour supply, rendering the overall response of labour supply ambiguous.

## 4. DYNAMICS

Externalities not only create a divergence between the long-run competitive equilibrium and the socially optimal outcome, but they also affect the transitional dynamics. This section studies the convergence of the economy to the steady state in the presence of externalities. In particular, we will compare the transition of the competitive economy and the socially optimal path in response to an exogenous shock, say in technology, which has the effect of increasing the steady-state stock of capital. As noted, in the presence of a positive production externality, ignored by the private sector, this will lead to the long-run under-accumulation of capital in the decentralized economy.

We will focus primarily on an economy with exogenous labour supply, in which case (9.2a)–(9.2g) implies that the dynamics of the decentralized equilibrium can be described by:

$$U_x(X^*, X^*) = \bar{\lambda}^* \tag{9.2a'}$$

$$C'(I^*) = q^* \tag{9.2c}$$

$$\frac{F_k(K^*, K^*)}{q^*} + \frac{\dot{q}^*}{q^*} = r \tag{9.2e'}$$

$$\dot{K}^* = I^* \tag{9.2f}$$

$$\dot{B}^* = F(K^*, K) - X^* - C(I^*) + rB^*, \tag{9.2g'}$$

where $\bar{\lambda}^*$ is determined by the steady-state relationships (9.6). Following the same steps for the centrally planned economy leads to

$$U_x(\tilde{X}, \tilde{X}) + U_X(\tilde{X}, \tilde{X}) = \tilde{\lambda} \tag{9.4a'}$$

$$C'(\tilde{I}) = \tilde{q} \tag{9.4c}$$

$$\frac{F_k(\tilde{K}, \tilde{K}) + F_K(\tilde{K}, \tilde{K})}{\tilde{q}} + \frac{\dot{\tilde{q}}}{\tilde{q}} = r \tag{9.4e'}$$

$$\dot{\tilde{K}} = \tilde{I} \tag{9.4f}$$

$$\dot{\tilde{B}} = F(\tilde{K}, \tilde{K}, \tilde{L}) - \tilde{X} - C(\tilde{I}) + r\tilde{B}, \tag{9.4g'}$$

where $\tilde{\lambda}$ is determined by (9.7).

Suppose that only a consumption externality exists (that is, $F_K \equiv 0$). In that case we have seen from (9.6) that the steady state of the decentralized economy coincides with the social optimum. In particular, steady-state consumption in the decentralized economy coincides with its socially optimal level. But with the marginal utility of consumption being constant throughout the entire transition, it follows from (9.2a') and (9.4a') that consumption in both the decentralized and centrally planned economies remains constant throughout the transition, and remains equal to the socially optimal levels, that is, $X^*(t) = \bar{X}^* = \tilde{\bar{X}} = \tilde{X}(t)$, for all $t$. Since the rest of the equilibrium relationships in the two economies coincide, it follows that, with fixed labour supply, the consumption externality causes no effect during the transition. We thus obtain

**Proposition 3** In a small open economy with inelastic labour supply, consumption externalities have no effect on the resource allocation along the transitional dynamic path.

This result contrasts quite sharply with the corresponding result for a closed economy. In that case, Liu and Turnovsky (2003) showed that for a range of widely employed utility functions the consumption externality may affect the transitional paths for the decentralized and centrally planned economies identically, so that while there are effects, they are non-distortionary. However, in other cases they can affect the two transitional paths differentially, thereby generating real distortions.[12]

Consider now the case of a positive production externality. The linearized dynamics of capital accumulation in the decentralized economy are described by (9.3a) and (9.3b), where $\mu^* < 0$ is the solution to

$$\mu^{*2} - r\mu^* + I'(F_{kk}^* + F_{kK}^*) = 0. \qquad (9.3c')$$

Similarly, the 'internal' dynamics of the centrally planned economy are given by (9.5a) and (9.5b), where $\tilde{\mu} < 0$ is the solution to

$$\tilde{\mu}^2 - r\tilde{\mu} + I'(\tilde{F}_{kk} + 2\tilde{F}_{kK} + \tilde{F}_{KK}) = 0. \qquad (9.5c')$$

Since $I'(q^*) = I'(\tilde{q}) = I'(1)$, the deviation of the path of capital stock in the decentralized economy from the social optimum depends upon the deviation of $\mu^*$ from $\tilde{\mu}$. Linearizing (9.3c') about (9.5c') yields

$$\mu^* - \tilde{\mu} \approx \frac{I'}{2\tilde{\mu} - r}\left[(\tilde{F}_{kK} + \tilde{F}_{KK}) - \frac{(\tilde{F}_{kkk} + 2\tilde{F}_{kkK} + \tilde{F}_{kKK})}{(\tilde{F}_{kK} + \tilde{F}_{KK})}\tilde{F}_K\right].$$

For plausible production functions, such as the Cobb–Douglas, we find $\mu^* - \tilde{\mu}$ to be positive, implying

$$0 > \mu^* > \tilde{\mu}.$$

With the transitional dynamics being a one-dimensional locus, the speed of which is fully captured by the unique stable eigenvalue, it follows that the decentralized economy converges at a suboptimally slow rate.[13] In particular, capital is accumulated too slowly.

Figure 9.1a illustrates the transitional paths for investment in the two economies. With $0 > \mu^* > \tilde{\mu}$, it follows by comparing (9.3b) and (9.5b) that the stable saddle path in the decentralized economy is flatter than it is in the centrally planned economy. In addition, if we compare the two economies in a situation in which they happen to have the same capital stock, $K(t)$ say, less than the steady-state value in either economy, subtracting (9.5b) from (9.3b), while noting $\bar{q}^* = \bar{\tilde{q}} = 1$, we obtain

$$q^*(t) - \tilde{q}(t) = C''[(\mu^* - \tilde{\mu})(K(t) - \bar{K}^*) - \tilde{\mu}(\bar{K}^* - \bar{\tilde{K}})] < 0. \qquad (9.13)$$

Investment in the decentralized economy is therefore occurring at a suboptimally low rate. Using the argument in the Appendix, the transitional path for bond accumulation in the decentralized economy, (9.3d), to a linear approximation coincides with that in the optimal economy and is illustrated by the common locus YY in Figure 9.1b.

The transitional dynamics can be compared as follows. Suppose that the two economies have the same stock of physical capital, $K_0$ say. The decentralized economy will have a corresponding value of $q$ given by the point A, lying below C for the centrally planned economy. Capital in the decentralized economy will accumulate along the path AB, lying below the optimal path CD. The positive production externality leads to the steady-state stock of capital in the decentralized economy B being less than the optimum, D. Corresponding to the initial given capital stock $K_0$, both economies have the same stock of foreign bonds, $B_0$. As capital is accumulated they both reduce their bond holdings along the locus YY. The decentralized economy converges to Q, which lies above the optimal stock of bonds at R.

With fixed labour supply, consumption remains fixed at its optimum throughout the transition, just as was the case for the consumption externality. But if labour supply is endogenous, the deviation in consumption from its optimum will vary along the transitional path. This can be seen by linearizing (9.2a) and (9.2b) about (9.4a) and (9.4b) to yield:

$$X^*(t) - \tilde{X}(t) = \frac{1}{D'}([-(U_{ll} + \tilde{\lambda}F_{LL}) + U_{xl}F_L](\bar{\lambda}^* - \bar{\tilde{\lambda}})$$
$$+ U_{xl}\tilde{\lambda}(F_{Lk} + F_{LK})(K^*(t) - \tilde{K}(t))$$

where $D' \equiv -(U_{xx} + U_{xX})(U_{ll} + \tilde{\lambda}F_{LL}) + U_{xl}(U_{lx} + U_{lX}) < 0$. The first term in the numerator is the deviation in consumption due to the deviation in the marginal utility, which remains constant along the transitional path. The second is due to the divergent path of capital.

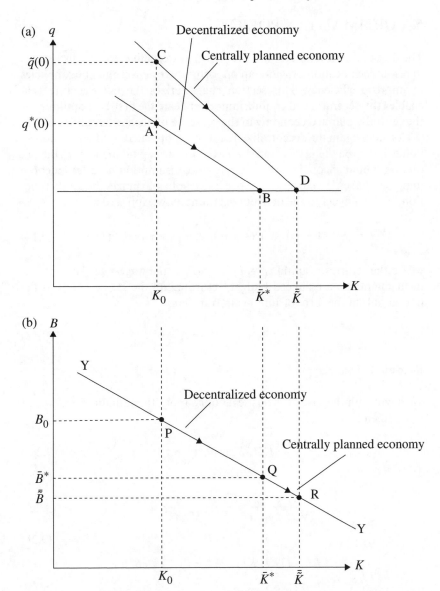

*Figure 9.1   Dynamic adjustment in presence of production externalities:*
*(a) investment paths for decentralized and centrally planned*
*economies; (b) time paths for asset accumulation in*
*decentralized and centrally planned economies*

## 5.   OPTIMAL TAX POLICY

The fact that consumption and production externalities create distortions in resource allocation provides an opportunity for government tax policies to improve efficiency. This section characterizes the tax structure that enables the decentralized equilibrium to replicate the first-best optimum of the centrally planned economy in the presence of such externalities.

Consider again the decentralized economy populated by identical households. Let $\tau_k$ be the tax rate on domestic private capital income, $\tau_w$ the tax rate on labour income, $\tau_c$ the tax rate on consumption, and let $v$ denote lump-sum taxes.[14] The representative household maximizes the utility function (9.1a), subject to the budget constraint, now expressed as

$$\dot{b} = rb + (1 - \tau_k)r_k k + (1 - \tau_w)wL - (1 + \tau_c)x - C(I) + v, \quad (9.14)$$

where the return to capital $r_k = F_k$, $w = F_L$ is the wage rate. The government maintains a balanced budget, returning all the tax revenues to the households in the form of lump-sum transfers:

$$\tau_k r_k K + \tau_w wL + \tau_c X = v \quad\quad\quad (9.15)$$

### Inelastic Labour Supply

We begin with the case of inelastic labour supply, the equilibrium of which is modified to

$$U_x(X^*, X^*) = \bar{\lambda}^*(1 + \tau_c) \quad\quad\quad (9.2a'')$$

$$C'(I^*) = q^* \quad\quad\quad (9.2c)$$

$$\frac{(1 - \tau_k)F_k(K^*, K^*)}{q^*} + \frac{\dot{q}^*}{q^*} = r \quad\quad\quad (9.2e'')$$

$$\dot{K}^* = I^* \quad\quad\quad (9.2f)$$

$$\dot{B}^* = F(K^*, K^*) - X^* - C(I^*) + rB^*, \quad\quad\quad (9.2g')$$

where $\bar{\lambda}^*$ is determined by the steady-state relationships, now modified to

$$U_x(\bar{X}^*, \bar{X}^*) = \bar{\lambda}^*(1 + \tau_c), \quad\quad\quad (9.6a')$$

$$(1 - \tau_k)F_k(\bar{K}^*, \bar{K}^*) = r, \quad\quad\quad (9.6b')$$

$$F(\bar{K}^*, \bar{K}^*) + r\bar{B}^* = \bar{X}^* \quad\quad\quad (9.6c')$$

$$B_0^* - \bar{B}^* = \left[ \frac{F_k(\bar{K}^*, \bar{K}^*) + F_K(\bar{K}^*, \bar{K}^*) - \mu^*}{\mu^* - r} \right] (K_0^* - \bar{K}^*) \qquad (9.6d')$$

$$\mu^{*2} - r\mu^* + I'[(1 - \tau_k)[F_{kk}(\bar{K}^*, \bar{K}^*) + F_{kK}(\bar{K}^*, \bar{K}^*)]] = 0. \qquad (9.6e')$$

The objective is to determine the tax structure that can replicate the dynamic equilibrium time path of the centrally planned economy, as described in (9.4a)–(9.4g'). Performing the comparison, it is straightforward to establish that setting

$$\tau_k(t) = -\frac{F_K(K^*, K^*)}{F_k(K^*, K^*)} \qquad (9.16a)$$

$$\tau_c(t) = a, \qquad (9.16b)$$

where $a$ is an arbitrary constant, will ensure that the decentralized economy will replicate the optimum throughout the entire transition.[15] The tax on capital is time-varying and will converge to a constant level as capital converges to its steady-state equilibrium value.[16] Equation (9.16a) asserts that the optimal tax on capital should be negative or positive according to whether the production externality is positive or negative. The arbitrariness of the consumption tax is because with fixed labour supply the distortion resulting from the consumption externality vanishes, so that the consumption tax acts like a lump-sum tax. Its value can therefore be set arbitrarily (including 0), being offset by the lump-sum rebate $v$ in (9.15).

We may summarize these results as follows:

**Proposition 4** In an economy with exogenous labour supply, the entire time path of the optimal resource allocation can be obtained by setting taxes at each instant of time in accordance with

$$\tau_k = -\frac{F_K}{F_k}; \quad \tau_c(t) = a,$$

where $a$ is arbitrary (possibly zero). As the economy approaches its steady state, the tax on capital income converges to its steady-state rate. With exogenous labour supply the tax on wage income can be set arbitrarily.

**Elastic Labour Supply**

When labour supply is endogenous, the equilibrium of the decentralized economy is now determined by the following conditions:

$$U_x(X^*, X^*, 1 - L^*) = (1 + \tau_c)\bar{\lambda}^* \qquad (9.2a')$$

$$U_l(X^*, X^*, 1 - L^*) = -(1 - \tau_w)\bar{\lambda}^* F_l(K^*, K^*, L^*) \qquad (9.2b')$$

$$C'(I^*) = q^* \qquad (9.2c)$$

$$\dot{\lambda}^* = 0, \text{ i.e. } \lambda^* = \bar{\lambda}^* \qquad (9.2d)$$

$$\frac{(1 - \tau_k)F_k(K^*, K^*, L^*)}{q^*} + \frac{\dot{q}^*}{q^*} = r \qquad (9.2e)$$

$$\dot{K}^* = I^* \qquad (9.2f)$$

$$\dot{B}^* = F(K^*, K^*, L^*) - X^* - C(I^*) + rB^* \qquad (9.2g)$$

which now needs to be compared to the corresponding relationships for the centrally planned economy, (9.3a)–(9.3d). Performing this comparison, it is straightforward to establish the following optimal taxation result.

**Proposition 5** In an economy with endogenous labour supply, the entire time path of the optimal resource allocation can be obtained by setting taxes at each instant of time in accordance with

$$\tau_k(t) = \frac{-F_K(K^*, K^*, L^*)}{F_k(K^*, K^*, L^*)}, \tau_w = \bar{\tau}_w,$$

and

$$\frac{1 + \tau_c(t)}{1 - \bar{\tau}_w} = \frac{U_X(X^*, X^*, L^*)}{U_x(X, X^*, L^*) + U_X(X^*, X^*, L^*)}.$$

The consumption and capital income taxes are time-varying and converge to constants as the economy converges to its steady state. Again, the tax on capital corrects for the distortion from the capital externality while the consumption tax corrects the distortion from the consumption externality. Although both forms of externalities generate distortions in labour supply, no active labour income tax is needed once the source of distortions is rectified. The labour income tax can therefore be set to zero. The government should subsidize capital investment if there is a positive capital externality, and should levy a positive capital income tax if there is a negative capital externality. Similarly, private consumption should be subsidized if there is a positive consumption externality and should be subject to taxes if there is a negative consumption externality. This tax configuration is essentially the same as obtained for a closed economy.

The endogeneity of labour supply introduces three differences worth emphasizing. First, with inelastic labour supply, the optimal consumption tax is purely arbitrary. However, when labour is elastically supplied, this arbitrariness disappears, once the fixed wage income tax is set. This is because $\lambda$ becomes important for the labour–leisure choice and needs to be mimicked as well to obtain the first-best optimum. Second, the arbitrariness of the tax on labour income with inelastic labour means that the first-best optimum in that case could in fact be reached with a uniform income tax, in which the incomes from capital and labour are taxed at the same varying rate. By contrast, with elastic labour supply, since the tax on labour income must remain fixed, these two components of income must necessarily be taxed at differential rates. This is because the capital income, which remains unchanged from the case where labour is supplied inelastically, is necessary to correct for the distortion to the capital market, while the labour market is distortion-free. Finally, because the consumption externality distorts the leisure–consumption trade-off, the consumption tax is no longer transitory, but must also remain in steady-state equilibrium.

## 6. TWO CONSUMPTION GOODS

We now augment the model to include two consumption goods, one that is produced domestically, the other imported. We assume that the country is large enough in the production of the domestic consumption good that it is able to influence its relative price, $\sigma$, say. We shall assume that both domestically produced consumption and the imported consumption good may yield consumption externalities. To keep things simple we shall compensate for this by assuming that labour is supplied inelastically. The extension we are considering is essentially that described by Turnovsky (1997), which in turn is based on Sen and Turnovsky (1989). The key difference is that the agent's utility function is now of the form

$$\int_0^\infty U(x, y, X, Y)e^{-\beta t}dt \qquad (9.17a)$$

where $x$ and $y$ are his own individual consumption levels of the domestic and imported goods and $X$ and $Y$ are the corresponding economy-wide average consumption levels.

The representative consumer–producer's decision is to choose $x$ and $y$, and the rates of accumulation of capital and traded bonds to maximize (9.17a) subject to the accumulation equations

$$\dot{b} = \frac{1}{\sigma}[F(k, K) - x - \sigma y - C(I) + \sigma rb] \qquad (9.17b)$$
$$\dot{k} = I, \qquad (9.17c)$$

where $\sigma$ is the real exchange rate, measured as the relative price of the imported good in terms of the domestic good, and $r$ is the foreign interest rate measured in terms of the foreign good, and initial conditions $k(0) = k_0$, $b(0) = b_0$. Equation (9.17b) describes the representative agent's instantaneous budget constraint expressed in terms of foreign output.

## Macroeconomic Equilibrium

As in the one-good model, the existence of a traded bond implies that the marginal utilities of wealth, expressed in terms of the traded bond, must remain constant through time. The main insight from introducing a second consumption good can be obtained by focusing on the steady-state relationships. In the case of the decentralized economy (denoted by an asterisk) these are described by:

$$U_x(X^*, Y^*, X^*, Y^*) = \frac{\bar{\lambda}^*}{\sigma^*}, \qquad (9.18a)$$

$$U_y(X^*, Y^*, X^*, Y^*) = \bar{\lambda}^* \qquad (9.18b)$$

$$F(K^*, K^*) = X^* + Z(\sigma^*) \qquad (9.18c)$$

$$Z(\sigma^*) + r^*\sigma^*B^* = \sigma^* Y^* \qquad (9.18d)$$

$$F_k(K^*, K^*) = r, \qquad (9.18e)$$

$$B_0 - B^* = \left[ \frac{\Omega^*}{\mu^* - r} \right](K_0 - K^*) \qquad (9.18f)$$

Equations (9.18a) and (9.18b) equate the marginal utility of the domestic and foreign consumption goods to the shadow value of capital expressed in terms of domestic and foreign output units, respectively. Equation (9.18c) describes clearance of the domestic output market, where $Z(\sigma^*)$ denotes exports, taken to be a positive function of $\sigma^*$, the relative price of foreign to domestic goods. Equation (9.18d) describes steady-state current account balance; the value of imports must equal the value of exports plus the interest earned on the holdings of foreign bonds. Equation (9.18e) is identical to (9.6b), while (9.18f) is analogous to (9.6d) and relates the equilibrium accumulation of bonds to that of capital. With the relative price being endogenous, the relationship between capital and bonds depends crucially upon the response of $\sigma$ to the evolving capital stock. In addition, we should point out that it incorporates the eigenvalue that is given by an equation similar (but not identical) to (9.6e) and is omitted. The derivation of (9.18f) is discussed at length in Turnovsky (1997, ch. 3), and under plausible assumptions we can assume $\Omega^* > 0$, yielding a negative relationship, as before.[17] Turnovsky also spells out in detail the dynamic structure which will drive the system to the steady state summarized by (9.18).

The analogous steady-state conditions for the planner's problem are

$$U_x(\tilde{X}, \tilde{Y}, \tilde{X}, \tilde{Y}) + U_X(\tilde{X}, \tilde{Y}, \tilde{X}, \tilde{Y}) = \frac{\tilde{\lambda}}{\tilde{\sigma}}, \qquad (9.19a)$$

$$U_y(\tilde{X}, \tilde{Y}, \tilde{X}, \tilde{Y}) + U_Y(\tilde{X}, \tilde{Y}, \tilde{X}, \tilde{Y}) = \tilde{\lambda} \qquad (9.19b)$$

$$F(\tilde{K}, \tilde{K}) = \tilde{X} + Z(\tilde{\sigma}) \qquad (9.19c)$$

$$Z(\tilde{\sigma}) + \tilde{r}\tilde{\sigma}\tilde{B} = \tilde{\sigma}\tilde{Y} \qquad (9.19d)$$

$$F_k(\tilde{K}, \tilde{K}) + F_K(\tilde{K}, \tilde{K}) = r, \qquad (9.19e)$$

$$B_0 - \tilde{B} = \left[\frac{\tilde{\Omega}}{\tilde{\mu} - r}\right](K_0 - \tilde{K}). \qquad (9.19f)$$

As before, (9.18f) and (9.19f) are the same to the first order of approximation, enabling us to write

$$B^* - \tilde{B} = \left[\frac{\tilde{\Omega}}{\tilde{\mu} - r}\right](K^* - \tilde{K}).$$

There are now three sources of externalities: consumption externalities from domestic and foreign goods, $U_X$, $U_Y$, and production externalities, $F_K$. Because of the relative price effect, both consumption externalities cause distortions, even when labour supply is fixed. Expanding (9.18) about (9.19) provides the expressions describing how the externalities impact on the equilibrium. In considering these results, we assume $Z' > Z/\sigma$, that is the price elasticity of the foreign demand for exports exceeds unity.[18] From the results reported in equations (9A.9) of the Appendix we observe the following.

The coefficient of $U_X$ is seen to have the following pattern. It is negative in equations (9A.9a) and (9A.9d), it is positive in equations (9A.9b) and (9A.9c), and it is zero in equations (9A.9e) and (9A.9f). The coefficient of $U_Y$ has the opposite sign patterns. The coefficients of $F_K$ are negative in equation (9A.9c), positive in equations (9A.9e) and (9A.9f) and ambiguous in (9A.9a), (9A.9b) and (9A.9d).

This leads to the following proposition relating the actual and socially optimal equilibria in the presence of consumption and production externalities.[19]

**Proposition 6** In a small open economy consuming a domestically produced and imported consumption good, but with fixed labour supply, the steady-state equilibrium has the following properties.

1. Consumption externalities associated with either the domestic good or the imported good have no effect on the equilibrium capital stock, output, or stock of foreign assets.

2. A positive consumption externality on the domestic good (that is, its preferences exhibit admiration ($U_X > 0$)), leads to a long-run real exchange rate that is too high ($\sigma^* > \tilde{\sigma}$). Domestic consumption of the domestic good is too low and that of the imported good is too high ($X^* < \tilde{X}$, $Y^* > \tilde{Y}$). In the case of jealousy these relationships are reversed.

3. A positive consumption externality on the imported good (that is, its preferences exhibit admiration ($U_Y > 0$), leads to a long-run equilibrium real exchange rate that is too low ($\sigma^* < \tilde{\sigma}$). Consumption of the domestic good is too high and that of the imported good is too low ($X^* > \tilde{X}$, $Y^* < \tilde{Y}$). In the case of jealousy these relationships are reversed.

4. If the production technology exhibits a positive aggregate capital externality ($F_K > 0$), equilibrium capital stock is below its long-run optimum, while the stock of foreign assets is too high ($K^* < \tilde{K}$, $B^* > \tilde{B}$). The real exchange rate is too low ($\sigma^* < \tilde{\sigma}$). Long-run consumption of either good may be either above or below its long-run optimal value. In the case of a negative production externality these relationships are reversed.

**Proof**    *See the Appendix.*

The following intuition for these results may be given. Consider first a positive domestic consumption externality, in which case the benefits of consuming the domestic good are undervalued. This causes an overconsumption of the imported good, and with output and foreign debt coinciding with their optimal levels, the real exchange rate is too high. Analogously, a positive imported consumption externality has the opposite effect. It leads to the undervaluation and therefore underconsumption of the imported good. With output and foreign debt remaining unchanged, the domestic real exchange rate is too low, causing an overconsumption of the domestic consumption good. In general, the net effect of consumption externalities in both goods depends upon their relative magnitudes, as measured by ($U_Y - \sigma U_X$).

The introduction of the imported consumption good and the adjustment in the relative price between them has important implications. It means that because of the relative price effect, even if the labour supply is fixed, consumption externalities do exert some effects. A positive consumption externality in either good leads to underconsumption of that good and a compensating overconsumption of the other good.

The effect of a positive production externality in the two-commodity world involves adjustments in production as well as in consumption. On the one hand, it leads to an under-accumulation of capital, and therefore underproduction, accompanied by an over-accumulation of foreign bonds. The underproduction of domestic output, together with the over-accumulation of foreign bonds, causes the real exchange to be too low. The underproduction of domestic output leads to the underconsumption of both goods, while the over-accumulation of foreign bonds, and therefore foreign income has the opposite effect, so that the net effect on consumption depends upon which effect dominates.

**Optimal Tax Policy**

Assume now that the domestic fiscal authority has at its disposal the ability to tax the two consumption goods, capital income and (the fixed) labour income in accordance with

$$\tau_k r K + \tau_w w \bar{L} + \tau_x X + \tau_y Y = v. \tag{9.15'}$$

The relevant modifications to the equilibrium consumption conditions in the decentralized economy are:

$$U_x(X^*, Y^*, X^*, Y^*) = \frac{\bar{\lambda}^*(1 + \tau_x)}{\sigma^*}, \tag{9.18a'}$$

$$U_y(X^*, Y^*, X^*, Y^*) = \bar{\lambda}^*(1 + \tau_y) \tag{9.18b'}$$

$$(1 - \tau_k)F_k(K^*, K^*) = r, \tag{9.18e}$$

Comparing these equations with the corresponding conditions in the centrally planned economy we can derive the following proposition characterizing the optimal taxation for the two-consumption-good economy.

**Proposition 7** In a small open economy that consumes both a domestically produced and an imported consumption good, but with fixed labour supply, the time path of the optimal resource allocation can be obtained by setting taxes at each instant of time in accordance with

$$\tau_k(t) = \frac{-F_K(K^*, K^*)}{F_k(K^*, K^*)}, \quad \frac{1 + \tau_y}{1 + \tau_x} = \frac{U_x + U_X}{U_x} \frac{U_y}{U_y + U_Y} = \frac{1 + (U_X/U_x)}{1 + (U_Y/U_y)}$$

The optimal tax on capital remains as given by (9.16a). The relative tax rates on the two consumption goods should therefore reflect the relative sizes of the two consumption externalities they generate, and any combination of the two tax rates satisfying the condition in the proposition will succeed in eliminating the distortions they create. Note that with capital accumulating over time, the domestic goods market clearance condition, (9.19c), requires consumption of both goods to vary over time. Thus, like the tax on capital, the consumption taxes are time-varying, even though the labour supply remains fixed.

In the case that only the imported consumption good generates an externality, we can set

$$\tau_y = -\frac{(U_Y/U_y)}{1 + (U_Y/U_y)}. \qquad (9.20a)$$

The imported good should therefore be subject to a tariff or a subsidy according to whether it causes jealousy or admiration. But it is also possible to correct for this externality by taxing the domestic good at the rate

$$\tau_x = \frac{U_Y}{U_y}. \qquad (9.20b)$$

Likewise, the admiration or jealousy caused by the domestic good can be corrected by imposing a tariff or subsidy on the imported good.

## 7.　CONCLUSIONS

This chapter has examined the effects of consumption and production externalities in a small open economy with accumulating capital. The main conclusions are the following. First, externalities as expressed by the first derivatives of the utility and production functions with respect to aggregate consumption and capital, respectively, are what matter in determining their qualitative effects. The responses, described by cross partial derivatives, and embodied in the notions of keeping up with the Joneses in the case of consumption externalities, are less important. Second, the extent to which consumption externalities matter depends crucially upon whether or not labour supply is fixed. If it is fixed, they have no effect on production or capital, either in the steady state or along the transitional path. With endogenous labour, positive consumption externalities lead to a steady state with an undersupply of both capital and labour, but an oversupply of foreign bonds; the net effect may be either underconsumption or overconsumption. The effects of production externalities are much more pervasive, in that irrespective of the nature of labour supply, they do exert long-run distortionary effects. Third, we have analysed the optimal taxation to correct for the distortions created by the externalities. In general we find that a combination of an appropriate consumption tax (or subsidy) to correct for the consumption externality, together with a capital income tax (or subsidy) to correct for the production distortion can easily achieve the social optimum. Finally, extending the model to include an imported, as well as a domestic, consumption good yields important differences. This gives rise to a relative price effect that may cause the consumption externality of either good to lead to overconsumption of one good to be accompanied by the underconsumption of the other. Appropriate consumption taxes may eliminate the distortions, thus providing a new motivation for a tariff.

## NOTES

\* This chapter is a revised version of the paper presented at the *Festschrift* honouring Peter Lloyd held at the University of Melbourne, 23 and 24 January 2003. The comments of the discussant, Peter Dixon, and an anonymous referee are gratefully acknowledged. This research was supported in part by the Castor endowment at the University of Washington. Revised version June 2003.

1. Ljungqvist and Uhlig (2000) also consider this and refer to it as 'catching up to the Joneses'. A few papers formulate the utility externality in terms of relative wealth rather than consumption; see, for example, Corneo and Jeanne (1997), Futagami and Shibata (1998).

2. That is, we abstract from population growth and accordingly: the Ramsey model is associated with a fixed long-run capital stock.

3. That is, they define keeping up with the Joneses as $d(U_x/U_l)/dX > 0$ and what they call running away from the Joneses as $d(U_x/U_l)/dX < 0$.

4. Thus if $U_X \equiv 0$ there is no externality to which the agent can respond. On the other hand, if the utility function is additively separable in aggregate consumption, any feelings of jealousy, for example, would have no impact on their individual behaviour. However, most widely adopted utility functions are non-separable, in which case the two types of externalities are not independent. For example, the constant elasticity utility function $U(x, X) \equiv (1/(1 - \gamma))(xX^\rho)^{1-\gamma}$ implies the relationship: $\text{sgn}(U_X) = \text{sgn}(\rho)$; $\text{sgn}(U_{xX}) = \text{sgn}(\rho(1 - \gamma))$. Thus if the intertemporal elasticity of substitution is less than 1 ($\gamma > 1$), the agent will keep up with the Joneses if and only if he is jealous.

5. As we shall presently show, at the optimum, $U_x + U_X$ equals the shadow value of capital and is presumably positive.

6. Characterizations of production externalities parallel to those suggested for consumption externalities, in terms of $F_K$ and $F_{Kk}$, can be made. In particular, at the optimum $F_k + F_K = r > 0$, where $r$ is the foreign interest rate.

7. For a discussion of this type of investment function in an international context, see Turnovsky (1997, chapter 3).

8. For notational convenience we shall denote $\partial L^*/\partial K^*$ by $L_K^*$ and analogously for other partial derivatives.

9. For convenience, we assume that both the decentralized and centrally planned economies start with the same initial stocks of assets, $K_0$, $B_0$.

10. See Liu and Turnovsky (2005).

11. When linearizing around the decentralized equilibrium, we should also add the restriction $F_{kK} + F_{KK} < 0$.

12. In particular, consumption externalities generate no distortions along the transitional path in a closed economy if and only if the utility function satisfies the condition: $(U_X/U_x)|_{x=X}$ is constant.

13. With a single stable eigenvalue, any variable, $z$ say, converges along the path $\dot{z} = \mu(\tilde{z} - z)$.
14. There are no taxes on interest income or on the capital gains component of capital income. These can be added but are not necessary.
15. Having set the tax on capital income in accordance with (9.16a), and thus replicated the optimal stocks of capital and bonds, (9.6c) and (9.7c) ensure the replication of the optimal consumption, independent of the consumption tax.
16. Setting the optimal tax on capital in accordance with (9.16a) also ensures that $\mu^* = \tilde{\mu}$.
17. The mechanism is somewhat different from before, depending particularly upon the adjustment in the relative price.
18. These results are also predicated on assumptions, noted in the Appendix, concerning the cross partial derivatives of the utility function.
19. In considering these results our definition of the real exchange rate, as the price of imported goods in terms of the domestic good, should be recalled.

# REFERENCES

Abel, A. (1990), 'Asset prices under habit formation and catching up with the Joneses', *American Economic Review* (Papers and Proceedings), **80**, 38–42.

Barro, R.J. (1990), 'Government spending in a simple model of endogenous growth', *Journal of Political Economy*, **98**, 103–25.

Carroll, C., Overland, J. and Weil, D. (1997), 'Comparison utility in a growth model', *Journal of Economic Growth*, **2**, 339–67.

Corneo, C. and Jeanne, O. (1997), 'On relative wealth effects and the optimality of growth', *Economics Letters*, **54**, 87–92.

Dupor, B. and Liu, W.F. (2003), 'Jealousy and equilibrium overconsumption', *American Economic Review*, **93**, 423–8.

Eicher, T.S. and Turnovsky, S.J. (2000), 'Scale, congestion, and growth', *Economica*, **67**, 325–46.

Fisher, W.H. and Hof, F.X. (2000), 'Conspicuous consumption, economic growth, and taxation: a generalization', *Journal of Economics (Zeitschrift für Nationalökonomie)*, **72**, 241–62.

Futagami, K. and Shibata, A. (1998), 'Keeping one step ahead of the Joneses: status and the distribution of wealth, and long-run growth', *Journal of Economic Behavior and Organization*, **36**, 93–111.

Gali, J. (1994), 'Keeping up with the Joneses: consumption externalities, portfolio choice, and asset prices', *Journal of Money, Credit, and Banking*, **26**, 1–8.

Judd, K.L. (1998), *Numerical Methods in Economics*, Cambridge, MA: MIT Press.

Liu, W.F. and Turnovsky, S.J. (2005), 'Consumption externalities, production externalities, and long-run macroeconomic efficiency, *Journal of Public Economics*, **89**, 1097–129.

Ljungqvist, L. and Uhlig, H. (2000), 'Tax policy and aggregate demand management under catching up with the Joneses', *American Economic Review*, **90**, 356–66.

Lloyd, P.J. (1973), 'Optimal intervention in a distortion-ridden open economy', *Economic Record*, **49**, 377–93.

Lloyd, P.J. (1974), 'A more general theory of price distortions in open economies', *Journal of International Economics*, **4**, 365–86.

Romer, P.M. (1986), 'Increasing returns and long-run growth', *Journal of Political Economy*, **94**, 1002–37.

Romer, P.M. (1989), 'Capital accumulation in the theory of long-run growth', in R.J. Barro (ed.), *Modern Business Cycle Theory*, Cambridge, MA: Harvard University Press, pp. 51–127.

Sen, P. and Turnovsky, S.J. (1989), 'Tariffs, capital accumulation, and the current account', *International Economic Review*, **30**, 811–31.

Turnovsky, S.J. (1996), 'Optimal tax, debt, and expenditure policies in a growing economy', *Journal of Public Economics*, **60**, 21–44.

Turnovsky, S.J. (1997), *International Macroeconomic Dynamics*, Cambridge, MA: MIT Press.

Turnovsky, S.J. (2000), 'Fiscal policy, elastic labor supply, and endogenous growth', *Journal of Monetary Economics*, **45**, 185–210.

## APPENDIX

### Linearization of (9.6d) about (9.7d')

The national intertemporal budget constraint in the decentralized economy is

$$B_0 - B^* = \left( \frac{F_k(K^*, K^*) + F_K(K^*, K^*) - \mu^*}{\mu^* - r} \right)(K_0 - K^*),$$

which for convenience we write as

$$B_0 - B^* = \left( \frac{F_k^* + F_K^* - \mu^*}{\mu^* - r} \right)(K_0 - K^*), \tag{9A.1a}$$

where

$$\mu^{*2} - r\mu^* + (F_{kk}^* + F_{kK}^*)I' = 0. \tag{9A.1b}$$

We wish to linearize this budget constraint about the corresponding budget constraint in the centrally planned economy

$$B_0 - \tilde{B} = \left( \frac{F_k(\tilde{K}, \tilde{K}) + F_K(\tilde{K}, \tilde{K}) - \tilde{\mu}}{\tilde{\mu} - r} \right)(K_0 - \tilde{K}) \equiv \left( \frac{\tilde{F}_k + \tilde{F}_K - \tilde{\mu}}{\tilde{\mu} - r} \right)(K_0 - \tilde{K}), \tag{9A.2a}$$

where

$$\tilde{\mu}^2 - r\tilde{\mu} + (\tilde{F}_{kk} + 2\tilde{F}_{kK} + \tilde{F}_{KK})I' = 0. \tag{9A.2b}$$

Note that since the steady-state values of $q$ are the same in the two economies, $I'$ is the same in both (9A.1b) and (9A.2b).

Expanding (9A.1a) about (9A.2a), we obtain

$$B_0 - B^* = \left( \frac{F_k^* + F_K^* - \mu^*}{\mu^* - r} \right)(K_0 - K^*) = \left( \frac{\tilde{F}_k + \tilde{F}_K - \tilde{\mu}}{\tilde{\mu} - r} \right)(K_0 - \tilde{K})$$

$$- \left[ \frac{\tilde{F}_k + \tilde{F}_K - \tilde{\mu}}{(\tilde{\mu} - r)^2} + \frac{1}{\tilde{\mu} - r} \right](\mu^* - \tilde{\mu}) + \left[ \left( \frac{\tilde{F}_{kk} + 2\tilde{F}_{kK} - \tilde{F}_{KK}}{\tilde{\mu} - r} \right)(K_0 - \tilde{K}) \right.$$

$$\left. - \left( \frac{\tilde{F}_k + \tilde{F}_K - \tilde{\mu}}{\tilde{\mu} - r} \right) \right](K^* - \tilde{K})(K_0 - \tilde{K}).$$

Substituting the equilibrium condition (9.7c), this simplifies to

$$B_0 - B^* = K^* - K_0 + \left( \frac{\tilde{F}_{kk} + 2\tilde{F}_{kK} - \tilde{F}_{KK}}{\tilde{\mu} - r} \right)(K_0 - \tilde{K})(K^* - \tilde{K}). \quad (9A.3)$$

Subtracting from the intertemporal budget constraint in the centrally planned economy,

$$B_0 - \tilde{B} = \tilde{K} - K_0$$

yields

$$B^* - \tilde{B} = -\left(1 + \left( \frac{\tilde{F}_{kk} + 2\tilde{F}_{kK} - \tilde{F}_{KK}}{\tilde{\mu} - r} \right)(K_0 - \tilde{K}) \right)(K^* - \tilde{K}), \quad (9A.4)$$

and rewriting (9A.2b) as

$$\left( \frac{\tilde{F}_{kk} + 2\tilde{F}_{kK} - \tilde{F}_{KK}}{\tilde{\mu} - r} \right) = -\frac{\tilde{\mu}}{I'},$$

(9A.4) simplifies to

$$B^* - \tilde{B} = -(1 - \tilde{\mu} C''(K_0 - \tilde{K}))(K^* - \tilde{K}).$$

Since $K_0 - \tilde{K}$ and $K^* - \tilde{K}$ are proportional to the underlying shocks the multiplicative term $(K_0 - \tilde{K})(K^* - \tilde{K})$ is of second order and should be dropped in our first-order approximation. Thus, to the first order we have

$$B^* - \tilde{B} = -(K^* - \tilde{K}). \quad (9A.5)$$

**Proof of Proposition 2**

Applying Taylor expansions to equations (9.9a)–(9.9e) around the optimal steady state $(\tilde{X}, \tilde{L}, \tilde{K}, \tilde{\lambda}, \tilde{B})$, and rearranging the terms, we obtain the following:

$$\begin{bmatrix} U_{xx} + U_{xX} & -U_{xl} & 0 & -1 & 0 \\ U_{lx} + U_{lX} & -(U_{ll} + \tilde{\lambda} F_{LL}) & -\tilde{\lambda}(F_{Lk} + F_{LK}) & -F_L & 0 \\ 0 & F_{kL} & F_{kk} + F_{kK} & 0 & 0 \\ -1 & F_L & r & 0 & r \\ 0 & 0 & (1 + \theta) & 0 & 1 \end{bmatrix}$$

$$\cdot \begin{bmatrix} X^* - \tilde{X} \\ L^* - \tilde{L} \\ K^* - \tilde{K} \\ \lambda^* - \tilde{\lambda} \\ B^* - \tilde{B} \end{bmatrix} = \begin{bmatrix} U_X \\ 0 \\ F_K \\ 0 \\ 0 \end{bmatrix} \qquad (9A.6)$$

where the derivatives appearing in (9A.6) are evaluated at the optimal (centrally planned) steady-state equilibrium. Let $D$ denote the determinant of the matrix on the left, hand side of equation (9A.1). It can be shown that $D > 0$. Solving for $X^* - \tilde{X}$, $L^* - \tilde{L}$, $K^* - \tilde{K}$, $B^* - \tilde{B}$ and $\lambda^* - \tilde{\lambda}$, we obtain

$$X^* - \tilde{X} = \frac{U_X F_L}{D}[F_L(F_{kk} + F_{kK}) + \theta F_{kL}]$$

$$+ \frac{F_K}{D}\left\{ - F_L\tilde{\lambda}(F_{Lk} + F_{LK}) + \theta r[U_{xl}F_L - (U_{ll} + \tilde{\lambda}F_{LL})] \right\} \quad (9A.7a)$$

$$L^* - \tilde{L} = \frac{U_X F_L}{D}(F_{kk} + F_{kK})$$

$$- \frac{F_K}{D}\{\tilde{\lambda}(F_{Lk} + F_{LK}) + \theta r(U_{lx} + U_{lX} - F_L(U_{xx} + U_{xX}))\} \quad (9A.7b)$$

$$K^* - \tilde{K} = -\frac{U_X F_{kL} F_L}{D} + \frac{F_K}{D}\{- F_L U_{xl} - (U_{lx} + U_{lX})F_L$$

$$+ (U_{ll} + F_{LL}\tilde{\lambda}) + F_L^2(U_{xx} + U_{XX})\} \quad (9A.7c)$$

$$B^* - \tilde{B} = -(1 + \theta)(K^* - \tilde{K}) \qquad (9A.7d)$$

$$\lambda^* - \tilde{\lambda} = -\frac{U_X}{D}\{(F_{kk} + F_{kK})[(U_{ll} + \tilde{\lambda}F_{LL}) - F_L(U_{lx} + U_{lX})]$$

$$- \theta r F_{kL}(U_{lx} + U_{lX})\}$$

$$+ \frac{F_K}{D}\{\tilde{\lambda}(F_{Lk} + F_{LK})(U_{lx} - F_L(U_{xx} + U_{xX}))$$

$$+ \theta r[U_{xl}(U_{lx} + U_{lX}) - (U_{xx} + U_{xX})(U_{ll} + \tilde{\lambda}F_{LL})]\} \quad (9A.7e)$$

**Proof of Proposition 6**

Applying Taylor expansions to equations (9.18a)–(9.18f) around the optimal steady state $(\tilde{X}, \tilde{L}, \tilde{K}, \tilde{\lambda}, \tilde{B})$ and rearranging the terms, we obtain the following:

$$
\begin{bmatrix}
U_{11} & U_{12} & \tilde{\lambda}/\tilde{\sigma}^2 & -1/\tilde{\sigma}^2 & 0 & 0 \\
U_{21} & U_{22} & 0 & -1 & 0 & 0 \\
-1 & 0 & -Z' & 0 & 0 & r \\
0 & -\tilde{\sigma} & (Z'-Z/\tilde{\sigma}) & 0 & r\tilde{\sigma} & 0 \\
0 & 0 & 0 & 0 & 1 & -\tilde{\Omega}/(\tilde{\mu}-r) \\
0 & 0 & 0 & 0 & 0 & F_{kk}+F_{kK}
\end{bmatrix}
$$

$$
\cdot
\begin{bmatrix}
X^*-\tilde{X} \\
Y^*-\tilde{Y} \\
\sigma^*-\tilde{\sigma} \\
\lambda^*-\tilde{\lambda} \\
B^*-\tilde{B} \\
K^*-\tilde{K}
\end{bmatrix}
=
\begin{bmatrix}
U_X \\
U_Y \\
0 \\
0 \\
0 \\
F_K
\end{bmatrix},
\tag{9A.8}
$$

where we assume $U_{11} \equiv U_{xx} + U_{xX} < 0$; $U_{12} \equiv U_{xy} + U_{xY} > 0$; $U_{21} \equiv U_{yx} + U_{yX} > 0$; $U_{22} \equiv U_{yy} + U_{yY} < 0$, and $U_{11}U_{22} - U_{12}U_{21} > 0$. Let $E'$ denote the determinant of the matrix on the left-hand side of equation (9A.8). It can be shown that

$$
E' = -(F_{kk}+F_{kK})E \equiv -(F_{kk}+F_{kK})\left[\left(Z'-\frac{Z}{\sigma}\right)\left(U_{12}-\frac{U_{22}}{\sigma}\right)\right.
$$

$$
\left. +\sigma\left[\frac{\lambda}{\sigma^2}+Z'\left(\frac{U_{21}}{\sigma}-U_{11}\right)\right]\right] > 0.
$$

Solving for $X^*-\tilde{X}$, $Y^*-\tilde{Y}$, $\sigma^*-\tilde{\sigma}$, $K^*-\tilde{K}$, $B^*-\tilde{B}$, and $\lambda^*-\tilde{\lambda}$, we obtain

$$
X^*-\tilde{X} = -\frac{U_X\sigma Z'}{E}+\frac{U_Y Z'}{E}
$$

$$
+\frac{F_K r}{E'}\left\{\frac{\Omega}{(\mu-r)}\sigma Z'\left[\frac{U_{22}}{\sigma}-U_{12}\right]-\left[\frac{\lambda}{\sigma}+\left(Z'-\frac{Z}{\sigma}\right)\left(U_{12}-\frac{U_{22}}{\sigma}\right)\right]\right\}
$$

$$
\tag{9A.9a}
$$

$$
Y^*-\tilde{Y} = \frac{U_X(Z'-Z/\sigma)}{E}-\frac{U_Y(Z'-Z/\sigma)}{\sigma E}-\frac{F_K r}{E'}\left\{\frac{\Omega\sigma}{(\mu-r)}\left[\frac{\lambda}{\sigma^2}+\right.\right.
$$

$$
\left.\left. Z'\left(\frac{U_{21}}{\sigma}-U_{11}\right)\right]+\left(Z'-\frac{Z}{\sigma}\right)\left(\frac{U_{21}}{\sigma}-U_{11}\right)\right\}
\tag{9A.9b}
$$

$$\sigma^* - \tilde{\sigma} = \frac{U_X}{E} - \frac{U_Y}{E} + \frac{F_K r \sigma}{E'} \left\{ \frac{\Omega}{\mu - r} \left( U_{12} - \frac{1}{\sigma} U_{22} \right) - \left( \frac{1}{\sigma} U_{21} - U_{11} \right) \right\} \quad \text{(9A.9c)}$$

$$\lambda^* - \tilde{\lambda} = \frac{U_X}{E} \left[ - Z'\sigma U_{21} + \left( Z' - \frac{Z}{\sigma} \right) U_{22} \right]$$

$$- \frac{U_Y}{E} \left[ \frac{\lambda}{\sigma} - Z'\sigma U_{11} + \left( Z' - \frac{Z}{\sigma} \right) U_{12} \right]$$

$$+ \frac{F_K r}{E'} \left\{ - \frac{\Omega \sigma}{\mu - r} \left[ - Z'(U_{11}U_{22} - U_{12}U_{21}) + \frac{\lambda}{\sigma^2} U_{21} \right] \right.$$

$$\left. + \left( Z' - \frac{Z}{\sigma} \right)(U_{11}U_{22} - U_{12}U_{21}) - \frac{\lambda}{\sigma} U_{21} \right\} \quad \text{(9A.9d)}$$

$$K^* - \tilde{K} = \frac{F_K}{F_{kk} + F_{kK}} < 0 \quad \text{(9A.9e)}$$

$$B^* - \tilde{B} = \frac{\Omega}{\mu - r} \frac{F_K}{F_{kk} + F_{kK}} > 0. \quad \text{(9A.9f)}$$

# 10. Explaining a dynamic CGE simulation with a trade-focused back-of-the-envelope analysis: the effects of eCommerce on Australia

**Peter B. Dixon and Maureen T. Rimmer**[*]

## 1. INTRODUCTION

This chapter was written in honour of Peter Lloyd for presentation on the occasion of his retirement. Together with Arndt, Corden, Gregory, Hazari, Kemp, Salter, Snape, Swan and Woodland, Lloyd is in a select group of economists that have made Australia a leading contributor over the last half century to the development and application of the theory of international trade.[1]

Reflecting the pre-eminence of its trade theorists, Australia's applied multi-sectoral modellers have also emphasized trade issues. The first multi-sectoral model for Australia was the path-breaking work of Evans (1972). The Evans model was devoted almost entirely to the analysis of the effects of changes in tariffs. Similarly, protection was the primary focus of Klijn's (1974) model and of the ORANI model (Dixon et al., 1977 and 1982). While the MONASH model (Dixon and Rimmer, 2002) has a broader range of applications than its predecessors, it retains a strong trade focus.

As measured by the share of trade in its GDP, Australia is not among the world's most trade-oriented nations. This makes the dominance of trade analysis in the work of Australia's theoretical and applied economists somewhat of a surprise. Nevertheless, the concentration on trade has been well justified.

Over many decades Lloyd and Australia's other leading trade economists, supported by multi-sectoral modellers, have demonstrated the importance to Australia's economic welfare of trade policy. But the importance of trade policy is not the only justification for their research on trade issues. Since the 1980s it has become apparent from applied multi-sector models that an understanding of the determinants of international commodity and capital flows is essential for the quantification of the effects of almost all economic policies, not just trade policies. Numerous examples can be found of ORANI and MONASH studies showing that the specification of international flows is critical in determining the simulated effects of non-trade-related shocks. A striking example from a recent MONASH study (Dixon and Rimmer, 1999) is the finding that the overall welfare effect of the introduction of the GST (goods and services tax) is heavily dependent on international tourism. Because tourism services are Australia's only major exports subject to the GST, the MONASH simulation showed the tourism sector to be a significant loser. The implication for Australian welfare of GST-induced damage to tourism was then shown to depend on the foreign elasticity of demand for tourism services and on the basecase (no GST) growth forecast for international tourist arrivals.

The remainder of this chapter has two objectives. The first is to provide an illustration of the importance of trade flows in the determination of the outcomes for Australia of shocks that are not directly related to trade. The example we have chosen is a MONASH-based analysis of the effects on Australia of the adoption of eCommerce.[2] The second is to demonstrate that the macro results from detailed models such as MONASH can be understood from back-of-the-envelope (BOTE) calculations with equations that are familiar from simple models used by trade theorists. Once the macro results are understood from these BOTE calculations, the justification of results for industries, occupations and regions becomes straightforward.

The chapter is organized as follows. Section 2 gives a brief overview of the MONASH model. Section 3 lists the shocks that we have used to represent the adoption of eCommerce. Section 4 provides BOTE explanations of the macro results. Sections 5, 6 and 7 discuss the results for industries, regions and occupations. Section 8 looks at the sensitivity of the results to changes in the assumed rate at which eCommerce is adopted. Section 9 contains concluding remarks.

## 2.   THE MONASH MODEL AND KEY ASSUMPTIONS IN THE POLICY SIMULATION

MONASH is a dynamic computable general equilibrium (CGE) model of the Australian economy (see Dixon and Rimmer, 2002). In standard applications, it is run with 112 industries. Via a suite of add-on programs, results can be generated for 57 sub-national regions (statistical divisions), 340 occupations and numerous types of households.

MONASH has evolved over the last 20 years from the comparative static ORANI model. Apart from the introduction of dynamics, the main advances in MONASH are associated with closures (choice of exogenous variables).[3] With different closures MONASH produces: estimates of changes in technologies and consumer preferences (historical closure); explanations of historical developments such as the rapid growth since the mid-1980s in Australia's international trade (decomposition closure); forecasts for industries, regions, occupations and households (forecast closure); and projections of the deviations from forecast paths that would be caused by the implementation of proposed policies and by other shocks to the economic environment (policy closure). The results to be described later in this chapter were generated by two MONASH simulations, one with a forecast closure and the other with a policy closure.

In forecast closures, we exogenize a wide variety of naturally endogenous variables for which forecasts are available from specialist groups. For example, we exogenize most macro variables and shock them with forecasts produced by macro forecasters such as Access Economics, and we exogenize export prices and quantities and shock them with forecasts produced by the Australian Bureau of Agricultural and Resource Economics and by the Bureau of Tourism Research. Exogenization of these naturally endogenous variables requires corresponding endogenization of naturally exogenous variables such as propensities to consume, invest and import, and the positions of export demand and supply curves. By using specialist forecasts we ensure that MONASH produces credible results, that is, results that are consistent with expert opinion. MONASH forecasts are also informed by extrapolations of recent trends in industry technologies and consumer preferences. These trends are derived from MONASH historical simulations in which the model is given sufficient freedom in the determination of technology and preference variables to allow it to reproduce historical movements in observable variables such as industry inputs and outputs and consumption by commodity.

In policy closures, naturally endogenous variables such as macro aggregates and export prices and quantities are endogenous. In policy simulations these variables must be endogenous so that they respond to the policy shocks. Naturally exogenous variables such as propensities to consume, invest and import, and the positions of export demand and supply curves are exogenous.

If all of the exogenous variables in a policy simulation are given the values that they had either endogenously or exogenously in the associated forecast simulation, then the policy simulation reproduces the forecast results. However, in policy simulations some of the exogenous variables are given different values from those in the forecast simulation. For example, in our eCommerce analysis, technology and preference variables in the policy simulation are moved away from the historical trend values adopted in the forecast simulation. The imposed deviations in these variables reflect judgements about the direct effects of eCommerce on technology and preferences. The comparison of policy results with forecast results then shows the effects of eCommerce on macro, industry, regional and occupational variables as deviations from explicit and realistic forecasts.

The use of realistic forecasts is important in policy analysis for two reasons. First, basecase forecasts of, for example, the relative sizes of industries and the commodity composition of exports affect the simulated values to the economy of shocks such as the adoption of eCommerce. Second, in cases where a policy is likely to cause a reduction in employment in an industry, the basecase forecast is critical in estimating adjustment costs. These costs depend on whether the adjustment will be handled by a reduced rate of hiring or an increased rate of firing.

The details of MONASH policy closures can be varied to introduce different macroeconomic assumptions. The main macro assumptions in the policy simulation (the effects of eCommerce) presented later in this chapter are as follows.

## Labour Market

We assume that workers are concerned with the real after-tax wage rate, that is, the wage rate less income taxes, deflated by the CPI. If the labour market strengthens, then we assume that the real after-tax wage rate rises in response to increased worker negotiating strength. More precisely, we assume that

$$\left\{\frac{W_{t,p}}{W_{t,f}}-1\right\} = \left\{\frac{W_{t-1,p}}{W_{t-1,f}}-1\right\} + \alpha\left\{\frac{E_{t,p}}{E_{t,f}} - \frac{LS_{t,p}}{LS_{t,f}}\right\}, \qquad (10.1)$$

where $W_{t,f}$, $E_{t,f}$ and $LS_{t,f}$ are the real after-tax wage rate, aggregate employment and the long-run labour supply in year $t$ in the basecase forecast simulation; $W_{t,p}$, $E_{t,p}$ and $LS_{t,p}$ are the real after-tax wage rate, aggregate employment and the long-run labour supply in year $t$ in the policy simulation, that is, the simulation with the eCommerce shocks; and $\alpha$ is a positive parameter.

Under (10.1), the real after-tax wage rate in a policy simulation moves further above its value in the forecast simulation if the ratio of policy employment to forecast employment is greater than the ratio of policy long-run labour supply to forecast long-run labour supply. Long-run labour supply is specified in MONASH policy simulations as a function of lagged real after-tax wage rates and various shift variables. In the policy simulation reported in this chapter, the elasticity of long-run labour supply to lagged real after-tax wage rates is zero. Thus, in the absence of supply shifts, $LS_{t,p}/LS_{t,f} = 1$, reducing (10.1) to

$$\left\{\frac{W_{t,p}}{W_{t,f}} - 1\right\} = \left\{\frac{W_{t-1,p}}{W_{t-1,f}} - 1\right\} + \alpha\left\{\frac{E_{t,p}}{E_{t,f}} - 1\right\}. \qquad (10.2)$$

Under (10.2), wages rise in policy relative to forecast whenever employment in policy is above its level in forecast. However, as will be apparent in Sections 3 and 4, we introduce shifts in long-run labour supply to represent time-saving by households from the use of eCommerce. If these shifts cause a deviation in long-run labour supply in year $t$ of $x$ per cent, then under (10.1), the policy-induced deviation in the real after-tax wage rate increases in year $t$ relative to year $t-1$ if and only if the policy-induced deviation in employment in year $t$ is more than $x$ per cent. While favourable shocks such as the adoption of eCommerce can temporarily produce positive gaps between employment and long-run labour supply, we can expect these gaps to close under (10.1) as wage rates rise thereby reducing labour demand. The rate at which gaps are closed is controlled largely by the parameter $\alpha$. In the policy simulation reported in this chapter, the value of $\alpha$ was set so that the short-run gap generated by any shock is substantially eliminated within five years of the shock. Our labour market specification can be summarized as short-run real-wage stickiness and long-run real-wage flexibility. It is consistent with conventional macroeconomic modelling in which the non-accelerating inflation rate of unemployment (NAIRU) is exogenous.

**Private Expenditure, Public Expenditure and Taxes**

The shocks considered in this chapter (the adoption of eCommerce) generate increases in national income, providing the potential for increases in private and public consumption. Consistent with the emphasis in recent years on small government, we assume that the eCommerce-induced percentage deviations in public consumption are half those in private consumption. For example, if in a particular year eCommerce generates a 2 per cent increase in real household disposable income, causing private consumption to be 2 per cent greater than it would otherwise have been, then we assume that public consumption is 1 per cent greater than it would otherwise have been. As well as adjusting the path of public consumption, we assume that the government adjusts the path of consumption taxes[4] so that the adoption of eCommerce does not affect the path of the public sector deficit.

**Rates of Return on Capital**

In simulations of the effects of changes in policy and other exogenous variables, MONASH allows for short-run divergences in after-tax rates of return on industry capital stocks from their levels in the basecase forecasts. Short-run increases/decreases in rates of return cause increases/decreases in investment and capital stocks, thereby gradually eroding the initial divergences in after-tax rates of return.

**Production Technologies**

MONASH contains variables describing: primary-factor and intermediate-input-saving technical change in current production; input-saving technical change in capital creation; input-saving technical change in the provision of margin services; and input-saving changes in household preferences.[5] In the policy simulation described in this chapter, all of these variables are exogenous. We move a selection of them away from their basecase forecast values to introduce the direct effects of eCommerce on technology and preferences.

## 3.  THE SHOCKS

In 1999, Kerry Barwise of the Allen Consulting Group (ACG), with sponsorship from the National Office for the Information Economy (NOIE) and several other organizations, chaired a series of meetings for people from business and government who were knowledgeable in the area of eCommerce. The aim of these meetings was to obtain a broad picture of the likely effects of adoption of eCommerce on the conduct of business. Our task was to lead the participants in the meetings towards a quantification of their views in terms of effects on variables describing technologies and preferences. After an iterative process, consisting of qualitative and anecdotal discussion by participants, quantitative suggestions from us and further discussion by participants, an agreed list of shocks to be applied to the MONASH model emerged.[6]

On the assumption that the adoption of eCommerce is a gradual process, we phased in the shocks to MONASH over ten years, beginning in 1998. We assumed that each shock operates in year 1 (1998) at a tenth of its eventual strength, in year 2 (1999) at two-tenths of its eventual strength and in year 10 (2007) and beyond at its full strength. The shocks, organized in 14 sets, are described below. For each set of shocks we provide an estimate of the full-strength direct GDP effect. For example, if a set of shocks saves 10 per cent of an industry's labour and the industry's labour represents 5 per cent of GDP, then the direct GDP effect is 0.5 per cent. This recognizes that the shock releases resources that can be used to generate a 0.5 per cent increase in GDP. We also note for each set of shocks the direct effect on consumption (combined private and public). In most cases this can be considered an indicator of the direct welfare effect of the set of shocks.

### Saving of Margins by Consumers (s1)

For books we assume that eCommerce will, after ten years, reduce retail margins by 30 per cent. For most other goods we assume reductions in retail margins of between 0 and 20 per cent. Overall, the average reduction in retail margins is 12.8. This is a saving to consumers of about $4.7 billion in 1996–97 prices, equivalent to about 0.95 per cent of GDP.

Reductions in retail margins are likely to require increases in wholesale margins. Rather than dealing with retailers, consumers will deal more directly with wholesalers. We assume that half the savings of retail margins are lost to consumers via increases in wholesale margins. This is a loss to consumers of about $2.35 billion in 1996–97 prices. Together the changes in retail and wholesale margins generate a gain in GDP of about $2.35 billion, that is 0.47 per cent of GDP.

All of the GDP gain generated by changes in margins is available for extra private and public consumption. Because private and public consumption are about 80 per cent of GDP, a gain in GDP of 0.47 per cent translates into a consumption gain of 0.60 per cent.

*GDP effect = 0.47%*
*Consumption and welfare effects = 0.60%*

### Saving of Time by Households (s2)

eCommerce reduces households' non-discretionary shopping time. In our simulation we assume that the time saved could generate labour income of half the net savings generated by the net reduction in consumer margins (the retail and wholesale margins discussed in s1), that is we assume there is a potential increase in labour supply worth $1.17 billion in 1996–97 prices (= 2.35/2). Of this potential increase in labour supply, we assume that half ($0.59 billion) is translated into extra leisure and half into extra labour supply. This represents an increase in labour supply of about 0.20 per cent, generating an increase in GDP of about 0.12 per cent and a corresponding increase in private and public consumption of 0.15 per cent (= 0.12/0.8).

In calculating welfare we include the increase in leisure. Thus the welfare effect is equivalent to an increase in consumption of 0.30 per cent.

*GDP effect = 0.12%*
*Consumption effect = 0.15%*
*Welfare effect = 0.30%*

### Purchase of eCommerce Equipment and Services by Households (s3)

We assume that households purchase eCommerce equipment and services worth 25 per cent of consumer-margin cost savings ($2.35 billion, s1). That is, consumers in year 10 purchase equipment and services worth $0.59 billion. We simulate this as a change in consumer preferences requiring extra expenditures on: (a) electronic equipment of $0.059 billion; (b) communications of $0.059 billion; (c) banking of $0.247 billion; (d) non-bank finance of $0.165 billion; and (e) business services of $0.059 billion.

Changes in consumer preferences have no direct effect on GDP. For welfare analysis we recognize that purchase of eCommerce equipment and services is an expense to consumers not a benefit.

*GDP effect = 0.00%*
*Consumption effect = 0.00%*
*Welfare effect = −0.15%*

### Saving of Margins by Industries (s4)

For most inputs to industries we assume that eCommerce will reduce wholesale and retail margins by 5 per cent over ten years. For consumer goods used as inputs to industries we assume that margins savings will be at the same rate as for households (s1). Under these assumptions the overall reduction in margins on inputs to industries is about $1.85 billion, approximately 5 per cent of wholesale and retail margins on inputs to current production and capital creation. This saving of margins in business translates to a direct GDP gain of about 0.37 per cent.

*GDP effect = 0.37%*
*Consumption and welfare effect = 0.46%*

### Saving of Labour by Industries in Buying Inputs (s5)

eCommerce will reduce shopping time not only for households but also for firms. We simulate this as a labour-saving technical change worth half the savings of margins by industries, that is half of effect (s4).

$$GDP \ effect = 0.19\%$$
$$Consumption \ and \ welfare \ effect = 0.23\%$$

## Purchases of eCommerce Equipment by Industries (s6)

As with households, we assume that industries must buy eCommerce equipment and services worth 25 per cent of their margins savings (s4). By the tenth year this is an annual cost to the economy of about 0.093 per cent of GDP.

$$GDP \ effect = -0.09\%$$
$$Consumption \ and \ welfare \ effect = -0.12\%$$

## Direct Labour-saving Technical Progress in Transport and Banking (s7)

We assume that over the period 1998 to 2007 eCommerce will reduce labour costs by 5 per cent in the Transport and Banking sectors (MONASH industries 93, 96, 97, 99 and 100).[7] These cost savings will arise from reductions in staff required to provide services to the public, for example, selling airline tickets.

$$GDP \ effect = 0.28\%$$
$$Consumption \ and \ welfare \ effect = 0.35\%$$

## Time-saving by Industries Dealing with the Transport and Banking Sectors (s8)

If industry $j$, where $j$ is any industry except ownership of dwellings (104), uses 10 per cent of the services sold by the banking sector (industries 99 and 100), then we assume that industry $j$ makes labour savings worth half of 10 per cent of the savings made by banking. A similar treatment is adopted with respect to industry purchases of services from the transport sector (industries 93, 96 and 97).

$$GDP \ effect = 0.06\%$$
$$Consumption \ and \ welfare \ effect = 0.08\%$$

## Time-saving by Households Dealing with the Transport and Banking Sectors (s9)

If households use 10 per cent of the services sold by industry $q$ ($q$ = 93, 96, 97, 99 and 100), then we assume that households save time worth half of 10 per cent of the direct savings made by industry $q$. We also assume that if ownership of dwellings uses 10 per cent of the services sold by industry $q$ ($q$ = 93, 96, 97, 99 and 100), then households receive a time-saving worth half of 10 per cent of the savings made by industry $q$. We assume that half of the time-saving made by households is devoted to labour and half is devoted to leisure.

*GDP effect = 0.01%*
*Consumption effect = 0.02%*
*Welfare effect = 0.04%*

### Additional Margins Savings by the Communications Industry (98) (s10)

As well as the margins savings outlined in s4, we assume that the communications industry will save an additional 20 per cent of the wholesale margins on all its purchases. The communication industry's participants in the NOIE-sponsored meetings felt that eCommerce will be particularly important in enabling the communications industry to buy directly from producers.

*GDP effect = 0.05%*
*Consumption and welfare effect = 0.06%*

### Saving of Particular Inputs (s11)

We assume that the banking sector (industries 99 and 100) will save 5 per cent of its inputs of paper products (commodities 49 and 50).

*GDP effect = 0.01%*
*Consumption and welfare effect = 0.02%*

We assume that business services (industry 103) will save 5 per cent of its inputs of paper (commodities 49 and 50), machinery and equipment (commodities 74 to 80) and financial and business services (commodities 101 to 105).

*GDP effect = 0.12%*
*Consumption and welfare effect = 0.15%*

We assume that the banking industry (99) will save 3 per cent of the costs of construction inputs to capital creation. eCommerce will reduce the need for constructing branch offices.

*GDP effect = 0.01%*
*Consumption and welfare effect = 0.01%*

**Twist in Favour of Imports (s12)**

eCommerce will increase awareness by Australian households and industries of foreign products. We represent this by a twist in preferences which at given prices increases the ratio of imports to purchases of domestic products by 5 per cent. In the MONASH simulation, the preference twist has no direct effect on consumer welfare. We introduce welfare effects in (s14), where we recognize that eCommerce will allow consumers to find imported products that satisfy their requirements at lower prices.

*GDP effect = 0.00%*
*Consumption and welfare effect = 0.00%*

**Increase in Foreign Awareness of Australian Products (s13)**

eCommerce will increase foreign awareness of many of Australia's manufactured commodities and of tourism opportunities in Australia. For most MONASH-manufactured commodities (25–48, 53–57, 59–85, 101–105) and for tourism we assume a vertical upward movement in foreign demand curves of 5 per cent. For commodities 49 and 50 (publishing and printing) we assume an upward movement of 10 per cent. For agricultural, mineral and standard processed food products, we assume movements of 0 per cent. For these traditional export commodities, it seems likely that foreign awareness will not be increased by eCommerce.

Combined, the shifts in export demand curves have an impact effect on the terms of trade of 2.4 per cent. With exports representing about 20 per cent of GDP, this terms-of-trade improvement is equivalent to a gift to consumers worth about 0.60 per cent (= 0.2 · 2.4/0.8) of private and public consumption.

*GDP effect = 0.00%*
*Consumption and welfare effect = 0.60%*

**Reductions in Foreign-currency c.i.f. Prices of Imports (s14)**

Sophisticated eCommerce in Australia will help Australian households get a better deal on imported products. We recognize this by assuming for most commodities that households will be able to save foreign margins worth 50 per cent of the margins that they save in Australia. For example, if we assume that saving of Australian margins reduces the price of clothing in Australia by 1 per cent, then we assume that shopping around using eCommerce reduces c.i.f. prices of imported clothes by 0.5 per cent. Participants in the NOIE-sponsored meetings felt that the import prices of books and commercial printing (commodities 49 and 50) are particularly susceptible to shopping around. For these commodities we assume that the percentage reductions in c.i.f. prices are equal to the percentage reductions in Australian prices caused by savings of Australian margins.

After 10 years the assumed reduction in average import prices caused by Australia's adoption of eCommerce is 0.76 per cent. With imports being about 25 per cent as large as private and public consumption, the reduction in import prices of 0.76 per cent has an impact effect on consumption of 0.19 per cent.

*GDP effect = 0.00%*
*Consumption and welfare effect = 0.19%*

**Aggregate Effects**

Adding over the 14 sets of shocks we obtain:

*GDP effect = 1.60%*
*Consumption effect = 2.80%*
*Welfare effect = 2.82%*

The GDP effect consists of a 1.47 per cent increase from technological improvements and a 0.13 per cent increase from additional labour supply.

## 4. MACRO RESULTS

Figures 10.1 to 10.5 contain macro results from the MONASH model for the effects of the 14 sets of shocks listed in Section 3. The figures show percentage deviations from the basecase forecasts. For example, Figure 10.1 implies that in 2007 real GDP will be 2.7 per cent higher if Australia embraces eCommerce (that is, experiences the 14 sets of shocks) than if it doesn't.

We explain the MONASH macro results via a trade-focused BOTE model in which Australia produces and exports grain (good $g$), imports vehicles (good $v$), consumes $g$ and $v$ and creates capital from $g$ and $v$.

The production function for good $g$ is of the form

$$Y = A \cdot F(K, L), \tag{10.3}$$

where $Y$ is output of grain; $K$ and $L$ are inputs of capital and labour; $F$ is a homogeneous function of degree one (constant returns to scale); and $A$ is a technology variable, with increases in $A$ representing technological improvements.

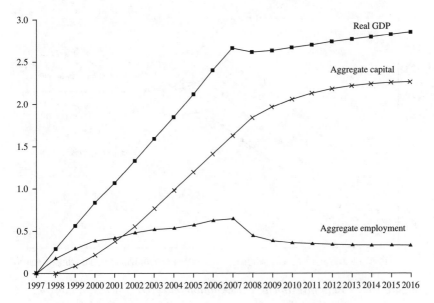

*Figure 10.1    Real GDP and factor inputs (% deviation from basecase
forecasts)*

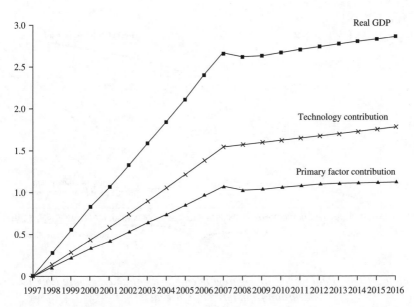

*Figure 10.2    Contributions to real GDP (% deviation from basecase
forecasts)*

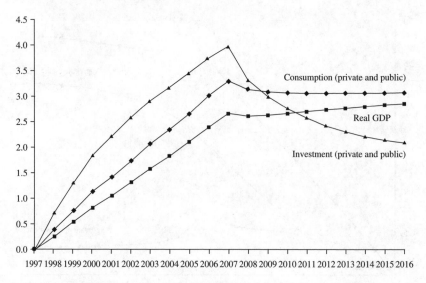

*Figure 10.3    Real investment, consumption and GDP (% deviation from basecase forecasts)*

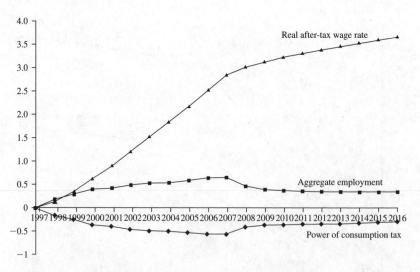

*Figure 10.4    Real wage rate, aggregate employment and consumption tax (% deviation from basecase forecasts)*

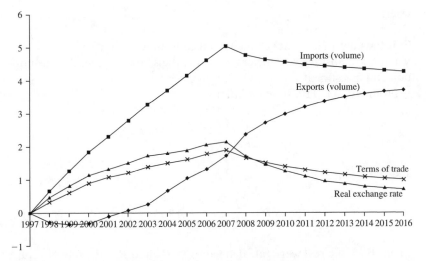

*Figure 10.5   Macro trade variables (% deviation from basecase forecasts)*

Assuming that factors are paid the values of their marginal products, we obtain

$$W = P_g \cdot A \cdot F_l \tag{10.4}$$

and

$$Q = P_g \cdot A \cdot F_k, \tag{10.5}$$

where:
$W$ is the wage rate;
$P_g$ is the price of grain;
$Q$ is the rental rate on capital; and
$F_k$ and $F_l$ are the first derivatives of $F$.

$F_k$ is a decreasing function of $K/L$ and $F_l$ is an increasing function of $K/L$.
    Next, we define the price deflators ($P_c$ and $P_i$) for consumption and investment by

$$P_c = P_g^\gamma \cdot P_v^{(1-\gamma)} \cdot T_c \tag{10.6}$$

and

$$P_i = P_g^\delta \cdot P_v^{(1-\delta)}, \tag{10.7}$$

where:

$P_v$ is the price of vehicles;

$T_c$ is the power (1 + rate) of the tax on consumption; and

γ and δ are positive parameters reflecting the share of grain in consumption and investment.

From (10.4) to (10.7) we find that

$$W_r = \frac{1}{T_c} \cdot \left(\frac{P_g}{P_v}\right)^{(1-\gamma)} \cdot A \cdot F_l \qquad (10.8)$$

and

$$R = \left(\frac{P_g}{P_v}\right)^{(1-\delta)} \cdot A \cdot F_k, \qquad (10.9)$$

where $W_r$ is the real wage rate defined as $W/P_c$; and $R$ is the rate of return on capital defined as the ratio of the rental price of capital ($Q$) to the asset price of capital ($P_j$).

Our simulation of the effects of eCommerce involves increases in $A$, $L$ and the terms of trade ($P_g/P_v$). In the long run, we expect rates of return in Australia to be unaffected by eCommerce. Thus via (10.9) we see that $F_k$ must decline and $K/L$ must increase. The increase in $K/L$ can be seen in Figure 10.1, where the long-run increase in $K$ is about 2.26 per cent and the long-run increase in $L$ is only about 0.33 per cent.

Most (0.22 per cent) of the long-run increase in $L$ arises from time-saving by households (shocks (s2) and (s9)). The rest is explained by the relationship between the eCommerce shocks and the basecase forecasts. Beyond 2007, there are no further eCommerce shocks to individual technology variables or to foreign-demand curves. Nevertheless, there are continuing increases in the aggregate eCommerce-induced improvement in technology and in the aggregate upward shift in foreign demand curves for Australian products. This is for two reasons. First, the eCommerce shocks produce technological improvements concentrated in parts of the economy (for example, banking) that are fast growing in our basecase forecasts. Second, the eCommerce-induced upward shifts in foreign-demand curves are concentrated in export markets (for example, tourism) that are fast growing in our basecase forecasts. In terms of our BOTE model it is as though $A$ and $P_g/P_c$ continue to receive positive shocks throughout the simulation period. This allows the employment deviation (0.33 per cent) to settle above the long-run supply deviation (0.22 per cent), despite continuing increases in $W_r$.

In MONASH, investors are modelled as responding cautiously to good news. Thus the movement to a higher value for $K/L$ is gradual. It is achieved over and beyond the ten-year period of favourable shocks from eCommerce adoption. In Figure 10.3 the deviation in investment increases for all of the ten years of eCommerce shocks and then tapers off. In year 1, investment is responding to the favourable shock in year 1; in year 2, investment is responding to the favourable shock in year 2 and continuing its response to the favourable shock in year 1; in year 10 investment is responding to the favourable shock in year 10 and continuing its response to the favourable shocks in previous years; in year 11 and subsequent years there are no further favourable shocks and investment is gradually completing its responses to the favourable shocks of years 1 to 10.

Increases in $A$, $K$ and $L$ generate an increase in $Y$ via (10.3). In percentage change terms, (10.3) can be written as:

$$y = a + S_k \cdot k + S_l \cdot l, \tag{10.10}$$

where:
$y$, $a$, $k$ and $l$ are the percentage deviations in $Y$, $A$, $K$ and $L$ caused by eCommerce; and $S_k$ and $S_l$ are the shares of $K$ and $L$ in GDP (approximately 0.4 and 0.6).

The shocks listed in Section 3 imply an increase in $A$ of about 1.5 per cent. With the long-run increases in $K$ and $L$ being 2.26 and 0.33 per cent, equation (10.10) gives

$$y = 1.5 + 0.4 \cdot 2.26 + 0.6 \cdot 0.33 = 2.60. \tag{10.11}$$

This is close to the long-run increase in GDP shown in Figure 10.1. Figure 10.2 uses (10.10) to disaggregate the percentage deviations in GDP into the technology contribution (the increase in $A$) and the primary factor contribution (the weighted average of the increases in $K$ and $L$). The contribution of technology continues to increase beyond the shock period because, as explained earlier, the eCommerce technology shocks are concentrated in parts of the economy showing fast growth in the basecase forecast.

With an increase in $K/L$, there is an increase in $F_l$. This, together with the increases in $P_g/P_v$ and $A$, produces a strong increase in the real wage rate (see (10.8) and Figure 10.4). The increase in the real wage rate is reinforced by a cut in consumption taxes (Figure 10.4). As mentioned in Section 2, we assume that consumption taxes adjust to stabilize the public sector budget. The fall in consumption taxes reflects reductions in unemployment benefits and our assumption that the eCommerce-induced percentage expansion in public consumption is half that of private consumption. The cut in consumption taxes is preserved into the long run but is reduced beyond 2007 as the employment deviation falls towards its eventual long-run level.

Employment in the short run overshoots its long-run level because of sticky adjustment in real wages to the shocks during the period 1998 to 2007.

The deviation path for private and public consumption (Figure 10.3) lies above that for GDP but has approximately the same shape. The gap between the consumption and GDP paths is mainly a reflection of the improvement in the terms of trade that allows increased consumption independently of increases in output. In the long run, the eCommerce-induced increase in private and public consumption is about 3 per cent. Four factors contribute to this increase:

1. The long-run increase in employment of 0.33 per cent. This produces additional GDP of 0.2 per cent (= 0.33 · 0.6) allowing an increase in private and public consumption of 0.25 per cent (= 0.2/0.8; recall that the ratio of private and public consumption to GDP is 0.8).

2. The long-run improvement in the terms of trade of 1 per cent (Figure 10.5). This allows additional consumption of 0.25 per cent (the value of exports is about 25 per cent of that of private and public consumption).

3. The improvement in technology, which by 2016 contributes 1.77 per cent to GDP (Figure 10.2). This allows additional consumption of 2.2 per cent (= 1.77/0.8).

4. The increase in the capital stock of 2.26 per cent. Although there is a long-run increase in domestic saving, this is sufficient to finance only a small fraction of the increase in the capital stock. Thus, most of the additional GDP derived from the additional capital stock accrues to foreigners. However, about 25 per cent accrues to the domestic economy through Australian taxes. With returns to capital representing about 40 per cent of GDP, the eCommerce-induced increase in capital allows an increase in private and public consumption in Australia of 0.3 per cent (= 2.26 · 0.4 · 0.25/0.8).

Up to 2008, the deviation path of investment, as well as consumption, lies above the deviation path of GDP. Consequently, the deviation path of imports must lie above that of exports (Figure 10.5). Beyond 2008, investment weakens as the adjustment in the $K/L$ ratio moves towards completion. Thus the gap between the import and export deviations narrows. The increase in exports beyond 2008 causes a reduction in the terms of trade (Figure 10.5). However, the deviation in the terms of trade remains positive reflecting the eCommerce-induced movements in foreign demand curves for exports and reductions in the prices of most imports.

The movements in exports and imports are facilitated by movements in the real exchange rate (Figure 10.5). During the early part of the simulation period in which there are large eCommerce-induced deviations in investment, the real exchange rate appreciates. Later, when investment weakens, the real exchange rate declines, thereby allowing an improvement in the real trade balance.

## 5. INDUSTRY AND SECTOR RESULTS

MONASH produces results for 112 industries. In Figure 10.6, these are aggregated and presented for 18 sectors. Results for industries and sectors can be explained as a combination of impact effects from the shocks and indirect effects from the macro movements already discussed.

### Entertainment (MONASH Industries 110–112), Rank 1

The entertainment sector is ranked first by output growth in the final year of our simulation. This sector benefits from growth in tourism exports and in consumption. Tourism exports grow strongly relative to other exports mainly because of shock s13. In s13 we stimulate all tourism exports, but only some non-traditional exports (manufacturing) and none of the traditional exports (agriculture and mining).

### Transport (MONASH Industries 93–98), Rank 2

This sector owes its high growth ranking to air transport (industry 96). Air transport benefits from tourism demand.

### Ownership of Dwellings (MONASH Industry 104), Rank 3

The output of this sector is the services provided by the housing stock. The housing stock receives a strong boost from eCommerce via the effect of eCommerce on consumption (Figure 10.3) combined with a relatively high expenditure elasticity of demand for housing.

### Construction (MONASH Industries 87–88), Rank 4

The output deviation in this sector follows closely that of investment (Figure 10.3). Investment increases strongly in the short run to facilitate the adjustment of the economy to a higher $K/L$ ratio. Even in the long run, investment is elevated, reflecting the need to maintain a larger capital stock than in the basecase forecast.

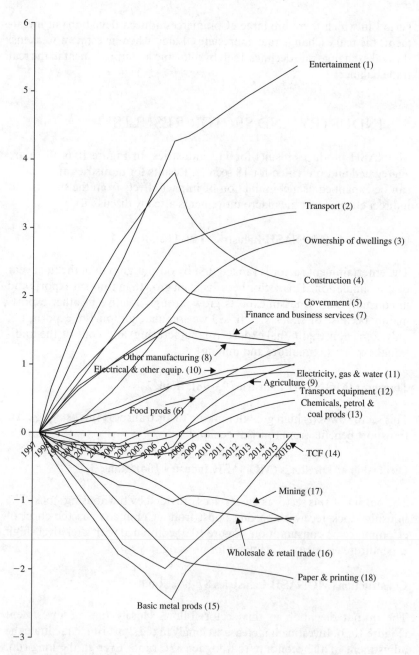

*Figure 10.6    Output by sector (rank in last year) (% deviation from basecase forecasts)*

### Government (MONASH Industries 105–109), Rank 5

This sector benefits from increased government consumption facilitated by increased overall income. We assume that the percentage deviation in government consumption is half that in private consumption.

### Food Products (MONASH Industries 18–29), Rank 6

This sector is adversely affected in the early part of the simulation period by real exchange rate appreciation. Later, as the real exchange rate weakens the sector's exports recover. Eventually the sector has a significant positive deviation in output reflecting growth in domestic consumption. Within the sector, standard export commodities (meat and sugar) perform poorly. Emerging exports (for example, other drinks, mainly wine) perform well via shock s13.

### Finance and Business Services (MONASH Industries 99–103), Rank 7

This sector achieves major cost reductions via eCommerce. However, expansion of the sector is limited by low price-sensitivities of demand and by the strong link between business services (industry 103) and wholesale and retail trade. As discussed below, activity in wholesale and retail trade contracts under the emergence of eCommerce.

### Other Manufacturing (MONASH Industries 40–43, 57–62, 79–83), Rank 8

This is a diverse group and the average outcome is not informative. Industries 40 to 43 and 57 to 62 consist mainly of materials used in building. The output paths for most of these industries are closely related to that of investment. Industries 80 to 82 (mainly rubber and plastic products) are highly exposed to import competition. They are adversely affected by real appreciation, especially in the early years of the simulation. Industries 79 and 83 (leather products and sporting equipment) perform well. They have considerable export potential that is enhanced by shock s13.

### Agriculture (MONASH Industries 1–11), Rank 9

Those industries in the sector that produce traditional export commodities (wool, grain and meat) perform poorly relative to those that produce food for the domestic market or inputs (for example, grapes) used in emerging export products. Traditional exports are harmed by real appreciation of the exchange rate and do not gain directly from eCommerce.

### Electrical and Other Equipment (MONASH Industries 72–78), Rank 10

Industries in this sector are influenced by a variety of factors. Industries 76 and 77 (agricultural and construction machinery) benefit from eCommerce via increased foreign awareness of their products. The other industries in the sector benefit from stronger investment and consumption but are harmed by increased competition from imports arising from a stronger real exchange rate.

### Electricity, Gas and Water (MONASH Industries 84–86), Rank 11

This sector achieves only moderate output deviations. While the outputs of electricity and gas benefit from expansion of consumption, they are damped by the negative deviations of energy-using sectors such as aluminium that are hurt by real appreciation.

### Transport Equipment (MONASH Industries 68–71), Rank 12

This sector is dominated by motor vehicles (industry 68). Output from the Australian motor vehicle industry is highly sensitive to the real exchange rate. In the early part of the simulation period the industry suffers from import competition brought about by a high real exchange rate. Later when the real exchange rate falls, the industry shows positive output deviations associated with increased activity in the economy.

### Chemicals, Petrol and Coal Products (MONASH Industries 49–56), Rank 13

This sector has a similar output deviation path to that of transport equipment. The sector contains several exchange-rate-sensitive import-competing industries including basic chemicals (industry 50), cosmetics (54), fertilizers (49) and explosives (55).

### Textiles, Clothing and Footwear (MONASH Industries 30–39), Rank 14

As with the previous two sectors, this sector is dominated by exchange-rate-sensitive import-competing industries.

**Basic Metal Products (MONASH Industries 63–64), Rank 15**

The main industry in this sector is aluminium (64). eCommerce has no direct beneficial effects on aluminium production. Aluminium output, which is heavily exported, is harmed by increases in real wages (reflected in real appreciation). Real wage increases arise from eCommerce-related productivity gains in the rest of the economy.

**Wholesale and Retail Trade (MONASH Industries 89–92), Rank 16**

The output deviation path for this sector is dominated by the negative result for retail trade (industry 90). Retail trade contracts because of eCommerce-related margin saving (shock s1).

**Mining (MONASH Industries 12–17), Rank 17**

As with basic metal products, this is an export-oriented sector that does not benefit directly from eCommerce but is harmed by higher real wages and real exchange rate.

**Paper and Printing (MONASH Industries 40–48), Rank 18**

This sector suffers from paper-saving changes in technology brought about by eCommerce (s11). In addition, some industries in the sector, particularly pulp, paper and paperboard (industry 44), face considerable import competition and are harmed by real appreciation.

## 6.   RESULTS FOR STATES, TERRITORIES AND STATISTICAL DIVISIONS

Figure 10.7 shows long-run eCommerce-induced deviations for gross state products (GSP) in Australia's six States and two Territories, together with the deviation in real GDP. All States and Territories show gains in output.

The region which is least stimulated is Western Australia. As explained in Section 5, eCommerce is likely to reduce activity in mining. Western Australia suffers relative to other regions because of the heavy representation of mining in its economy.

Queensland has a heavy concentration of mining and also export-oriented agriculture. This explains its relatively low ranking in Figure 10.7. An offset for Queensland, which means that it performs better than Western Australia, is its well-developed tourism industry.

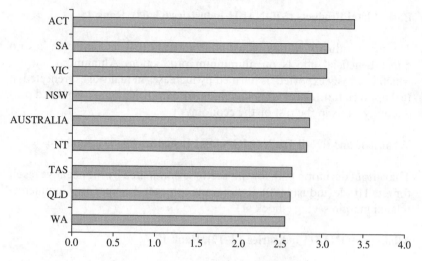

*Figure 10.7    GSPs for States and Territories and GDP for Australia in
2016 (% deviation from basecase forecasts)*

Like Queensland, Tasmania has over-representations in its economy of
traditional exports and of tourism. This gives it a performance under
eCommerce similar to that of Queensland. The Northern Territory also
has over-representations of traditional exports and of tourism. Its output
deviation under the eCommerce shocks is larger than those of Queensland
and Tasmania because the Territory, which has a relatively large government sector, benefits from the eCommerce-induced expansion in public
expenditure.

The industrial composition of the New South Wales economy is close to
that of Australia. Thus the deviation for GSP in NSW is close to that for
Australia's GDP.

Victoria and South Australia have above-average prospects under
eCommerce because neither state has a heavy reliance on traditional
exporting.

The ACT is the region of Australia with least reliance on traditional
exporting. This gives it the top ranking in Figure 10.7.

Figure 10.8 shows long-run employment deviations for Statistical
Divisions. These are relatively uniform, all lying in the range −0.16 to
1.38 per cent. The position of a Statistical Division within this range is
determined mainly by the shares of its economic activity accounted for by
tourism and traditional exports. The top three Statistical Divisions shown
in Figure 10.8, Far North (QLD), Morton (QLD) and Kimberley (WA), all

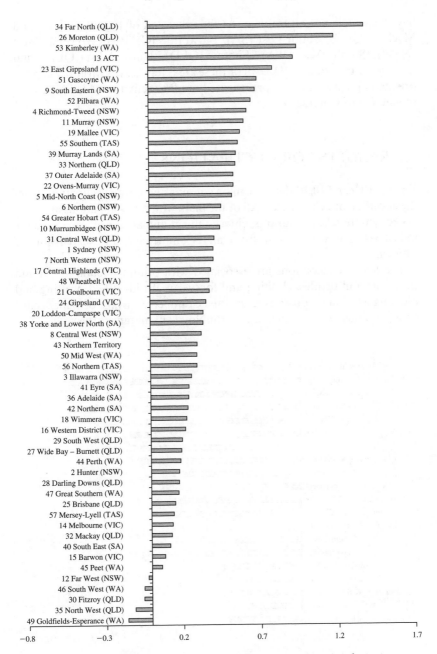

*Figure 10.8    Employment by Statistical Division in 2016 (% deviation from basecase forecasts)*

have heavy reliance on tourism. At the other end of Figure 10.8, we find Mackay (QLD), South East (SA), Barwon (VIC), Peel (WA), Far West (NSW), South West (WA), Fitzroy (QLD), North West (QLD) and Goldfields-Esperance (WA). All of these areas rely heavily on either export-oriented agriculture or export-oriented mining, activities which have least to gain from eCommerce.

## 7. RESULTS FOR OCCUPATIONS

Figures 10.9 and 10.10 show the main winning and losing occupations from the adoption of eCommerce. All of the main winning occupations are associated with hotels, restaurants, entertainment and air travel. These are the industries that will benefit from an eCommerce-related expansion of tourism.

The losing occupations are associated with printing, retailing, ground transport and textiles, clothing and footwear. We identified printing and retailing as losing industries reflecting eCommerce savings of paper (hard copy) and savings of retail margins. Employment in transport is reduced by

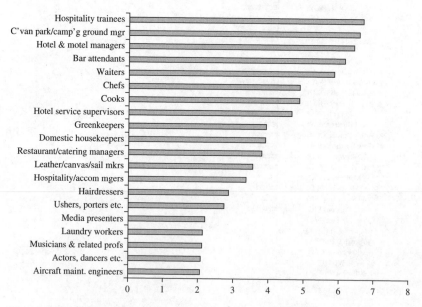

*Figure 10.9   The main winning occupations in 2016 (% deviation from basecase forecasts)*

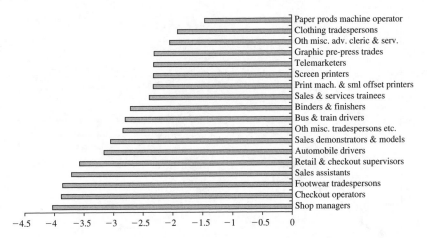

*Figure 10.10   The main losing occupations in 2016 (% deviation from basecase forecasts)*

eCommerce-related labour-saving technical change. The TCF sector is harmed by real appreciation associated with eCommerce-related increases in real wage rates.

## 8.   THE COSTS OF LAGGING AND THE BENEFITS OF LEADING

Officials from NOIE were interested in the effects on our results of slow and fast adoption of eCommerce in Australia relative to the rate of adoption in the rest of the world.

A danger for Australia from lagging behind the rest of the world is loss of market share in tourism and advanced manufactures to competitor countries. In terms of the sets of shocks listed in Section 3, Australia would miss out on all or part of s13; in other words Australia would miss the opportunity to increase foreign awareness of Australian products.

Figure 10.11 shows the paths of consumption (private and public combined) in three MONASH simulations: the standard simulation of the effects of eCommerce already discussed in the previous sections; a simulation in which Australia lags other countries in adopting eCommerce; and a simulation in which Australia leads other countries. In the lag simulation we assume that Australia increases foreign awareness of its products (s13) at half the rate assumed in the standard simulation, and in the lead simulation we assume that Australia increases foreign awareness of its products

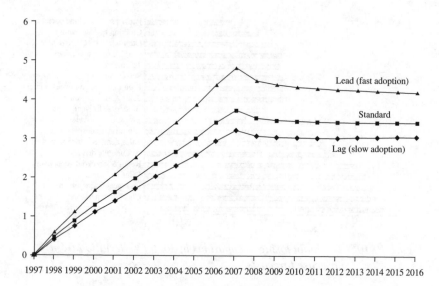

*Figure 10.11    Consumption in standard, lead and lag simulations
             (% deviation from basecase forecasts)*

at twice the rate assumed in the standard simulation. In the lag simulation we assume that the loss of market share relative to the standard simulation is permanent. That is, after the assumed ten-year adoption period, the eCommerce-induced increase in foreign demands for Australian products is permanently left at half the value it had in the standard simulation. Similarly, in the lead simulation we assume that the eCommerce-induced gain in foreign demands for Australian products is permanently left at twice the value it had in the standard simulation.

As could be anticipated from the consumption/welfare effect noted at the end of our discussion of s13 in Section 3, the long-run deviation in consumption in the lag simulation is about 0.3 percentage points below that in the standard simulation and the long-run deviation in consumption in the lead simulation is about 0.6 percentage points above that in the standard simulation.

With a discount rate of 5 per cent, the present value of the cost of lagging (the gap between the standard and lag simulation paths in Figure 10.11) is about 6.6 per cent of a year's consumption. The present value of gaining extra market share by leading is about 13.9 per cent of a year's consumption.

## 9.   CONCLUDING REMARKS

We present two groups of concluding remarks. The first concerns the effects of eCommerce and the second concerns the influence of trade economists on CGE modelling in Australia.

### Effects of eCommerce

In this chapter we have represented the direct effects of the adoption of eCommerce as shocks to 14 sets of technology, preference and trade variables in the MONASH model. The shocks were suggested in discussions with groups of people knowledgeable in the operation of eCommerce and drawn from sectors of the economy most likely to be directly affected by eCommerce. The group discussions produced quantifications of many of the effects identified qualitatively in recent papers by Freebain (2001), Dunt and Harper (2002) and Madden and Coble-Neal (2002).

   The main direct effects of eCommerce quantified in the group discussions involve: reductions in the use of retail margins in facilitating the flow of goods and services from producers to households; reductions in the use of wholesale and retail margins in facilitating the flow of goods and services between businesses; improvements in labour efficiency, especially in the finance and transport sectors; increases in the awareness of Australians of some foreign products and similar increases in the awareness of foreigners of some Australian products; reductions in the prices paid by Australians for some foreign products; and saving of shopping time by both businesses and households. We also allowed in our simulations for the creation of an eCommerce industry growing over the next ten years to an annual level of output of about $1 billion (1996/97 prices). This industry will provide equipment, training and software.

   In scaling the shocks we attempted to be conservative. Nevertheless, the MONASH simulations show major benefits for the Australian economy. Under our assumptions, eCommerce will, after ten years, allow a sustained increase in private and public consumption of about 3 per cent.[8]

   It is hard to think of changes in the way we do business that have simulated growth dividends as big as that shown for eCommerce. The only example that comes to mind is the Industry Commission's simulation of the Hilmer reforms (Industry Commission, 1995). By adopting a very broad view of the savings that could be attributed to the successful implementation of Hilmer, the Commission found a GDP gain of about 5 per cent.[9] Other microeconomic reforms such as tariff cuts generate relatively negligible gains. For example, in their final report on the Motor Vehicle Inquiry of 1997, the Industry Commission (1997) showed a sustainable consumption gain from the proposed reduction in car tariffs of about 0.3 per cent.

At the micro level, the MONASH results reveal no serious eCommerce-related adjustment problems. The long-run results show that eCommerce will increase the outputs of most sectors. The main exceptions are primary-product exporters and retail trade that are projected to suffer small output losses. eCommerce is not likely to raise foreign awareness of Australia's agricultural and mineral products but it is likely to harm the agricultural and mining industries by strengthening Australia's real exchange rate. Retail trade will be adversely affected by reductions in retail margins per unit of consumer sales. The sectors showing greatest expansion from eCommerce are associated with private consumption (which expands strongly in response to eCommerce-generated increases in real income) and tourism (which benefits from the expansion in domestic consumption and from an upward shift in foreign demand).

Consistent with the sectoral results, MONASH shows eCommerce-generated employment gains in tourism-related occupations such as hospitality trainee and hotel manager. Employment losses are shown for retail occupations with the largest being 4 per cent for shop managers. An employment loss of this size phased in over the period of our simulations does not pose an adjustment problem.

eCommerce will have a relatively uniform stimulatory effect across Australia's States and Territories. The ACT shows the greatest long-run expansion in output (3.4 per cent) and WA the smallest (2.5 per cent). These results largely reflect differences between the two regions in dependence on traditional exports. The ACT also benefits from expansion in public consumption. At the sub-state level, nearly all statistical divisions show eCommerce-induced long-run increases in employment. Employment increases are particularly pronounced in regions specializing in tourism (for example, Far North Queensland). A few mining and agricultural regions (for example, Goldfields-Esperance in WA and Fitzroy in Queensland) show small employment losses.

## Trade Economists and CGE Modelling in Australia

A common criticism of CGE models is that their results are unintelligible. Rauscher (1999) comments that 'To many economists, computable general equilibrium (CGE) models are a bit dubious. They are huge, they are complex, and they appear to be large black boxes that produce results that cannot be traced to an accessibly small set of simple assumptions or axioms'.[10] Rauscher then goes on to congratulate the GTAP group (Hertel, 1997) on their attempts to interpret CGE results.

In North America, CGE modelling is generally regarded as an outgrowth of the formalization of the Walrasian system undertaken by Arrow, Debreu and other mathematical theorists in the 1950s and 1960s. This was made clear with the award in 1991 by the American Economic Association (AEA) of a distinguished fellowship to Herbert Scarf, a prominent mathematical theorist in the mould of Arrow and Debreu. In part, the fellowship citation read 'Scarf's path-breaking technique for the computation of equilibrium prices has resulted in a new sub-discipline of economics: the study of applied general equilibrium models' (*American Economic Review*, vol. 82, no. 4, September 1992).[11]

People working in the Arrow–Debreu–Scarf tradition pay little attention to practical interpretation of results, and for most applied economists the formalization of the Walrasian system is arcane. Given the central position of North America in economic research, it is then not surprising that CGE models are widely regarded as black boxes.

While CGE modelling in Australia owes much to the USA,[12] it has developed in a totally different way. The antecedents of Evans (1972) were the multi-sectoral planning models of the 1950s and 1960s (for example, Sandee, 1960 and Manne, 1963). These were formulated and solved as linear and non-linear programming problems. The antecedents of ORANI and MONASH were Johansen's (1960) model of multisectoral growth in Norway and Armington's (1969 and 1970) model of multilateral trade. With these antecedents, the Australian CGE modelling effort has been focused sharply on practical issues, enabling Australian CGE modellers to participate in the ongoing economic policy debate to a greater extent than modellers in other countries. To facilitate their participation, they have developed BOTE models as a way of explaining their results to economists with no particular interest in CGE modelling.

As illustrated in this chapter, these BOTE models draw heavily on Australia's tradition of research in international trade and, as required by Rauscher, they have allowed Australian CGE modellers to trace their results 'to an accessibly small set of simple assumptions or axioms'. Because of the influence of Peter Lloyd and other Australian trade economists, simple trade models are a common language for communication among Australian economists. Thus the international trade tradition in Australian economics has made Australia a fertile ground for CGE modelling. This perhaps explains the pervasiveness of CGE modelling in Australian policy advising.

# NOTES

\* We thank John Freebairn for useful comments on an earlier draft.
1. For an excellent survey of analysis by Australian economists of trade issues (particularly protection in Australia) see Lloyd (1978).
2. Our work on eCommerce was originally performed for the National Office for the Information Economy (NOIE). Non-technical descriptions of MONASH eCommerce results prepared by the Allen Consulting Group can be found in NOIE (2000a, 2000b and 2001).
3. CGE models contain more variables than equations. In solving these models, they must be 'closed' by setting the values of $n-m$ variables exogenously where $n$ and $m$ are the numbers of variables and equations. Considerable flexibility in applications can be achieved by varying the closure. For example, short-run conditions can be simulated with exogenous real wage rates and endogenous employment. For long-run simulations employment becomes exogenous and real wage rates endogenous.
4. Alternatively we could have assumed adjustments in income tax rates. Our results would have been little affected.
5. These variables are the $A$s in production and utility functions of the form $F(X_1/A_1, \ldots, X_n/A_n)$, where the $X$s are quantities of inputs or consumption.
6. Litan and Rivlin (2001) describe a rather similar process for finding out about the direct effects of eCommerce in the USA. However, they stopped with the direct technology effects. They did not use an economic model to translate these effects into ultimate effects.
7. The MONASH industry and commodity categories used in the present study can be seen in NOIE (2000a, Tables A3 and A1).
8. Litan and Rivlin (2001) produced a smaller estimate for the USA, 1 to 2 per cent. However, as mentioned in note 6, their study stopped with the direct technology effects. It did not include trade-awareness effects or apply an economic model.
9. Quiggin (1997) argues cogently that the Commission's study exaggerates the benefits of the Hilmer reforms.
10. We thank Tony Meagher for drawing our attention to this quotation.
11. Dixon and Parmenter (1996, pp. 6 and 7) argue that the AEA misrepresents Scarf's contribution.
12. The major building block in all practical CGE models is an input–output table of the type first formulated by Leontief (1936) at Harvard University. Two of Australia's early CGE modellers, Evans and Dixon, completed their PhDs at Harvard under Leontief's supervision. It is also interesting to note that possibly the two most prominent policy-focused CGE modellers in the USA, Dale Jorgenson and Sherman Robinson, also completed their PhDs at Harvard in the 1950s and 1960s at the height of Leontief's influence. Both work outside the Arrow–Debreu–Scarf tradition.

# REFERENCES

Armington, Paul S. (1969), 'The geographic pattern of trade and the effects of price changes', *IMF Staff Papers*, **XVI**, 176–99.
Armington, Paul S. (1970), 'Adjustment of trade balances: some experiments with a model of trade among many countries', *IMF Staff Papers*, **XVII**, 488–523.
Dixon, P.B. and Parmenter, B.R. (1996), 'Computable general equilibrium modelling for policy analysis and forecasting', in H.M. Amman, D.A. Kendrick and J. Rust (eds), *Handbook in Computational Economics*, Volume 1, Amsterdam: Elsevier, pp. 3–85.

Dixon, P.B. and Rimmer, M.T. (1999), 'Changes in indirect taxes in Australia: a dynamic general equilibrium analysis', *Australian Economic Review*, **32** (4), 327–48.

Dixon, P.B. and Rimmer, M.T. (2002), *Dynamic General Equilibrium Modelling for Forecasting and Policy: a Practical Guide and Documentation of MONASH*, Contributions to Economic Analysis 256, Amsterdam: North-Holland.

Dixon, P.B., Parmenter, B.R., Ryland, G.J. and Sutton, J. (1977), *ORANI, A General Equilibrium Model of the Australian Economy: Current Specification and Illustrations of Use for Policy Analysis*, Volume 2 of the First Progress Report of the IMPACT Project, Canberra: Australian Government Publishing Service.

Dixon, P.B., Parmenter, B.R., Sutton, J. and Vincent, D.P. (1982), *ORANI: A Multisectoral Model of the Australian Economy*, Contributions to Economic Analysis 142, Amsterdam: North-Holland.

Dunt, E.S. and Harper, I.R. (2002), 'E-Commerce and the Australian economy', *Economic Record*, **78**, 327–42.

Evans, H.D. (1972), *A General Equilibrium Analysis of Protection: The Effects of Protection in Australia*, Contributions to Economic Analysis 76, Amsterdam: North-Holland.

Freebain, J. (2001), 'Some market effects of e-commerce', *Singapore Economic Review*, **46** (1), 49–62.

Hertel, T.W. (ed.) (1997), *Global Trade Analysis: Modeling and Applications*, Cambridge, UK: Cambridge University Press.

Industry Commission (1995), *The Growth and Revenue Implications of Hilmer and Related Reforms: A Report by the Industry Commission to the Council of Australian Governments, Final Report*, Canberra: Australian Government Publishing Service, March.

Industry Commission (1997), *The Automotive Industry*, volumes I and II, Industry Commission Report No. 58, Canberra: Australian Government Publishing Service, May.

Johansen, L. (1960), *A Multisectoral Study of Economic Growth*, Amsterdam: North-Holland (enlarged edn, 1974).

Klijn, Nico (1974), 'Revaluation and changes in tariff protection – the short term effects with special reference to agriculture', paper presented at the Australian Agricultural Economics Society 18th Conference, Perth.

Leontief, W.W. (1936), 'Quantitative input–output relations in the economic system of the United States', *Review of Economics and Statistics*, **18** (3), 105–25.

Litan, R.E. and Rivlin, A.M. (2001), 'Projecting the economic impact of the internet', *American Economic Review*, AEA Papers and Proceedings, **91**, 313–17.

Lloyd, P.J. (1978), 'Protection policy', in F.H. Gruen (ed.), *Surveys of Australian Economics*, volume 1, Sydney: George Allen and Unwin, pp. 241–96.

Madden, G. and Coble-Neal, G. (2002), 'Internet economics and policy: an Australian perspective', *Economic Record*, **78**, 343–57.

Manne, A.S. (1963), 'Key sectors of the Mexican economy 1960–1970', in A.S. Manne and H.M. Markowitz (eds), *Studies in Process Analysis*, New York: Wiley, pp. 379–400.

National Office for the Information Economy (2000a), *E-commerce Beyond 2000, Final Report*, Canberra: Commonwealth of Australia.

National Office for the Information Economy (2000b), *E-commerce Across Australia*, Canberra: Commonwealth of Australia.

National Office for the Information Economy (2001), *The Current State of Play 2001*, Canberra: Commonwealth of Australia.

Quiggin, J. (1997), 'Estimating the benefits of Hilmer and related reforms', *Australian Economic Review*, **30** (3), 256–72.

Rauscher, M. (1999), 'Review of global trade analysis: modeling and applications', *Economic Journal*, **109**, F799–800.

Sandee, J. (1960), *A Long-Term Planning Model for India*, New York: Asia Publishing House and Calcutta: Statistical Publishing Company.

# 11. Trade liberalization, resource degradation and industrial pollution in developing countries

**Ian Coxhead and Sisira Jayasuriya[1]**

## 1. INTRODUCTION

Economic growth and trade are generally said to have three types of environmental effects: scale effects, associated with increases in the overall size of the economy; technique effects due to changes in production technology; and composition effects, capturing induced changes in the structure of production and factor demand (World Bank, 1992; Grossman and Krueger, 1993). Of these, the first is unambiguously negative (in the sense of creating more pollution or increasing demands on depletable natural resource stocks), and the second is most likely to be positive since new technologies are by and large cleaner than old. Aggregate empirical studies of the non-linear relationship between income and pollution or demands on depletable resource stocks (the search for an 'environmental Kuznets curve (EKC)' as in, for example, Antweiler et al., 2001) are driven by the changing relative importance of these two. But for many purposes, the greater interest is in the sign of the composition effect, about which there are no general prior hypotheses. Whereas scale and technique effects determine the shape of the EKC, changes in the structure of production – the sources of composition effects – displace it vertically, and as such may have more immediate medium-run environmental impacts.

The composition effect is of particular importance in studies of trade policy reform since the primary effects of such reform are felt through changes in relative prices, which in turn stimulate the reallocation of resources among productive activities. To the extent that different activities have varying propensities to pollute or to make use of depletable resources, changing the structure of production can have significant environmental effects. This is particularly true, of course, in developing economies with large agricultural and natural resource industries and protected heavy industrial sectors. In addition, they also alter factor rewards and income distribution, with consequences for poverty. These environmental and income distributional effects are critically affected by some of the common structural features of developing countries, such as the limited degree of spatial and sectoral factor mobility and the absence or poor enforcement of property rights over natural resources.

Because discussions of trade liberalization and its environmental and distributional outcomes evoke strong political and emotive responses, there is a premium on analytical rigour and careful drawing out of policy conclusions. The economy-wide ramifications of major policy reforms and shocks imply the need for an explicitly general equilibrium analytical approach. At the same time, it is also important to ensure that key structural and institutional features of these economies are adequately taken into consideration in analytical work. Unfortunately much theoretical work assumes overly simple economic structures to focus on an analytically interesting issue, while much empirical work either lacks rigorous theoretical underpinnings or is based on econometric results from cross-sectional country data. In both cases, they can lend support to misleading policy conclusions.

The recent history of economic development in a group of natural resource-rich developing market economies of Asia-Pacific (Indonesia, Malaysia, the Philippines, Sri Lanka, Thailand and increasingly, Vietnam) provides a laboratory of sorts for comparative study of development policies and for some illuminating case studies for the interaction of growth, policy reforms, trade and the environment. A half-century ago, they shared many similarities in initial resource and factor endowment and economic structure but they differ markedly today in terms of their state of development, level of industrialization and economic structure (Table 11.1).

Their divergent trends in the second half of the twentieth century, as summarized by the growth rates in Table 11.1, can be attributed in part to differences in policy regimes. In agriculture, all countries initially taxed farm output heavily to finance industrialization (especially Thailand, a food exporter); these policies too have been relaxed, but in many cases later, and more slowly, than industrial policies. Historically, the net price-increasing effects of food import restrictions and related interventions were insufficient to offset the prevailing anti-agriculture bias of industrial promotion policies (Krueger et al., 1988). In a very significant shift, however, this policy bias was inverted in the 1990s, as significant progress was made in manufacturing but not agricultural import trade liberalization. WTO trade policy rules bind import tariffs for manufactures, but are considerably more lenient where developing-country agricultural imports are concerned.[2]

Finally, while continuing high protection has done little to reduce production of import-competing crops, globalization and capital-deepening have also fuelled massive expansion of plantations producing industrial

*Table 11.1    GDP growth rates and shares of major sectors (per cent), developing Asian countries*

| Country | GDP growth[a] | Years | Agric. | Industry | (Mfg) | Services |
|---|---|---|---|---|---|---|
| Indonesia | 3.97 | 1960–80 | 42 | 23 | 10 | 35 |
| | | 1981–90 | 22 | 37 | 16 | 40 |
| | | 1991–00 | 18 | 43 | 24 | 40 |
| Malaysia | 4.12 | 1960–80 | 29 | 30 | 14 | 41 |
| | | 1981–90 | 20 | 39 | 21 | 41 |
| | | 1991–00 | 13 | 42 | 27 | 45 |
| Philippines | 1.04 | 1960–80 | 28 | 31 | 23 | 41 |
| | | 1981–90 | 24 | 36 | 25 | 40 |
| | | 1991–00 | 20 | 32 | 23 | 48 |
| Thailand | 4.34 | 1960–80 | 29 | 25 | 17 | 46 |
| | | 1981–90 | 17 | 33 | 24 | 50 |
| | | 1991–00 | 11 | 39 | 29 | 50 |
| Vietnam | 5.37[b] | 1960–80 | .. | .. | .. | .. |
| | | 1981–90 | 40 | 29 | 26 | 32 |
| | | 1991–00 | 29 | 30 | 20 | 41 |
| Sri Lanka | 2.99 | 1960–80 | 30 | 24 | 17 | 47 |
| | | 1981–90 | 27 | 27 | 15 | 46 |
| | | 1991–00 | 23 | 26 | 16 | 50 |

*Notes:*
[a]  Real per capita income (1995 US$), annual average 1970–2000.
[b]  1991–2000.
..= not available.

*Source:*   World Bank: World Development Indicators 2001.

crops. In Southeast Asia, the area planted to coffee has risen by more than 300 per cent since 1980, while for oil palm the increase is more than 500 per cent.[3] New land for expanding crops has been obtained primarily through the conversion of forests, where enforcement of property rights remains costly and controversial (Gérard and Ruf, 2001; Vincent et al., 1997; Ha, 2001). Deforestation rates in tropical Asia are the world's highest (Table 11.2). These trends, however, mask substantial variation in country-specific conditions, and may mean quite different environmental responses to similar policy changes.

In this chapter we consider the environmental and welfare effects of several types of reforms, in general, and with specific reference to some 'representative' developing Asian economies. The policy experiments themselves mimic, in stylized fashion, the ending of ISI policies through the

*Table 11.2　Estimated changes in natural forest and plantation cover*

| Region | 1990 ('000 ha) | | 2000 ('000 ha) | | Average annual change of natural forest | |
|---|---|---|---|---|---|---|
| | Nat. forest | Plantation | Nat. forest | Plantation | '000 ha | Per cent |
| Africa | 697 882 | 4 415 | 641 828 | 8 038 | −5 589 | −0.8 |
| Oceania | 36 201 | 149 | 34 869 | 263 | −133 | −0.4 |
| S. America | 903 199 | 7 279 | 863 739 | 10 455 | −3 946 | −0.4 |
| Asia | 495 340 | 56 117 | 431 422 | 115 873 | −6 392 | −1.3 |
| Tropical | 289 820 | 22 486 | 233 448 | 54 624 | −5 637 | −1.9 |
| Temperate | 205 520 | 33 631 | 197 974 | 61 249 | −755 | −0.4 |

*Source:*　World Resources Institute calculations from FAO data (Mathews, 2001).

relaxation of tariffs on industrial manufactures as well as the liberalization of import restrictions on food, a major issue on the current policy agenda in many food-importing Asian developing countries. While our main focus is on policy changes and their environmental outcomes, we also consider implications for other potentially important policy concerns, such as aggregate real income and the welfare of the poor. We show that specific characteristics of the economic structure are critical for the environmental and income distributional outcomes of the major policy changes that are currently on the agenda and that simple generalizations can be quite misleading. In particular, under a variety of circumstances, both manufacturing and agricultural trade liberalization can be both pro-environment and pro-poor, but greater access to developed-country markets for labour-intensive manufactures of developing countries may determine whether agricultural trade liberalization will benefit the poor or not.

## 2.　THE INTERSECTORAL TRANSMISSION OF ECONOMIC SHOCKS

In this section we provide a geometric illustration of the main mechanisms by which a shock in one sector or region of a stylised developing economy is transmitted to others in a general equilibrium setting. The goal is to take account of key economic and spatial features of developing economies and to differentiate among types of environmental issue – primarily, between industrial emissions and deforestation that occurs at the agricultural frontier, and to highlight the direct and indirect impacts of price and policy changes and the nature of adjustments that they call forth. We begin with a base case model that captures many of the stylized facts of Asian developing economies. The formal structure of the model is presented in the Appendix, and developed more fully in Coxhead and Jayasuriya (2003).

## Trade Policy, Migration and Environment with Open-access Forests

Imagine an economy comprising two sub-economies, manufacturing and agriculture. Manufacturing ($M$) is an H–O–S (Heckscher–Ohlin–Samuelson) sub-economy with mobile $L$ and $K$ used to produce an import-competing good $H$, and an exportable $X$. The assumption that factors are intersectorally mobile tends to be a reasonable one in most manufacturing activities, at least in the medium run, but can be easily altered to allow for short-run factor-specificity as an extreme case. Agriculture ($A$) is produced in two 'regions', 'upland' and 'lowland', with different land types, denoted by $T$ in upland and $N$ in lowland. These land-type differences reflect differences in elevation, soil type, access to irrigation and other agro-climatic factors; in most Asian countries, rice, the main food staple, is grown primarily in low lying, fully or partially submerged land (that is often irrigated), while 'uplands' or 'dry lands' are cultivated to perennials – often tree crops like tea, rubber and oil palm – as well as to food crops under rain-fed conditions.[4] The manufacturing sub-economy has two sectors, one with a low capital-to-labour ratio ($k$) and one with high $k$. The high $k$ sector is import-competing and may receive protection; the low $k$ sector is export-oriented and is not initially protected. We assume that the high $k$ sector is also more emissions-intensive. These assumptions on emissions and the bias of trade policy capture Asian realities, albeit in highly simplified form. Lowland agriculture produces food, which may be protected if this economy is a net food importer, or unprotected if it is a net exporter. Upland agriculture may also produce food (in which case the same product is produced in two spatially and technologically distinct sectors) or tree crops for export. In uplands, land is 'produced' by converting forests; for simplicity, we assume that the forest products themselves are of negligible value. More importantly, the forest is an open-access resource. Consumers value its existence, but upland farmers need not take this into account, nor spend to acquire the forest area, when making agricultural land expansion decisions. Clearing forest requires labour only. Labour is mobile among all activities: upland agriculture (and forest clearing), lowland agriculture, and manufacturing. The two manufacturing sectors also share a mobile factor, capital. Each agricultural sector uses land, assumed specific to the sector.

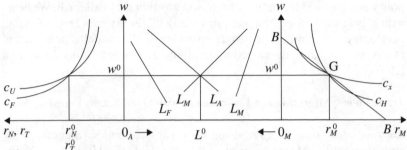

Panel (a): Agriculture    Panel (b): Labour market   Panel (c): Manufacturing

*Figure 11.1   Equilibrium of a four-sector, two-region economy*

Commodity prices are exogenously fixed, and may differ from world market prices by measures such as tariffs, export taxes or quantitative restrictions. Tariff/tax revenues are assumed to be redistributed in lump-sum fashion, and given the small-country assumption, have no impact on base commodity prices. We want to know the effects of a change in some price or tax policy on production in each sector and on the returns to manufacturing capital and land in each agricultural sector. We assume constant returns to scale, perfect competition in both goods and factor markets, and complete markets for all factors except $T$, the land endowment in uplands. Therefore, the primary mechanism for transmittal of policy or other shocks throughout the economy is the labour market.

Figure 11.1 captures the main structural features of the economy just described. The central panel (b) shows an economy-wide labour market, with the width of the panel denoting the economy's total labour endowment. Employment in agriculture is measured to the right from $0_A$, and that in manufacturing to the left from $0_M$. Labour demand curves for $M$ and $A$ sub-economies are constructed by horizontal addition of those for the respective sectors, as shown. In the initial equilibrium, the economy-wide wage ($w$) is given by the intersection of the $L_A$ and $L_M$ curves.

On the right-hand side of the diagram, panel (c) shows unit cost (i.e. zero profit) curves for each manufacturing sector under the assumption of constant returns to scale. This panel differs from the usual dual Lerner–Pearce diagram in that we are supposing wages to be set economy-wide rather than purely within the manufacturing sector. Product prices and the wage determine the set of feasible manufacturing industries and the location of their unit cost curves. In this space, the line $BB$ has slope $-k$, the negative of the manufacturing sector capital–labour ratio. An increase in $k$ increases the slope of this line, and a value of $k$ higher than the slope of a tangent to $c_H$ at the intersection of the unit cost curves (point G) implies specialization in capital-intensive production.[5] For a given wage, we can read off the equilibrium return to $M$ sector capital, $r_M$, on the horizontal axis.

Panel (a) shows the analogous cost curves for the two agricultural sectors. The horizontal axis shows unit returns to land in each agricultural region, $r_U$ and $r_F$. These, being region-specific, are not required to be equal, though for convenience we have chosen units of land so as to equate them in the initial equilibrium.

Absence of property rights in upland land means that profit-maximizing upland producers use upland land up to the point at which its average product is equal to average cost (Gordon, 1954). We can capture this in the figure, by interpreting the curve $L_A$ in panel (b) as the horizontal sum of labour demands in lowland and upland agriculture, noting that under open access to forests, upland labour demand exceeds the quantity that would be observed if property rights were enforced. In the initial equilibrium, open access means that there is overuse of labour in upland; were property rights enforced, the total labour demand curve in agriculture would lie to the left of $L_A$.

In manufacturing, we assume that producers in the dirty industry are not penalized for emissions – another form of property rights failure, this time for clean air and water. Unlike the case of forest, however, 'free disposal' of air and water pollutants leaves producers on their marginal curves, producing a pure externality.

## Policy Shocks and Outcomes

How do factor prices and the structure of production respond to a change in some policy or product price? To see the working of the model, let the labour-intensive manufacture be the numeraire good, and set $p^X = 1$. Now consider an increase in the price of upland agriculture, $p^U$. As shown in Figure 11.2, this displaces the demand for upland labour vertically upwards in panel (b) by the amount of the price rise. The aggregate agricultural labour demand curve is displaced vertically by the price change times the upland share in agricultural employment. With no change in manufacturing prices, the aggregate labour market response is clear: labour is withdrawn from manufacturing and moves into agriculture; within agriculture as a whole, it is reallocated from lowland to upland production.

As a result of the price change, production in upland rises and that in lowland falls. For the lowland, where the quantity of land is fixed, the output change can be read directly from the horizontal axis in panel (b); it is proportional to the reduction in labour use at the new, higher wage. For the upland sector, we suppose that new land may be brought

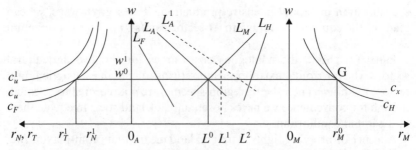

Panel (a): Agriculture    Panel (b): Labour market   Panel (c): Manufacturing

*Figure 11.2   Increase in upland agricultural price*

into production through forest clearing. However, as long as the labour required for forest conversion is directly proportional to that required for upland production, the increase in upland farmed area is still proportional to the shift in labour demand. Returns to land in each agricultural region are altered, as seen in panel (a): that in upland rises, and that in lowland must fall.

At the original wage and price levels, the withdrawal of labour from $M$ has predictable Rybczinski effects; that is, there is a lowering of the aggregate $K/L$ in manufacturing (in terms of Figure 11.1, the line $BB$ becomes steeper) and the labour-intensive sector contracts while $H$ expands. As long as the quantity of labour withdrawn is relatively small, the manufacturing economy remains within its original cone of diversification with the return to capital unchanged at $r_M^0$.

This is not an equilibrium, however, as the increase in agricultural labour demand also exerts upward pressure on the economy-wide wage. With constant output prices, the productivity of labour in $M$ must rise to match the wage increase. As a consequence, the $M$ sector's aggregate labour demand falls and the $L_M$ curve in panel (b) moves to the right. In the new equilibrium the sectoral labour allocation will lie between $L^1$ and $L^2$ and the wage between $w^0$ and $w^1$; the precise outcomes will depend on the extent to which the $M$ industries in aggregate release additional labour. Within manufacturing, both the quantity and price effects of the economy-wide labour market adjustment will reduce the output of the labour-intensive sector; the output of the capital-intensive sector may rise or fall. The return on $M$-sector capital must also fall.

The environmental effects of the agricultural price increase can be inferred from the adjustments shown in the diagram. In manufacturing, we assume that the capital-intensive sector pollutes while the labour-intensive sector does not. The 'dirty' $H$ sector expands relative to the 'clean' $X$ sector, so the overall emissions-intensity of manufacturing must rise. Whether total emissions rise or fall depends on whether dirty-sector output expands in absolute terms or not. In agriculture, we assume lowland production to be 'clean' while upland production makes use of open-access forest to generate land. The price rise for upland agriculture increases demand for land, thus raising the return to labour used in clearing forest as well. Moreover, the release of some labour from manufacturing reduces costs in upland production and forest clearing, thus further increasing the deforestation response. Looking across the economy as a whole, the price rise is an environmental lose–lose proposition (more deforestation, more emissions) if $H$ expands, or a lose–win proposition if $H$ contracts.

**Changing Tariffs on ISI Sectors**

Other variations on Figure 11.1 can be used to consider other price and policy changes. One is the effects of a fall in the domestic price of $H$, due, for example, to the relaxation of tariffs as ISI policies favouring heavy industry are abandoned. In many respects this is exactly the reverse of the story just told. At constant wages, the tariff reduction displaces $c_H$ inwards, so the new intersection of $M$ sector unit cost curves in panel (c) is above and to the left of G. At the lower tariff rate, $X$-sector output expands and $H$ contracts. At the original economy-wide wage, the $M$ sector increases its labour demand overall; this in turn bids up the wage and reduce profits in all agricultural activities, including land clearing. The environmental outcomes associated with the tariff reform are clear and unambiguous: manufacturing becomes less emissions-intensive as the dirty industry contracts, and there is less deforestation due to the higher cost of land clearing. Reducing the tariff is an environmental win–win policy move, even with open-access forests.

**Changing Protection for Food Producers**

In a third experiment, consider the situation in which food producers are initially protected from import competition, a scenario that is relevant to many developing Asian countries now contemplating agricultural trade liberalization (Anderson, 1992).

If food is produced in lowland only, then relaxing barriers to food imports can have mixed environmental effects despite higher national income. An inward shift of the lowland unit cost curve in panel (a) of Figure 11.1, and the corresponding downward displacement of the $L_F$ and $L_A$ curves in panel (b), will reduce the wage, lowering costs in other sectors. Deforestation in upland will expand, while in manufacturing there will be positive Rybczinski effects reinforced by the falling wage; the labour-intensive $X$ sector will expand while $H$ may expand or contract. The overall environmental outcome is thus mixed: there is more land clearing in upland, while the $M$ sector as a whole becomes less emissions-intensive (and emissions may even fall absolutely).

For many countries, however, it is more appropriate to think of food as produced in both agricultural regions. For example, irrigated rice in lowland and rain-fed rice or corn in upland has been a common in farming systems of the Philippines. Under this assumption, a lower food price displaces $L_A$ down by the amount of the price change and shifts both $c_F$ and $c_U$ in toward $0_A$. Lowering import barriers on food will then have a direct pro-forest effect by reducing incentives to expand agricultural land, but at the same time will further lower the cost of land clearing, thus indirectly contributing to more deforestation. Whether deforestation will rise or fall on balance will depend significantly on the extent to which manufacturing sectors take up extra labour as product wages fall. The presence of a large, very labour-intensive $X$ sector will increase the chance that reducing the protection on food will not have a large land-clearing effect; conversely, if food policy is relaxed in an economy with mainly capital-intensive ISI manufacturing, the wage-driven decline in land-clearing costs will be correspondingly higher. In a nutshell, the environmental consequences of the food policy change will depend on initial economic structure, not only in agriculture, but economy-wide.

An important side effect of both food policy scenarios is that while the real wage must rise (since labour absorption in non-food sectors restricts the drop in the wage to less than that of the food price), the real incomes of some groups in the economy may fall. In particular, rural households who derive most of their income from labour and land may experience increased poverty if their losses from declining land returns outweigh their gains from higher wages and cheaper food. This presents a policy dilemma that is familiar to students of large, poor, agrarian Asian economies undergoing or contemplating agricultural trade liberalization. Our analysis stresses the importance of economy-wide labour market adjustments to poverty outcomes, with the clear implication that policy reform packages, rather than piecemeal efforts at sectoral level, may be the key to simultaneous poverty reduction and environmental improvement.[6]

## Reform of Property Rights

Finally, recall from the discussion of Figure 11.1 that because there is open access to forests for conversion to upland land, the privately optimal labour allocation in upland agriculture equates average, rather than marginal, costs and returns. Thus the curve $L_A$ in panel (b) of the figure is equal to the horizontal sum of labour's value marginal product in lowland agriculture and its average product in upland. It follows that enforcing property rights in forests, which reduces the rents earned from land clearing, displaces the $L_A$ curve to the left – in the limiting case, to the point at which it is simply the sum of the upland and lowland marginal (that is, labour demand) curves, and property rights in forest are fully enforced. In panel (c), an increased manufacturing sector labour endowment and lower economy-wide wage will once more reduce the overall emissions-intensity of manufacturing production, and – if these effects are large enough that $H$ output contracts absolutely – even reduce it in absolute terms.

It is now clear that, other things equal, enforcement of forest property rights will hurt the poor disproportionately. Not only do upland farmers (typically the poorest group in any developing-country population) lose rents formerly earned on 'free' land, but the economy-wide wage decline associated with restricting access to upland will potentially hurt all wage-earners. Enforcing property rights in upland land amounts to the reversal of internal migration policies, widely adopted in insular Southeast Asia beginning in the 1950s, in which governments subsidized the movement of poor landless families to the agricultural frontier, where their labour productivity could be enhanced by access to supposedly abundant forest-covered lands. If governments are to pursue environmental protection simultaneously with poverty alleviation, the declaration of protected forest areas and other legal and institutional innovations restricting the growth of upland agriculture will have to be accompanied by policies that increase labour productivity elsewhere in the economy. ISI policies, where they persist, are obvious candidates for relaxation in order to achieve growth with environmental protection and poverty alleviation. Reducing protectionist policies for lowland (food) agriculture may, in contrast, have the opposite effects.

The analysis so far has explored direct and indirect effects of sectoral interventions when major component parts of the economy are linked by an integrated labour market. Through both price and quantity changes, labour market adjustments to a sector-specific price or policy shock convey cost signals to producers in other sectors or regions. In manufacturing, the standard Rybczinski effects associated with labour endowment changes in a Heckscher–Ohlin–Samuelson economy are augmented by economy-wide wage adjustments. On the environmental front, wage and labour force changes may alter incentives to deforest (labour may migrate to or away from the frontier) and to engage in relatively capital-intensive 'dirty' manufacturing production. These effects may be accompanied by changes in real incomes, potentially raising additional challenges when poverty alleviation is a policy target.

## 3.  ECONOMIC STRUCTURE AND ENVIRONMENT IN SOME STYLIZED ASIAN ECONOMIES

### Protection and Environment in the 'Jeepney' Economy

The model outlined above is capable of many permutations, each reflecting a different economic structure and set of policies. One is the case of an economy producing food in both agricultural regions, in addition to the two types of manufacturing industry, capital-intensive ISI and labour-intensive exportables. This configuration is a stylization of many developing Asian economies before the recent era of globalization, and in honour of the Philippine economy before liberalization in the Ramos era (1992–98) we call this the 'jeepney' economy. (The jeepney, a locally made adaptation of Second World War era military jeeps, is an early and colourful example of import substitution in Asian manufacturing.)

Consider a tariff on capital-intensive manufactures in the jeepney economy. With other product prices fixed, this increases the relative profitability of ISI production, and labour and capital are transferred to the protected sector; its output goes up, and the manufacturing sector as a whole becomes more emissions-intensive. Within manufacturing, however, the tariff raises the return to capital and lowers that to labour in the usual Stolper–Samuelson fashion. With a constant food price, labour is drawn into agriculture with lower wages. The cost of land clearing for upland agriculture falls, so the tariff also increases deforestation pressures. Net migration of labour into uplands, as a response to declining productivity and earnings potential in manufacturing, is a well-documented feature of ISI regimes (for example, Cruz and Francisco, 1993); the tariff is one factor giving rise to the increased population pressure on upland resources that is often identified as a cause of deforestation.

Second, consider agricultural protectionism, for example that which is motivated by concerns about food self-sufficiency as a source of food security. Higher food sector protectionism draws labour out of manufacturing, and the Rybczinski theorem tells us that the manufacturing industry experiencing the largest relative output decline will be the labour-intensive, export-oriented one. Both upland and lowland agriculture will expand. Lowland, however, is constrained by a fixed land endowment; in uplands, the higher food price increases the return to forest clearing to create new lands. In Asia, high and increasing rates of protection for corn and other cereals grown largely in uplands and non-irrigated areas has been associated with agricultural expansion at the forest margin (Coxhead et al., 2002; Coxhead, 2000). Thus protection for food producers increases deforestation and reduces the output of labour-intensive manufactures. The emissions-intensity of manufactures rises, but overall industrial pollution may rise or fall since the sector as a whole will contract.

The combination of industrial protection and agricultural protection in the jeepney economy thus favours both emissions-intensive industrial development and deforestation at the upland agricultural margin. Whether total industrial emissions are higher or lower relative to free trade depends on parameter values. Accordingly, if economy-wide labour markets matter, the solution to the environment–economic growth trade-off must involve trade policy liberalization.

### The 'Becak' Economy

The becak is a tricycle rickshaw once common in Indonesia, and the becak economy is so named because it has characteristics representative of that country's economy. (It is appropriately labour-intensive, and though its progress on the flat is slow and steady, it goes downhill very easily.) In stylized form, it differs from the jeepney economy only in that upland agriculture produces tree crops for export rather than food. As in the earlier case, the land frontier is open in the sense that forest can be freely converted to fuel agricultural expansion, in spite of negative externalities generated by forest clearing. Such negative externalities with transboundary dimensions are particularly pertinent in the Indonesian case, where widespread forest burning to establish oil palm and other plantations since the late 1990s has generated significant pollution in the form of smoke, or 'haze' through much of Indonesia as well as many other neighbouring countries of (Schweltheim and Glover, 1999).

With tree crops exportable, manufacturing protection again releases labour to both agricultural sectors. The rate of expansion at the frontier depends on tree-cutting technology (in a more sophisticated model, it would matter whether the forests had previously been logged, and thus made more readily accessible to colonizing farmers; see Angelsen, 1995). Protection for food producers, in the becak economy, causes the lowland region to expand, raising labour demand; this promotes downslope migration and discourages deforestation at the upland frontier. As before, the protection for food producers also draws labour out of the manufacturing sector, reducing the relative size of the exportable goods sector and increasing emissions-intensity. By comparison with the jeepney economy, in the becak economy agricultural protectionism tends to diminish pressures on forests.

## The 'Tuk-tuk' and 'Cyclo' Economies

Another interesting case is that in which food is exported rather than import-competing. This is the case with Thailand and, more recently, Vietnam. In Thailand, food is produced in both agricultural regions; in Vietnam it is produced primarily in lowland only, with plantation crops occupying the uplands and the forest margin. Continuing the transport metaphor, we can think of these variants as the 'tuk-tuk' and 'cyclo' economies respectively; the tuk-tuk is a three-wheeled motorcycle that can be seen tearing along Bangkok streets at speeds that are high relative to its stability, rather like the growth of the Thai economy. The cyclo may be thought of as just the same, only built by a state corporation and lacking a motor.

In both economies, industrial protectionism has the same effects as already described. Additions to the labour force must find employment in agriculture rather than industry, and with an open land frontier, engage in deforestation. This process ended in Thailand in the 1990s, after several decades of unfettered harvesting of forests for both timber and agricultural land, during which time forest cover diminished dramatically. In Vietnam, 'push' migration of this kind was apparent in the 1980s and early 1990s, although it is more likely a failure of industrial growth, rather than protection for non-labour-intensive sectors, that was the prime mover.

In both economies, trade and related policy reforms have seen huge increases in manufacturing sector activity, especially in the most labour-intensive industries. In the Thai case this has been accompanied by extraordinary rates of outmigration from the countryside, and especially from the forest frontier areas, with the total agricultural area diminishing by more than 10 per cent between 1989 and 1996 (Coxhead and Jiraporn, 1999). In Vietnam, however, the opening of the economy has caused a land race at the forest frontier. Between 1989 and 2000, Vietnam's harvested coffee area increased by a factor of more than one hundred, from 42 000 ha to 477 000 ha[7] as the country became the world's second-largest coffee exporter, and other crops such as mulberry and tea have also experienced rapid area growth (Ha, 2001).

These sketches, although obviously quite incomplete, nevertheless provide indicators of some of the ways in which apparently minor variations in economic structure can be associated with very substantial differences in the ways in which apparently similar policy reforms influence the use of environmental and natural resources. If nothing else, they do indicate clearly that even within a relatively homogeneous subset of developing resource-rich economies, there are no grounds for supposing the existence of a common set of environmental and natural resource depletion trends in the course of economic growth. Reading further between the lines, they also suggest some tentative conclusions concerning development with incomplete property rights in natural resources. Open access to forest is a more severe problem when other labour-intensive sectors in the economy fail to grow. In the language of the EKC literature, a capital-intensive industrialization strategy may induce composition effects that displace upward its EKC, not only for industrial emissions, but also for deforestation. Pro-environment development strategies inherently address more than one target, and as such must involve more than one instrument.

## 4. SOME CONCLUDING REMARKS

Debate on the environmental effects of trade liberalization in developing countries continues to grow in intensity, but theorizing on the underlying economics lags behind the empirical literature. The analytical model in this chapter is a useful tool for understanding the general equilibrium sources and consequences of policy changes. These can have intersectoral effects, of a sign and a magnitude determined by the initial structure of the economy being examined, and importantly, the same shock could well have opposed environmental effects in two different economic types. This finding undermines analyses of the trade–growth–environment relationship that rely on uniform assumptions about economic structure in different economies. A second finding is that different types of environmental damage – in our example, industrial emissions and deforestation at the agricultural frontier – respond differently to economic shocks. A third point is that when environmental externalities coexist with policy-induced distortions, partial policy liberalization may have negative effects on aggregate welfare or environmental problems, or income distribution and poverty.

None of these findings is new in the trade literature, but they have yet to emerge as clearly understood facets of the analysis of economy–environment relationships in developing economies. But these analytical results can play an important role in highlighting the lack of generality of conclusions reached in papers in the trade–environment literature that provide support for those who argue that trade liberalization is likely to be anti-environment (see, for example, Deacon, 1995). As we have shown, moving away from a pure specific factor model is sufficient to generate results that immediately undermine the generality of the trade liberalization–anti-environment relationship.

Any further extension of the model to bring it closer to the empirical reality of developing countries introduces new sources of ambiguity about the trade–environment relationship. Consider, for example, the case in which agriculture in either or both regions consists of two distinct sectors, cash crops and subsistence crops. The former are grown for export as well as domestic consumption; the latter are grown only for the home market; thus, their prices depend on domestic demand and supply. Suppose further that subsistence crops compete directly with forest land (a common example is the case in which rice, sugar and other internationally traded crops are grown in irrigated lowlands, while coarse grains and vegetables for the home market are grown mainly in uplands, at the forest margin). In this scenario, trade liberalization lowers the relative price of manufactures, and this raises the real wage, as predicted by Stolper–Samuelson. The output price effect on its own causes both agricultural sectors to expand. However, the higher wage has differential effects within agriculture. If the subsistence crop sector is labour-intensive relative to cash crops (as is often the case in developing economies), then costs in that sector rise by more than costs in cash crops. So long as the demand for subsistence crops is relatively inelastic with respect to incomes, the net effect of trade liberalization is a contraction of the subsistence sector. Since this is the sector that competes with forestry for land, deforestation is reduced.

Of course, a different set of assumptions about sectoral factor intensity might generate the opposite result. Our point is that the effects of trade liberalization on deforestation must be evaluated on a case-by-case basis. While the appeal of simple and elegant models is beyond dispute, in the highly charged atmosphere of current debates on trade and the environment it should be emphasized that the impact of trade policy on deforestation will vary greatly with the specific circumstances of individual countries.

We conclude with some remarks on the EKC. A great deal of energy has been expended on the so-called theoretical underpinnings of this relationship (for example, Andreoni and Levinson, 1998) and on empirical exercises purporting to test for its existence (for a recent survey, see Anriquez, 2002). The very concept of an EKC is problematic: it inevitably refers to trends in the emissions of a single pollutant or the depletion of a single natural resource stock, there being no meaningful index of 'environment'. More fundamentally, however, the modelling in this chapter underscores the argument that the EKC is a concept with almost no usable normative or policy content. Theoretical EKC models typically abstract from the composition effect that has been the main focus of our study. Empirical analyses nearly all rely on cross-country data, using models that reduce country-specific market, policy and institutional features to mere caricatures at best. Our approach, by contrast, directly identifies the economic, institutional and policy determinants of changes in individual measures of resource depletion or environmental quality. It does so in a general way that explicitly recognizes potential inter-country differences in economic structure, policies and institutional arrangements. More than this, it identifies the indirect, intersectoral determinants of environmental change, their interactions with conventional indicators of economic well-being, and provides a road map (albeit a large-scale one) for empirical and policy-oriented research at the country level.

In spite of our claim to relatively greater generality, the model we have presented merits extension in a number of areas. Foremost among these is to examine both comparative static and dynamic effects of trade as well as investment liberalization. As a first step in this direction, the model in Section 3 permits derivation of implied changes in rates of return to capital in manufacturing and (with some minor elaborations) in each agricultural region. The implications of policy changes for investment incentives by sector and region can thus be derived, opening the way to a longer-run analysis in which net international capital flows by sector and region alter the environmental and welfare outcomes we have described. This will be an important extension if we are to consider empirical phenomena with substantive environmental implications, such as the rapid expansion of Indonesia's oil palm industry. A second extension is to relax the assumption of a unified, flexible-wage labour market. Transactions costs and institutional barriers to wage adjustment are characteristic of many developing economies, as is persistent (equilibrium) unemployment. Amending the model to include these features, as in Corden and Findlay's (1975) restatement of the Harris–Todaro migration model, is fairly straightforward, as an inspection of Figures 11.1 and 11.2 makes clear. Finally, bringing in non-traded goods in explicit fashion will add complexity and realism, although at some cost in terms of the clarity of exposition. These three subjects are the focus of our ongoing research in this area.

## NOTES

1. The authors would like to thank Peter Warr, Max Corden, participants at the conference in honour of Peter Lloyd (University of Melbourne, January 2003), and participants at the European Association of Environmental and Resource Economists (Bilbao, Spain, June 2003) for their helpful comments on earlier drafts. Remaining errors are ours alone.
2. As a result, very high levels of protection for cereals have persisted in Asia even after major trade reforms in other sectors, and rice, corn, and other staples are now among the region's most heavily protected commodities (WTO, 1998–2001). Until the mid-1990s wave of WTO accessions by developing economies, the use of quantitative restrictions (QRs) and other non-market barriers to restrict food imports in the name of food security (or more specifically, food self-sufficiency) was widespread in Asia (see Coxhead, 2003), agricultural trade liberalization lags far behind progress – even on paper – in regional pacts such as the ASEAN Free Trade Agreement and the Free Trade Agreement of the Americas. Thus in the Philippines, for example, the effective rate of protection for manufacturing declined from 32 per cent to 15 per cent between 1990 and 2000, whereas that for agriculture fell only

from 32 per cent to 24 per cent (Aldaba and Cororaton, 2001). In 2000, the Philippines' implicit tariff on rice and corn was 43 per cent while the median value for manufactures other than food processing was under 10 per cent (ibid.). Indonesia, another net food importer, liberalized trade in a very wide range of commodities in the 1990s but excluded rice, the main staple cereal, imports of which remain under the control of a state trading agency 'to guarantee its supply to the population at affordable prices and to ensure food security' (Government of Indonesia, cited in WTO, 1998).

3. FAO data reported in Coxhead (2003).
4. Conversion of 'uplands' to 'lowlands' is technically feasible but costly, sometimes prohibitively so, and even when converted differences in key agro-climatic factors result in continuing productivity differences that justify treating these as essentially two different land types.
5. Output in each of the M sectors can also be computed from the diagram, by drawing lines tangential to each unit cost curve at the point of intersection and calculating sectoral employment shares of capital and labour along each axis. See Mussa (1979).
6. For an empirical exploration of this question using an applied general equilibrium model, see Coxhead and Jayasuriya (2003).
7. Source: FAO data accessed at www.fao.org/faostat, 17 January 2003.

# REFERENCES

Aldaba, R.A.M. and Cororaton, C.B. (2001), 'Trade liberalization and pollution: Evidence from the Philippines', unpublished manuscript, Manila: Philippine Institute for Development Studies.

Anderson, Kym (1992), 'The standard welfare economics of policies avecting trade and the environment', in Kym Anderson and Richard Blackhurst (eds) *The Greening of World Trade Issues*, Ann Arbor: University of Michigan Press, pp. 25–48.

Andreoni, J. and Levinson, A. (1998), 'The simple analytics of the environmental Kuznets Curve', NBER Working Paper No. W6739.

Angelsen, A. (1995), 'Shifting cultivation and "deforestation": a study from Indonesia', *World Development*, 23 (10), 1713–29.

Anriquez, G. (2002), 'Trade and the environment: An economic literature survey', Working Paper No. 02–16, Department of Agricultural and Resource Economics, University of Maryland.

Antweiler, W., Copeland, B.R. and Taylor, M.S. (2001), 'Is free trade good for the environment?', *American Economic Review*, 91 (4), 877–908.

Corden, W.M. and Findlay, R.F. (1975), 'Urban unemployment, intersectoral capital mobility, and development policy', *Economica*, 43, 59–78.

Coxhead, I. (2000), 'The consequences of Philippine food self-sufficiency policies for economic welfare and agricultural land degradation', *World Development*, 28 (1), 111–28.

Coxhead, I. (2003), 'Development and the environment in Asia: a survey of recent literature', *Asian-Pacific Economic Literature*, 17 (1), 22–54.

Coxhead, I. and Jayasuriya, S. (2003), *The Open Economy and the Environment: Development, Trade and Resources in Asia*, Cheltenham, UK and Northampton, USA: Edward Elgar.

Coxhead, I. and Plangpraphan Jiraporn (1999), 'Economic boom, financial bust, and the decline of Thai agriculture: was growth in the 1990s too fast?', *Chulalongkorn Journal of Economics*, 11 (1), 76–96.

Coxhead, I., Shively, G.E. and Shuai, X. (2002), 'Development policies, resource constraints, and agricultural expansion on the Philippine land frontier', *Environment and Development Economics*, **7**, 341–63.

Cruz, W. and Francisco, H.A. (1993), 'Poverty, population pressure and deforestation in the Philippines', paper presented at a workshop on Economy-wide Policies and the Environment, World Bank, Washington, DC, 14–15 December.

Deacon, R. (1995), 'Assessing the relationship between government policy and deforestation', *Journal of Environmental Economics and Management*, **28** (1), 1–18.

Dixit, A. and Norman, V.W. (1980), *Theory of International Trade*, Cambridge: Cambridge University Press.

Gérard, F. and Ruf, F. (2001), *Agriculture in Crisis: People, Commodities and Natural Resources in Indonesia, 1996–2000*, Montpellier, France: CIRAD, and Richmond, UK: Curzon.

Gordon, H.S. (1954), 'The economic theory of a common-property resource: the fishery', *Journal of Political Economy*, **62** (2), 124–42.

Grossman G. and Krueger, A.B. (1993), 'The environmental impacts of a North American Free Trade Agreement', in P. Garber (ed.), *The U.S.–Mexico Free Trade Agreement*, Cambridge, MA: MIT Press, pp. 13–56.

Ha, Dang Thanh (2001), 'Balancing economic development and environmental protection: challenges for the uplands of Vietnam', paper presented at the SANREM Research Synthesis conference, Athens, GA, USA, 28–30 November.

Krueger, A.O., Schiff, M. and Valdés, A. (1988), 'Agricultural incentives in developing countries: measuring the effect of sectoral and economy-wide policies', *World Bank Economic Review*, **2** (3), 255–71.

Lloyd, P.J. and Schweinberger, A.G. (1988), 'Trade expenditure functions and the gains from trade', *Journal of International Economics*, **24**, 275–97.

Lopez, R. and Niklitschek, M. (1991), 'Dual economic growth in poor tropical areas', *Journal of Development Economics*, **36** (2), 189–211.

Mathews, E. (2001), Understanding the FRA 2000, Forest Briefing No.1, World Resources Institute, March. Accessed at http://www.wri.org/pdf/fra2000.pdf.

Mussa, M. (1979), 'The two-sector model in terms of its dual: a geometric exposition', *Journal of International Economics*, **9**, 513–26.

Schwetheilm, J. and Glover, D. (1999), 'Causes and impacts of the fires', in D. Glover and T. Jessup (eds), *Indonesia's Fires and Haze: The Cost of Catastrophe*, Singapore: Institute for Southeast Asian Studies, and Canada: International Development Research Center, pp. 1–13.

Vincent, J.R., Rozali Md. Ali, and Associates (1997), *Environment and Development in a Resource-Rich Economy: Malaysia Under the New Economic Policy*, Cambridge, MA: Harvard Institute for International Development, and Kuala Lumpur: Institute of Strategic and International Studies.

World Bank (1992), *World Development Report 1992*, Washington, DC: The World Bank.

WTO (World Trade Organization) (1998), *Trade Policy Review: Review of Indonesia: TPRB's Evaluation*, press release (7 December 1998), accessed May 24 2002 at www.wto.org.

WTO (World Trade Organization) (1998–2001), *Trade Policy Review* (various countries), Geneva: WTO, accessed December 2001 at www.wto.org.

# APPENDIX: GENERAL EQUILIBRIUM ANALYSIS

The analysis in the text captures what is arguably the primary mechanism for intersectoral transfer of shocks, the labour market. We now present a more complete model, taking account of the requirement that aggregate expenditures and income be equal in equilibrium (and thus, by Walras's law, ensuring that the current account is also in balance). For this analysis we introduce the model in algebraic form, using the trade expenditure function (Dixit and Norman, 1980; Lloyd and Schweinberger, 1988). This enables us to evaluate reforms for their effects not only on the environment but also on a measure of consumer welfare. We retain a comparative static approach, while recognizing that under some circumstances the transitional dynamics of adjustment to a shock may produce somewhat different outcomes.

The structure of the model is similar to that developed in Section 2.[1] Since labour is the only factor mobile among all sectors, for analytical purposes manufacturing is a separate H–O–S economy, but with both its labour endowment and wage determined by an economy-wide labour market equilibrium condition. For a given quantity of labour in manufacturing, the two agricultural sectors, each with specific land and mobile labour, are like a Ricardo–Viner–Jones specific-factors economy. With the help of these analytical constructs we can evaluate the impacts of price and policy shocks as well as the direction of changes in environmental and natural resource depletion externalities. As before, we make the simplifying assumption that environmental damages affect the economy only through consumer preferences rather than through intersectoral effects on production costs.[2]

The economy consists of producers making resource allocation decisions in a competitive market environment, with the exceptions that, as before, the forest resource may be freely depleted to create upland land, and factories in 'dirty' manufacturing ($H$) may emit pollution without penalty. Following Lopez and Niklitschek (1991), we suppose that each unit of upland, $T$, is cleared from forest using the input of a constant quantity $\alpha$ of labour; thus $T = \alpha L$. Industrial emissions, $J$, are produced in constant proportion to the output of $H$, that is, $J = \beta y^H$, $\beta > 0$. We assume an initial policy distortion in the form of a tariff on imports of the output produced in the dirty industry. All industries compete for a common (and fixed) pool of labour, $L = L^U + L^F + L^M$. Prices (assumed exogenous) for each good are $p^U$ and $p^F$ for upland and lowland agriculture respectively, and $p^H$ and $p^X$ respectively for the import-competing (dirty) and exportable (clean) manufactures. By the choice of a numeraire, $p^X = 1$. The quantities of lowland land, $N$, and manufacturing capital, $K$, are assumed exogenously fixed. Using this notation we define revenue functions for each sector or region:

| | |
|---|---|
| Lowland (food): | $Q(L^F, N, p^F)$ |
| Upland: | $R(L^U - \alpha T, T, p^U)$ |
| Manufacturing: | $S(L - L^F - L^U, K, p^H)$. |

The functions $Q$, $R$ and $S$ each give the maximum revenue earned by sectoral or regional producers for given prices, technologies and factor endowments. These functions are non-decreasing and homogeneous of degree one in prices and endowments. By the envelope theorem their partial derivatives with respect to prices are sectoral outputs, and partial derivatives with respect to factor endowments are shadow factor prices. We now write income from production as the sum of sectoral and regional revenues:

$$I = Q(L^F, N, p^F) + R(L^U - -\alpha T, T, p^U) \\ + S(L - L^F - L^U, K, p^H). \tag{11A.1}$$

Sectoral outputs and factor prices are obtained by the envelope theorem, from the output price and factor quantity derivatives of the sectoral and regional revenue functions.

Consumer preferences and behaviour are captured by a conventional conditional expenditure function, in which the quantities of industrial emissions, $J$, and the amount of standing forest cleared for agriculture, $T$, enter as exogenous quantities:

$$E = E(\mathbf{p}, J, T, \upsilon) \tag{11A.2}$$

where $\mathbf{p}$ is the vector $(p^F, p^U, p^H, 1)$. This embodies all the information on the preferences of a utility-maximizing representative consumer with utility function $\upsilon(F, U, H, X; J, T)$, with $\upsilon_F > 0$, $\upsilon_U > 0$, $\upsilon_H > 0$, $\upsilon_X > 0$, $\upsilon_J \leq 0$, $\upsilon_T \leq 0$. To simplify the analysis we have assumed that utility is separable between marketed goods and environmental bads.

As a notational convention we write the derivatives of $Q$, $R$, $S$ and $E$ with respect to prices using the symbols for each sector, for example, $E_M = \partial E/\partial p^H$, $E_{HF} = \partial^2 E/\partial p^H \partial p^F$, and so on; derivatives with respect to factors are written (for example) $R_T = \partial R/\partial T$. By the properties of the revenue and expenditure functions and the envelope theorem, $R_U$ is the supply of upland output, $Q_N$ is the shadow value of lowland, $E_H$ is domestic demand for import-competing manufactures, $E_T$ is the negative of willingness to pay for standing forest, $E_\upsilon$ is the reciprocal of the marginal utility of income, and so on. Finally we introduce a single policy measure. The initial domestic price of $H$ is increased by a tariff, given by $t^H = p^H - \bar{p}^H$, where the bar indicates a world price in domestic currency terms.

The aggregate budget constraint of this economy, with tariff income equal to the tariff rate multiplied by excess domestic demand for $H$, is:

$$E = I + t^H(E_H - S_H). \tag{11A.3}$$

There is full employment in equilibrium, so the usual marginal productivity condition for labour requires that the following conditions hold:

$$Q_L = R_L \tag{11A.4}$$

$$R_L = S_L \tag{11A.5}$$

$$R_T - \alpha R_L = 0. \tag{11A.6}$$

Condition (11A.6) ensures that in the upland, labour used in land clearing and in production is of equal value at the margin. It is thus a property of the model that since labour is the only input to land clearing, any shock that raises labour productivity in upland production also generates pressures for deforestation.[3] The solution to equations (11A.3)–(11A.6) yields equilibrium values of real income, $L^F$, $L^U$ and $T$, each as a function of $(p, t^H, L, N, K)$; from these we can calculate changes in $L^M$ as well as sectoral and regional outputs, the wage, and industrial emissions.

In the remainder of this section we use this model to explore the general equilibrium effects of some price and policy changes. For clarity, and to conserve space, we do not provide complete comparative static solutions (Appendix A.2 sketches the procedure, and see Coxhead and Jayasuriya (2003) for complete solutions to an analogous model). The results presented below rely mainly on differentiation of (11A.3), and are largely sufficient to indicate the nature of each complete solution.

## Effects of a Tariff Change

The real income effect of a small increase in the tariff is found by totally differentiating (11A.3), using (11A.2) and (11A.1) and setting changes in the exogenous prices and quantities, $L$, $K$, $N$, $p^U$ and $p^F$, to zero. Defining net imports $Z_H = (E_H - S_H)$, and using (11A.4) and (11A.5) to eliminate some terms, we obtain:

$$\gamma dv + E_J dJ + E_T dT = t^H Z_{HH} dt^H - t^H S_{HL} dL^M, \tag{11A.7}$$

where $\gamma = E_v - t^H E_{Hv} > 0$ and $dL^M = -(dL^F + dL^U)$. The first term on the left-hand side provides a measure of change in the real income of the representative consumer; the second and third terms capture the utility effects of changes in each of the environmental variables. If we ignore environmental damages for a moment by setting $E_J = E_T = 0$, then (11A.7) yields a measure of the change in real income due to the tariff rise. The first term on the right-hand side is the familiar deadweight loss due to a reallocation of resources within the manufacturing sector as a whole; it is negative as $Z_{HH} = (E_{HH} - S_{HH}) < 0$. The second term captures an additional efficiency loss due to the reallocation of labour from agriculture to manufacturing. This term is negative, depending on whether the tariff causes labour to flow into or out of the $M$ sector as a whole. Converting the relevant parts of (11A.7) to proportional changes rather that the absolute changes shown (see below) yields an expression in which we see that the magnitude of the environmental and welfare changes due to the tariff depend on the magnitude of the $H$ sector in relation to overall income and expenditures, the tariff as a percentage of $p^H$, the capital-intensity of the $H$ sector relative to manufacturing as a whole, the elasticities of domestic excess demand for $H$ with respect to own price, and the elasticity of the economy-wide wage with respect to $p^H$.

Now consider the environmental terms on the left-hand side of (11A.7). If, as we have assumed, $H$ is the only polluting industry in $M$, then emissions $J$ must increase with the tariff, and any gain (or loss) in consumer welfare from consumption of marketed goods is augmented by additional losses due to increased consumption of emissions. Whether the tariff causes deforestation to increase or decline (and thus $T$ to fall or rise) depends, in this model, on whether there is a net labour inflow or outflow to upland agriculture – as was demonstrated in Section 2.[4] Thus deforestation impacts depend on the tariff and on the characteristics of the sector(s) to which it is applied, even if these are spatially distant from the frontier and linked to upland production only in indirect fashion.

**Derivation of Equation (11A.7) in Elasticity Form**

Ignoring the two environmental terms on the left-hand side, equation (11A.7) relates changes in consumer real income directly to changes in the tariff, and indirectly to intersectoral labour flows induced by the tariff change. The direct term is negative; the indirect term is of indeterminate sign. The magnitudes of both are of interest when we consider tariff change in economies with different initial structure (relative size of sectors, and so on). Converting from absolute to relative changes of variables yields expressions whose parameters are readily given economic interpretation. Taking the direct tariff term first, we have

$$t^H Z_{HH} dt^H = t^H \frac{\partial Z_H}{\partial p^H} dt^H$$

$$= t^H \cdot \varepsilon^H \cdot \frac{Z_H}{p^H} dt^H,$$

where $\varepsilon^H$ is the elasticity of excess demand for $H$ with respect to own price. Dividing (11A.7) by initial total expenditure $E$ gives, for the direct tariff term:

$$\varepsilon^H \cdot \frac{Z_H}{E} \cdot \frac{t^H}{p^H} \cdot dt^H, \tag{11A.8}$$

which is the elasticity of excess demand ($<0$) times excess demand as a fraction of total expenditures, times the tariff as a fraction of domestic price, times the tariff change. The direct tariff effect will be larger, the greater in absolute value is each of these terms.

The indirect term can be similarly reinterpreted:

$$t^H S_{HL} dL^M = t^H \frac{\partial S_H}{\partial L^M} dL^M;$$

then, using Hotelling's lemma to obtain $S_H = y^H$, the output of sector $H$, and Young's theorem (symmetry of second partial derivatives), we have:

$$t^H \frac{\partial y^H}{\partial L^M} dL^M = t^H \frac{\partial w}{\partial p^H} dL^M,$$

or, after dividing through by $E$ and some minor manipulation,

$$\frac{t^H}{p^H} \cdot \varphi^{LH} \cdot \frac{wL^H}{E} \cdot \lambda_{LH}^{-1} \frac{dL^M}{L^M}, \tag{11A.9}$$

where $\varphi^{LH} < 0$ is the elasticity of the wage with respect to $p^H$, and $\lambda_{LH}$ is the share of $H$ sector in total manufacturing employment. The sign of $dL^M/L^M$ is determined in general equilibrium by the simultaneous solution to equations (11A.3) – (11A.6), and will depend on the relative magnitudes of the tariff-induced changes in relative prices and wages. If $dL^M/L^M > 0$, the migration of additional labour into manufacturing as the result of the tariff exacerbates the existing misallocation of resources in the economy, and thus further reduces real income. Expression (11A.9) says that the welfare loss from labour transfers due to the tariff is greater, the higher is the tariff in relation to domestic price, the greater is the (absolute value of the) wage elasticity, and the larger is the wage bill in $H$ in relation to total income. The effect is diminished in proportion to the share of $H$-sector employment in total manufacturing employment. For $E_J$ and $E_T \neq 0$, the overall welfare effect of the tariff depends on these direct and indirect real income effects as well as endogenous changes in $J$ and $T$.

## Appendix Notes

1. The model and analysis in this section is a substantive variation on that in Coxhead and Jayasuriya (2003). Some of its features, notably the modelling of forest clearing in upland, are drawn from Lopez and Niklitschek (1991).
2. Coxhead and Jayasuriya (2003) explore production externalities in a similar model.
3. This rather stark assumption is made for convenience only, and an extension to the model could provide for labour–land substitution in upland. In other work (Coxhead and Jayasuriya, 2003) we permit such substitution by modelling upland production with more than one output and different factor proportions.
4. If there were non-traded final goods in the economy, there would be additional substitution terms in (11A.6) due to endogenous price changes. We explore these in Coxhead and Jayasuriya (2003, ch. 4).

# Index

Abd-el-Rahman, K. 150
Abel, A. 185, 188
Abrego, L. 86
ACT 246, 252
*ad valorem* tax distortion 66, 68, 70–75
adjustment
    for aggregate payments imbalance
        148–9
    to trade expansion 148, 155
admiration 188–9, 200–201
affiliate sales, cross-border 150
agglomeration 48, 56–61, 61–2
aggregate effects 234
aggregate payments imbalance,
    adjustment for 148–9
aggregation, categorical 148–9, 157
agricultural protection 265–6, 268–9,
    269
agriculture 51, 53–4
    environmental effects in developing
        countries 258–9, 261–73
    MONASH model 242, 243–4
    STEs 162–4, 166–78
Allais, M. 65
Allen, R.G.D. 70
Alston, J.M. 166–7, 174
American Economic Association
    (AEA) 253
Amiti, M. 48
Anderson, K. 265
Andreoni, J. 272
Angelsen, A. 269
Anriquez, G. 272
Antonelli matrix 66, 70, 75, 79, 83
Antweiler, W. 257
Aquino, A. 149
arbitrage 128–30
Argentina 173
Armington, P.S. 253
Arrow, K.J. 29, 34, 253
Asia Pacific Economic Cooperation
    (APEC) 155

Asian developing countries 257–81
asymmetry in customs unions 100–101,
    104–5
Atkinson, A.B. 66, 68, 78
Australia 164, 173
    effects of eCommerce 223–56
    states, territories and statistical
        divisions 245–8, 252
Australian Wheat Board 168
Austria 85
autarky 10

back-of-the-envelope (BOTE)
    calculations 224, 234–41, 253
Bagwell, K. 165
Balassa, B. 148
banking sector 231–2
Barro, R.J. 186
Barros, P.P. 121, 123, 124
Barwise, K. 228
basic metal products 242, 245
Baumol, W.J. 78
'becak' economy 269
Bergstrand, J.H. 149
Bertrand, T.J. 47
Beta function 8–10
bilateral trade liberalization 120
Boiteaux, M. 65
Bolivia 47
Bond, E. 21, 35, 38
bonds, traded 190–92, 194, 195–6,
    199–201, 204, 205, 210–11, 212
Brander, J.A. 151, 152, 156, 165
Brülhart, M. 149, 150
budget constraint 52, 190, 206
Burbidge, J. 87

Cairns Group 164
Canada 164, 166–7, 173–7
Canadian Wheat Board 166–7, 168,
    173